D0856016

River towns in the Great West

River towns in the
Great West

The structure of provincial urbanization in the American Midwest, 1820–1870

TIMOTHY R. MAHONEY

University of Nebraska, Lincoln

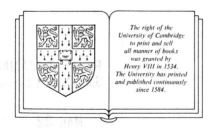

The right of the
University of Cambridge
to print and sell
all manner of books
was granted by
Henry VIII in 1534.
The University has printed
and published continuously
since 1584.

CAMBRIDGE UNIVERSITY PRESS

Cambridge

New York   Port Chester   Melbourne   Sydney

Published by the Press Syndicate of the University of Cambridge
The Pitt Building, Trumpington Street, Cambridge CB2 1RP
40 West 20th Street, New York, NY 10011, USA
10 Stamford Road, Oakleigh, Melbourne 3166, Australia

First published 1990

Printed in the United States of America

Library of Congress Cataloging-in-Publication Data
Mahoney, Timothy R., 1953-
River towns in the Great West: the structure of provincial
urbanization in the American Midwest, 1820-1870 / Timothy R. Mahoney.
    p. cm.
ISBN 0–521–36130–3
1. Cities and towns – Middle West – History – 19th century.
2. Urbanization – Middle West – History – 19th century. 3. Land
settlement – Middle West – History – 19th century. I. Title.
HT123.5.M53M34 1990
307.76'0977–dc20   89–32208

British Library Cataloguing in Publication Data
Mahoney, Timothy R.
River towns in the Great West: the structure of
provincial urbanization in the American Midwest, 1820–1870.
1. United States. Midwestern states.
Urbanisation, history
I. Title
307.7'6'0977

ISBN 0–521–36130–3   hard covers

To my father,
Thomas W. Mahoney,
and the memory of my mother,
Marianne S. Mahoney

Contents

Figures and tables

Figures

Tables

Acknowledgments

History books, like the lives described in them, are shaped by the conditions in which they were written. Much of this work was written during a period of part-time academic employment between 1981 and 1986. Therefore, its completion owes special thanks to those who offered me a living and some support during those years, including Daniel Headrick, Barbara Sciaccahitano, Richard Farrell, and Jon Sumida. Additional support was provided by the American Historical Association, which awarded me a Beveridge grant in 1985. Above all, I would like to thank the members of the Department of History at the University of Nebraska, Lincoln, who, in welcoming me as a colleague, provided the support necessary for the completion of this project. I would especially like to acknowledge Benjamin Rader, the chairman of the Department of History; the dean of the College of Arts and Sciences; and the Research Council for two grants, one to buy a personal computer and the other to defray the costs of the mapwork. Thanks are also due to Les Howard for doing the maps.

The many others who provided help and support of different kinds through the course of this project include the librarians, archivists, and staff at the following institutions: the Regenstein Library at the University of Chicago; the Newberry Library; the state historical societies of Wisconsin, Iowa, Illinois, Missouri, Ohio, Indiana, and New York; and the local historical societies or public libraries in St. Louis, Alton, Quincy, Hannibal, Keokuk, Davenport, Rock Island, Galena, and Dubuque. I owe special thanks to Kathleen Conzen, William McNeil, Michael Conzen, and Frank Smith for useful discussions of the material. I would also like to thank my brother Robert Mahoney for editorial assistance throughout.

PART I

Human geography and the structure of regional life

1

Introduction and "topographical description"

Introduction

In the middle of the nineteenth century the Ohio and Mississippi river valleys were considered by most travelers an essential part of any American tour. Yet, as has recently been argued, most British travelers were disoriented by the landscape they encountered. [1] More comfortable with the traditional categories of reference for appreciating scenery, they judged the relatively featureless western landscape to be boring and uninteresting. Composed of low-relief prairies, hills, moraines, and ravines, broken occasionally by clusters or lines of trees and long, shallow, meandering rivers, only to give way to more trees, more prairie swells or flat expanses, followed by more rivers and underbrush in various combinations and seemingly endless repetition – the midwestern topography offers a landscape that can numb the mind with tedium and bring on disorientation. Repetition tends to blur out the details, and landscape, as a feature to be analyzed, is reduced to pure space, measured by the passage of time to traverse it, which often has to be endured to the point of nervous exhaustion. The symptoms, though varied, seem clear: anxiety, boredom, a vague unfocused introspection, languor, or depression. Some travelers made the best of it and stressed the hypnotic, or peaceful, sense engendered by the breadth of the landscape and its seeming stillness. [2] Others found the solitude and quiet awe-inspiring and sensed vast natural forces at work. But such high-spiritedness, felt more often by American poets or travelers who saw practical opportunities in the land, was foreign to most and seems so forced as to appear as a rationalization to defend against the harpies of boredom. Whether one wants to call this cognitive response a kind of "horror vacui" or a low-level agoraphobia, it is an emotional response that, in reappearing time

---

1 Christopher Mulvery, *Anglo-American Landscapes: A Study of Nineteenth Century Anglo-American Travel Literature* (Cambridge, 1983), 211–43.
2 Ibid., 216.

and time again in the region's literature, history, and public discourse, and still continually referred to today, seems certainly to exist.[3] The pervasiveness of this attitude is reflected in the responses of both residents and outsiders toward the land and region. The rapidity in which early settlers picked up stakes and moved on again may indicate a half-conscious response to an ever-beckoning flat horizon promising a more hospitable environment beyond. A kind of wanderlust – a continual interest in what is going on outside the region, a sense of being beyond or outside the mainstream or the center – has pervaded regional culture and life. In many cases, this perspective has led to social and cultural openness. In others it has fostered a bitter, defensive, and resentful provincialism. So too, the abundance of rather unscenic landscape may have encouraged residents to view the land practically, as a resource to exploit for economic ends, and not as an environment to live in and appreciate. Nature in the Midwest is not a picturesque garden: The climate is variable and often harsh, and the flora and fauna not very distinctive. As a result, the environment is viewed as a vast unity of undifferentiated space to be used and developed by similar kinds of people using the most efficient methods.[4]

From their first encounter with the prairies, travelers, settlers, government surveyors, speculators, town planners, and railroad men were apparently unable or unwilling to discern the natural contours of the land. Consequently, they created a geometric landscape of base lines, meridians, sections and townships, county grids, and town plats with numbered streets and alphabetically ordered names; railroad lines and roads that followed these markings; and rivers calibrated by distances above and below certain places, studded with numbered islands, or docks and levees, interspersed in a sequentially understood linear arrangement. The vastness of the area to be covered necessitated repetition simply to encompass it within the coordinates of an ordered system.[5]

To some extent, the ability to organize space so efficiently was a consequence of the environment and topography. The inclination may have existed elsewhere but the terrain was not suited to such arrangements. Yet, in

3 Barbara Novak, *Nature and Culture* (New Haven, 1980) 34–44; *An Open Land: Photographs of the Midwest, 1852–1982,* ed. Victoria Post Ranney, cur. Rhonda\ McKinney (New York, 1983).
4 Mulvey, *Anglo-American Landscapes,* 215–31.
5 Scholars have viewed the effects of the flat terrain in different ways. See Michael P. Conzen, "American Urban System in the Nineteenth Century," in *Geography and the Urban Environment: Progress in Research and Applications,* 6 vols., ed. D. T. Herbert and R. J. Johnston (Chichester, 1978–84), 4: 333; John Jakle, *Images of the Ohio Valley: A Historical Geography of Travel* (New York, 1977), 9; and John Brinckerhoff Jackson, *Discovering the Vernacular Landscape* (New Haven, 1984), 32. Also see Robert Geddes, "The Forest's Edge," in *Architectural Design Profile* (London, 1982), 11; John Mack Faragher, *Sugar Creek: Life on the Illinois Prairie* (New Haven, 1986), 42; and Cullom Davis, "Illinois: Crossroads and Cross Section," in *Heartland* ed. James H. Madison (Bloomington, Ind., 1988), 127–57.

imposing repetitious arrangements onto a relatively undifferentiated topography, early settlers and planners encouraged – even steered events into – repetitious social, economic, and political patterns across the region. In time, scholars of the region, conditioned by this repetition of social, economic, and political life across the area, emphasized what was similar in each town's, city's, or state's history and reinforced the perception that the culture and society, like the land, were uniform. Not surprisingly, local history, which seeks to understand what is unique about any one place's history, as well as what is universal in it, would find such a consensual agenda rather barren ground on which to develop. This same consensual agenda has continued to work against the development of any strong sense of regional self-consciousness in the Midwest by focusing on those aspects of midwestern life that were derived and remained continuous to life in the East. The Midwest, from such a perspective, is seen as a re-creation of the social, institutional, economic, and political life of the East in the West and, therefore, as a redundancy rather than some kind of new reality.

To combat this tendency, historians seem to have two options. First, they can narrow the range of their categories of topographical analysis and, in doing so, demonstrate that neither the landscape, the climate, nor the flora and fauna in the Midwest are as uniform as generally perceived. If one narrows the range of one's categories of analysis and sharpens one's eye for detail, variation becomes apparent. The vast prairies are actually a patchwork of different topographical and geological zones. The climate varies significantly from north to south and east to west. The openness of the region's boundaries to other regions and cultures has enabled people from all over the country and the world to enter it, creating dramatic urban and rural social, cultural, and political diversity. By emphasizing diversity, analysis shifts toward trying to explain variation and, by counteracting the consensual agenda, encourages the development of a true local history. The consensus tradition remains so strong, however, that such a tactic amid perceived uniformity still seems to involve splitting hairs and consequently to be parochial, redundant, even antiquarian. To break through the impressions of sameness and to discern variation and diversity across the region, one must do more; the historian must imagine, if possible, a new region defined by new or different criteria.

A fruitful approach would be to change the criteria by which one defines a region from topographical or ethnic features to patterns of human activity organized systemically across space. Economies, urban systems, transport networks, patterns of settlement, and social networks can provide a frame of reference for a regional study as readily as topographical features or climate. Of these systems, urbanization casts the widest net in drawing various phenomena into an explanatory framework. Urbanization could be defined as the concentration of population around some kind of economic, military, religious, or political establishment. In modern times, the motive force behind this concentration has been primarily economic. In the Midwest, most towns began with the decision of some farmer or peddler to specialize as a middleman or merchant among the people in the neighborhood. By drawing people to some central location, the merchant thus triggered the development of a market for goods and services and encourged others to specialize in craft production and the provision of services. Specialization brought competition, which triggered more specialization and, by creating internal efficiencies, stimulated economic development. In time, clustering intensified to the point at which larger, successful firms, seeking to gain control of regional as well as local markets, increased production to a point at which economies of scale were achieved. When these economies were exhausted, they sought external economies to stay ahead of the competition; they would hire out work, or contract certain aspects of the production process to specialized producers, or even sell wastes or by-products to other specialized producers who would use the raw materials to produce another finished product.

Either way, small firms became large and clustering intensified, generating even greater external economies. The transport system, and flow of raw materials, capital, and labor that supported these large firms, reinforced the agglomeration advantages of the city over the town or country, drawing entire regions within their sphere. As a result, village and city, town and metropolis became interconnected, as did merchants, farmers, manufacturers, and laborers. In time, the space controlled by the network of roads, rivers, and information flows among towns and cities defined the structure of an urban region. Like beads on a string, cities are the points of interaction and contact, and they provide the sparks of growth and development that define the region. [6]

This breadth, of course, has been the basis of its appeal as a subject of study by urban historians for the last two generations. Traditionally, urban historians have employed three methods to try to understand the multilevel dynamics of the urbanization process. Most prevalent has been the case study or urban biography of a town or city. As a sample, the case study works best, if one assumes the universality of the process and limits generalizations to other places with similar functions in similar circumstances. Those urban historians uneasy with the single-case approach broadened their sample to include several cases among towns or cities with the same or different functions, with the intention of increasing the varieties of urban phenomena examined or compared and deepening their understanding of the process in general. [7]

6 Fernand Braudel, *The Mediterranean and the Mediterranean World in the Age of Phillip II*, trans. Sian Reynolds (New York, 1972), 23.
7 Among the more recent comparative urban histories, see Gary Nash, *The Urban Crucible* (Cambridge, Mass., 1979; abridged ed., 1986); and William H. Pease and Jane H. Pease, *The Web of Progress: Private Values and Public Styles in Boston and Charleston, 1828–1845* (New York, 1985).

More recently, some historians and historical geographers have argued that the diversity of urbanization is best appreciated and able to be explained by examining urban systems as a whole and, in particular, trying to understand the interaction among towns and cities within the sytem. [8]

From such a regional systemic perspective, it becomes clear that in spite of similarities among towns throughout a system, change at any town or city results from an interaction of local processes with regional forces of economic change. Ironically, by emphasizing the diversity of experiences and interaction among towns and cities across a complex urban economic system, the regional perspective provides new impetus for local history. By focusing on how local reality interacted with regional forces, it demonstrates more clearly that any local economy or society evolves not by the repetition of some universal process of development, but rather by the intersection of a local echo of that process with regional but external forces that over time shape, alter, and divert the course of local change. Gradually, the local economy and society becomes a kind of composite, built up by different episodes of activity, usually related to some interaction with the regional system outside, specific to itself, and providing a unique local context that can help explain the divergence of local events or phenomena from those in other towns.

Moreover, by examining regional dynamics, local events can be placed in a larger context and their true social or economic character known. For example, as regional forces concentrated at the entrepôts, more hinterland towns responded to entrepôt – but for them, outside – directives. Hence, not only did local life become more discontinuous, uneven, and distinctive from other towns once like it, but it also became more vulnerable to and dependent on outside decisions. It became more insecure, unable to control its own development – a subtle change that altered how almost any local event would be interpreted or understood. To find a relevant locale, which does more then repeat other case studies, requires therefore that one place local history in a regional context. [9] The study of a regional process of urbanization thus provides a seamless web of explanation, among different processes, levels of

8 Allan Pred, *Urban Growth and City Systems in the United States, 1840–1860* (Cambridge, Mass., 1980); James Vance, *The Merchant's World* (Englewood Cliffs, N. J., 1970); Michael P. Conzen, "Capital Flows and the Developing Urban Hierarchy: State Banking in Wisconsin, 1854–1895," *Economic Geography* 51 (October 1975): 321–8; Edward K. Muller, "Selective Urban Growth in the Mid-Ohio Valley, 1800–1860," *Geographic Review* 66 (1976): 178–99; Allan Pred, *Urban Growth and the Circulation of Information* (Cambridge, Mass., 1973); Michael P. Conzen, "The Making of Urban Systems in the United States, 1840–1910," *Annals, Association of American Geographers* 67 (1977): 88–108; John C. Hudson, "The Plains Country Town," in *The Great Plains: Environment and Culture*, ed. B. W. Blouet and Frederick Luebke (Lincoln, Neb., 1979), 99–118. On regionalism, see David Goldfield, "The New Regionalism," *Journal of Urban History* 10, no. 2 (February 1984): 171–86.
9 Timothy R. Mahoney, "Urban History in a Regional Context: River Towns on the Upper Mississippi, 1840–60," *Journal of American History* 72, no. 3 (September 1985): 318–39.

reality, and units of organization, upon which a broader "total history" may be based. This analysis of the urban economic system that spread across the upper Midwest in the middle of the nineteenth century and then was transformed by the dramatic rearrangement of economic activity across the area has, in view of these remarks, three primary goals: to demonstrate the validity of defining a region by systemic, functional, or structural criteria; to establish a broad explanatory context to understand the development and evolution of a provincial regional society and culture; and to bridge the gap between generalized regional studies and what has been called a "true" local history.

To have any chance of differentiating a region defined topographically from one defined systemically, however, one must still know something about the contours of the physical environment. As William Cronon recently demonstrated with regard to seventeenth-century New England, human activities continually interact with the environment. [10] As part of an ecosystem, with its own natural forces of change and process, man adjusts, responds, uses, controls, and is, in turn, shaped, limited, and forced into new strategies, either by the changes he has already wrought in the environment or by environmental changes that have taken place independent of human interaction. The relative power of either side to act or be acted upon depends on the character of the environmental features and human technology, willpower, and knowledge. It is imperative, as James Malin long ago suggested, and Robert Swierengra reminds us, that we emphasize this two-way interaction in order to avoid the simplistic notion that a confrontation between the two forces resulted in one or the other becoming dominant. [11] Walter Prescott Webb, in describing the harsh environment of the Great Plains and its impact on Easternens, drifted close to environmental determinism. [12] One must be careful, in a systemic approach, of not erring in the opposite direction, however, and discounting the role of the land, rivers, and climate in shaping regional life, as perhaps some studies of the progress of modern agriculture, water control, and technology have done. [13] Whether one emphasizes the environment as it is changed by human intervention or the human response to the environment, each must be viewed as one side of an ongoing process with no end point of equilibrium beyond which historical change ceases to occur.

In this study of a regional economic and urban system, the focus will be primarily on the human response. But because those studied are

10 William Cronon, *Changes in the Land: Indians, Colonists, and the Ecology of New England* (New York, 1983), 1–15.
11 James C. Malin, *History and Ecology: Studies of the Grassland*, ed. Robert Swierengra (Lincoln, Neb., 1984), XV–XXIII. 1–17.
12 Ibid., 84–9; Walter Prescott Webb, *The Great Plains* (Boston, 1952).
13 Allan Bogue, *From Prairie to Corn Belt* (Chicago, 1962).

predominantly agricultural workers, expanding into a new region with insufficient data, technology, and economic and social support, their interaction with the new environment was especially intense.[14] The study of the exact character of that environment I will leave to the environmental historians.[15] I will refer only to those larger-scale hydrologic, climatic, topographical, and geological features to which Easterners had to accustom themselves and that had, therefore, a significant impact in shaping the human geographical pattern of economic and social activity.

To differentiate between a purer analysis of the physical environment and the geographical study of human interactions within the context of that environment's geographic arrangement, either in settling, occupying, traversing, or initiating economic activity across it, it will perhaps be useful to preface our analysis of regional life in the nineteenth century with a topographical description surveying the character of the environmental processes that distinguish midwestern topography from that in the East.

A "topographical description"

Geologists tell us, and every midwestern schoolchild knows, that the character of the land beyond the Appalachian Mountains was formed by the advance and retreat of a succession of glaciers between fifty thousand and ten thousand years ago. Acting not unlike century-long winters, these great sheets or rivers of ice eroded, rearranged, and redeposited vast amounts of soil and rock, leaving in their wake a relatively smooth deep layer of new land atop older geological formations, as well as a dramatically altered drainage system of lakes and rivers. Therefore, when crossing the Appalachians, immigrants, much like their ancestors or predecessors in the seventeenth and eighteenth centuries who emigrated from Europe to the Atlantic coast of America, were literally entering a new or immature environment that the forces of wind, water, and ice had hardly had a moment, in geological time, to shape.

Geologists have understood for some time how a glacier advances and retreats across land surface, creating topographical diversity within the general uniformity across its path. When the leading edge of a glacier stops, for instance, it will generally begin to deposit the debris and soil trapped within it onto the backside of a ridge of plowed land, risen in its advance, and form a *terminal* moraine. If a glacier is especially thick and heavy – and some glaciers reached a mile or two in depth – then it will dig deeper into the surface, shoveling larger pieces of earth in front of it. When such a glacier slows down

14 Cronon, *Changes in the Land*, 1–15; Malin, *Studies of Grassland*, 1–11.
15 Michael O'Brian, ed., *Grassland, Forest, and Historical Settlement: An Analysis of Dynamics in Northeast Missouri* (Lincoln, Neb., 1984).

and stops, the piles of stones and debris in front of it form hills, knobs, hummocks, the result being somewhat irregular *push* or *sump* moraines.[16] But most of the geological impact of the glacier occurs as it melts and retreats across the land it has covered and scraped clean under its weight. As it recedes, sheets of water flow down its front onto the land, depositing debris and soil in low swells or meadows, often called outwash plains or *kame* moraines. The heaviest debris within the glacier drops more vertically downward, building up behind the terminal moraine, enhancing its size and extent even further. As the glacier further recedes, often unevenly – slowing down, speeding up, then perhaps stopping – it leaves in its tracks, other, less prominent moraines, roughly parallel to the terminal moraine, until the point at which most of the debris dug up from its heaviest and furthest extent has been redeposited; then lightened of its load, it retreats with a cleaner scrape to the north.[17]

Any significant glacier, therefore, in the course of its advance, will level the land, fill in valleys, scrape off hilltops, and smooth uneven surfaces and then, in the wake of its retreat, will leave a series of ridges, decreasing in size, extent, and depth from its furthest advance. The extent of these morainic systems depended on the size of the glacier. Vast and deep glaciers could lay down moraines extending across half the continent, whereas lesser glaciers, digging less deeply into the land, would leave smaller, narrower, shallower moraines along the paths of least resistance in the river valleys and low-lying areas of a region. By such movements, unified glaciers could split into "lobes," each of which advanced across a narrower range of territory, sometimes intersecting and creating dense, chaotic, irregular networks of smaller moraines.[18]

The real complexity of the apparently unified midwestern topography derived from the fact that at least six different glaciers of varying size and extent surged south out of Canada and then retreated, each leaving behind them a new layer of soil, new systems of moraines, and new drainage flows on top of those left by previous glaciers. The result was the superimposition of the topographical effects of each glacier on one another, resulting in a more varied, complex topography than at first meets the eye. Of primary significance to the contemporary landscape are the last two glaciers, the Illinoisan and the Wisconsin, which in their gradual advance and halting, uneven retreat across the region laid down the famous "Prairie Peninsula" (Figure 1.1).

Although theoretically presented on many maps as a great triangle of rich land extending out from the High Plains east across central Illinois, Indiana, and into Ohio, the Prairie Peninsula was, in fact, formed by the deposit of varying layers of soil from south to north by different glaciers as they advanced

16 Nevin M. Fenneman, *Physiography of Eastern United States* (New York and London, 1938), 477.
17 Ibid., 455, 473–9.
18 Ibid., 481–6.

Figure 1.1. The Prairie Peninsula and the upper Mississippi River valley.

and retreated along a front from the western slope of the Missouri River valley
to the headwaters of the Ohio River.[19] After two earlier glaciers had already
extended south to the line of the Missouri and Ohio river valleys and, in their
drain-off, created the ancestors of both modern rivers, the Illinoisan glacier
moved south and covered a narrower area whose western border approximated
the later Mississippi River valley and whose southern extent shadowed the

19 Ibid., 454; John H. Garland, ed., *The North American Midwest: A Regional Geography* (New
York, 1955), 93–6.

Ohio River valley, thus reinforcing the action of earlier glaciers. The furthest
extent of the Illinoisan glacier deposited a moraine on a line from western Lake
Erie, near Toledo, south to the headwaters of the Scioto River southeast of
Columbus, Ohio, and then south to the Ohio River. The front edge of the
glacier then ran along the Ohio until just east of New Albany, Indiana, where
it arched north toward northern Brown County and then turned sharply
southwest back toward the river, intersecting it a few miles above the mouth of
the Wabash River in Posey County, Indiana. It then roughly followed the line
of the Great Bend of the Ohio River and the Mississippi River, briefly crossing
the Mississippi River and running parallel and about twenty miles west of the
course of the river from a point near the mouth of the Des Moines River, in
Iowa, north to the bank opposite the mouth of the Rock River in Illinois. It
was this ridge left by the retreating glacier through which the Mississippi
River, later shifting its channel to the east, would cut its valley, forming the
upper and lower rapids. [20]
    The impact of the Wisconsin glacier, which began to recede sixteen
thousand years ago, but did not finally vacate the region until as recently as ten
thousand years ago, was to add considerable complexity to the two level plains
deposited by the Kansas and Illinoisan glaciers, west and east of the
Mississippi River respectively. [21] As a thinner glacier, the Wisconsin ice sheet
advanced in a series of lobes rather than in a broad advance on all fronts. One
double-front lobe advanced from the northwest across the troughs or valleys
that would form Lakes Huron and Michigan and then moved south on a joint
front reaching the line of the Shelbyville moraine, stretching across east central
Illinois and south central Indiana and Ohio. Galesburg, Peoria, and
Springfield, Illinois, and Cincinnati, Ohio, all lie within a few miles of this
important topographical feature. But as the glacier was slow to recede, and
several times readvanced to the south, it deposited in roughly parallel lines
shallower moraines to the north and east of the Shelbyville moraine. These
included the Bloomington, Union City, Fackerton, Late Wisconsin, Defiance,
and Kalamazoo moraines running from south to north into central Michigan.
There the intersection of lobes coming from the east and west added to the
complexity of that area's terrain. A similar intersection of different lobes
created the complex terrain around the Wisconsin Kettle moraine. But this
glacier advanced no further west, leaving the rest of Wisconsin and Illinois
uncovered. Far to the northwest, however, another lobe plunged south from
the Minnesota River valley as far as the headwaters of the Des Moines River,

20 Fenneman, *Physiography of Eastern United States*, 454, 474, 577; W. N. Logan, ed., *Handbook
   of Indiana Geology* (Indianapolis, 1922), 19, 66; Elliot Downing, *A Naturalist in the Great
   Lakes Region* (Chicago, 1914), 62, 65.
21 Fenneman, *Physiography of Eastern United States*, 474, 485.

near the modern site of Des Moines, Iowa. This glacier's advance is marked by the Bemis moraine on the east and the Altamont moraine on the west. [22]

Therefore, rather than a distinct unified geological feature, created by a single geological event, the Prairie Peninsula was built up, from east to west, by a series of different glaciers, depositing layers of different thickness at various locations over a broad zone across which most of the glaciers, at some point, reached their furthest southerly extent. That the line of furthest extent reached by different glaciers in both east and west happened to be approximately the same (which also roughly corresponds to the area of subfreezing winters) gradually created the topographical appearance of a broad connected swath of richer, newer land stretching from west to east between the infertile lands of the far north and the older, less fertile lands south beyond the reach of the glaciers. To the east of the Mississippi the base of the peninsula was laid down by the Illinoisan glacier. To the west, the Kansas glacier laid down slightly newer soil. The Wisconsin glacier then built up the eastern and western areas, south to within fifty miles of their previously farthest southern extent. As a result, the soil is richest on the northeast tip and northwest base of the peninsula, with a swath of rich soil in between. Rather than extending out from the High Plains like a peninsula, therefore, it forms a broad concave plateau, through the center of which the Mississippi River cuts its path to the south. [23]

While the glaciers rearranged the physiographic surface of the land over which they advanced and retreated, they also rearranged the lakes and rivers that drained their massive runoff. As the glaciers melted along their lines of farthest advance, they left outwash moraines, hills, and knobs to their south, which occasionally formed troughs into which flowed excess runoff, forming small river valleys. The earliest glaciers had left the Ohio, Missouri, and Mississippi rivers as the major arteries across the new land in just this way. As each subsequent glacier moved south and covered each valley (but particularly the Mississippi) with debris, the subsequent drain-off flowed down the former valley, and toward these valleys across the newly formed till plains, to carve out new valleys and eroded terrain. As the glaciers retreated further north, the source of this drain-off became more concentrated, sharpening the cutting power of the water. On the northeast, the deep furrow of a valley of an older river running from south to north was filled to the brim to form Lake Michigan. As the glacier melt continued, however, the water level apparently rose higher than the ridges to the south of the lake's edge were able to hold and torrents of water rushed down the Illinois River valley to carve its broad, deep

22 Garland, *The North American Midwest*, 94.
23 Ibid., 95.

path. Further west, beyond the higher ground of the driftless area, excess water from the retreating glacier followed a series of glacial lakes in Minnesota into the trough of the Mississippi River. Later, as the glacier moved further north and its runoff was drawn into the drainage basin of Hudson Bay, the southward push of water slowed to a trickle. Lake Michigan, meanwhile, receded within its morainic rim and the Illinois River was cut off from its water supply as well. In each case, the severing of river-water supply from extensive lake systems in the north would leave only the precipitation falling across their drainage area as a source of water. [24]

It seems that at first, the legacy of the glaciers continued to be most directly exerted by the cool, wet climate following the ice age. North and west winds blowing across the receding glaciers cooled the moisture-laden air and brought copious amounts of rain below the melt line. Over the centuries, as the climate warmed with the retreat of the glaciers, however, the source of moisture increasingly came from southerly subtropical winds off the Gulf of Mexico. In more recent times, these winds, which prevail in the late spring, summer, and early fall, clashed with the now drier surges of cold air from the Arctic to bring a highly variable, seasonal pattern of precipitation, which only declined in annual volume and intensity as one traveled west and north into the continental interior.

The volatility and variability of this climatic pattern – which still characterizes the region – was, of course, a legacy of the level lands created by the glaciers, and their great runoff in the north below the glacial extent line. [25] The topographical openness of the region assured wind currents from each of the three major directions dominant in a prevailing westerly pattern. With the elimination of the moisture-laden maritime air from the Pacific by the Rocky Mountains, however, the contrast of the variable flows of northern and southern winds was exacerbated, resulting in the variable seasonal pattern of precipitation. Furthermore, the reliance on the intersection of seasonal wind flows from the north or south, rather than directly off the sea, could, if one or both of the currents of winds failed to materialize, result in unusual periods of heavy rains or drought. This variation was further exacerbated by the fact that much of the region lay above the freeze line in winter: The relatively lower precipitation of the winter was locked up on or in the ground, and its effect concentrated in the spring runoff, the same time at which the rains brought in by the southerly winds increased. [26]

24 Fenneman, *Physiography of Eastern United States*, 468–72, 487–95.
25 Robert E. Warren, "The Physical Environment: A Context for Frontier Settlement," in O'Brien, *Forest, Grassland, and Historical Settlement* 95–8; Norman J. Rosenberg, "The Climate of the Great Plains Region of the United States," *Great Plains Quarterly* 7, no. 1 (Winter 1987): 22-32.
26 Reid Bryson and Kenneth F. Hare, *The Climates of North America* (New York, 1974).

But it was in the end the level, poorly drained, vast, and treeless landscape left behind by the glaciers that gave this variable pattern of precipitation its volatile environmental effect. Had the land been mountainous, uneven, heavily forested, or even stony, or had it been rock-covered, with deep aquifers beneath it, any amount of precipitation would probably have run off into a series of short, locally fed streams and rivers. But the flat, clay, glacial prairies prevented much drainage beneath the surface, while allowing water to run off toward lower ground across extensive areas. That enormous amounts of water were once trapped on the surface is evident from the numerous contemporary accounts of vast "wet prairies" that settlers encountered in the interior of Illinois in the nineteenth century. Water not trapped on the surface or in marshes sought lower ground and carved troughs and valleys through the deep prairie loam. These loam-filled outflows naturally moved toward the largest valleys created by older glaciers, reinforcing the regional drainage system.

Thus, from all directions, water flowed toward only a few major channels, putting enormous pressure on them. In the spring these valleys routinely overflowed, the water carving newer banks and channels. Given its reliance on uneven precipitation, however, this rush through the system left only minimal water to flow through it for the rest of the year. By middle summer lighter water flows deposited heavy amounts of loam in the valleys, which for a while blanketed the riverbanks in rich soil, but later filled in parts of the river and facilitated the near drying up of the rivers. It was this dramatic interaction between the character of the land and that of the rivers to which Easterners would have to respond in order to forge effectively a new economy and society in the early nineteenth century. The length, variable water flow, and alluvial character of the rivers directly mirrored the relatively level, alluvial, poorly drained, treeless, loose-soil surface of the land and the variable climate through which they ran. The discovery of these mechanisms and the natural flow of environmental processes from the land to the rivers occurred haltingly, but settlers moving west after 1810 gradually adjusted. My first task will be to explore the progress of these discoveries and the manner in which the knowledge gained from experience was used to shape individual and aggregate actions in forming a regional economic and social system between 1810 and 1840. The order in which this analysis proceeds is not crucial, for the discovery of different realities occurred simultaneously and unevenly. But to cast the broadest net in searching for the underlying forces that shaped regional development, we will look first at the settlement and occupation of the land, just up to the point at which regional economic activity became pervasive, and then focus in more detail on the sequence of man's actions and responses to the vast variable rivers that flowed through the region,   and examine how the character of this encounter, experienced by different people, affected the subsequent pattern of human activity in the region.

2

The land takes shape: the process of settlement

The great prairie plain that extends from the Allegheny River and Ohio River valleys on the east and south, west beyond the Missouri River, forms a geological and topographical patchwork of smaller prairies of different sizes, with varying soil quality, vegetation, drainage, and climate. Today, the differentiation of agricultural and industrial activity across the region reflects the contours of this topographical and environmental diversity. Such an alignment, however, evolved only through a long historical process of land-use differentiation that followed the course of settlement and economic and social development.

At first, the process through which farmers sorted out the most efficient uses of the land across the Midwest was interwined – indeed, at times, submerged – in the dynamics of mass migration and settlement. Before farmers could begin to formulate precise market strategies and differentiate land use according to topography, location, and market orientation of their farms, they first had to find a suitable plot of ground, clear the land, till it, live on it, and try to market a few crops. The latter process, given the broad choice in locating a farm and the uncertainty about what factors made for a good farm, was far less precise, systematic, and rational than the former. For any individual or group, the choice of where to settle was complicated by a wide range of factors and variables. In addition to goals, intentions, decision-making power, and behavior, access to transportation, economic interests and assets, cultural values, timing, and luck also affected the ability of settlers to reach certain destinations. Thus, all these factors shaped settlement patterns, and even if they were relatively equal, the quality of a plot of ground was judged by several different variables. In spite of such difficulties, however, settlers did try to balance a variety of factors and variables in choosing where to locate in the West. Consequently, an understanding of how the relative weight of these factors shifted and caused changes in the settlement patterns of the Midwest as settlers moved from east to west could provide the historian of a regional system with a point of departure for an investigation of the underlying forces of both local and regional economic and urban development.

16

Both contemporary guidebook writers and immigrants implied in words and actions that if sufficient information, transportation, and economic support had been available, the settlement of the trans-Appalachian West could have occurred in a rational, more efficient order. The best any settler could do in achieving this goal, however, William Amphlett suggested, was "after due regard to the healthfulness of a settlement, [to] look out for a combination of as many advantages as may be found together on any given point." [1] He sensed that most immigrants, although aware that the land near them was probably not the best, chose to temporarily settle on inferior lands just to get a footing, establish a farm, and gain some experience. Then they could leisurely look around or, if immediately dissatisfied, move around over the course of several years until they found a place they liked. It was not only the complexity of the factors involved or the cost in energy expended but also the size of the region that precluded a rational strategy and replaced it with a trial-and-error process. One could not, as Amphlett remarked "take a ride over a state so easily as over an English county and examine its advantages. ... The length of the voyage, and the wearisomeness of the long journey, make him [the immigrant] very desirous of a home for himself and his family. He is tired of American taverns, their accommodations, and their high charges, and at last he is generally left to chance for his final lot." Settlers were, he thought, more inclined to take a chance and accept what was available near where they landed, secure in the knowledge that if in a few years they were dissatisfied, they could easily move on. [2]

A few guidebook writers thought, however, that if one had the time, energy, and money, an effort to make an informed choice by studying the range of lands available would be amply repaid with a maximum return in farming and land-value appreciation. Morris Birkbeck, for one, though as early as 1818 unsuccessful in finding any first-rate land left in Ohio, felt himself "repaid by the pleasure of our ride through a fine portion of the country, and especially by the information we pick up as we pass along. It is by multiplied observations that we must qualify ourselves to make a good final choice." [3] According to such rationalists, to choose correctly, or at least wisely, one should study and analyze the different characteristics that made for a first-rate piece of land, decide which variable or two were most important, and then almost secretly travel around as much of the country as one could before deciding on some general area. Having done that, the more careful land prospectors would study

1 William Amphlett, *The emigrant's directory to the western states of North America* (London, 1819), 194–5.
2 Ibid., 166, 194–5.
3 Morris Birkbeck, *Notes on a journey in America from the coast of Virginia to the territory of Illinois* (London, 1818), 73, 115; John Woods, *Two Years Residence on the English Prairie of Illinois*, ed. Paul M. Angle (Chicago, 1968), 178–9; William Oliver, *Eight months in Illinois; with information to emigrants* (Newcastle-upon-Tyne, 1843), 94, 126.

the maps in the regional land office to pinpoint which sections and townships were still available for sale and then, often accompanied by an informed guide or surveyor, proceed to walk around the chosen townships to test the soil, water, and drainage and observe the vegetation, trees, agriculture, and climate. Having decided, one would rush back to the office and lay a claim to a specific section. Given the vast number of potential sites, and the number of variables involved, this was about the best one could do, and most immigrants seemed to accept this fact. It was sufficient for most rationalists, therefore, to provide an immigrant with a general destination. Once there he could then study the local maps, walk the land, and make his own decision.

Among the many general descriptions of the early West in immigrant guidebooks, Edmund Dana's *Geographical sketches on the western country: designed for emigrants and settlers . . .* , published in 1819, stands out among the first generation of western guides for its detail, precision, and its sophisticated use of data to make rather complex multivariate locational decisions. [4] For the historian, therefore, his work provides an opportunity to compare impressions with actual settlement and thus to interpret and explain the early course of regional settlement. In the course of his detailed descriptions of most of the areas west of the state of Ohio, Dana mentions at least eight variables as relevant in determining a location's suitability for profitable settlement: climate, the availability of ground water, the availability of timber, drainage, topography, the quality of the soil, the legal security of one's claim, and access to a market. What strikes one in reading Dana's report of each area is that he seems to highlight only those characteristics of each place that seem worthy of special mention, positively or negatively. One may assume from this that he considered the other variables of average quality. Moreover, rather than having a settler look for a site with the greatest number of positive variables, Dana was aware that some variables were of greater or lesser importance than others: Because a cluster of positive attributes could, in certain circumstances, be outweighed by negative ones, decisions had to be made by balancing positive and negative variables of different weights.

Theoretically, as implied by Dana's mention (or nonmention) of some characteristics, the variable with the greatest weight is the one whose values vary most within the area under analysis. Varying most, settlers tended to value it more and attached critical importance to it in making a decision. As a result, its pattern across a region would, given the relative weights of other variables, strongly influence the pattern of locational decisions and settlement. In recognizing this, Dana also implicitly pinpointed a primary mechanism by

4 Edmund Dana, *Geographical sketches on the western country: designed for emigrants and settlers . . . including a particular description of unsold public lands, collected from a variety of authentic sources. Also, a list of the principal roads* (Cincinnati, 1819).

which change in the pattern of settlement occurred across a region as it was slowly "created" by man's occupation of land. No doubt, the broad range of values of the critical variable across an area would elicit a response, usually decreasing the range of variation, if possible, and thus reducing the critical weight of that variable in relation to others. As the range of values of one variable narrowed, another variable would gradually become more critical and thus have the greatest weight in decision making until it too was controlled by the settlers' responses to it.

In a similar way, the expansion of the area settled increased the range of values of each variable and could, by increasing the range of one variable as opposed to another, shift the relative weights among them, change the critical variable upon which decisions were made, and thus reorient the pattern of settlement. In either case, expansion and development shifted the relative weights among variables, which in turn shifted gradually the decision-making patterns of subsequent immigration. The subtle process by which variables interacted in the course of decision making and response was the motive force behind the aggregate shifts in certain patterns of the system's spatial arrangements; in this case, shifting patterns of settlement would foreshadow and ultimately cause dramatic structural shifts in the region's urban or economic system.

One can simulate such a mechanism at work by employing Dana's data, supplemented where necessary by estimates of variables at different locations derived from other sources, to arrive at an attractiveness index or score for each area of the West in the 1820s. Because we are using incomplete nominal or ordinal data, we are limited to assigning each range of values for each variable on a similar one-to-ten scale, then adding up the scores of the different variables of each area to arrive at a cumulative attractiveness index. This number, of course, has no arithmetic significance but is simply a sum that allows us to compare it with other sums achieved in the same way and to arrive at some sense of the relative value of different areas. In Table 2.1 the range of values for each variable as described by Edmund Dana is assigned a high or low score from ten down to one. In each case a positive attribute is scored high, a negative one is scored low, while missing data or no mention of a value is arbitrarily assigned a median score so as to cancel out other missing data and yet not skew the general score for a piece of land too high or too low. Among the variables cited, soil quality, topography, and timber are given the most consideration and thus have the most finely differentiated degrees of positive or negative values. Indeed, Dana mentions no less than twenty-one gradations of soil quality across the region, of which the most common ten, ranging from "superior" to "sterile," were used as values to score a plot of land. [5]

5 Ibid.

Table 2.1. *The attractiveness to settlers of western locations as assessed by Edmund Dana in 1819*

Location	QSL	TOP	MKT	WAT	DRE	TBR	CTE	CLM	Total
American Bottom	10	5	4	8	(5)	(8)	(3)	(9)	52
Bluffs above American Bottom	4	3	4	(5)	(6)	(7)	(7)	(8)	44
Southern Illinois River Valley	3	3	4	(5)	(5)	(8)	(6)	(6)	40
Military Tract northeast	10	5	3	(5)	(7)	6	(5)	5	46
Between Big and Little Wabash	6	3	5	7	3	(6)	(8)	(8)	46
Northeast Illinois	9	8	3	7	2	2	(5)	(3)	39
Vicinity of Carlisle, Ill.	8	8	4	2	9	2	7	10	50
12 miles northeast of Parasaw Creek, Ill.	5	5	6	(4)	2	9	3	(8)	42
Wabash Bottoms, Ind.	8	4	6	(5)	3	(5)	(4)	(8)	43
Above Alton, Ill.	5	5	4	5	6	7	(7)	(8)	47
Near Edwardsville, Ill.	(7)	(6)	4	(7)	(8)	(7)	(7)	6	52
Outside Carlisle, Ill.	8	7	4	5	(8)	(7)	(7)	10	56
Near Macoupin Creek, Ill.	4	4	3	7	(8)	(6)	(5)	8	45
East of Macoupin Creek	10	9	3	7	(8)	(6)	(5)	(7)	55
Illinois River 30 miles above Alton	4	(5)	3	3	(8)	3	(6)	(5)	37
Sangamon Valley, Ill.	7	8	1	5	(6)	8	(5)	3	43
Salt River, Mo.	6	(5)	1	(5)	(7)	(7)	(5)	7	43
Along Missouri River	3	2	3	(5)	(5)	(6)	(4)	(4)	32
Behind Cape Girardeau, Mo.	5	8	4	(5)	(6)	(7)	(5)	(8)	48
Florrissant Valley, Mo.	8	7	4	(7)	(6)	(8)	(5)	(8)	53

	QSL	TOP	MKT	WAT	DRE	TBR	CTE	CLM	
Around St. Genevieve, Mo.	3	3	4	(5)	(8)	(5)	(5)	(8)	41
Bottoms near St. Genevieve	8	7	4	(5)	(6)	(8)	(4)	(8)	50
Howard County Mo., High Ground	8	8	1	7	(8)	9	(7)	(7)	55
Missouri Bottoms, Howard County, Mo.	10	7	1	(5)	(6)	7	(5)	(7)	48
Northeast Indiana, Plein River	2	4	3	(5)	1	2	(5)	(3)	23
Tippecanoe Valley, Ind.	10	8	6	(7)	(7)	4	(7)	(3)	49
Around Vincennes, Ind.	8	8	8	(6)	(6)	(7)	(7)	(9)	57
Near Corydon, Ind.	1	1	10	(5)	(8)	(8)	(4)	(8)	43
Ohio Bottoms, Ind.	7	4	4	(5)	(5)	(10)	(7)	(7)	55
Around Hamilton, Ohio	(8)	(6)	(10)	(7)	(6)	(5)	(5)	(9)	56

Note: QSL = quality of soil; TOP = topography; MKT = market access; WAT = quality of water; DRE = drainage; TBR = availability of timber; CTE = climate, healthiness; CLM = security of land claim.

Rankings by number, going from best (10) to worst (1), are given for each variable. Quality of soil: 10, superior; 9, exceedingly rich; 8, excellent; 7, strong, fertile; 6, good; 5, middling, ordinary; 4, second-rate; 3, thin; 2, infertile; 1, sterile. Topography: 10, high elevated; 9, gentle swells; 8, prairie; 7, moderately elevated; 6, high bottoms; 5, low, flat bottom; 4, low, uniform; 3, broken, hills; 2, rugged, holes; 1, barren, rough. Market access: 10, strong profits; 8, good profit; 7, occasional profits; 6, break even; 5, occasional risk; 4, some risk; 2, great risk; 1, outside. Quality of water: 8, plentiful water; 7, well watered; 6, very good; 5, good; 4, scarce; 3, poor; 2, tainted; 1, none. Drainage: 10, dry; 9, very well drained; 8, well drained; 7, moist; 6, above floods; 5, occasionally inundated; 4, damp; 3, annually inundated; 2, occasionally cold and wet; 1, wet. Availability of timber: 10, bottom forest; 9, handsome forest; 8, interspersed; 7, mixed prairie and forest; 6, wide-skirts of forest; 5, fringe; 4, scattered; 3, some timber; 2, scarce; 1, none. Climate, healthiness: 10, very temperate; 9, salubrious; 8, moderate; 7, temperate; 6, variable; 5, changeable; 4, extremes; 3, harsh; 2, unhealthy; 1, deleterious. Security of land claim: 10, surveyed and just opened; 9, surveyed and being settled; 8, surveyed and settled; 7, preemption claims; 6, some speculators; 5, speculators; 4, to be surveyed; 3, ceded but unsurveyed; 2, squatters; questionable; 1, outside U.S. territory.

All missing data or implied to be fine were scored 5. Numbers in parentheses indicate estimated or implied.

His examination and assessment of soil seems to have been based on a combination of soil color and texture, terrain, and the kind of vegetation each supported. The best soils were dark, almost black, while ordinary soils were brown and gray and poorer soils became sandy and of a lighter texture. It was generally assumed that vegetation and, in particular, the growth of trees correlated directly to soil quality. But the relationship between soil and tree growth was not, as many were beginning to realize, a direct or certain one. Black soil could support both a heavy forest, as it did on the bottoms, or no timber at all, as was the case across the uplands of the Miami and Scioto rivers in Ohio and across areas of the northern Military Tract in Illinois. Moreover, heavy, rich forests, such as those north of Cincinnati, as described by Kilbourn in 1815, and across the southeastern corner of Ohio before 1815 stood on less fertile, even barren, soils that thinly covered the uneven ground. [6] Despite these anomalies, however, it was still generally assumed that tree growth was an indicator of the richness of the soil: Softwood and fruit trees flourished in the rich black bottom-land soils; harder-wood trees, such as hickory, elm, maple, and oak did best on the drier, less rich soils between the river bottoms and the open prairies; and pines, small stunted trees, and shrubbery were all that sterile and poor sandy or wet soils could maintain. [7]

Dana's soil descriptions reflect, however, the shifting opinions on the factors that created good soil, and thus on the ideas of where to look for it. It was generally assumed that there was a kind of circular cause and effect between vegetation and soil quality. Good soil grew good trees, which, in turn, by means of their decay and renewal from year to year, reinforced the quality of the soil. On the bottom lands, floods, with their deposits of silt, further replenished the soil. But Dana's examination of soil quality across Illinois suggested an interesting relationship between the topography of the land and the quality of its soil. Flat land, whether along a river bottom or across the open prairies, seemed to contain the richest soils. Second-rate soils predominated on rolling terrain with shallow gullies and low hills. Higher hills

6 John Kilbourn, *The Ohio gazetteer, or topographical dictionary; containing a description of the several counties, towns, villages, settlements, roads, rivers, lakes, springs, mines, and etc. in the state of Ohio* (Columbus, Ohio, 1819), 18–19.
7 Ibid., 19; John Bradbury, *Travels in the interior of America, in the years 1809, 1810, and 1811; including a description of upper Louisiana, together with the states of Ohio, Kentucky, Indiana, and Tennessee, with Illinois and western Territories* (Liverpool and London, 1817), 307–8; William Darby, *The emigrant's guide to the western and southwestern states and territories comprising a geographical and statistical description of the states* (New York, 1818), 217; Daniel Drake, *Natural and statistical view, or picture of Cincinnati and the Miami country illustrated by maps* (Cincinnati, 1815), 34; David Dale Owen, *Report of a geological exploration of part of Iowa, Wisconsin, and Illinois* (Washington, D.C., 1844); Sir Charles Lyell, *Travels in North America*, 2 vols. (New York, 1845; reprint, New York, 1978) 2: 62–3; Barbara Novak, *Nature and Culture* (New York, 1980), 47–77.

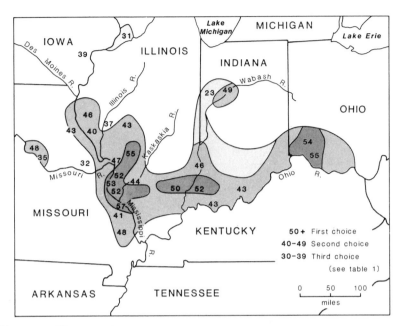

Figure 2.1. The attractiveness of western locations for settlement as assessed by Edmund Dana in 1819.

or bluffs, ridges and ravines, "knobs" and sinkholes invariably seem to have been areas of poor or sterile soil. In observing the alluvial character of both the bottom lands and the prairies, Dana joined others, particularly Kilbourn, Bradbury, and Darby, all writing before 1820, in arguing that the prairies may have been laid down by the action of water and that their soil was, in fact, quite fertile, in spite of the lack of trees. [8]

Plotted out on a regional map, the various cumulative scores arrived at for different areas present a cognitive map of Edmund Dana's West (Figure 2.1). The immediate hinterland of Cincinnati, the area around Vincennes, Indiana, the English Prairie in southeast Illinois, and, of course, the American Bottom opposite St. Louis achieved the highest scores. Somewhat surprisingly, the recently settled Boonslick country in central Missouri, also scored high. Not everyone could acquire a plot of ground in the premium areas, however, as was apparently the situation in central Ohio as early as 1818. Nevertheless, outside

8 Jervis Cutler, *A topographical description of the state of Ohio, Indiana territory, Louisiana. Comprehending the Ohio and Mississippi Rivers, and their Principal Tributary streams* (Boston, 1812), 39; Drake, *Natural and statistical view of Cincinnati*, 73–75; Oliver, *Eight months in Illinois*, 109.

of these specific regions of optimum attractiveness lay much broader areas of the West that would still provide one with a good choice, better than most land back East.[9] Most of southern Illinois and eastern Missouri, but especially the area behind Cape Girardeau, west along the Missouri river, and north of Alton, Illinois, and the area along the southern Illinois River, and most of southern Indiana provided, according to Dana's analysis, numerous opportunities for a good locational choice. In fact, according to Dana, the only lands in the West not recommended were either too near the water or beyond the range of the current regional produce market. These included the area to the northwest of the Wabash River valley, the high ground north of the Sangamon River valley in central Illinois, and the farthest northern reaches of the interior Military Tract in west central Illinois.

These figures confirm, ironically however, the misgivings of other guide writers about the possibility or need for such a rational approach to choosing a location. After all, if such a vast area scored about the same, the mix of variables must be so complex that no decision could gain any real advantage. Only by experience could one really get to know the land and climate, as well as one's own preferences, and thereby make an optimum choice based on one's own needs. Nevertheless, Dana's figures do pinpoint several premium areas amid the generally attractive lands across the West. By analyzing the mix of variables that made these areas attractive, we can better appreciate the difficulty in balancing positive and negative variables as one tried to make a decision on where to settle.

For example, despite the exceedingly high fertility of the American Bottom, the area was only about as attractive as less fertile areas around Vincennes, Cincinnati, or Howard County, Missouri, because of its poor ground water, inadequate drainage, and unhealthy climate. The bottoms along the Missouri River in Howard County were able to counteract a less advantageous market location by having considerably better drainage, a healthy climate, and soil of almost equal fertility. Meanwhile, the uneven, second-rate, forested land behind Cincinnati scored as high as each of these richer western areas because of its proximity to a major market center with a strong demand for produce. The nearby bottom lands along the Ohio, however, although close to Cincinnati and having richer soil than interior areas north of the city, were compromised by their tendency to flood regularly. This negative factor resulted in an even stronger disincentive to settlement along the Wabash bottom lands, which, in spite of their rich soil, were liable to annual

9 Michael J. O'Brien, "The Roots of Frontier Expansion," in *Grassland, Forest, and Historical Settlement; An Analysis of Dynamics in Northeast Missouri*, ed. Michael J. O'Brien (Lincoln, Neb., 1984), 74–77; Birkbeck, *Notes on a journey in America*, 69–72; Woods, *Two Years Residence on the English Prairie*, xxix.

inundations and thus impractical for agriculture. In this case, strong scores on each of the other variables were counteracted by a very low score in healthfulness and drainage. Indeed, so strong was the disincentive to settle along the Wabash that these rich bottom lands were considered to be equally attractive to settlers as the poor, hilly lands behind Corydon, Indiana, the value of which came only from their proximity to nearby markets.

Among the broad range of areas that scored on the second level of attractiveness, a variety of combinations of different variables also existed. The very rich lands across the prairies of north central Ohio, Indiana, and Illinois were simply beyond the range of the market and thus unlikely to provide remunerative farming for years to come. In Illinois this disincentive was exacerbated by uncertain land titles, a factor that seemed to negate all other positive attributes, as it had once in western Kentucky and extreme southern Illinois. Dana believed that there was no security in squatting and invariably recommended that a settler choose a less rich tract of land where one's claim was secure, such as in eastern Missouri or further south along the Sangamon River in Illinois, rather than risk occupying an unsecured plot of very rich land. Indeed, the average scores for each variable at a variety of locations along the Missouri coast, as well as along the Ohio in southern Indiana, made both areas a haven for more conservative types wanting to make a safe choice. Not surprisingly, these areas were also heavily settled by immigrants interested in the richer lands nearby and who settled there so as to be in a position to occupy the land immediately after it was surveyed and the titles cleared.

Dana was the first to admit, however, that the West that he saw according to the criteria of attractiveness was still years, if not decades, from becoming a reality. Actual settlement patterns in 1819 still clustered much further east, with only a few thousand "strays," "leftovers," or pioneers drifting down the Ohio and taking up residence across from St. Louis in the Illinois country. The discrepancy between his assessment of western lands and the actual pattern of settlement indicates that some of the variables by which land was judged had considerably more weight; in certain cases they could even preclude the relevance of other variables. One need only compare the pattern of individual variables across the West with the known pattern of settlement in 1820 to discern the relative importance of market access, the availability of timber, and the quality of the soil.

Dana believed, for example, that the richest soils in the region, and indeed in the country as a whole, had yet to be encountered by the wave of immigration. From authentic sources, as well as his own observations as a resident and surveyor of the Military Tract, Dana argued that the richest soils in the West were located across the north central part of the tract. In his more general guide he seems only to have been aware of the first swath of rich soil running along the east bank of the Mississippi behind the future site of Quincy.

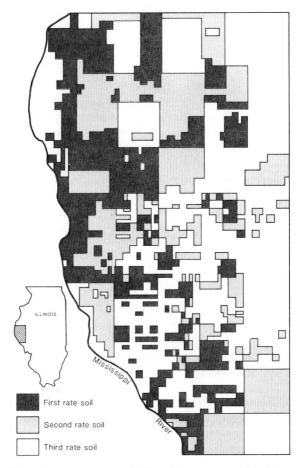

First rate soil

Second rate soil

Third rate soil

Figure 2.2. Soil quality of the western Military Tract as assessed by Edmund Dana in 1819.

However, in a far more detailed analysis of the bounty lands of the Military Tract, also published in 1819, and clearly reflecting his belief that one could determine the premium locations in an area and efficiently guide settlers to them, he also pinpointed another band of rich soil that cut a northwest to southeast swath across the future area of Knox County and intersected the west bank of the Illinois River near the site of Fort Clark (the future site of Peoria).[10] Further east he described, in addition to a similar swath of rich land crossing the Wabash River valley, another band of rich soil that skirted the

10 Edmund Dana, *A description of the bounty lands in the state of Illinois: also, the principal roads and routes, by land and water, through the territory of the United States* (Cincinnati, 1819).

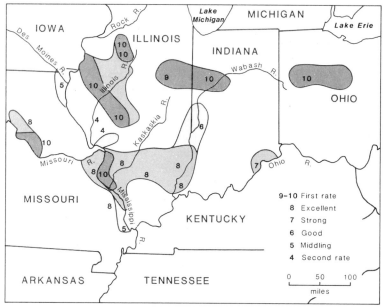

Figure 2.3. Soil quality in the West as assessed by Edmund Dana in 1819.

northern edge of the Wabash valley where the river turned southward after having run east to west from its source in western Ohio (Figures 2.2 and 2.3).

Whether Dana was aware that these rich areas of land were geologically connected to a broader area of rich alluvial soil is unclear. He did, however, note that the stretch of fertile interior land in Ohio seemed to be located just below a "ridge" of high land that ran across north central Indiana and Ohio and then turned sharply northeastward toward central New York.[11] The existence of this ridge of valuable land, forming the edge of a fertile plateau stretching across the uplands of the Miami River valley, had been widely known of from early reports in Ohio. Cutler observed that this area of good soil, sixty by one hundred milesl, commenced just north of Chillicothe. He described the land as bona fide prairie with deep, dry, rich soil, covered with tall grass (toward which drovers from Kentucky were already driving their cattle) and supporting a few trees.[12] This line, and the attention it drew from guides and geologists became, soon thereafter, something of a topographical landmark across the state. And so too would the parallel moraines that continued west across Indiana and Illinois. It is a fact of considerable interest that there, on maps that interpret Dana's data twenty years before it was

11 Dana, *Geographical sketches on the western country*, 16.
12 Cutler, *A topographical description*, 38–9.

settled and another twenty before it came entirely under cultivation as one of the richest areas in America, lies the faint impression of the Shelbyville moraine and the edge of the Prairie Peninsula. [13]

Dana was considerably less precise in determining the relative market access enjoyed by different areas in the West in 1819. In general he seems to have accepted the spreading opinion that whatever regional market activity existed before the crash of 1819, its spatial orientation was undergoing a dramatic change as a result of the recent initiation of steamboating and the gradual western shift of settlement. Sufficient descriptive evidence indicates that as early as 1815 Cincinnati had begun to draw in wheat supplies from a forty-to fifty-mile-wide hinterland in Ohio, Indiana, and Kentucky and to export significant amounts of flour and wheat to New Orleans. [14] So too, Cramer argues, had such activity recently begun as far upriver as Wheeling, Charlestown, and Maysville. To the west, however, the early shipping of produce upriver to Pittsburgh or Cincinnati, and activity occurring as early as 1810, was according to Darby "in decline" and instead "shifting towards the natural outlet [downstream] to Natchez and New Orleans." Louisville merchants, we are told, also shipped goods south. The presence of steamboats at Shippingport, Kentucky, further indicates increased Ohio River contacts with New Orleans. So too, we have evidence that the residents of the English Prairie settlement increasingly viewed New Orleans, and not Cincinnati, as the outlet for whatever goods they had to export, although Elias Fordham's mention of freight going east to Pittsburgh suggests that that trade still continued even as trade to the west and south increased. [15]

Unfortunately, with no production figures from before 1810, and few market quotations from local newspapers, it is difficult to give anything more than a general description of the market access afforded any location in the variable produce trades of the time. One way is to take average freight rates by wagon or steamboat and calculate the cost of transport between central markets and various points upriver or downriver. One could then compare, given the central-market price, local-market prices to the generally accepted break-even cost of production per bushel and determine whether shipments could have been made profitably from that distance. In Chapter 5, the

13 Allan Bogue, *From Prairie to Corn Belt* (Chicago, 1962); Robert E. Warren, "The Physical Environment: A Context of Frontier Settlement," in O'Brien, *Grassland, Forest, and Historical Settlement*, 95–134, esp. 95–7.

14 Beverly Bond, Jr., *The Civilization of the Old Northwest: A Study of Political, Social, and Economic Development, 1788–1812* (New York, 1934; reprint, St. Clair Shores, Mich. 1970), 390–6; Richard Wade, *The Urban Frontier* (Chicago, 1959); Robert Leslie Jones, *History of Agriculture in Ohio to 1880* (Kent, Ohio, 1983), 60; George Flower, *History of the English Settlement in Edwards County, Illinois* (Chicago, 1882), 278.

15 Zadoc Cramer, *The Navigator*, Cincinnati (1806): 47, 50, 59; ibid. (1808): 20, 72, 79, 87; ibid. (1814); Darby, *The emigrant's guide to the western and southwestern states and territories*, 207, 216, 217, 226.

contours of the region's economic geography will be precisely mapped out for the period after 1830. Before 1820, however, the paucity of data forces one into considerably more risky extrapolations and estimates.

For the earlier period I have been able to find only one set of reliable figures on the relative cost of land and river freights. In 1818 Elias Pym Fordham estimated the cost of shipment to market from the English Prairie settlement in southeastern Illinois.[16] Interestingly, downriver freight rates by keel boat actually seem to have been lower than rates for steamboats twenty-five years later because the time of merchants was less valuable, given the less volatile and sensitive markets, and the cost of waterpower was considerably less than maintaining a speed of six to ten miles per hour with the current by feeding wood to a high-pressure boiler. Upstream barge rates, in contrast, were about twice those of later rates for upstream steamboat freight.[17] The cost of travel by land across the English Prairie, still without roads, was in comparison very high. Fordham estimated that it cost about two and a half cents per bushel per mile to carry wheat, a figure, if correct, that is four to five times comparable costs in the 1850s.[18] Further east, in Cincinnati's hinterland, where roads were somewhat better, rates were probably half those in Illinois.

If one plots these different transport costs across a map of the Ohio River valley, the causes for the breaking in half of the flow of produce in the valley – one-half heading east toward the market in Cincinnati, the rest drifting west down the Ohio and Mississipi toward New Orleans – are readily apparent. For example, when the price of wheat was about one dollar in New Orleans, the local price at Cincinnati (estimated as the New Orleans price minus downriver freight rates) was about twenty-three cents. Given the fact that most farmers considered their break-even cost of production at about thirty cents per bushel, such a local price indicates that only local trade was occurring. Therefore, any farmers upstream and downstream, from any distance, would be discouraged from marketing their grain in Cincinnati. And yet, further downstream, in the vicinity of Shawneetown, Illinois, or Louisville, from which points the cost of transport downstream to New Orleans stood at about sixty cents, local farmers could technically have sent their produce south and made a small profit. Often, given the limited immigrant demand for one's produce, especially in low-immigration years (which seemed to correlate with lower prices), such southerly trade was the only viable economic action to take, aside from letting the crop rot in the fields or feeding it to livestock and trying to drive them to

16 Elias Pym Fordham, *Personal Narrative of Travels in Virginia, Maryland, Pennsylvania, Ohio, Indiana, Kentucky, and of a Residence in the Illinois Territory, 1817–18,* ed. Frederic Austin Ogg (Cleveland, 1906), 117–18.
17 R. Carlyle Buley, *The Old Northwest: The Pioneer Period, 1815–1840* (Bloomington, Ind., 1951), 427–9.
18 Fordham, *A Residence in Illinois,* 118.

Cincinnati overland. Likewise, shipments from around St. Louis could, in an average-price year, generate a modest profit (Figure 2.5).

When the New Orleans market was higher – say, for instance, at a dollar and a half – market prices at Cincinnati would be somewhere around seventy cents per bushel. At that rate, farmers from as far north and east as Pittsburgh but only as far west as Madison, Indiana, could ship produce to the Queen City markets. Below Madison, hardly one hundred miles west of Cincinnati on the Ohio, the alternative, in a medium-price year, shifted dramatically in New Orleans's favor. When prices at New Orleans stood at a dollar and a half, most farmers in southern Indiana were still within profitable shipping range, but now beyond the profitable range of shipping their produce upstream to Cincinnati. Thus, as farmers moved into the southern Wabash valley, along the Ohio in Illinois and Indiana, and up the Mississippi, the drift of the "natural outlet" with the river currents, instead of back against them, became more and more apparent. This fact was recognized by Birkbeck, who when traveling down the Ohio, remarked that he "felt himself actually approximating to Europe as we proceeded to the west" on account of the contacts between the western fringe of the valley and New Orleans.[19]

Another variable that Dana identified as important in choosing a good site was the availability of timber. As already noted, and described by Dana, Kilbourn, Drake, Birkbeck, and others, the heavy forest that covered the Alleghenies lined the banks of the Ohio River from Pittsburgh to Cincinnati, and extended inland, in some places, more than a hundred miles. To the north, however, settlers were already observing that the timber became thinner and indeed gave way to mostly open ground above Zanesville, Ohio, and especially west and north of the Miami and Scioto river valleys.[20] Further west, a heavy forest, containing a variety of fine timber, covered the hilly terrain between the White and Ohio rivers in southern Indiana. Beyond the Wabash, the trees thinned out again and gave way, gradually, to more open prairies, at first no more than meadows, but eventually, to the north and west of the English Prairie and above the National Road, to vast open treeless plains. Further west and south, timber continued to line the Ohio, parts of the Mississippi and Missouri river bottoms, as well as the Flourissant and Salt river valleys in Missouri. But the further west one traveled, the narrower the bands of timber along the rivers became. Dana also noted that as these bottom-land forests thinned out, their exotic and subtropical trees gave way to more temperate-

19 Birkbeck, *Notes on a journey in America*, 80; John Mack Faragher, *Sugar Creek: Life on the Illinois Prairie* (New Haven, 1986), 102–5.
20 Kilbourn, *Ohio gazetteer, or topographical dictionary*, 17; Culter, *A topographical description of the State of Ohio*, 38–9; Bond, *Civilization of the Old Northwest*, 395; Jones, *Agriculture in Ohio*, 123; Birkbeck, *Notes on a journey in America*, 60–2, 66; Woods, *Two Years Residence on the English Prairie*, 172, 178.

zone hickories, elms, maples, and oaks.[21] Brian Birch's modern analysis of
eastern Illinois shows that these stands of river-bottom timber gave way to a
fringe of less dense woods and then a mixture of woods and meadows, either in
a variegated pattern (which Dana referred to as "mixed") or in differentiated
patches of thick handsome woods and wide, increasingly larger prairies covered
in grass and shrubs, interspersed with only an occasional tree within a few
miles of the western tributaries of the Wabash. On the American Bottom, a
similar mixture of trees and meadows near the river was reinforced by a heavy
stand of timber extending inland beyond Carlyle, at which point the woods
began to thin out.[22] Robert Warren, in his recent analysis of the original
vegetation in the Salt River valley in Missouri, documents a similar pattern,
although there the prairies began within a mile or two of the river.[23]

Dana himself recorded this pattern in his detailed analysis of the Military
Tract, just across the Mississippi from the Salt River valley. In the narrow
southern peninsula of the tract between the Illinois and the Mississippi rivers,
Dana found, as one still finds today, a relatively thick forest on uneven, hilly
ground. Several miles north, these stands of timber were increasingly limited
to the river bottoms, whereas "mixtures" and "interspersals" of timber and
prairie became more common on the higher ground. Throughout the area
behind the future site of Quincy, he found spacious prairies skirted with stands
of timber of varying widths, which narrowed as one traveled north. In one
instance he noted that the trees and open land were arranged in patches, as if
the trees were intentionally planted "reservations of spacious wood lots" amid
a cultivated landscape, an observation similar to that made earlier by Cutler
about northwestern Ohio.[24] Twenty to forty miles further north, in present-day
Hancock County, however, the timber became increasingly scarce, appearing
as isolated, small, and thus often hardly visible islands amid vast open prairies.
Yet only in two instances did he record "scarcely a tree as far as the eye can
reach," those places being near the respective centers of Hancock and Henry
counties. The great treeless expanses of prairie to the east and north remained,
in 1819, beyond his purveyance.[25]

By comparing each of these regionwide patterns with the pattern of
population density as mapped out in the 1890 census, we can gain a sense of

21 Samuel R. Brown, *The western gazetteer; or, emigrant's directory, containing a geographical
    description of the western states and territories* (Auburn, N.Y., 1817), 20.
22 Brian P. Birch, "British Evaluation of the Forest Openings and Prairie Edges of the
    North-Central States, 1800–1850," in *The Frontier: Comparative Studies*, ed. William W.
    Savage, Jr., and Stephen I. Thompson (Norman, Okla., 1979), 167–72.
23 Dana, *Geographical sketches on the western country*, 137, 145–6, 292–3; Birch, "British
    Evaluations of the Forest Openings," 170; Warren, "The Physical Environment: A Context
    for Frontier Development," in O'Brien, *Grassland, Forest, and Historical Settlement*, 113–29.
24 Dana, *A description of the bounty lands in the state of Illinois*, 18–20, 32–3; Cutler, *A
    topographical description of the State of Ohio*, 38.
25 Dana, *A description of the bounty lands in the state of Illinois*, 6, 18–20, 33–3.

the relative impact of each pattern on collective locational decisions. [26] The relative importance of each is, apparently, rather clear. The concentration of settlement in a narrow band along the Ohio River and across southern Illinois up to the northern edge of the American Bottom and across into the Boonslick territory in central Missouri seems to ignore the pattern of soil quality across the region. The fit between population and pattern of timber is somewhat closer. Perhaps settlers, in spite of Dana's evidence (which, by the way, most of them probably never saw) were, as Birch argues concerning English settlers, convinced that good trees meant good soil and a healthy environment and thus followed the trees. Their avoidance of western Kentucky would be understandable in this light. Even so, a number of forested areas remained unsettled – in particular, northwestern Ohio, the extreme southern tip of Illinois, and southwestern Missouri. In any case, Douglas McManis argues, correctly I believe, that the emphasis on timber naturally waned in the 1820s and 1830s as settlers moved out onto land having a thinner growth of timber and, through experience, refuted the theory. [27] The fit between the shape of the market and the pattern of settlement was even closer. Indeed, in some places, the line at which population density thinned out to under two persons per square mile and the edge of occasional market participation seem to shadow each other. From this general evidence it would seem that the majority of immigrants in the early West paid most attention, in making their locational decisions, to a mix of timber availability and market access.

The general data seem, therefore, to suggest a shift in which variables most settlers considered most important in making a locational choice. As settlers moved west, and market agriculture increased, market access and land quality (which was directly related to crop yield) increased in importance at the expense of timber, and began to direct the general pattern of settlement. Such evidence may be taken as demonstrating the increasing dominance of the market in regional life during this period. Or it may reflect earlier limitations that prevented settlers from settling according to market criteria or precluded market-oriented action, thus focusing attention on other factors that waned over the course of the 1820s and 1830s.

There is some evidence that in the early period, economic, time, and transport limitations may have made the entire immigration process unresponsive to rational choices. Within any migration chain, for example, the

26 Frederick Merk, *History of the Westward Movement* (New York, 1978), 167, 191–2; Birch, "British Evaluations of the Forest Openings," 171; Charles O. Paulin, *Atlas of the Historical Geography of the United States* (New York, 1932), 76; James E. Davis, *Frontier America, 1800 –1840: A Comparative Demographic Analysis of the Settlement Process* (Glendale, Calif., 1977), 34–8.
27 Douglas R. McManis, *The Initial Evaluation and Utilization of the Illinois Prairies, 1815–40* (Chicago, 1964), 76–85; Richard K. Vedder and Lowell E. Gallaway, "Migration and the Old

experiences of those at the front of the settlement process are filtered back to those behind them on the trail. As this occurs and the recommended path proves most efficient (and the locational choices prove themselves), the path of migration becomes a beaten track that anyone, without much thought, can follow until they find a location for a farm that is suitable, according to the current preferences of which variable is most important.

The point to be made is that the internal decision-making dynamics of this process were basically programmed, or irrational, or even blind. Having just followed those in front of them, later immigrants who did not just fill in where the first settlers had located a few years earlier, but moved past them, did so from the end of the migration chain, a fact that limited the direction of their next steps and their range of locational choices. The fact that at the end of a trip they often had little money or food left further narrowed their range of choices. Within the context of such a process, the vast open lands of the West were not judged on the basis of their various characteristics, and then sought out, but simply on the extent to which the next open land the immigrants came to met basic criteria for a farm – which amounts to saying that migration flows tended to follow the paths of least resistance across the topography of a region and that previous migration patterns combined with topography almost to determine the lands the settler would directly encounter, come near to, or bypass entirely. Obviously, the density and pattern of such movement were determined to a great extent by the dominant means of transportation. In the case of the West before 1820, most transport was by wagon, foot, or barge. The former traffic would be steered along the major roads crossing the river, whereas the barge traffic would naturally be drawn down the Ohio straight toward the west bank of the Mississippi and the American Bottom. [28]

Limited economic resources and simple, self-sufficient goals among the majority of settlers before 1820 give further support to such a geographic explanation. Several contemporaries reported on how the lack of resources restrained immigrants from shopping around, the basis of a rational strategy. William Amphlett argued that most settlers – tired, out of money, desirous of getting established – would finally give themselves up to the luck of the draw and take what was nearest and best at most reasonable prices. Nor could immigrants expect much financial help from relatives; indeed, during the early years of settlement, the reverse was often the case. In addition, few migrants could risk the extensive cost of purchasing land after arrival, calculated by one writer as equal to four or five times one's annual average income. [29] Van Zandt described the usual predicament of new settlers: "Having expended large sums

Northwest," in *Essays in Nineteenth Century Economic History: The Old Northwest*, ed. David C. Klingaman and Richard K. Vedder (Athens, Ohio, 1975), 159–76.
28 Davis, *Frontier America*, 46.
29 Amphlett, *The emigrant's directory*, 165–6.

of money on the road and having labored under serious difficulties arising from their ignorance of the country, and thereby exposing themselves to a loss of a season, which in the circumstances of some of them was hardly to be redeemed," or of property – which, in Cramer's words, "few individuals could bear the loss of" – most settlers were, in Flint's words, "in a hurry to commence operations for the provisions of their families." The result, not surprisingly, was a series of mistakes, poorly chosen locations, and accidents, forcing one to move again only a few years after settling down.[30] This economic pressure, which encouraged one to move quickly and efficiently to one's new chosen home, explains to some extent the utilitarian, practical leanness of Cramer's *Navigator* and other river and road guides. Most settlers had to pack up, travel, buy their new farm, and, if not break ground, then at least begin preparations for the following season, all within the year, or face economic calamity.[31]

But even if one had the time and money to view the country, or read and study Cramer's, Van Zandt's, Brown's, or Dana's guides, there was, given the economic goals of most immigrants, little interest in maximizing one's long-term profits by searching out the very best plot of land across an area, as defined by environmental and geological characteristics. In the first place, Dana indicates that even soil in the West that he ranked barren and thin could produce a fine crop of small grains at yields equal to or slightly higher than those received back East.[32] Second-rate soils in the West, which included most of Indiana and Illinois, could produce a fine crop. The average in Ohio ranged from 25 to 45 bushels per acre, which in an average year exceeded eastern yields by 40 to 50 percent. On less fertile ground 30 bushels was more common, while on the most fertile bottoms some farmers reported yields as high as 50 bushels of wheat an acre.[33] The impact of the rich bottom lands was especially apparent in corn culture. From an average of from 30 to 50 bushels a year on average soil in an average year, Fordham noted yields could range as high as 80 bushels per acre. Woods regarded 60 to 80 bushels per acre as a "good crop," even though he only had about 50 bushels or less from his first two harvests on the English Prairie. In very wet years yields could range even higher. Woods claimed that he heard of someone getting as much as 132

---

30 Nicholas Biddle Van Zandt, *A full description of the soil, water, timber, and prairies of each lot, or quarter section of the military lands between the Mississippi and Illinois Rivers* (Washington, D.C. 1818), iii; Cramer, *The Navigator* (1808): 14; Timothy Flint, *The history and geography of the Mississippi Valley* (Cincinnati, 1832), 35.

31 For a discussion of the costs of emigration thirty years later, see John Mack Faragher, *Women and Men on the Overland Trail* (New Haven, 1980), 20–4.

32 Cramer, *The Navigator* (1814); Brown, *The western gazetteer;* Van Zandt, *A full description of the military lands;* Dana, *Geographical sketches on the western country,* 7, 65–85, 109–24, 134–47, 290–9.

33 *Ibid.,* 66, 84–5, 136. On eastern yields, see Samuel Blodget, *Economica* (Philadelphia, 1806; reprint, New York, 1964), 97.

bushels an acre, while Kilbourn reported that 100 bushels an acre was not uncommon on the Ohio River bottoms.[34] Such yields far outstripped the capacity of any land in the East. Indeed, all soils above "thin" (or a two in our ranking system) generated yields as high as the best lands in the East and more than provided for the needs of a farmer and his family, no matter his choice of land. The choice of location, in short, was not very critical in determining whether one would be able to provide for oneself. The ability to do that was assumed at almost any location across the region.

But if this was the case, why then would immigrants have wanted to move west in the first place? Apparently farmers saw it as a chance to purchase a larger farm than that back East, which would appreciate in time; by selling it at some future point, they would be able to pay for an even larger farm further west, thus providing for their families' futures. That many immigrants had such motives on their minds is evident in comments in contemporary guidebooks: "The most radical fault committed by emigrants respecting the land is the purchase of too much. The probable rise in the price of the land is no excuse for this error. Where one man has gained by the augmentation in the value of the land, fifty have become rich by its fruits."[35] Another guide writer argued that in buying such large sections of land, farmers then planted much more than they could possibly handle during the harvesttime, which resulted in an increase in weed and pest problems and a decline in yields over time.[36] In some guide writers' eyes, farmers were trying to have their cake and eat it too. High yields would produce surpluses in a burgeoning market, and that market would appreciate the value of unsold lands, thus rapidly increasing their capital and enabling them to buy even more land further west. This strategy could best be carried out, not surprisingly, near the line of settlement. There, strong demand from incoming settlers for produce and land would bid up the value of both. Thus, as has been argued was the case in the Military Tract, the marketability of land played an important role in determining its cost, and that role was often more affected by its economic location than by its characteristics.[37]

Given these dynamics, there was a strong incentive to settle out at the fringe of settlement, rather than either closer to the center of regional development or too far out beyond the line of such settlement. In the former place, land would

34 Fordham, *A Residence in Illinois*, 119; Woods, *Two Years Residence on the English Prairie*, 152; Drake, *Natural and statistical view of Cincinnati*, 34; Bond, *The Civilization of the Old Northwest*, 320–1; Kilbourn, *The Ohio gazetteer, or topographical dictionary*, 20; Blodget, *Economica*, 97; Darby, *The emigrant's guide to the western and southwestern states and territories*, 304; Frederick Taylor, *A sketch of the military bounty tract of Illinois* (Philadelphia, 1839), 12.
35 Darby, *The emigrant's guide to the western and southwestern states and territories*, 298.
36 Drake, *Natural and statistical view of Cincinnati*, 57.
37 Siyoung Park, "Perception of Land Quality and Settlement of North Pike County, 1821–36," *Western Illinois Regional Studies* 3 (1980): 5–21.

cost just as much as in the East, enabling one to buy only as much as one had had before, and given the cost of immigration, perhaps even less. Moreover, as Darby warned, nearer the center, as the best lands were taken, settlers would begin to skip west. Locally, the result was a decline in demand pressure on local land values and a slowing in their appreciation. To settle on higher-priced ground near a town or city, therefore, was to stake one's economic future on the growth of the nearby urban place and not on the appreciation of land values caused by rural in-migration. Birkbeck clearly understood this when, on finding a large area of land south along the Scioto River still available for settlement, he went out to examine it and, as expected, found that it had been passed over because it was inferior to land immediately adjacent to it.

If one ventured too far out beyond the line of settlement, however, one might have to wait a considerable period of time for the appreciation of land values to occur. While waiting for the slow-to-come appreciation, one would suffer from high transport costs to market and thus sacrifice significant potential profits over the course of several years. In addition, the chances of misjudging the path of migration, at such a distance from the main flow of settlement, were real. One could find, in later years, that the plot one believed would be right in the path of settlement was now off to the side or remote from the most prosperous towns in the area. This, eventually, was the fate of the English Prairie settlement, as the National Road drew traffic, the flow of immigration, and rising land values to the north and west. [38]

The premium location lay somewhere between these two extremes: directly in the path of migration, and within reach of markets, allowing a farmer to combine both profits of production and appreciation of land values to augment his capital. The attempts by farmers to find this zone just out in front of the line of settlement help explain the highly controlled movement of settlement across a region. Moreover, the passing-by of this zone also helps explain why people were so quick to give up their newly acquired lands as soon as yields began to level off. When great profits were to be made in Illinois in the late 1840s, recent settlers streamed out of Ohio and Indiana. Likewise, when Iowa was the place to go after 1850, numerous recent Illinois settlers joined in the rush. And again, just before and after the Civil War, when Kansas, Nebraska, and western Iowa were rapidly growing, settlers from eastern Iowa and Illinois did not hestitate to move again. [39]

38 Woods, *Two Years Residence on the English Prairie*, 178–9; Darby, *The emigrant's guide to the Western and southwestern states and territories*, 207; Birkbeck, *Notes on a journey in America*, 69–72, 80.
39 Richard Easterlin, "Population Change and Farm Settlement in the Northern United States," *Journal of Economic History* 31, no. 1 (March 1976): 45–74, esp. 54, 63–9; For aggregate data, see Eleanor Myers, comp., *A Migration Study of Thirty-Two States and Four Organized Territories Comprising the United States in 1850 Based upon the Federal Census of 1850* (Syracuse, N.Y., 1977).

So long as immigration stayed within distinct, tightly defined paths, and the goals of most immigrants centered on providing self-sufficiency and acquiring most of their profit from the appreciation of land, one can assume that neither economic nor environmental factors had a very strong effect on the regional pattern of locational decisions. As has been shown elsewhere, immigration into Ohio and southern Indiana did, in fact, follow one or two very narrowly defined paths. But as immigration moved west across a broader territory encompassing a wider range of environmental and economic diversity (i.e., more variation in cost of transport because of greater distances), these few tight chains of migration extended outward in length, multiplied in number and thus in destinations, and gradually diffused across different areas of the region. As Dana's analysis indicates, there were by 1820 several major roads and river routes leading to several different places of considerable attractiveness to settlers. [40] One could go north toward central Ohio, northwest up the Wabash and into central Indiana, overland across southern Illinois into the Sangamon country, or continue on the Vincennes – St. Louis road into Missouri, around the "Cape of Cairo" onto the American Bottom, north along the Mississippi or Illinois into the Military Tract, or west along the Missouri toward the Boonslick country, or north into the Salt River valley, or even further north toward the Lead Region. Immigration no longer meant simply following the one or two beaten tracks across a relatively compact area.

As choices increased, the percentage of immigrants on one of these paths declined. The inevitable result was that the risks involved in choosing a correct location escalated, forcing settlers to become much more aware of the range of lands before them. This new need is documented by the sudden increase in western guidebooks between 1816 and 1819, most of which included sections on the Illinois country and the Mississippi River valley. [41] Logically, therefore, the pattern of settlement, as it moved west, would begin to reflect this greater sensitivity to a place's attractiveness as rationally determined by weighing the relative importance of different variables.

In addition, the broader area of land west of Ohio altered the range of values among different variables. Better soils, fewer trees, larger more useful rivers, and greater distances all eventually changed the decision-making patterns of settlers. Between 1810 and 1825 the primary weight still lay with environmental variables. But as people moved west, and the technology of transport

40 Dana, *A description of the bounty lands in the state of Illinois*, 48–60.
41 This increase in guidebooks is evident in any general bibliography on the period. For example, see Buley, *The Old Northwest: Pioneer Period, 1815–1840*, 638–40, 642–3. Of the thirty-five guidebooks cited, only five were published between 1801 and 1817, and seven in 1817 and 1818. Among the thirty-seven travel books, none was published between 1801 and 1812; only three appeared between 1812 and 1817, but there were fourteen between 1817 and 1821. Of these, nine were published in 1819, more than two times the number of travel books on the West published in any other year between 1801 and 1840.

improved, the impact of economic factors on the aggregate patterns of settlement increased. Theoretically one should be able to demonstrate this by simply repeating our analysis of 1819 for subsequent census years between 1820 and 1860. Because no guidebook after 1820 ever matched Dana's accuracy or detail, use of the 1819 maps of the relative distribution of different environmental variables across the region remains valid. Only an updated analysis of the economic extent of the marketplace, as altered by new transportation networks, would be necessary. A comparison of these maps with later population-density maps, therefore, will provide a reasonably sensitive indicator of the shifting relative importance of different factors in making a locational decision.

A comparison of the various geographic patterns suggests that over time the correlation between settlement pattern and the pattern of timber growth weakened. This seems to have been the almost inevitable consequence of a population moving across a region with fewer trees. At first, open areas may have been resisted for a variety of reasons. But as soon as settlers took up open lands and found them suitable to their needs, the relative importance of timber declined.[42] The lower cost of preparing the farm for cultivation combined with the increasing availability of timber from market sources further eroded its critical power to affect settlement decisions.[43] In Illinois, in fact, the movement out onto the prairies, besides seeming to dismiss the traditional importance of timber, also increased the awareness of the importance of soil quality. And, all other variables being equal, so too did the expansion of the transport system amplify the importance of good soil in generating a farm surplus by placing a greater premium on yields. Therefore, as settlers moved west, the river-oriented contours of the market continued to deepen, and shape the pattern of settlement even more directly.

This changing sensibility in the aggregate pattern can be documented with data from more detailed studies of local settlement patterns across the region during the period. What strikes one, for example, about the settlement pattern in Kentucky, the place of departure for a large portion of immigrants to Ohio, Indiana, Illinois, and Missouri, is how little, before 1810, it was oriented toward the rivers. In part this was due to the limited number of rivers across the state and the fact that migration into the territory came generally from the south, thereby delaying settlers' encounter with the Ohio River. The fact that the richest lands in Kentucky are "inland," at the center of the Blue Grass Plateau, further helped to draw population toward the middle of the state. Indeed, only after the plateau was fully settled did settlers begin to move down

42 Davis, *Frontier America*, 29–33; Merk, *History of the Westward Movement*, 191–2.
43 Agnes M. Larson, *A History of the White Pine Industry in Minnesota* (Minneapolis, 1949), 105–7, 122–5; Walter A. Blair, *A Raft Pilot's Log: A History of the Great Rafting Industry on the Upper Mississippi River, 1840–1915* (Cleveland, 1930) 256–65.

onto the riverbanks in west central Kentucky. But the riverside locations did not give a farmer any market advantage over those further in the interior, on account of the prevalence of flash floods, annual inundations, and wet soil laced with salt. Therefore, those away from the river and salt licks, despite their relatively poor market locations, continued to prosper in the burgeoning regional market, reinforcing development on the state's central plateau. Those unable to find land on the plateau and disappointed by the efforts of river-bottom farming were inevitably diverted north across the Ohio in search of good high ground away from the river on which to locate their new farm. [44]

The settlers who approached southern Ohio from the south seemed, therefore, to assume, on the basis of their Kentucky experiences, that the river bottoms tended to be deleterious, indeed dangerous, places containing marginal soil. A few salt licks near the river on the Ohio side tended to reinforce this impression. As a result, after the Indian cessions of the late 1790s, Kentuckians moved across the Ohio at each of the convenient fording places and quickly spread inland looking for the best lands. Meanwhile, from the east two other paths of entrance into Ohio reinforced the tendency to bypass the river bottoms and move inland. John Jakle, in his analysis of numerous travel books and logs of Ohio immigrants, indicates that many of the immigrants from Maryland and Pennsylvania followed the Cumberland Road west and north and entered Ohio on Zane's Trace, later the National Road, which ran west from Wheeling along a high, dry ridge of fertile land toward the site of Zanesville and then west southwest toward Cincinnati. [45] Eventually, many of these settlers turned south toward the river, but many, having arrived from the direction they did, were impressed by the land they encountered and settled far away from the Ohio along the upper reach of its north-bank tributaries.

Meanwhile, those who arrived by river initially settled along the Ohio River bottoms and founded several river towns. But given the narrowness of the bottoms, these lands were quickly filled and subsequent arrivals were deflected north in search of land as fertile as that along the rivers. As a result, settlement scattered across a much larger area away from the river. By 1820, as population-density maps clearly show, a band of heavier population settlement had moved far to the north of the knobs and hills that skirted the river. The result was to leave the hilly forested area of southwestern Ohio, though settled and brought into marginal cultivation, in a kind of "eddy" bypassed by the

---

44 O'Brien, "The Roots of Frontier Expansion," in O'Brien, *Grassland, Forest, and Historical Settlement*, 59–73; Dana, *Geographical sketches on the western country*, 88–92.
45 John Jakle, *Images of the Ohio Valley: A Historical Geography of Travel* (New York, 1977), 168–72. This is the same route taken in Birkbeck, *Notes on a journey in America*, and Oliver, *Eight months in Illinois*, as well as in Richard Mason Lee, *A narrative of Richard Mason Lee in the pioneer West, 1819* (New York, 1819).

main migration paths of the period, a pattern that deprived the river towns along the north bank of the Ohio of the economic support needed to counteract the growth of both Pittsburgh and Cincinnati. In between the settled areas of interior Kentucky and Ohio, therefore, lay the Ohio River, a topographical feature to be crossed or forded at Steubenville, Marietta, Portsmouth, or Maysville or traveled down just long enough to find the next road into the interior; it was not yet the central artery along which the currents of a regional system had begun to flow. The arrangement of the road system on either side of the river provides evidence of the secondary role played by the river in the early trans-Appalachian West. [46]

As settlers began to seek out land above the river bottoms a bit further west in Ohio and Kentucky, growing attitudes against settling on a heavily wooded track were reinforced. Brian Birch has argued that the general result of the settlers' experiences in Ohio was to encourage them to settle out toward the edge of the trees and the prairies beyond, rather than deep in the woods that extended inland from the rivers for a considerable distance in some places. [47] As early as 1810 Bradbury had spoken positively of the advantage of locating nearer to the open prairies or meadows. [48] Birkbeck apparently saw proof enough of the habitability of the prairies in traveling west toward Illinois. Along the National Road, and north and west of Chillicothe, Ohio, he observed numerous settlements on high ground at the edges of small prairies. In addition, it seems likely that he heard of similar settlement patterns amid the open forests and meadows of central Kentucky. [49]

Brian Birch argues that Englishmen in particular were accustomed to lightly timbered landscapes and sought them out when making their locational choices. For Morris Birkbeck, this tendency may have been reinforced by his almost obsessive concern for the "healthfulness" of the land, which discounted in his mind almost all forested riverside locations. But Englishmen were not the only ones choosing to locate near the edge of a prairie. On his 1818 map of the English Prairie settlement, Elias Pym Fordham "indicated by dots, the entries made by *American* backswoodsmen" (emphasis added). Each of the entries was conspicuously and ironically located on a prairie in the western half of the section. [50] Whether they simply followed the lead of Birkbeck and his settlers, or vice versa, is unclear. What matters is that more and more settlers were, for different reasons, being told to avoid the immediate river bottoms and seek out higher, drier, less timbered ground out near a prairie's

46 Jakle, *Images of the Ohio Valley*, 168–72
47 Birch, "British Evaluations of the Forest Openings," 172–5.
48 Bradbury, *Travels in the interior of America*, 308.
49 Birkbeck, *Notes on a journey in America*, 60–2, 64–6, 110, 123.
50 Birch, "British Evaluations of the Forest Openings," 172–84; Birkbeck, *Notes on a journey in America*, 66, 73, 76, 77, 85, 97, 110, 111, 115–16, 122, 123; Fordham, *A Residence in Illinois*, 116–117; Faragher, *Sugar Creek*, 66.

edge. For most immigrants, therefore, it seems that the word of mouth, based on the experiences of numerous settlers' locational choices, was filtering through the immigration chain and affecting subsequent choices as early as the late 1810s.

Even when settled, one continued the decision-making process by comparing word-of-mouth information with one's own experiences. An especially interesting dialogue took place among the residents of the English Prairie in the late 1810s. What is interesting here is that after having chosen their location according to certain safe criteria, settlers were forced to respond to an erosion of these assumptions caused by more and more settlers entering the area around them. In choosing a location on a prairie twelve to fifteen miles from a river and forty miles from a river port, Birkbeck and his followers were aware that in making their choice with a premium emphasis on good soil, a mix of trees and prairie, and a healthful environment, they had compromised on other factors that many considered important. Examples of John Woods's writing indicate how difficult it was to balance different variables and be really satisfied with one's choice. In commenting on the features of the settlement Woods invariably compared its characteristics to other places nearby: "Our land is not so rich, no timber so large as on the river bottoms, but it will bear as good wheat, corn, and grass as a person would wish, beside having that great advantage, health." Or again: "There is an English settlement in Indiana about ten miles back from Evansville, better watered, and nearer the markets than we, but it is in the woods and land is inferior to ours."

Sometimes his comparisons take on a complaining tone: "On the Mississippi I might perhaps have found as good or better land, and been nearer to water carriage, but by all accounts, not so favorable as to health; then the expense of getting my luggage there would have been considerable and I should, most probably, have been surrounded by total strangers." [51]

These last remarks seem to be responding to a tendency in the 1810s for people further west to settle closer to the rivers, in spite of its dangers and inconveniences. Where riverside locations were not very valuable or, as in eastern Ohio, settlers avoided the bottoms, the issue, and thus the question of choice, was never very serious. But as men moved west and encountered the wider, richer bottoms of the lower Ohio and upper Mississippi valleys, the pull toward the river became harder and harder to resist. Birkbeck, too, recognized the trend toward the rivers:

> The first settlers, needy people, and ignorant of the dangers they were incurring, found good land along the course of the rivers, and there they naturally fixed their cabins; near enough to the stream to dip out of it with a bowl, provided they could escape the flood. The founders of

51 Woods, *Two Years Residence on the English Prairie*, 178–79.

towns seem to have generally chosen their situations on similar
principles; preferring convenience and profit to salubrity. [52]

This increasingly fatal attraction, based on practical reasons, and inclining
toward the increasingly better prospects for marketing farm produce along the
rivers, became more evident as the path of migration, rather than turning
north up the Wabash valley into western Indiana and eastern Illinois, was
drawn into the relentless pull of the currents of trade that the flatboats and
early steamboats were taking downriver toward the Mississippi, "the Missouri
coast," and New Orleans. Zadoc Cramer, through his annual or biannual
updating of his famous *Navigator*, contributed to this southwestern orientation
in regional perspective. As early as the revised edition of 1802, Cramer
inserted a ribbon map of the lower Mississippi to New Orleans, and in placing
it behind the more familiar and detailed map of the Ohio, all but pulled the
reader cognitively to the southwest. [53] In reading the *Navigator* today, one can
still be drawn into the linear spatial perspective of the river traveler. As if
navigating downriver, guide in hand, we learn to recognize the topography and
hydrology of the river and, more important, how to navigate it. The land one
passes by drifts away as one follows the endless shifts of the channels from one
side of the river to the other and mentally navigates around obstacles –
sometimes unreported depending on the writer's ability to recognize them –
such as sandbars, planters and sawyers, whirlpools, outwash surges, rocks and
debris, and rapids. One's cognitive map of the West inevitably becomes
rivercentric, viewing settlements and lands from their orientation to the river.
As an almost universal experience of travelers further west, it must certainly
have affected subsequent settlement patterns in the Mississippi River valley.

More important, as Americans began to venture west just before and
especially just after the War of 1812 – boating down the Ohio and turning
north, as recommended by Cramer's guide – they encountered the settlements
of French Illinois. Given their ideas on where to settle in relation to the river,
they must have been surprised at how close the French settlements were to the
river. St. Genevieve, Cape Girardeau, Kaskaskia, Prairie du Rocher, and
Cahokia all were located on the river bottoms within the apparent flood plain,
while only St. Louis occupied an elevated site along the west bank, across from
the bottoms and below the mouth of the Missouri. What struck them perhaps
even more was evidence, recently corroborated, of a viable market system with
trade among the towns as well as between St. Louis and points upriver and
downriver, implying that an economy and society had developed near the river.
Between 1807 and 1813 scores of Americans settled rudimentary farms on the

52 Birkbeck, *Notes on a journey in America*, 76.
53 Cramer, *The Navigator* (1802): 40.

bottom lands that the French had not yet occupied or that were too low or too close to the marshes and no doubt discovered the true reasons for the pattern of French settlement: The soil along the bottoms was richer than any yet encountered in the West or, for that matter, in the whole of the United States.

The 1807 and 1813 records of preemption rights granted to early squatters in Illinois to claim a piece of land upon completion of the offical survey (1815) indicate the very earliest settlement patterns in the region (Figure 2.4). [54] Compared with the information about the soil quality as described by Dana in his 1819 guide, or the pattern of timber as shown on a map from 1826 by G. V. Collot, the quality of the soil was now a more important factor than the presence of timber. The Collot map, for example, indicates large open meadows stretching south of Cahokia past the Indian mounds that still rise above the river plain today, as well as several smaller meadows a mile or two north. A later General Land Survey indicated a similar pattern of "interspersals," to use Dana's word, of forest and meadow. In fact, one of these meadows, located just north of Horseshoe Pond (sections 3 and 4 north of the base line, and 9 west of the Third Principal Meridian) was already referred to as "Six Mile Prairie." And yet this area, along with the "low and flat" banks along the river across from St. Louis, was where settlers concentrated their claims. Indeed, more than half the tracts claimed in 1813 were only partially timbered, indicating a declining preference for timber. [55]

Instead, the settlement pattern seemed to follow the geography of soil quality along the bottoms and up across the bluffs. In general, soil quality was richest in a parallel band along the river to within a half mile or so of the bluffs. There, beyond the flood plain, and across the eroded bluffs, soil quality declined considerably, only to improve again, several miles behind the bluffs. The soil between the sites of Alton and Edwasrdsville, for example, was second-rate, with more poor-quality tracts toward the west than east. Further south, across the Kaskaskia River valley, the hilly broken ground supported mediocre soil. The only geological features of note in this area were several outcroppings of surface coal along the bluffs near Edwardsville and across the hills near the source of the Big Muddy River. [56]

54 Raymond Hammes, "Squatters in Territorial Illinois: The First Americans to Settle Outside the American Bottom after the Revolutionary War," *Illinois Libraries* 59, no.5 (May 1977): 319–27; Raymond Hammes, ed., ibid., 328–44; "The Report of 1807, Including Cover Letter and Index," Raymond Hammes, ed., "The Preemption Report of 1813," ibid., 345–82.
55 Dana, *Geographical Sketches on the Western Country*, 135–6; Hammes, "The Preemption Report of 1813," 380, 382; General George G. V. Collot, "Map of the Country of the Illinois" (Paris, 1826), in *Indian Villages of the Illinois Country, Part I: Atlas*, by Sarah Jones Tucker (Springfield, Ill., 1942; reprint, 1974), plate XXVIII.
56 Hammes, "The Preemption Report of 1813." Specific data are located as follows: "nine crops," 381: "eight crops," 350, 380; "six crops," 349, 362; "3–4 crops," 352, 372, 380; Dana, *Geographical sketches on the western country*, 134–6.

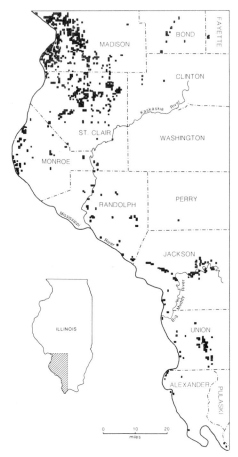

Figure 2.4. Settlers' preemption claims in southwestern Illinois, 1813.

There was a strong correlation between the pattern of soil quality and the early pattern of squatter settlements. The rich tracts on Cabane Island (sometimes referred to as "Cabarass" or "Carraber" Island), Big Island, and along the river in front of the "Six Mile Prairie" were fully occupied by 1813 and, given the amount of evidence presented for each decree of preemption, apparently hotly contested for. The less rich lands on the rise in front of Edwardsville were the second-best choices and also quite densely claimed, if not yet occupied or "improved." Fewer settlers were scattered across the less rich land between the bottoms and the bluffs, while settlement beyond the bluffs concentrated around the better tracts of land around the site of Belleville, Illinois, and along the edges of the Looking Glass Prairie, some nineteen miles east of the river.

The other less concentrated clusters of settlement followed the initial impulses of settlers around St. Louis and sought the best lands along the bottoms of the Mississippi or its larger nearby tributaries. In Monroe County there was, as yet, sufficient vacant land along the river for all settlers looking for a farm site. Further south, the Kaskaskia River valley was settled in what would become (as the evidence of the Salt River settlement a decade later would indicate) a classic pattern. First settlers followed the entire course of the river looking for a combination of the finest lands along the bottoms and the best timber. The result was a scattering of settlements both on the bottoms and on the adjacent higher ground from the mouth to the source of the river valley. Clusters of settlers near the modern sites of Murphysboro and Jonesboro, Illinois, were explained, in the 1813 record, by mention of one settler being near "ye coal bank." The general evidence suggests that American squatters paid more attention to soil than to timber in making their initial choices on the American Bottom and, consequently, located closer to the river than settlers generally were doing back in the Ohio River valley.

And yet, if one views the pattern across the entire area of exemption claims, extending nearly 150 miles from north to south, what strikes one is not so much the correlation between settlement and soil quality but the simple fact that three out of four squatters located within 20 miles of Fort St. Louis, the maximum distance generally considered profitable in transporting goods to a market. Although the economics of such a rudimentary market are hardly known, what is evident from the 1813 report is that several of the people who had located their farms near St. Louis were growing crops or providing supplies for the consumption of the nearby trading and communications post. Chief among these was Pierre Chouteau, an important entrepreneur in fur trading and early founder of St. Louis who "carried at different seasons fruit and grain to St. Louis" from his "orchard and garden" on Big Island. Joseph Williams planted corn and tobacco on another island plot. John Baumie, located on the riverbank just opposite the island, "made shingles and dug coal for sale." John Singleton, who located nearby, had also "cut cord wood and made shingles" as early as 1811. Less specific is the market activity of the numerous settlers who simply "cultivated" or "improved" their farms, or "built a cabin" or "dug a well" on their land. Nor is one able to read any market activity into the actions of the farmer who purchased a plot near the coal banks "for a wagon and two horses."[57]

57 Hammes, "The preemption Report of 1813." Specific data are located as follows: "Big Island," 347–9, 351, 365, 369, 375–6, 379, 381; "Island Cabarais," 359; "Carraber Island," 368; "Near ye coal bank," 356. Data on marketing activity are as follows: "coal," 381, 365, 347; "corncrib," 378; "dig a well," 376, 371; "wagon and two horses," 372.

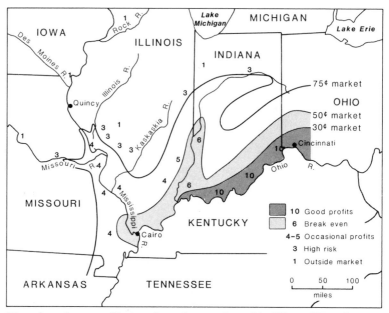

Figure 2.5. Access to Cincinnati market as estimated by Edmund Dana in 1819.

Another locational factor may have been the desire to settle near one of the roads that crossed the area from the east toward St. Louis. Most of the interior farms were located on the bluffs north of modern-day Collinsville, Illinois, where once the National Road, and now Interstate Highway 70, cut through the bluffs in its progress toward St. Louis. Another cluster lay near an old road that ran between southern Illinois and St. Louis at the place where it crosses the Fairview Heights just north of modern Belleville, Illinois (State Highway 161 follows the route today). Significantly, at the center of this cluster of farms was the estate of John Messinger, a surveyor, witness to numerous claims in the preemption report, and later an important mapmaker, who published, with John M. Peck (the gazetteer), some of the finest early state maps of Illinois. [58] In either case, it seems that economic factors played a stronger role than soil quality, given the fact that some questionable tracts near St. Louis were occupied, while good land at some distance from St. Louis remained unclaimed (Figure 2.5).

The sudden increase in the importance of market access, timber supply, and soil quality gave the settlement patterns of the American Bottom, the Missouri Coast, and nearby settled areas of Missouri and Illinois a distinctive

58 Ibid., John Messinger," 367; Messinger served as witness to legal claims twenty-two times within the document. See 346, 348–52, 255–6, 359, 361, 363, 365, 370, 372, 380, 381.

rivercentric appearance, quite different from that back east along the Ohio. In a way, this new settlement pattern became the basis of a new focus in regional life during the 1820s and 1830s, a focus that the steamboat would reinforce for more than a generation. The abundance of riverside land on both the Missouri and Mississippi rivers, in contrast to the limited supply back in Ohio, enabled supply to meet demand continually during the period. In fact, with the subsequent opening of Indian land cessions, such as the Black Hawk Purchase, further north along the rivers, that supply continued to grow. Any pressure by subsequent immigrants to push beyond settled riverside areas further south in the region tended to be diffused north along the rivers rather than inland beyond the line of furthest settlement near the edge of the prairies. In addition, it has been argued that the ever-larger scale of the prairies that encircled the river valleys as one moved north and west across the region may have proved a deterent to movement away from the rivers and reinforced riverside settlement.

Certainly across from the American Bottom on the Missouri Coast, riverside settlement ruled the day. The Edward Huttawa map of 1844 shows, for example, that the majority of pregrid land claims had been made directly adjacent to the Mississippi and its tributaries. Land claims stretched along the river both to the north and south of Cape Girardeau, St. Louis, and St. Genevieve, along both sides of the Little and Whitewater rivers in the hinterland of New Madrid, and north along the Mississippi River in Pike County, Missouri, near the mouth of the Salt River. Similar riverside concentration characterized the early settlement pattern in the Boonslick country. In Howard County, settlement lined the river bottoms because the Cooper Bottom was "close to or adjoined the river link with the larger population centers downstream." Within a few years, this preference for soil quality and market orientation was reinforced by further economic development: The town of Franklin, Missouri, was established at the center of this cluster and settlement soon surrounded this new link to the outside market. The early establishment of this town and the transport-cost advantages it brought to the area enabled subsequent settlers to move further from the river, occupying as they did two areas of prairie land with fine soil in the south central and northwestern parts of the county. This intial cluster of economic activity enabled Franklin to become briefly, between 1821 and 1826, the northern terminus of the Sant Fe trail and a regional market center – thus further emphasizing the tendency for settlement to now follow an economic geography delineated by market criteria.

A similar pattern, although it was slower to develop on account of its distance from the market, occurred along the Salt River in northeastern Missouri (southwest of Hannibal). There settlers moved up the full length of the river in search of quality soil and timber along the riverbanks. To some extent this pattern was stretched out even further because the bottoms, in some places, were only several hundred feet wide and timber, along most of the river, gave out within a mile. Even across the river in the Military Tract, where the best land was in the interior, settlement doggedly stuck to the fringes of the rivers. In fact, Dana felt the need to remind readers repeatedly of the futility of riverside settlement in an effort to reverse the recent trend, but only after he himself had tried to settle down by the river and been washed out at least twice. Dana indicated several settlements along the river in Calhoun County. A few years later, the first settlements in Pike County and Adams County also located on the best available soil as near as possible to the Mississippi.

As settlement spread north through the region, this pattern was repeated over and over again: All the plots along the tributary river would be taken up; a few subsequent settlers would push as much as a mile off the river, to the edge of the timber and the prairies; then subsequent settlers would move down along the river, leaving the line of settlement in place for most of the 1820s and early 1830s. Indeed, so prevalent had this settlement pattern become that by 1831 Timothy Flint could routinely remark that "a deep bottom, fertile soil, a position on the margins of a boatable or navigable stream; these are apt to be the determining elements of a settler's choice." From the "Cape of Cairo," north to the lower rapids, from the Boonslick country on the west to the tributaries of the Illinois River on the east and north, settlement and subsequent town and economic development hugged the rivers between 1815 and 1835, making them the center of the newly opened "Great West." [59]

To some extent, the hesitation to advance onto the prairies reflected a basic concern that prairie land would not make a good farm. The limited timber was interpreted by many as evidence of poor soil, and insufficient drainage and poor groundwater viewed as deleterious to health. Moreover, prairies were routinely viewed, as late as the middle 1830s, as "barren, empty, lonely, and dismal" heaths, "vast steppes," or "interminable waste(s) of grass and weed." Many settlers, by their hesitation, seemed to concur with Eliza Steele's opinion: "the dearth of water, wood, and stone will prevent them [the prairies] from being thickly settled except in the vicinity of the rivers." To advance into the interior (or as one punster put it, "inferior") areas was to face a harsh, primitive life. Even Edmund Dana, who in his detailed survey of the Military Tract indicated broad areas of fertile prairie soil, also indicated that many

59 Jacqueline A. Ferguson and Michael O'Brien, "General Patterns of Settlement and Growth in the Central Salt River Valley," in O'Brien, *Grassland, Forest, and Historical Settlement*, 148–70. Edward Huttawa, *Sectional Map of the State of Missouri, Compiled from U.S. Surveys and Other Sources* (St. Louis, 1844) (Geography and Map Division of the Library of Congress); O'Brien, "The Roots of Frontier Expansion," in O'Brien, *Grassland, Forest, and Historical Settlement*, 85–8; Dana, *A description of the bounty lands in the state of Illinois*, 17–46; Flint, *The history and geography of the Mississippi Valley*, 37.

tracts of prairie remained uninhabitable because of too much surface water or too little timber. Whatever the cause, throughout the lower river valley, most settlers hugged the rivers and settled where the forest and prairie intersected; few if any ventured out onto open treeless terrain. [60]

Soon after 1830, in each of the townships examined, settlers universally changed their minds. As noted, settlement in St. Clair County (to the east of St. Louis) had pushed eastward to about three miles east of Belleville, or about twelve miles east of St. Louis. Only in 1830 did newly arriving immigrants settle on the next section to the east. Significantly, however, once this barrier was breached and open ground occupied, settlement swept across the entire township and county, onto the prairies of Clinton and Washington counties in only four years. A similar rush occurred in Sangamon County between 1833 and 1835. In the Salt River valley, settlement moved from the forest–prairie fringe across the prairies between 1830 and 1834. Much further north, the line of settlement behind Peoria, which had stayed within a few miles of the river through the late 1820s, raced northwestward across Peoria County and onto the high, treeless prairies of Knox County by the mid-1830s. A similar dynamic occurred in Scott County, Iowa, a few years later. Indeed, throughout the region, new settlers arrived and rushed onto the prairies in the course of the 1830s boom. Whole townships, even entire counties were claimed by settlers within a few short years. [61]

From a broader perspective, it seems evident, however, that this rapid occupancy of the prairies only occurred where the land occupied was accessible to the market. The general pattern of settlement across the region tended to follow closely the extent of the market access, as determined by the cost of transport by land or water from any point in the region (Figure 2.6). Therefore, the further north one traveled, the fewer miles from the river settlement extended. One historian of settlement has shown that in south central Illinois, the prairies were occupied in almost direct relation to their proximity to the market. Another found the same relationship in eastern Missouri, and yet another once suggested that "the percentage of lands in farms decreased in proportion to the distance of the land from the river." This general correlation was confirmed by Robert Swierenga's analysis of the geography of the timing of the first land entries in eastern Iowa, which clearly

---

60 *The Western Mirror* (St. Louis), June 1837; H. A. Porter, *Rock Island and its surroundings in 1853* (Rock Island, Ill., 1854), 23; Eliza Steele, *A summer journey in the West* (New York, 1841), 132, 136.
61 McManis, *Initial Evaluation and Utilization of the Illinois Prairies, 1815–40*, 70–1, 66–9; Ferguson and O'Brien, "Patterns of Settlement and Growth," in O'Brien, *Grassland, Forest, and Historical Settlement*, 164–76; Theodore Carlson, *The Illinois Military Tract: A Study of Land Occupation, Utilization and Tenure*, Illinois Studies in the Social Sciences, vol. 32, no. 2 (Urbana, Ill., 1951), 3, 8, 10; Ronald Rayman, "The Blackhawk Purchase: Stimulus to Settlement of Iowa, 1832–51," *Western Illinois Regional Studies* 8 (Fall 1980): 141–53.

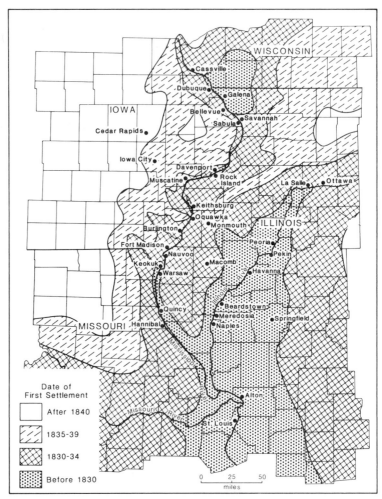

Figure 2.6. Pattern of first settlement across the upper Mississippi River valley, 1825–50.

shows waves moving across the state from east to west in the 1840s and 1850s. [62]

In addition, there seems to be a general pattern in which, on a regional or valleywide scale, land was increasingly valued primarily according to its proximity to the market and that various plots were occupied in direct relation

62 McManis, *The Initial Evalution and Utilization of the Illinois Prairies*, 82–9; Robert P. Swierengra, *Pioneers and Profits* (Ames, Iowa, 1968), appendix 4, 234–5; Carlson, *Military Tract*, 8–10.

to their relative value. Thus, as settlement in the south pushed into the interior and market forces, expressed through rising land-transport costs, began to favor movement further into the interior, subsequent settlers moved upriver to locate on land that was closer to the river (although farther from St. Louis by river) and thus suffered less transport-cost burden than the next-best plot of land available in the south. Hence, as settlement in the south reached a point of diminishing returns, it flowed north along the rivers. A similar mechanism seems to have been at work in the timing between the settlement of eastern Illinois, or parts of the Military Tract and eastern Iowa. In the mid-1840s, settlement further into the interior of the Military Tract had stalled due to unfavorable transport costs. Subsequent settlers thus rushed into relatively more accessible lands closer to the river, but further from St. Louis, in eastern Iowa. As the Swierengra maps have demonstrated, this advance continued to about 1852, then slowed briefly, before sweeping west across the state in the next land boom. [63] Meanwhile, settlement in the interior of the Military Tract remained stalled until about the same time, and then, being equal in value to even the next-best lands in interior Iowa, settlement filled in the Military Tract, causing long stagnant towns such as Macomb, Monmouth, and Carthage to come to life. The distribution of population across the region in 1850 reinforces the impression that settlement was determined by the economics of transportation, and then by the value of the soil and the availability of other amenities necessary to farm successfully (Figure 2.7).

As this economic-geographic dynamic deepened between 1830 and 1850, perceptions of the land were transformed as well. As more land was opened, people more readily succumbed to monotony and repetition, and began to perceive the land as space to be occupied rather than as a place to live. One can discern this changing sensibility, as early as 1819, in Edmund Dana's detailed description of the soil quality of the Military Tract. What strikes one about Dana's analysis, at first, is its remarkable detail. Through the first part of his analysis he seems to be relying entirely on personal observation: He had walked the land and observed it in detail. As the land broadens in area and features wash out, however, Dana inevitably fatigues and begins to describe the land more generally. Whole townships are increasingly described in less detail than his earlier descriptions of sections and half-sections further south. The land increasingly is viewed not as a landscape or environment, to walk and observe and, in time, to become intertwined with one's life, but as so much of a commodity to be marketed. Before our eyes, topography dissolves into nonspecific undifferentiated space. [64] As settlement rapidly spread across the region, others certainly were affected in the same way. As a result, people

63 Swierengra, *Pioneers and Profits*, appendix 4, 234–5.
64 Dana, *A description of the bounty lands*, 17–46.

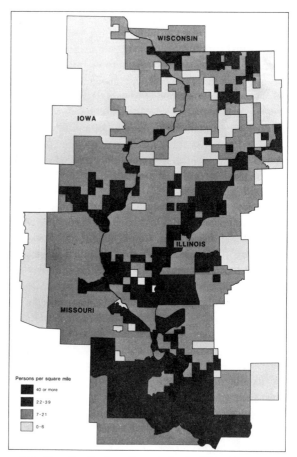

Figure 2.7. The distribution of population in "The Great West," 1850.

tended to view the land in more practical, economic terms, which, in turn, fed the primarily economic occupation of the vast prairies on both sides of the river. The land, in short, passed from those who sought to live on it, inhabit it, make it their home, and absorb its reality into their culture, to those who, from both towns and farms, sought to own it, use it, and often abuse it for their own goals – in particular, making a profit.

This broad, market-oriented regional trend seemed to have reached its fullest extent between about 1848 and 1853. Inevitably, about this time, the ability of the steamboat to extend the range of the market further inland faced diminishing returns. As settlers pushed further inland, they found themselves moving beyond the limits of the river-based market. Again settlement stalled, but in the face of growing demand, land prices rose and settlement again surged out further onto the unclaimed land, intensifying pressure on the system to accommodate to the transport needs of these farmers.

The combination of rising produce prices and fertile soil enabled many recent settlers out on the edges of the settled areas to generate impressive production figures. As a result, many merchants and entrepreneurs, at first considering these people beyond their range, sought to establish connections with these new areas of burgeoning wealth. The railroad-construction boom of the mid-1850s can be viewed as an effort to gain control over this new inland wealth. The result was to increase access to the interior, open it up for further settlement, and cause a boom in land prices. [65] Throughout the mid-1850s, the fastest-growing counties and cities, the most rapid rates of settlement, and the most intensive interest from speculators and investors were all in interior, as opposed to riverside, counties. The market still, of course, shaped settlement patterns, but it was the market now that had a new shape.

In summation, a pattern of settlement based on the individual settler's personal, local, self-sufficient struggle to gain a living from the land was, during the 1830s, rapidly overrun by settlement patterns based on the movement of settlers, operating in regional markets and acting according to economic criteria. As this happened, the indigenous vernacular culture in which individuals had felt a strong affinity with the land, achieved through an intensive experience on it, was uprooted and cast adrift by settlers acting in economically arranged space. [66] The result was to foster the development of a utilitarian, shrewdly economic, short-term, and practical attitude toward the land. Men trod on it more lightly, never sinking their roots very deeply, and thus knew it and experienced it in a relatively superficial way. This was a trend of human habitation that the land itself, lacking many of the qualities that make a place easier to inhabit, experience, and enjoy, could do little to impede.

Schematically, this transformation of the spatial arrangement of regional life should be viewed not as one pattern evolving or developing out of another, but rather as a broader, regional pattern of settlement arranged according to economically determined geographic factors, overrunning an earlier local pattern of settlement based on environmental and topographical factors. At first this new pattern may have appeared around early towns or cities or along interregional roads that, in the course of earlier development, had achieved some centrality on the basis of environmental and geographic advantages. But by the 1830s waves of population, moving from south and east to north and west, swept across the region, county by county, driven on by the broad expansion of the regional market at St. Louis. The early or intermediate settlement patterns were, therefore, absorbed, bypassed, or simply left behind

65 Faragher, *Women and Men on the Overland Trail*, 41–4.
66 Alexis de Tocqueville, *Democracy in America*, ed. J. P. Mayer (Garden City, N.Y., 1969), 50–6.

by the new patterns. Once the land was occupied according to
economic-geographic criteria, however, subsequent shifts in spatial
arrangements would reflect the shifting weight of different economic variables
within the same economic-geographic context. In either case, the pattern of
settlement, which was gradually translated into economic power, formed the
economic basis of different areas within the region at any time, and across the
whole of the region over a broader period.

   In general, the movement from south to north, and from east to west,
formed a deep underlying reality in the shifting relationships among settlers,
farmers, merchants, and businessmen during the steamboat period. On a
broader level, the wealth derived from such land would provide power and
wealth for the region. For the Midwest, as for other agricultural plains, the
land thus became a source of power; but in its wealth it also became a source of
trouble. For, as Braudel once remarked, such land is "obliged to live and
produce for the outside world, not for its own sake. This is both a condition of
its importance and a cause of its subordination and troubles."[67] In the
Midwest, for so many to move onto the land, cultivate, and bring crops to
market so quickly, required outside investment, a liberal land policy, enormous
capital outlays for transportation networks, and a variety of financial services
from entrepreneurs, investors, and speculators back East.[68] The underlying
potential of becoming subordinate to eastern powers would also, therefore,
shape the economic, social, and cultural life of any regional system that
developed across this rich agricultural area.

67 Fernand Braudel, *The Mediterranean and the Mediterranean World in the Age of Phillip II*,
   trans. Sian Reynolds (New York, 1972), 85.
68 John Denis Haeger, *The Investment Frontier: New York Businessmen and the Economic
   Development of the Old Northwest* (Albany, N.Y., 1981).

3

Encountering the rivers

Among the thousands of encounters settlers had with the Mississippi River in the nineteenth century, two types of experiences predominated. Either the river was a physical presence, an environment on or near which one lived, and to which one integrated the rhythms, strategies, and patterns of one's life, or it was an economic channel of trade that by its use influenced life far beyond its banks. As the focal point of certain economies, its environmental rhythms, its topography, and its geography have indirectly or directly defined the patterns of regional social and economic life. To the former, the river was, and to many remains, a predominantly local presence. To the latter, it became a regional economic force. But to both it provided the context from which to understand the land as a place and perceive the region around one as an organized system in space.

The water's edge: the river bottoms

To live by the river was to live by the pressure points of the region's hydrography, where floods and freshets actively reshaped the land, damaging and destroying on the one hand, reforming and enriching on the other. In *The history and geography of the Mississippi Valley*, Timothy Flint vividly described what it was like to be near the Mississippi below the mouth of the Missouri at flood tide:

> The bosom of the river is covered with prodigious boils or swells that rise with a whirling motion and a convex surface, two or three rods in diameter and with no inconsiderable noise, whirling a boat perceptibly from its track. In its course, accidental circumstances shift the impetus of its current and propel it upon the point of an island, bend, or sandbar, and sweep away the tender alluvial soil of the bends, with all their trees and deposit the soil in another place. At the season of high waters nothing is more familiar to the ear of the people who live along the river

than the deep crash of a land slip in which smaller or larger masses of soil
on the banks, with all the trees, are plunged into the river. [1]

The risks of life on the bottoms were, from the earliest settlement of the
West, clearly recognized. The optimum scenario by which the full benefits of
such a life could be gained went something like this. A brief moderate
midspring flood would cover the ground and deposit a rich layer of silt on
one's farm. For the sake of better soil after the ground was able to dry out a
little, the inconvenience of having to move one's household goods to the roof
and livestock to higher ground, or to have to evacuate oneself and one's family
beyond the flood waters, was generally accepted. When the flood subsided, a
routine cleanup and a few weeks drying would put the farm in a fine state for a
late-spring or early-summer planting. At season's end, losses incurred from the
flood were offset by the higher yields derived from such "river farming." The
annual result would be a small surplus and a slight gain before preparing for
next season.

The risk, of course, was that the river and climate would not follow this
schedule. A flood higher or lower, or earlier or later, than normal could easily
negate the advantages of living on the bottoms. A higher or earlier flood could
sweep one's farm clean rather than depositing topsoil, drown one's livestock, or
destroy one's farmstead and fences. Often, such flood damage could set back a
farmer five to ten years in the development of his farm. A later than normal
flood could leave one's fields too wet too late in the spring and thus force a late
planting, with its reduced yields, or no planting at all. And no flood or a low
flood would fail to provide the benefits necessary, in any year, to offset the
recognized negative aspects of living along the river. [2]

One's opinion on whether to risk living by the river depended, as in other
decisions, on one's earlier experiences, the timing of one's migration, and the
area being considered for settlement. In the 1810s, for example, Kentuckians
who moved north into Ohio and southern Indiana had learned from their
experiences of trying to live near the notorious rivers in Kentucky to stay
above the bottom lands. [3] The volatility of spring floods along the tributaries of
the Ohio River in Ohio and Indiana reinforced a tendency to settle on higher
ground. [4] As early as 1806 Zadoc Cramer warned settlers to stay away from the
Muskingum, Little Miami, Scioto, White, and Wabash rivers, each of which
were prone to flash flooding throughout the year, and more extensive floods in

1 Timothy Flint, *The history and geography of the Mississippi Valley* (Cincinnati, 1832), 32.
2 Ellesa Clay High, *Past Titan Rock: Journeys into an Appalachian Valley* (Lexington, 1984), 30,
  31, 77, 123–34.
3 Daniel Drake, *Natural and statistical view, or picture of Cincinnati and the Miami country
  illustrated by maps* (Cincinnati, 1815), 63; Sir Charles Lyell, *Travels in North America* (New
  York, 1845), 2: 59.
4 High, *Past Titan Rock*, 30–31, 77, 123–4.

the spring. [5] Apparently, however, settlers coming from the East, as opposed to areas south of the Ohio, increasingly failed to heed Cramer's advice. In part, Cramer blamed this wave of bottom-land settlement on a series of several low-water years during which numerous towns were established right on the flood plain. [6] Not suprisingly, new settlers tended to ignore warnings of floods when none occurred. When in 1811 and 1812, however, more normal floods returned, the damage was extensive. [7] Cramer urgently described the danger of several town sites and again encouraged settlers to avoid the bottoms, noting that it was now evident that after years of low water and minimal flooding that "seasons of high water and hard winters [were] again returning to the western country." [8] Further west, a similar need for reeducation seems to have also been necessary after a decade of low water. Cramer described the danger in the following way:

> [Forty or fifty] years ago, it was observed by an inhabitant of Louisiana that the Mississippi began decreasing in its risings and continued to decrease gradually for 20 years. And these last 20 years it has been observed by a gentleman of accuracy to increase yearly and by such gradual steps as to be generally not noticed. In consequence, the banks have, within 10 years back, got a considerable population, which is now obliged to retreat, half ruined, and abandon totally the fertile farms formed with much labor and difficulty. In the risings of the Mississippi in 1811, the inhabitants were much injured, but in 1813, all have been obliged to fly, except those protected by strong levees. [9]

Edmund Dana, in his 1819 *Geographical sketches on the western country,* echoed Cramer's concern, stating that the Ohio bottoms in Indiana and Illinois were "incapable of being improved" because of destructive floods "every five or six years." Yet Dana seems to have accepted the decision of some settlers along the Ohio to take the calculated risk. Upriver, for example, he considered most inundations a "mere inconvenience" occurring every few years. In addition, he recognized evidence that suggested that fear of the river was often overstated. For instance, he noted that the town of Lawrenceburgh, Indiana, was divided between those who had "dreadful apprehensions of the evils of the overflowing water" and the older settlers who claimed that the fear was more imaginary than real and that the floods were less frequent than supposed. [10] Certainly the floods of 1811–15, which Cramer emphasized, encouraged

5 Zadoc Cramer, *The Navigator,* Cincinnati (1806): 59.
6 Ibid. (1802): 49, ibid. (1806): 59.
7 Ibid. (1817): 80, 85, 87, 93, 96, 104, 129.
8 Ibid. (1817): 87.
9 Ibid.
10 Edmund Dana, *Geographical sketches on the western country: designed for emigrants and settlers. . . including a particular description of unsold public lands, collected from a variety of authentic sources. Also, a list of the principal Roads* (Cincinnati, 1819), 34, 138, 115.

abandonment of the bottoms. Still, the older settlers argued that these floods might only be temporary, and that abandonment of the rich bottoms would mean the loss of their wealth for the sake of avoiding a few years of misfortune.

Nevertheless, in the half-decade of high water between 1811 and 1816, at least two towns, Madison and Edinburgh, Indiana, decided to relocate above the flood plain rather than endure the periodic floods. Other towns contemplated and debated relocation. As Cramer reported, the townspeople of Marietta, Ohio, were unable to reach a decision. Cincinnati also stood too low, but the upland spread of most of the residential sections of the prosperous town eased concern. This was not the case at Shawneetown, Illinois, where annual inundations "for a series of successive springs had carried away the fences from the cleared lands till at length, they [the town's residents] have surrendered and ceased to cultivate them." Nevertheless, much to Morris Birkbeck's disdain, the town stayed put, rebuilding itself after each flood. One can imagine him shaking his head while writing: "Shawneetown evinces the pertinacious adhesion of the human animal to the spot where it had once fixed itself. The Ohio, with its annual overflowings, is unable to wash away the inhabitants" – although it had done a respectable job of washing away the buildings of the town. Further southwest the new inhabitants of Cairo were even more stubborn, and in 1816, rather than abandon the site, they "raised a few houses on piles of wood and ... 'kept the town,' as the boatmen phrased it, on a vast flatboat a hundred feet in length."[11] This stubbornness in locating towns along the river could be taken as an indication of the growing emphasis on economic factors rather than a concern for safety.[12]

After 1820, and further west down the Ohio, the weighing of potential gains versus losses in deciding to settle along the river seems to have increasingly tipped in favor of the former.[13] As the regional market evolved, and transport costs began to affect the value of one's produce, the potential advantages of being near the river increased, and forgoing those potential returns for the sake of safety became harder to do.[14] Thus, when settlers turned north around the Great Bend at Cairo and arrived at the American Bottom, they generally dispensed with lessons learned on the Ohio and settled along the river. The reason for this change in strategy, as noted, was the incomparable richness of the soil, its abundance, and its proximity to markets. Settler after settler

11 Ibid., 115, 117; Cramer, *The Navigator* (1817): 87, 104; Morris Birkbeck, *Notes on a journey in America from the coast of Virginia to the territory of Illinois* (London, 1818). 76–7, 122–3; Timothy Flint, *Recollections of the last ten years in the valley of the Mississippi* (Boston, 1826), 242.

12 Abner D. Jones, *Illinois and the West* (Boston, 1838), 23; *A History of Mercer County, Illinois* (Chicago, 1882), 46; J. P. Walton, ed., *Scraps of old Muscatine Containing facts and stories told at Old Settlers meetings and other places* (Muscatine, Iowa, 1893), 20.

13 William V. Pooley, "The Settlement of Illinois, from 1830 to 1850," *Bulletin of the University of Wisconsin*, History Series 1 (May 1908): 309.

14 James Hall, *Letters from the West* (London, 1828), 177.

between 1815 and 1830 located along the bottoms, willing to risk the dangers of living beside a much larger, more powerful river.[15] Moreover, the lack of serious flooding between 1816 and 1826 induced early settlers to consider such conditions normal and, as Cramer feared, spurred more bottom-land settlement.[16]

The floods of 1826 and 1832 only briefly dampened the enthusiasm for the bottoms. One supposes that the high agricultural yields combined with the relative infrequency of the floods still seemed a good risk, especially considering the fact that the nearest dry ground was considerably less fertile. Besides, the flood of 1826 was the first serious one that many settlers had encountered, and usually one had to suffer a series of floods, as happened on the Ohio, to become convinced of the fruitlessness of staying on the bottom land.[17] Through the late 1820s and the 1830s, therefore, the tide of settlement on the low ground continued, reinforced, as we have seen, by the developing market activity in the area.

The residents spread across the American Bottom and the lowlands to the north experienced this grim lesson on the counteracting forces of nature between 1844 and 1851. During that seven-year period a succession of unprecedented floods caused such extensive damage along the river that all but the most stubborn of the river people were forced from the bottom lands, thus bringing settlement patterns along the Mississippi in line with those that had evolved along the Ohio a generation before. The destruction of the Great Flood of 1844 was reported in detail. When the crest of late June hit the river below the confluence of the Missouri, the entire American Bottom was covered by six to ten feet of rampaging water. One Davenport reporter observed how amid the torrent one could see distant farmhouses, knocked off their foundations, being swept along with the current, and vast piles of wood, hundreds of livestock, and untold amounts of dry goods carried away. According to one report five hundred people abandoned the lowlands across from St. Louis and around Alton, while the towns on the American Bottom, in particular the old town of Kaskaskia, were abandoned and given up by many for lost. In this old town, the curious tale of a daring steamboat rescue of a group of nuns from a convent roof indicates the depth of the water.[18] But the fact that most stores and homes in town were destroyed and that the river eventually carved a new channel out to the east of town attests to the power of

---

15 Dana, *Geographical sketches on the western country*, 136.
16 Raymond Hammes, ed., "The Pre-Emption Report of 1813," *Illinois Libraries* 59, no. 5 (May 1977): 345–82, esp. 345–52
17 Edmund Dana, *A description of the bounty lands in the state of Illinois: also, the principal roads and routes, by land and water, through the territory of the United States* (Cincinnati, 1819), 6, 18.
18 *Burlington Hawkeye*, July 12, 1843; *A History of Jackson County, Illinois* (Philadelphia, 1878), 19.

the flood tide. Cahokia, meanwhile, was apparently visible only by chimneys protruding above the water, while Harrisonville was so badly struck that it never recovered and, in fact, was eventually sucked into the main channel of the river.[19] Unlike previous floods, the flood of 1844 convinced many residents that the bottoms were no longer habitable because few seem to have returned to reclaim their destroyed farms. Population of the bottoms continued to decline after similar inundations in 1845, 1846, 1849, and 1851.

Further north, along tributaries such as the Illinois, Rock, Des Moines, and Fever rivers, and wherever the bluffs along the Mississippi opened up into a gentle slope or bottom land, the relative emptiness of the riverbanks, inhabited only by a few "river people" living in shacks or log cabins, attests to the lessons learned during the "shower times" between 1844 and 1851. There, as elsewhere, scores of original settlers and towns had located too low and were forced to retreat to higher ground. The experience of the founders of Rockingham, Iowa, just south of Davenport, was repeated numerous times. Having been settled in early summer, the town got going in its first year, 1832, only to find during the next spring, that it was located too far below the average level of flood stage. Towns such as Galena, Warsaw, Rock Island, Alton, and Davenport all quickly moved to higher ground after experiencing a few floods that rose into Main Street. These concerns were even more of a problem at St. Louis, Burlington, Hannibal, Keokuk, and Dubuque, where an average rise in the river would flood stores on the wharf and bring trade to a halt. But in each of these towns floods of sufficient height to cover Main Street were infrequent enough, and the advantages of locating at the riverbank so great, that merchants and townspeople learned to live with it as best they could.[20]

Intertwined with these practical and economic concerns in locating on the bottoms was the growing concern that bottom lands were also a considerable threat to one's health. Like locational strategies, however, concern over health seems to have run in cycles. For example, between 1802 and 1818, the health of the country was one of the underlying concerns of most guidebooks. For Birkbeck, Woods, Oliver, and Darby, finding a healthy location was the sine qua non of deciding where to settle. As early as 1802 Cramer noted that the high water formed and supplied extensive riverside swamps and marshes along the Ohio and the American Bottom "which provides the nurseries of myriads of mosquitoes and other insects of no small inconvenience to the traveller and

19 *St. Louis Gazette*, June 27, 1844; *A History of Randolph, Monroe, and Perry Counties* (Philadelphia, 1883), 414.
20 Dana, *A description of the bounty lands in the state of Illinois*, 25; *The History of Jo Daviess County, Illinois* (Chicago, 1879), 255; James D. Burrows, "Fifty years in Iowa Being the Personal Reminiscences of J. M. D. Burrows," in *The Early Day of Rock Island and Davenport: The Narrative of J. W. Spencer and J. M. D. Burrows*, ed. Milo Quaife (Chicago, 1942), 262.

never failing as a source of grievious diseases to the inhabitants."[21] Brown, in 1817, merely advised that settlers move to higher ground, until they were "naturalized to the climate." Edmund Dana, in commenting on several rivers in Indiana, in particular the White River, noted that he would avoid it on account of its languid current and heavy overgrowth that prevented the sun from dispelling disease-laden miasmas. About the same time, Jones lamented that, in spite of their fertility, the bottoms were uninhabitable because there is "so much disease and death in these fertile bottoms."[22]

Among these early Cassandras of the threat of disease, few were more outspoken than Morris Birkbeck. As we have noted, he believed that in making locational choices, most American farmers and town founders had the wrong priorities, choosing "convenience and profit over salubrity" and thus were "bad calculators after all." The pervasive result was that there were too many towns set too low to the river, and too many people living along the forested bottom lands who were exposed to moist, stagnant air, insufficient and putrefied ground water, decaying vegetation, and disease-festering flood residues. As a result, sickness was pervasive in the country and the death rate higher than necessary. To avoid disease and to "afford the best security for health," Birkbeck emphasized that one need only to find an "elevated situation on absorbent soil, not buried too deeply in heavy timber," criteria that he believed the English Prairie settlement in southeastern Illinois satisfied.[23]

During the 1820s, however, the apparent impact of such warnings on the actual decisions of settlers seems to have been minimal. Indeed, after 1820, and especially after 1830, references to the health dangers of living on the bottoms became so routine, and were apparently so widely disregarded, that some guidebook writers began to shift their strategy. One still tried to discourage settlers from locating along the bottoms, if not to avoid the floods, then to decrease the chances for disease; but in the same breath, as if admitting that such advice was almost pointless, they proceeded to offer some advice on how to minimize the dangers for those who intended to settle on the bottoms anyway. Timothy Flint, in 1832, noted that the bottoms were indeed unhealthy and found it ironic that such rich land should have been "appended, as a drawback to that advantage, in being generally sickly." But he continued, it was becoming clear that "the bluffs were more unhealthy than the bottoms or prairies they overlook" – a fact, he claimed, "amply demonstrated on the

21 Cramer, *The Navigator* (1802): 13.
22 Samuel Brown, *The western gazetteer; or emigrant's directory, containing a geographical description of the western states and territories* (Auburn, N.Y., 1817), 354; Dana, *Geographical sketches on the western country*, 31–2; Jones, *Illinois and the West*, 68, 73, 82.
23 Birkbeck, *Notes on a journey in America*, 76, 66, 77, 73.

Ohio bluffs and bottoms, on the margins of the alluvial prairies of the Upper Mississippi, wherever a high bluff overlooks a bottom." [24]

In general, as residents became more aware of this supposed "medical topography" and accepted it as an environmental reality, concern about health focused on how to take sufficient precaution against such an unhealthy environment (the counter implication being that proper habits could minimize the threat of disease). William Darby, in 1819, suggested that "exposure to night air" was the primary cause of disease in the West. In addition, he cited the immigration experience in general as weakening one's defenses and increasing susceptibility to illness: "a want of rest" facilitated contagion, while a "perplexity of mind" weakened one's natural defenses. "Death," he warned, "can be traced from disappointed hopes." It was in the context of such ideas that a kind of "seasoning" period was recommended before one start heavy work. Years later, Timothy Flint still believed that the propensity for Westerners to reside in small open cabins accounted for a considerable proportion of the region's alleged unhealthiness. [25] Others, more specifically, suggested that postflood debris contributed to disease and that the bottoms must be allowed to dry fully before being reoccupied. For example, the carcasses of dead animals, such as those that were strewn "in incredible numbers on the bottom between Alton and St. Louis" in August 1844 after the Great Flood, were viewed by some as obvious incubators of disease. [26] Others focused their attention on the mosquitoes and other insects that rose up off the river on late summer nights, and encouraged people to guard themselves against them.

As it turns out, the settlers who suspected the direct correlation between river proximity, insects, and disease were half-correct. It now seems apparent that deaths caused by the alluvial environment were significant enough to cause higher death rates per age and sex cohorts in riverside counties than in interior counties. But in general these higher death rates did not significantly increase the overall regional death rate, which given the younger population, was still lower than that back East. Chief among the river-associated diseases were malaria, yellow fever, and various agues resulting from a moist atmosphere. But over time, improvements in hygiene, living conditions, clothing, work patterns, and medical care caused a decline in the relative impact of these diseases. Nevertheless, the belief that the causes of disease

---

24 Flint, *The history and geography of the Mississippi Valley*, 37, 38.
25 Daniel Drake, *Cincinnati as it is* (Cincinnati, 1851), table of contents; Franc B. Wilkie, *Davenport, past and present; including the early history and personal and anecdotal reminiscences of Davenport* (Davenport, Iowa, 1858), 233; William Darby, *The emigrant's guide to the western and southwestern states and territories comprising a geographical and statistical description of the states* (New York, 1818) 297; Flint, *The history and geography of the Mississippi Valley*, 37.
26 *Davenport Gazette*, August 1, 1844.

were concentrated along the rivers imposed a distinctive "medical topography" on the economic and social perceptions of the region. [27]

In addition, the river bottoms, because of their proximity to the transient population along the river, were viewed as being socially uncertain. As Birkbeck again argued:

> There are 2000 people regularly employed as boatsmen on the Ohio and they are proverbially ferocious and abandoned in their habits.... People who settle along the line of this grand navigation, generally possess or acquire similar habits; and thus the profligacy of manners seems inseparable from the population of the banks of the great rivers. It is remarked everywhere that inland navigators are worse than sailors.

Of course, having stated his case, Birkbeck was certain to find evidence in support. At Mount Vernon, Ohio, for example, he found "people of a cast confirming my aversion to a settlement in the immediate vicinity of a large navigable river." And at Shawneetown he, like others, found considerable evidence of "river barbarism."[28] John Woods also tended to view society as more mixed near the rivers and thus full of strangers and not to be trusted. Richard Lee Mason, after finding society polite and well educated on the plain in central Ohio, seemed delighted in finding "real Ohios" near the river. They were "real savages in appearance and manners, destitute of every degree of politeness."[29]

Twenty years later such observations passed for truisms. Oliver stated as fact that "the population on the great rivers is mixed and of doubtful character while much of that on the prairies and agricultural districts consists of decent people of simple manners." These were not simply an outsider's prejudices or fears. He apparently picked up such ideas from the people themselves, the ferryman across from Terre Haute, Indiana, for example, who when hearing that Oliver had crossed the bottoms at night, responded with shock: "Why you're lucky you're alive after coming over that bottom at night! Why just the other night someone was murdered between here and Paris [the nearest town]. I wouldn't pass through that bottom after sundown for $50!"[30] To be suspicious of river people had become part of the region's social geography. They were increasingly perceived as social outcasts, recluses, misfits, transients, or river "hillbillies" who had willfully withdrawn themselves into

27 James E. Davis, *Frontier America, 1800–1840: A Comparative Demographic Analysis of the Settlement Process* (Glendale, Calif. 1977), 115–8; Charles E. Rosenberg, *The Cholera Years: The United States in 1832, 1849, 1866 (Chicago, 1962)*.

28 Birkbeck, *Notes on a journey in America*, 85, 111, 123.

29 John Woods, *Two Years Residence on the English Prairie of Illinois*, ed. Paul M. Angle (Chicago, 1968), 129; Richard Lee Mason, *A Narrative of Richard Lee Mason in the pioneer west* (New York, 1819), 26.

30 William Oliver, *Eight months in Illinois; with information to emigrants* (Newcastle-upon-Tyne, 1843), 79, 106.

the isolation and secretiveness of the bottoms. The fact, as Pooley and Gates argue, that a great majority of these people came from Kentucky only reinforced the impression. In some cases, such as the Cave in the Rock gang of the 1800s, the National Road gang of the 1820s, and the Bonney gang of the 1840s, the reality matched the impression.[31] The exploits of such gangs fed the imagination of upland residents, some of whom, notably Samuel Clemens of Hannibal, Missouri, would later repopulate the riverside with thieves, runaways, vagabonds, and cutthroats, who lived in a fabulous landscape of islands, coves, secret caves, and deep forests, their evil deeds shrouded by the mists and fogs of the river.

That the advance of such a pejorative attitude toward the bottoms should have accompanied the expansion of settlement out onto the prairies and the rearrangement of regional activity according to the prairie topography and environment should come as no surprise. The railroad-based land economy was, in contrast to that of the bottoms, free from floods, able to operate at any season, relatively freer from disease, and more spacious and thus able to support larger farms operable by labor-saving machinery. There was a progressiveness and security to life on the prairies that the bottoms could never provide. And the more evident these advantages, the clearer the disadvantages of the older life along the bottoms became. Life on the land was based on newer ideas, newer impulses, and new parameters, each of which dramatically affected the history of the region. One way of recognizing and emphasizing this was to denigrate the old ways and patterns of life.

Yet the break was never as clean as one might suppose. The old patterns of the river-based economy were still, for example, reflected in the arrangement of nodal points of the new railroad system. Even though the river was a route of only minor importance in the new system, trade still came within reach of the river and had to deal with it. Moreover, the evacuation of the land along the bottoms made them convenient locations for subsequent uses. The old riverfronts of Davenport, Dubuque, Alton, St. Louis, Quincy, Hannibal, LeClaire, and Burlington, as well as other towns, and the bottom land in between were routinely taken up by the railroads and covered with railroad yards and support buildings. Around these transport centers clustered manufacturing firms, mills, warehouses, and storage areas, all of which served to keep the towns down by the river and leave them open to the ravages of the river. Having freed themselves from the rhythms of the river's rise and fall, the towns only reattached themselves to the same environmental forces, indirectly drawing the river back into the patterns of regional life. Later, the increase in barge traffic would further reinforce the lingering influence of the river on the regional system. Finally, the survival of the old towns and ports along the

31 Edward Bonney, *The banditti of the prairies* (Chicago, 1881); Oliver, *Eight months in Illinois*, 108–12.

river, the last runs of the Northern Line Packet boats, and the survival of steamboat excursions continued to outline the land and reinforce and nurture rivercentric biases and attitudes toward the open lands long after the land had become the dominant factor in the structure of the regional economy. Nevertheless, the topography of the land was sufficiently different to give rise to new strategies, impulses, and patterns of interaction that did much to shape anew the course of regional economic and social history.

The "dominion of the waters"

The reach and extent of the rivers' role in regional life was expanded by their transformation into channels of travel and trade by the steamboat. The dominance of the steamboat gradually forced most regional development to depend on the river. As a result, the geography of the river, the seasonal timing of its water flow, and the impact that its variable water level had on the extent of possible navigation affected, indeed shaped, the structure of the developing regional economic urban system. Thus, even places far from the rivers were influenced by their rhythms, by the rivercentric perspectives toward space and topography they created, and by strategies of actions geared toward the rivercentric and southern bias of the economy.

It was the length of western rivers, compared with those in the East and in Europe that set them qualitatively above other rivers and their topographical features. Their length, from the first human contacts with the area, provided relatively unobstructed, rapid travel. To be on a great river was akin to driving on a modern interstate highway. One could bypass, with limited interaction, most of the life of the land through which one passed. In contrast to traveling through the country, and experiencing it, one seemed to travel above, or around, or outside it, never really encountering it, immune from all the delays and hinderances of travel off the main road. Moreover, one could travel, with limited obstructions on these interstate or interregional channels, across great distances, dramatically expanding the range of one's reach and contact across continental space without yet having gained actual control over or interacted with the various local cultures or economies that existed in the bypassed region.

This detached quality of western river travel is evident from the very first voyages of Joliet and Marquette in the seventeenth century to the anxiety-ridden response of polite English tourists as recently described by Christopher Mulvey. By remaining on the river, many journeys became merely extended river voyages or cruises, in which the travelers reported what they saw from the river. The journals of Johnathan Carver, Henry Schoolcraft, Stephen Long, Lewis and Clark, and Zebulon Pike all have this extended quality. [32] On the one hand, one is amazed by how far they traveled at such early dates, using such rudimentary boats. On the other hand, one is struck by how little of the region, aside from its riverside facade, they actually saw or encountered. It is as if they were content to trace imprecise lines across early blank maps in order to establish the borders, the limits, and the range of the vast areas of unknown territory – areas that would remain blank white spaces on contemporary maps for another generation.

From the very beginning, therefore, the great rivers of the West had an interstate, interregional, indeed, a national quality about them. No locality, region, or area could alone claim to control or be defined exclusively by their presence. Contemporaries made this point in an endless variety of ways, realizing that in the West each local area was by virtue of its proximity to the Mississippi River system "bound – as with a cord – to national interests." [33] The Mississippi and its tributaries were, to the same commentator, "the great thoroughfares of trade and commerce" of a vast "interior empire." The river was invariably described as the "nation's river," the "bond of union," control of which was a "national work" and whose interegional extent would naturally integrate local and national interests. [34] The only comparable contemporary travel experience was that of an ocean passage, and many observers were quick to draw the comparison. One perceived the Mississippi River system as the "arms of the ocean... interlocking the Atlantic and Pacific, the Gulf and Hudson's Bay, ...constituting a system of navigation whose aggregate is thrice the breadth of the Atlantic Ocean." To others it was the great "liquid highway," the "continental river," even "an ocean of water." [35] John C. Calhoun, in arguing for the inclusion of western waters into the national waters of the United States, remarked that "the invention of the Fulton [steamboat] has, for all practical purposes, converted the Mississippi with all its tributaries, into an inland sea. It is manifest that it is beyond the power of individual states

32 Each of these journals has been reprinted several times. For the originals, see Johnathan Carver, *Travels through the interior parts of North America in the years 1766, 1767, and 1768* (London, 1778); Henry R. Schoolcraft, *Summary narrative of an exploratory expedition to the sources of the Mississippi River, in 1820; resumed and completed, by the discovery of its origin in Itasca Lake, in 1832... with... all the official reports and scientific papers of both expeditions* (Philadelphia, 1855): Meriwether Lewis and William Clark, *The travels of captains Lewis and Clark from St. Louis by way of the Missouri and Columbia Rivers to the Pacific Ocean performed in the years 1804–1806* (London, 1809): Stephen H. Long, *Voyage in a six-oared skiff to the falls of St. Anthony in 1817* (Philadelphia, 1820); Zebulon Pike, *An account of expeditions to the sources of the Mississippi, and through the western parts of Louisiana, to the sources of the Arkansas, Kansas, La Platte, and Pierre Juan Rivers* (Philadelphia, 1810).
33 *Illinois State Gazette*, February 15, 1844.
34 John M. Peck, *A gazetteer of Illinois* (Philadelphia, 1837), 62.
35 *Dubuque Daily Miner's Express*, November 14, 1852; *Galena Daily Advertiser*, May 21, 1849; William Prescott Smith, *The book of the great railway celebration of 1857* (New York, 1858), 94; *Dubuque Miner's Express*, November 6, 1850.

to supervise it."[36] In the West, whatever local society or economy developed, it would always be viewed in the context of a wider unified reality and thus almost always forced to interact and respond to forces of a regional and national origin.

The interregional character of the river systems in the West was reinforced by the continental scale of the environmental processes that determined the flow, depth, and character of the rivers. By their very extent the water flow and character of western rivers reflected the complex ecological role the river played in regard to larger environmental processes, such as climate, topography, and vegetation. As men entered the valley and used the river to achieve their economic and social goals, they inevitably became aware of these vast environmental mechanisms that established the level of the water and thus its usefulness. As they did, their regional perspective on events was widened even further.

The Mississippi River, by reason of its length, size, and centrality, was the benchmark against which all other rivers in the system were measured. As a river type, hydrologists describe the Mississippi as an "alluvial" river – that is, it exists primarily to drain excess water off the land through which it flows and thus its flow of water is directly related to the seasonal variation in precipitation across its drainage area. On a local level, the mechanism of water flow and its relation to the changes of the seasons would have been common knowledge to anyone who had lived in a temperate continental climate. What newcomers to the West had to adjust to was the broader extent of the relevant factors that affected water flow, and hence the greater variability in water flow from season to season and year to year as well as the more complex mechanisms that, on such a scale, had to coincide to create extreme high- or low-water conditions. Unfortunately, as a seminar on western river hydrology and its interaction with the environment, the Ohio River, the river Westerners obviously first encountered, was only of limited help in understanding the ways of the Mississippi. Although considerably longer than any river east of the Appalachians, the Ohio's topography and seasonal water flow followed eastern and European patterns. Like other rivers whose entire drainage area was in a similar climatic zone, and in which snow was unlikely to stay on the ground for more than a few weeks in midwinter, spring runoff approached almost all points of the river's course at about the same time. Thus, in a spring with heavy rain or a sudden thaw of heavy snow cover, a large flood would rush into the river at all points and move en masse, without much accumulative buildup along the way down the river channel. As a result, this flood would move early, usually in March or the first week of April, and

---

36 Alex Anderson, *The Mississippi and Its Tributaries* (Washington, D.C., 1890), 33.

quickly, often taking less than ten days to pass through the river system. Although on a larger scale, its flow was similar to that of numerous smaller rivers and streams.

Once this flood had passed, the water flow for the rest of the year relied on the variable but progressively lighter rainfall of spring and summer, the result being that the river gradually lost its water, experiencing almost every year an extended period of low water by midsummer. The impetuous, quick, violent nature of the river, characterized by one observer as a "thundershower river," in time limited its economic usefulness. Zadoc Cramer had to write a special guide, as early as 1801, to lead travelers through the landscape of sloughs, sandbanks, bars, shifting channels, and islands that obstructed the river for months at a time. Such difficulties often encouraged early immigrants to move north across the river at one of numerous fording points between Pittsburgh and Maysville before moving west on a parallel track. Hence the river, on account of its difficult channel, often reverted to the more parochial, local, fragmented reality of shorter streams, another aspect of the river that seemed familar to newcomers in the West. [37]

One can imagine the surprise of rivermen and travelers, Cramer's *Navigator* in hand, when their local catchall assumptions about water flows failed to predict the rise and fall of the Mississippi. [38] Although collectively the "mysteries of the river's workings" gave way to a concerted effort to study and understand its movements as steamboat traffic increased and the variability of the water became more of an economic factor, each person still had to face this rude awakening themselves. Expressions of surprise that the river was not working as expected were a continual chorus in contemporary literature and writing. Light rains that precipitated floods, heavy rains that had no effect, heavy winters followed by low-water spring seasons, droughts combined with high water, or rain and continued low water – these were the environmental realities that puzzled eastern observers and that new efforts at empirical observation sought to explain so as to lessen the risks involved in operating on the river.

In the Mississippi valley one had to broaden one's range of observations to be able to judge the likelihood of a change in the water level: Just as the river extended across great distances, so too did the water flowing past one's wharf at any time come from very far away, meaning that its level was determined by a variety of forces across a considerable area. To discern a pattern that permitted predicting the state of the water, contemporaries began to accumulate

---

37 Adolphus M. Hart, *History of the Mississippi Valley*, (Cincinnati, 1853), 147; Zadoc Cramer, *The Navigator* (1801).

38 For recent comments on the use of *The Navigator*, see Jonathan Raban, *Old Glory: An American Voyage* (New York, 1981); *Galena Daily Advertiser*, June 17, 1842; *Keokuk Gate City*, June 4, 1855.

data about the length and severity of winters, the quantity of the spring rains, and the incidences of flood in a piecemeal, unsystematic, and after-the-fact way. In doing so they began to understand the complex environmental interaction between the timing and quantity of precipitation and the occurrence of a great flood. Until 1844, however, the incidence of damaging floods similar to those on the Ohio was rare. Few settlers remembered the great flood in 1785, a year memorialized as "l'année des grand eaux" in French Illinois. A few more recalled the important flood of 1826 and its lesser successor of 1832. But a series of dry years combined with a rapid increase in migration insured that few settlers in the late 1830s had an awareness of the powers of the Mississippi's floods.[39] In spring 1844, however, a period of unprecedented rainfall, the heaviest in memory, sent torrents of water into the river system. Two more rainy years followed, threatening huge floods in each year. By 1852, the apparent change in the climate seemed so clear that one contemporary referred to it as the "shower times," so as to contrast the period with the drier and more "normal" periods of precipitation that preceded and followed this unusual wet spell.[40]

That the shower times of 1844–51 were, indeed, a period of relatively high water is evident in the general records of the annual average level of the river in each year between 1839 and 1858 as gathered from river-town newspapers (Figure 3.1). Though impressionistic, it is apparent that dry and wet periods seemed to alternate in intervals of five to seven years. More precise precipitation records from eastern Iowa during the same period indicate a similar curve in the rise and fall of precipitation. The wettest year since record keeping had begun in the previous decade, and the wettest in memory for those years before, was 1844. It was followed by three straight above-normal years. After a return to a more normal level of annual rainfall in 1848–50, the spell of heavy rain reestablished itself with substantially above-normal rainfall through the summer of 1850 and into the midpart of 1851. In the latter year, more than twice the annual average rainfall, an incredible seventy-five inches, deluged eastern Iowa, flooding fields, roads, towns, and rivers alike.[41] Thereafter, heavy rainfall abated and, as often happens, the cycle went into reverse by bringing three consecutive dry years, the driest spell between summer 1854 and fall 1854 developing into an extensive drought. Normal rainfall in the late 1850s was broken only by the wetter-than-normal spring of 1858. On a general level, the rise and fall of the upper Mississippi and the periodicty of rainfall are parallel. Yet the match is not exact, suggesting a less

39 *Lloyd's Steamboat Register* (New York, 1856), 256–8.
40 *Peoria Weekly Democratic Union*, June 4, 1858.
41 *Iowa, Home for Immigrants* (Des Moines, 1870; reprint, Iowa City, 1970), 63; H. S. Hyatt, *Manufacturing, agricultural and industrial resources of Iowa* (Des Moines, 1872) 22, 24; for modern substantiation of these data, see Reid Bryson and Kenneth Hare, *The Climates of North America* (New York, 1974), 43–7.

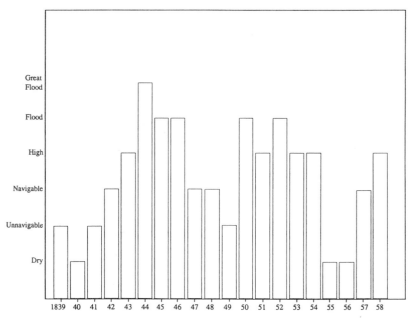

Figure 3.1. Mean annual variation of the water level on the upper Mississippi River, 1839–58.

than mechanical relationship between the two. Indeed, in some years higher rainfall caused smaller rises on the river than occurred in normal rainfall years, whereas in other years normal rainfall amounts brought a flood of some importance downriver. How to explain such anamolies?

Part of the explanation seems to lie in the relationship between the length and severity of the winters between 1834 and 1860, as measured by the opening and closing of navigation from various locations on the river. Again a less than random pattern is evident (Figure 3.2). What immediately strikes one is the range of variance in the midwestern winter. Then as now, winter across the Midwest could range from bitter cold and snowy winters extending from November to April, to relatively short two- or three-week cold and snowy spells amid several months of relatively mild and wet weather. The timing of the short open winters in which the river did not freeze is especially interesting. There was hardly a winter at all in 1836–7, 1843–4, 1850–1, 1857–8, 1858–9, and 1862–3. Interestingly, such easy winters occurred about every six or seven years and in four out of six instances preceded springs with above-average rainfall and extensive flooding across the region. In contrast, the long winters of 1837–8, 1842–3 (one of the severest winters in history, matched only recently by the winter of 1979–80), and 1861–2 each ushered in

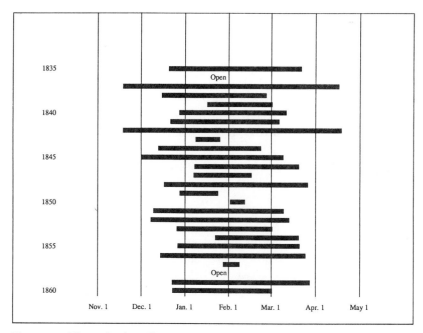

Figure 3.2. The navigation off-season at the upper rapids of the Mississppi, 1835–60.

relatively normal years in terms of precipitation and flooding.[42] So much for the correlation between a heavy winter and the expectations of high water. Nor did a heavy winter and above-normal spring rains necessarily assure a flood. If anything, an easy and open winter followed by heavy spring rains seems to have been the most likely harbinger of a difficult spring along the river.

Contemporary "riverologists" came to recognize this relationship as they realized the thermospatial complexity by which the environment released its water into the main river channel in order to insure a steady-bank high river without a major flood. A winter of average length, retreating isotherm by isotherm to the north, thus releasing the water from one tributary river after another from south to north into the main channel, was the climatic–environmental mechanism that maintained a steady flow of high water for months at a time. And in most years the system generally worked, thus preventing major flooding. But for a winter to depart early, or all at once all along the river from south to north, and then to be accompanied by a scattering of heavy rain across the region, spelled trouble in the system's

42 Among the more helpful reports of navigation's closing and opening, see Increase A. Lapham, *Wisconsin: its geography and topography, history, geology and mineralogy* (Milwaukee, 1846), 76; Harry E. Downer, *History of Davenport and Scott County, Iowa* (Chicago, 1910), annual reports.

hydrolics. As early as 1817 Zadoc Cramer sensed that there was some such mechanism regulating the flow of this massive river system, even though it had been twenty years or more since the last great flood. Referring to a report by William Dunbar of the American Philosophical Society, he noted that the extended six-month rise in the water was due to "its being supplied by so many climes, the two extremes being frequently extended by the early autumnal and winter rains in the southern latitudes, and by the protraction of the northern winter, which retards the dissolution of immense accumulations of snow in the cold regions." [43]

In 1837, an observer in St. Louis articulated the beauty of the process in more detail. To him, the orderly advance of the spring thaw to the north released, one by one, the waters of the important tributaries into the Mississippi: first, the Ohio, swollen by the Cumberland and the Tennessee; next, the Illinois, the Des Moines, the Iowa, and the smaller streams of eastern Iowa; then, the Rock and the Wisconsin – all sending their crests into the main river. After these had passed St. Louis, contributing to an extended period of high water, the waters still locked up by the late-arriving spring in the north woods of Minnesota and Wisconsin surged down the Mississippi to reinforce the faltering water supply from the expended tributaries farther south. And then, as if there were not beauty enough in this sequence, came the final late surge of cold water from the Missouri, having traveled 1,500 miles from the Rockies, to reach the Mississippi above St. Louis in early June. In the course of this annually anticipated "June Rise," the wharf at St. Louis was routinely flooded, boats jostled at their moorings, carters and draymen were sent scurrying to higher ground, and riverside stores were briefly submerged, but flooding that caused serious damage was seldom a problem. [44]

So long as the sequence remained in place, that is. It was when the "natural order of things" went awry that a flood threatened – usually when two or three rivers that normally flowed sequentially into the Mississippi discharged their waters simultaneoulsy. The lack of any serious winter freeze, of course, left the system to rely entirely on precipitation patterns. And because rainfall was generally more pervasive and less orderly in its runoff than the gradual movement of the spring thaw to the north, water could enter the system from all sources at once, causing a significant overflow of the main channel. [45]

The first chance to substantiate these theories, which one assumes were based on recollections of the few settlers who had experienced large floods before the 1830s, occurred in 1844 along the entire river system. By that year,

43 Cramer, *The Navigator* (1817): 137.
44 *The Western Mirror* (St. Louis), February 1, 1837; John Thomas Scharf, *A History of St. Louis city and county*, 2 vols. (Philadelphia, 1883), 1129–30.
45 Cramer, *The Navigator* (1808): 137; also in John Reynolds, *Sketches of the country, on the northern route from Belleville, Illinois, to the city of New York* (Belleville, Ill., 1854), 47.

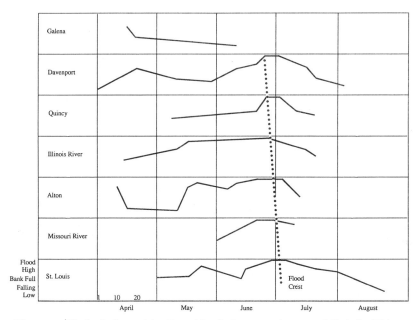

Figure 3.3. The hydrology of the Great Flood of 1844 on the upper Mississippi River.

increased population and the extensive use of steamboats for trade and travel had encouraged numerous merchants, local newspaper editors, and amateur natural scientists, or "riverologists," to improve their methods of observation. Directrixes were installed at St. Louis and Cairo, and water gauges at Alton, Quincy, and Galena. Most river-town newspapers carried, by 1842, regular updates on the "state of the river" from all parts of the system. Such improvements combined to insure a more precise analysis of any new flood event. Quickly passing were the days when taking the temperature of the water or observing the wildlife and vegetation along the banks or even the debris and boats in the water sufficed to enable riverside merchants to guess what the system was doing and thus predict what was to come (Figure 3.3). [46]

After an early spring and an unusually early opening of navigation along the upper river, high water from Minnesota arrived from Galena, Illinois, in mid-April 1844. Ten days later this moderate crest passed by Burlington, Iowa. When it reached the mouth of the Illinois River, this northern rise picked up the rise coming out of the Illinois and in the first week of May passed in front of Alton. The tardiness of the Illinois rise was due to the

46 Richard Edwards, *Edwards's great West and her commercial metropolis, embracing a general view of the West and a complete history of St. Louis* (St. Louis, 1860), 383–4; Scharf, *St. Louis*, 1129–30.

"heaviest rains in fifty years" in central Illinois and eastern Iowa. The rise downstream peaked at St. Louis on May 23, a few weeks earlier than usual. [47]

In the wake of this early flow of high water, the river in front of Alton and St. Louis fell for two weeks, prompting many to comment that it had all just been a "June rise" come in May. Meanwhile, heavy rains continued in central Illinois, swelling the Illinois River at Peoria past flood stage on June 18. By this time, the rains were having a similar effect in the main channel as well, evidenced by the fact that after falling for three weeks water up and down the river was suddenly "at a stand" and even rising slowly. The swiftness of the Illinois River flood, so unexpected this late, is evident by its appearance at the mouth of the Illinois by June 21. The same day water levels at Alton began to rise "at an alarming rate!" On June 26 the record crest was moving past the mouth of the Missouri River at the very moment, as fate would have it, when that river's traditionally later rise was reaching the Mississippi two weeks late. [48]

All the week before, the water in front of St. Louis had been rising steadily. The double crest from upriver combined with the surge of water from the Missouri to form an unprecedented flood crest that slammed into St. Louis late on June 26. By midday on June 27, a crest forty-five feet high, rising to a height of twenty feet in the stores along Front Street, swamped the waterfront and caused considerable damage. To the east and south the American Bottom was transformed into a vast lake, thirty miles long and six to ten miles across, ranging from five to twenty feet deep. Reinforced by further rain-fed surges from upriver, the water remained at this remarkable height for two weeks, not falling back to its banks until July 15. Meanwhile, high water downriver submerged Cairo and points south until well past the beginning of August (Figure 3.4) [49]

In this flood, the lateness and geographic extent of the heavy rains were the primary catalysts of natural disaster. If anything, the earlier than normal arrival of the spring waters only lulled river-town observers into a false confidence, thus exacerbating the alarm when the rain-fed crest of late June started to head south. Ironically, had the upper Mississippi thaw come down at its usual time, the floods would probably have been even more destructive to

---

47 See 1844 weekly files of *Davenport Gazette, Warsaw (Illinois) Signal, Quincy Whig*, and *Alton Telegraph*.
48 *St. Louis Republican*, May–July 1844.
49 Scharf, *St. Louis*, 1130; Edwards, *Edwards's great West and her commercial metropolis*, 384; William D. Skidman, *The western metropolis, or St. Louis in 1846* (St. Louis, 1846), 58; and Andrew Atkinson Abbott Humphreys, *A Report on the Mississippi River* (St. Louis, 1861), 513–15. Also see Glen Holt, "The Shaping of St. Louis, 1763–1860" (Ph.D. dissertation, University of Chicago, 1975), 291–4.

Figure 3.4. High water at Cairo, Illinois, in 1844.

the south of St. Louis. The very next year the scenario, although it seemed similar, was in fact quite different. In that case, the earlier than normal arrival of the upper Mississippi (again) combined with the punctual runoffs from tributaries in Illinois and Iowa to concentrate flood pressure on the middle part of the valley. At Quincy water rose to within ten feet of the 1844 record, while south of the Missouri it failed to pick up the yet-to-arrive crest from the Rockies. In 1846, it was the Missouri crest that arrived early and, by combining with the orderly flow from upriver, flooded St. Louis's wharf.[50] In 1852 only a late-spring thaw out west kept the 1844 scenario from being repeated. An early wet spring sent a rush of water toward St. Louis, but in contrast to 1844, it did not pick up the simultaneous crest from the Missouri until after it had passed to the south. Only in 1858 did an open spring combine with heavy rains to send a series of crests simultaneously into the main channel. An unprecedented surge of water submerged St. Louis's wharf and the entire American Bottom and sent a record forty-seven-foot crest of water, four feet higher than in 1844, rushing over the levee at Cairo.[51]

Observing the river in such detail was essential to people living in the steamboat age. The river was their lifeline to the outside. By affecting the time and cost of travel and transport, the water level could, as we will see, dramatically affect the patterns of social and economic activity. But even before and after the dominance of the steamboat, which was the practical purpose for river watching, observing the river and being aware of its changes played an important role in the lives of "river people" and those who lived in towns along the rivers. To watch the river, read its moods, and try to unlock its "mysteries" (which many older settlers believed unfathomable) was to immerse oneself in the workings of a vast ecological, hydrologic, and climatic process in which the timeless forces of nature interacted. No wonder so many observers responded to the river with such emotion during the romantic age. One can still feel the sense of awe in descriptions of great floods, the torrents of water, the debris, the danger, and the mystery of life on and along the river. Traveler after traveler, lucky enough to arrive at the river during floodtide, responded to the spectacle with excitement. If such a response did not exist, how can anyone explain the exotic image of thousands upon thousands of people crowding onto rooftops and perching from balconies and steeples of St. Louis or camping out along the high cliffs at Alton in June 1844 watching the "sublime spectacle" of the "ocean river" "rushing to the sea"; "its water carrying whole trees, houses, remains of boats," the roar of the turbulent

50 *Quincy Whig*, June 25, July 2, July 10, July 27, 1845.
51 *Galena Daily Advertiser*, May 20, May 24, 1852; *Keokuk Gate City*, April 16, April 21, June 17, July 1, July 3–4, July 8–11, July 17, 1858; John M. Landsen, *A History of Cairo, Illinois* (Chicago, 1910), 72, 80; Downer, *History of Davenport and Scott County, Iowa*, 121.

water, according to one observer, mixing with the shouts and expressions of wonder and awe from the assembled audience? [52]

Rivers within rivers

The water flow of western rivers did more than simply reflect the climate and drainage patterns of the land through which they ran. The water that flowed toward the rivers actively altered and reshaped the character of the land off which it drained. As alluvial rivers, drawing their water off the land, the rivers of the West carried off tons of topsoil and sediment every year. Rushing through their respective valleys, crests of high water were capable of much more: They could erode banks; sweep away islands and forests, farmland and towns; forge new channels; create new islands and sloughs; and, as the rush of the spring flood passed and their currents slowed, deposit deep rich soil from up north onto the still-flooded bottom lands along the main channel of the river. As the water continued to run out during the early summer, currents slowed further, and debris and soil, rather than being washed downstream, were deposited locally in the river channel. Trees, either individually as planters or sawyers or in great "rafts," became lodged in low-water sloughs and in the channel, thus creating eddies. [53] Whether formed by the action of the stagnant water circling around a sawyer, by a whirlpool under the point of the confluence of a tributary into the main channel (called a "chute") [54] or by the natural turns of the current itself, such eddies accelerated the deposit of soil across or along the river channel as "wing bars" or dams, sandbars, shoals, or islands, and further slowed the current behind them.

One contemporary anticipated modern understanding of the relationship between current and silting by observing that "when the main river rises, say an inch a day, whatever is thrown loose onto its surface floats upwards and is carried out with the current, while a contrary effect follows from a contrary cause." [55] In time, these soil-covered piles of debris grew into extensive sandbars, which, as the water continued to fall, soon "reared their white crests" above the water and began visibly to fill in the channel. [56] Low water represented more than a mere drop in water level to reveal the shallow uneven bottom of the river. In a very real way, it also represented the repossession of

---

52 Daniel S. Curtiss, *Western portraiture, and emigrant's guide* (New York, 1852), 329; W. T. Norton, *History of Alton to 1861* (Alton, Ill., n.d.), 6; Edwards, *Edwards's great West and her commercial metropolis*, 385; *Burlington Hawkeye*, July 12, 1844; *Dubuque Miner's Express*, November 6, 1850.

53 Peck, *Gazetteer of Illinois*, 295.

54 *Appleton's southern and western traveller's guide* (New York, 1852), 47.

55 *History of Jackson County, Illinois*, 23; *Dubuque Miner's Express*, January 29, 1853.

56 *Galena Daily Advertiser*, June 29, 1852.

the river by the land, in which much of the erosion and deep carving of the channel achieved in the spring was counteracted by silting so as to maintain the river channel, year after year, in much the same condition. It was, in short, another part of the process by which water and land interacted to shape the environment, a process in which, as in others, the land will almost always take its due.

In general, the tendency for water to run out and silting in to begin varied indirectly with the duration of the high water. Therefore, the upper river and tributaries to the north experienced low-water problems long before the main channel near St. Louis was affected. The upper Ohio tended to dry out earlier than the lower Ohio, while the Ohio in general had low-water difficulties before they were felt on the Mississippi. Likewise, the tributaries along the north bank of the Ohio were noted for the speed in which they became shallow, unnavigable streams for most of the summer. The tributaries of the Mississippi experienced similar problems, deriving from similar causes. The Rock, the Des Moines, and the Kaskaskia, among others, were annually obstructed by sandbars for all but a brief period of high water in the spring. And even then, navigation was often impossible for years at a time. The formation of a bar across the Des Moines River, for example, halted navigation for several years in the late 1840s.[57] The Illinois River, however, almost always had a navigation season, but was known for its sluggish current, "reposing in its bed with the tranquility of a lake," as one traveler put it, and by midsummer it was usually broken by a string of sandbars into a series of torpid algae-covered pools of water.[58] As early as 1839, the bars in front of Peoria's wharf prevented further navigation and, for a while, "were too numerous for the dredging machines to remove."[59] Further north, the silting in of the Fever River, Galena's lifeline to the outside, was an even more serious problem. Once a deep clear stream and easily navigable up beyond Galena, it was gradually filled in with debris, silt and soil that had washed off the overmined and undercultivated hills, ravines, and banks along the river. By the early 1850s dredging operations became increasingly necessary. But within a decade the main channel had silted in entirely.[60]

In the main channel of the Mississippi and Ohio rivers, the impact of low water was exacerbated by the presence of three important geological obstructions. Early settlers were frustrated enough in finding that during a

57 William Petersen, *The Story of Iowa*, 2 vols. (Chicago, 1952), 1: 516–18; *A History of Keokuk from Its Founding in 1820 to Date* (Keokuk, Iowa 1906), 6.
58 Eliza Steele, *A summer journey in the West* (New York, 1841), 164.
59 *Peoria Register and Northwestern Gazette*, September 14, 1839.
60 Sylvester W. McMaster, *60 years on the upper Mississippi. My life and experiences* (Rock Island, Ill., 1893), 7, 14, 17; David Dale Owen, *Report of a geological exploration of Part of Iowa, Wisconsin, and Illinois* (Washington, D.C., 1844), 10; *U.S. Engineer's Report on Harbors and Rivers* (Washington, D.C., 1872), 44–5.

considerable portion of the year the rapids in front of Louisville needed a drop in water level of only a few feet before passage became very difficult and eventually impossible.[61] As early as 1810, explorers venturing up the Mississippi north of St. Louis discovered two extensive chains of rocks cutting across the main channel of the river and forming rapids just above the future sites of Keokuk and Davenport, Iowa. Anthony Nau, drawing from the notes of Zebulon Pike, shows clearly the location of the rough water around Rock Island in his 1810 map.[62] Meanwhile, traders on the upper river moving between St. Louis and three forts in the Indian country between 1815 and 1820 reported the impact of these rapids on river travel. In 1819 a group of Army engineers, among whom was the young Robert E. Lee, did the first topographical survey of the upper rapids at Rock Island.[63]

Not until the early 1820s, however, after the initiation of steamboat traffic to Galena from St. Louis, did upriver captains begin to comprehend the fateful reality that the range of rising and falling water in the main channel above and below the rapids corresponded to water levels on the rapids that were often insufficent to float a boat over, thus causing, in the course of a normal fall in the river, the blockage of the channel for months at a time. For example, while the river stood at a navigable ten to fifteen feet at Burlington or Quincy, five feet of clear water covered the rapids, sufficient to float medium-sized steamboats. But as the water level above and below the rapids dropped, say to nine feet (the depth the Army Corps of Engineers considered sufficient to set as their goal in their channel digging and lock and dam project in the twentieth century),[64] the depth of the water over the rapids fell toward three feet, the point at which most boats began to rub bottom. At this stage, most captains would have to halt at Keokuk or Davenport, lighten the ship of passengers and freight, and then "lighter" the boat through the narrow shallow channel between the rocks. A further drop to twenty-eight inches would require boats to unload almost all of their freight and passengers to get over. But even at this level it was a squeeze for medium-sized boats, involving considerable dragging along the bottom. At twenty-four inches, few if any captains would even attempt to cross. At that water level, corresponding to a still-navigable five to

61 Cramer, *The Navigator* (1802): 37; ibid. (1808): 14. Also see Thomas Hutchins, cartographer, "The New Map of the Western Parts of Virginia, Pennsylvania, Maryland, and North Carolina Comprehending the River Ohio" (London, 1778), in *Indian Villages of the Illinois Country Part 1: Atlas*, by Sarah Jones Tucker (Springfield, Ill., 1942, reprint, 1974), XXIX.
62 Anthony Nau, cartographer, "A Sketch of the Mississippi from the Town of St. Louis to Its Source in Upper Red Cedar Lake Taken from the Notes of Zebulon Montgomery Pike" (1810), in Tucker, Atlas, XXXII.
63 Phillip Scarpino, *Great River: An Environmental History of the Upper Mississippi, 1890–1950* (Columbia, Mo., 1985), 14–15, 4–5.
64 *Navigation Charts of the Upper Mississippi River* (Chicago, 1978); *The Upper Mississippi Comprehensive Study, Main Report*, vol. 1 (Chicago, 1972).

six feet in the main channel, the rapids completely blocked passage and navigation was halted. [65]

The length and severity of the natural blockade depended on how much water had run through the system in the spring and how much precipitation since had replenished the system's water supply. Those years with the worst conditions tended to match the troughs in the water-flow chart mentioned earlier. Several low-water troughs were reached in the dry late 1830s. In 1838 record low water on the upper river persisted all summer long. By August 24, 1839, the water at Rock Island "was lower than ever recorded," one observer remarking that "our noble river is fast approaching a lean and slippery pantaloon, its course almost run dry . . . not a thing of life, but zig-zag, all used up." [66] A drought of similar proportions struck the upper river between 1854 and 1856. In the late summer of 1854 a "two year low" at Quincy was followed by record low water the following spring at Keokuk. In summer 1855 navigation was difficult for all but the smallest boats. The next year brought much of the same, save for a trickle of water that washed through the system in late August 1856, prompting one despairing traveler to note that: "the river is so low it displays vast amounts of sand I never saw before. Our route was a meandering one around these sandy plains." And so it remained on through 1857 and into the spring of 1858 when, at last, heavy rains broke the dry spell. [67]

Not surprisingly, the Ohio's low-water spells were more frequent, though still longer and severer in the dry periods of the late 1810s, late 1830s, and the mid-1850s. The great dry spell of 1819 has been blamed directly for delaying the mails and exacerbating the western financial collapse of that year. [68] It was soon followed by an even more extensive drying up of the river in 1821 and 1822. Other years of low-water navigation on the Ohio included 1838 and 1841. [69] And the droughts of 1854, 1855, and 1856, which had such a deleterious effect on navigation on the upper Mississippi, had an even severer effect on the Ohio. Indeed, Louis C. Hunter claimed that the frustrations with the river caused by the drought of 1854 encouraged Cincinnatians to invest heavily in the railroad and forsake the river for good. [70] In such a year, when wagons could cross the dry river bed, and farmers and merchants sent goods out by road rather than by river, while small local boats bumped from bar to

65 Curtiss, *Western portraiture, and emigrant's guide*, 379; *Keokuk Gate City*, May 11, 1855; July 31, 1857.
66 *Rock Island Banner*, August 24, August 31, 1839; *Iowa Patriot* (Davenport), July 11, July 18, August 22, 1839.
67 *Keokuk Gate City*, June 5, 1855; *Quincy Whig*, June 6, 1854; also see *Keokuk Gate City*, May 11, June 1, June 4, September 5, September 15, September 20, 1856.
68 R. Carlyle Buley, *The Old Northwest: The Pioneer Period, 1815–1840* (Bloomington, Ind., 1951), 434.
69 Louis C. Hunter, *Steamboating on Western Rivers* (Cambridge, Mass., 1949), 219–25.
70 Ibid.; Norman J. Rosenberg, *North American Droughts* (Denver, 1978). 13–18.

bar and between the rapids, travel, exchange, and communication reoriented itself according to the contours of the land.

These north-to-south variations in the spring water level, and its extension into the summer, were reinforced by the variable impact that winter could have on river conditions across the system. Steamboat captains, then and now, in much the same way as farmers measure the length of an area's growing season, knew that the further north one traveled beyond St. Louis, the earlier the river could be closed by ice. Moving from the north, almost like a "little ice age," the Arctic cold usually froze the river at St. Paul in the last week of November. At Galena, the Fever River usually froze about December 10. Davenport merchants had about ten extra days to get their winter stocks in and make last shipments to the south before the ice closed in. At Quincy, the end of navigation on account of ice usually coincided with the town's Christmas celebration. Below Alton, however, the closing of the river because of ice was, in most years, just a passing condition of a week or so. At St. Louis, ice before New Year's Eve was rare. And when the river did freeze, which John M. Peck in 1837 claimed to have happened frequently, it rarely lasted for more than two weeks.[71] In 1854, when navigation was closed from Christmas Day through February 14, a situation helped by the low water, it was considered one of the "longest embargoes of navigation in many years." Further south, on the broader, deeper southern river, occasional ice floes obstructed the river around Cairo, but the actual freezing of the river was an extreme rarity.[72]

With the arrival of spring, navigation opened first where it had been closed only most recently. As noted, the inconvenience at St. Louis usually was over within two weeks. But at Keokuk, seventy-five days was considered the normal length of closed navigation, and the ice bridge across the river, which formed on the rapids, usually broke about March 1. At Galena and Dubuque the wait lasted into mid-March, whereas at St. Paul, which remained above the ice line for four months a year, the first boat from the south usually arrived about April 1.[73]

As in so many other environmental mechanisms that affected use of the land or water across this region, what the northward advance of the spring thaw gave to the river system in providing a prolonged supply of water, it took back with a vengeance first in the running out of the water and the silting in of the river channels during the long dry summers and then in the refreezing of the river from the north with the readvance of winter. The former brought unity, whereas the latter fragmented and constricted the river system into separate

71 Peck, *Gazetteer of Illinois*, 39.
72 *Quincy Whig*, February 15, 1854: Landsen, *The History of Cairo*, 244.
73 Alfred T. Andreas, *A. T. Andreas' Illustrated historical atlas of the state of Iowa* (Chicago, 1875; reprint, Iowa City, 1974), 386.

areas of activity. Cumulatively, the result was a hydrographic–spatial pattern in which the duration of "navigability" on local waters varied significantly from place to place across the system. To the north, the winter embargo was long, the spring rise late and quick to run out, and the summer low-water period long and uneven and followed by an early close of navigation. At Dubuque or Galena, ten weeks of unobstructed navigation from early April to mid-June and another brief spell in October or November was the usual extent of the river season for profitable trade. As one traveled south, however, the winter embargo ended earlier and was followed by a more extended series of rises off tributaries above, thus prolonging summer water and enabling fall rains more quickly to bring the channel back to a navigable state until a brief stoppage of traffic by ice sometime around January 1. At St. Louis, navigation was usually underway by late January; the spring rise began in late February and extended through its peak in June, and then might fall toward a brief period of low water in early September, followed by an extended fall navigation season. Therefore, whereas the river was navigable up north or on the far reaches of the Ohio for three to four months a year, increasing to four to six months of the year along the central areas of the river, the navigation season in the zone where the three great rivers of interior North America intersected swelled to nine and ten months and, in many years, to a full twelve months without a break from there to the gulf. Such diversity, with a natural bias toward the south, formed the underlying hydrographic and geographic reality that shaped men's actions across the region and thus ultimately shaped the structures of economic and social interaction.

The fact that the hydrographic character paralleled its geological division by obstructions at the lower rapids and the falls of the Ohio, only reinforced the distinctive reality of each segment of the river system. Just as the rapids separated distinctive geological and topographical zones, and coincided with critical variations in temperature and precipitation, so too they separated different rivers, with different water flows, patterns and rhythms. It is not surprising, as a result, to encounter significantly different patterns of settlement, land use, urban settlement, and patterns of economic activity as well, each in a way representing itself as a distinct subsystem within the larger river-related economic system. Indeed, one might perceive each of these areas as a series of pools or "rivers within rivers," across which any intent of regional expansion would have to deal.

The core of the system, extending from the bend of Cairo and north to the lower rapids, and dominated by packets running to and from each and every point, had its own distinctive and differentiating characteristics. The waters of this region, on account of the confluence of numerous tributaries, were perhaps the most volatile, turbulent, and dangerous of the river system. One stretch of the river south of the mouth of the Missouri was called the graveyard on account of the numerous boats that went down over the years. [74] It was within this stretch of the river that boats from the north encountered the floating palaces of the south. Because smaller boats were unable to compete with the large, and because the large were unable to steam any further north without risk to their hulls and cargoes on account of shallow water, the regional scale of interaction in the center of the valley was reinforced. Here, economic activity paralleled the interaction of environmental and natural forces. It became an area of larger-scale regional and continental exchange. Sometimes this central St. Louis-dominated river would, on account of high water, extend its direct influence as far east as the falls of the Ohio. At other times, the Ohio River system could infiltrate this central area all the way to the lower rapids by means of Ohio River boats simply passing the functional entrepôt at St. Louis. [75] This broader central river, extending between Cincinnati and the lower rapids, at the center of which lay the bend of Cairo and the American Bottom along with St. Louis, was, in many ways, the river of the Grand Tour described in countless travel books of the time. (Figure 3.5). [76]

Less distinctive was the short curving river between the rapids, a less turbulent, wide-open river strewn with islands, a river of through passage from north to south and back. This stretch of the river, usually perceived as a kind of prelude to the majesty of the upper river, gained its identity primarily during low water, when on account of the blockage of navigation, its towns became active transport depots from which passengers and freight were shuttled around the rapids or put onto stage lines to reach their destination. Travel, in this stretch of the river was, as a result, often slow, broken, discontinuous, and frustrating. Later, as rail lines reached the river, the towns in this area would become the transshipping points for passengers heading east and west, further cutting the river in two and continuing its role as a breakpoint in the course of the river system.

Finally there was the northern river, the true upper Mississippi, with its scenery, romance, and adventure, a contrast in almost every way to the river below the rapids. Here the river was narrow, calm, and clear, (except on Lake Pepin); lined by high scenic bluffs, which still draw excursion boats today; less prone to severe flooding but more liable to low water, given the lateness of the spring and the earliness of the winter. Because the river is so far north, and has such a brief navigable water flow, its scenic and recreational features would almost always exceed its practical use in a regional or local economy.

---

74 Jones, *Illinois and the West*, 40–41.
75 *Davenport Gazette*, April 14, 1842.
76 Christopher Mulvey, *Anglo-American Landscapes: A Study of Nineteenth Century Anglo-American Literature* (Cambridge, Eng., 1983).

As the water rose and fell in the river system, each of these separate rivers, dominated by one or more major river-town ports and controlling trading and transport networks distinctive to themselves, would be opened to and closed from contact with other parts of the system. As water rose, contacts with places farther away increased, competition among towns intensified, steamboat lines intersected and competed more actively, the speed of travel accelerated, and the range of contacts affecting local life broadened, becoming regional in scale. But as the water fell, all but the local traffic within the adjacent pool was cut off; trade and exchange were constricted to local needs and efforts, social and political activities narrowed and became less diverse, contacts with the outside were delayed, even cut off; and town life in general turned inward, focusing on local matters and the parochial concerns of their immediate hinterland.

Figure 3.5. Normal water level at Cairo, Illinois, in 1844.

PART II

The human system

4

Towns, roads, steamboat routes, and the development of a regional system

To move from human geography to an analysis of the regional systems created across the early Midwest is to shift our attention from the long-term, stable, persisting realities of regional life to the day-to-day, year-to-year efforts of individuals and groups to make a living, establish social and political lives, and contribute to the development of town or county culture. Not surprisingly, both individual and group efforts initially focused on economic development. Most immigrants had, as we have shown, come west for economic reasons and thus perceived the land and the environment as capital or wealth and viewed most of their actions in economic terms. This perspective manifested itself not only in the gradual reorientation of settlement activity according to economic criteria, but also in the efforts by settlers to found scores, if not hundreds, of towns and then to connect them by establishing steamboat lines, building roads, and improving communications. From such actions would eventually emerge a coherent regional system that would serve as the context for the evolution of a distinctive regional society and culture. In focusing on the regional system, I hope to demonstrate that just as most individual economic activity was defined according to regional rather than to individual or aggregate dynamics and criteria, so too local society, culture, and politics in nineteeth-century America can best and most accurately be understood in their regional, rather than local or national, context.

Towns

The establishment of towns was deeply imbedded in the process of settlement between 1800 and 1850. Some towns, which began as early forts or trading posts, were indeed the "spearheads of the frontier." They existed before their hinterlands were settled, controlled extensive trading operations across the West before the region was populated, and therefore had considerable advantages in becoming the centers of economic activity once the market developed. Few of the towns founded across the West belonged to this group, however. Further east, and in the earlier years of the settlement of the trans-Appalachian West, many towns were in fact founded and developed after the area had been settled. The mercantile services provided by towns were demanded only when settlers, after years of self-sufficient local activity, began to seek outlets to the regional marketplace. In time, however, as the market economy became more pervasive, and more farmers sought outlets for their produce, towns were increasingly laid out at the same time or even just before the occupancy of an area.

Just when this reversal in the sequence of development occurred is difficult to say. Throughout Ohio and Kentucky the founding of towns followed the settlement of an area by a few years. In the early 1830s, in Pike County, Illinois (in the southern part of the Military Tract), and in nearby Sangamon County most towns were still founded after the land had been settled.[1] But just to the north and west, and within a few years of 1830, towns were increasingly being laid out before people arrived to use them. By the 1834–6 economic boom, settlers no longer demanded towns, but rather prospective new towns, which had been established by speculators and investors demanded and even competed for settlers.[2] Consequently, while land surveyors and travelers searched for good land to settle and farm, they also actively began to seek out those sites that they thought would support a town.

John Bradbury, as early as 1812, traveled around the West and remarked on the number of "places which, from the nature of things, must become the sites of towns." But then assuming that "a person of judgement and observation would easily point out these places," he felt it unnecessary to do so.[3] John Woods, expressed similar assumptions when he noted a number of towns that "had nothing to recommend them except the opinion of their proprietors." Birkbeck also commented on the prospects of different towns, noting that one town "was not likely to thrive" or another "seemed to have great promise." So too, William Oliver scoffed at the ludicrous speculations of paper towns and claimed that he could tell a town with a future when he saw one.[4] Edmund Dana's comments on the future site of Quincy indicate some of the criteria used to make such judgments. To his mind, the bluff along the river in Adams

---

1 Juliet E. K. Walker, "Entrepreneurial Ventures in the Origin of Nineteenth Century Agricultural Towns, Pike County, 1823–1880," *Illinois Historical Journal* 68 (Spring 1985): 45–64.

2 Morris Birkbeck, *Notes on a journey in America from the coast of Virginia to the territory of Illinois* (London, 1818), 98–100; John Mack Faragher, *Sugar Creek: Life on the Illinois Prairie* (New Haven, 1987), 173–6.

3 John Bradbury, *Travels in the interior of America, in the Years 1809, 1810, and 1811; including a description of upper Louisiana, together with the states of Ohio, Kentucky, Indiana, and Tennessee, with Illinois and western Territories* (Liverpool and London, 1817), 324.

4 John Woods, *Two Years Residence on the English Prairie of Illinois*, ed. Paul M. Angle (Chicago, 1968), 80; William Oliver, *Eight months in Illinois: with information to emigrants* (Newcastle-upon-Tyne, 1843), 21.

County provided an ideal site for a town because it was on the Mississippi; it was high, dry, above the miry bottom lands that extended north and south of the site for many miles; its surface was level; and it was supplied with springs of good water. Moreover, the rich quality of the soil would provide the economic basis of any town. In addition, he and others believed its geographic location to be the most convenient for crossing the Mississippi, on a route from Sangamon County to the Boonslick and Salt River settlements in Missouri, making this location ideal for a ferry site. The fact that the location was also a full day or more north of St. Louis on the river, made it an ideal stopover and supply depot for river traffic. [5]

Not surprisingly, a favorable environment, good soil, good drainage, a sufficient height above the flood plain, and access to good drinking water were important in Dana's positive assessment of this town site. The reasons for each of these criteria are evident. The high ground and good climate would enable townspeople to prosper without suffering from flood damage or poor health. The good soil and water in the vicinity would attract farmers to settle the area around the town and thus trigger market activity. A good location near roads or river routes further enhanced its attractiveness, giving it the potential for being a convenient market, transport, and communications center. [6]

On such spatial and geographic locational criteria, Dana seems to have had fairly set ideas. For example, of the eighteen locations across the Military Tract that he pinpointed as favorable for a town site, twelve (67 percent) were on the Mississippi and only two on the Illinois River. Each of the chosen sites was high, dry, and surrounded by good soil. It was not Dana's expectation that the Mississippi would become the dominant line of trade that explains the bias toward sites along its shores. Rather the "miry bottoms" along the west bank of the Illinois from northern Brown County north to Fort Clark simply precluded riverside urban settlement. Indeed, the site of Peoria was the only elevated site along the Illinois that met the prerequisites for town development. A town site, therefore, needed to combine access to the river, with a site high enough to avoid the flooding and disease environment associated with the bottoms. [7]

Not all such favorable locations supported successful towns, however. Nor did Dana pinpoint each of these good sites along the Mississippi as favorable to town development. Rather he seems to have selected certain sites over others on the basis of their distance from other towns or cities, given the current or expected means of transport, and the population of the area. Quincy's location

5 Edmund Dana, *A description of the bounty lands in the state of Illinois: also the principal roads and routes, by land and water, through the territory of the United States* (Cincinnati, 1819), 25.
6 Definition of "ancien regime" from Fernand Braudel, *The Wheels of Commerce* (New York, 1984), 245; Diane Lindstrom, *Economic Development in the Philadelphia Region, 1810–1850* (New York, 1978), chap. 1.
7 Dana, *A description of the bounty lands in the state of Illinois*, 8, 23, 25–8, 30–4.

was valuable not just because of its topographical and geographic advantages. Its location a day north by boat from St. Louis further enhanced its potential as a market and transport center, because both a depot and stopover point were needed at that distance from the center. The fact that there was no elevated town site along the river for fifty miles in either direction reinforced the spatial advantage of this site. Predictably, the first town established in Adams County (Quincy) was situated on this site in 1821. [8]

Similar spatial concerns informed his other predictions as to where towns would develop in the Military Tract. To the north, between the lower and upper rapids, he believed that small depots or towns would develop every twenty to thirty miles along the river. A town near the site of Fort Edwards was an obvious choice, being at the foot of the rapids. Given that location, and the time needed to cross the rapids, he felt that other towns would be located between Montebello and Nauvoo, and Nauvoo and Appanoose, Illinois. Although he underestimated the barrier the rapids would present, and set the nearest towns too far north, he correctly anticipated the spacing between them. Back to the south he also expected that smaller local depots would develop along the river at intervals of fifteen to twenty miles in Pike and Calhoun counties. But he did not expect any of these towns, given the lack of a back country, to be important. Curiously, he chose to locate his own town speculation of "Bountyville, Illinois," on the river in northwest Calhoun County. [9]

Across the interior of the Military Tract, Dana's spatial comments focused on four sites he suggested as suitable for inland towns. Stopover points on the roads crossing from the Illinois to the Mississippi were clearly required. Given the difficulty of land transport, he believed that such towns should be located about four to five hours apart by wagon, or about twelve to fifteen miles from each other. South of the base line, this meant that a town would be needed about halfway between the two rivers. North of the base line, towns would be needed at this distance from each river, the distance in between being about the same. East of Quincy, he chose a site at the current Adams–Brown county line: Later the town of Clayton was laid out nearby. From the east, he suggested town sites on the high ground above Sugar Creek in east central Schuyler County, and on the level prairie between the East Fork and Spoon rivers in the northeastern part of McDonough County. In time, Rushville and Macomb, Illinois, were located about nine miles south of both of these locations, perhaps to accommodate requirements that county seats be near the center of counties, but at almost exactly the same distance apart. That Dana

8 Siyoung Park, "Land Speculation in Western Illinois, Pike County, 1821–1835," *Journal of the Illinois State Historical Society* 77 (Summer 1984): 115–28, 121.

9 Dana, *A description of the bounty lands in the state of Illinois*, 18.

could anticipate the spacing of towns with some accuracy indicates his rudimentary grasp of the spatial–economic requirements of urban nodal development.[10]

Other contemporaries expressed a similar awareness of space. To John Woods, the proximity of the two towns on the English Prairie settlement was clear: "The evil of two villages so near to each other had been great. For had they been united there would have been better taverns, stores, and etc." The inevitable result of founding two less efficient units was that one would fail and the other succed, and in this case he thought Bonpas "not likely to thrive" because "Oxford was laid out about a mile from it at the mouth of the Bonpas, on the banks of the Big Wabash and thus was better situated for trade." The failure of both towns, in the end, indicates that within the market range of both depots there must have been another town with greater locational and market advantages.[11]

Given the remarks of Dana and others, it seems that by 1820 the general rule of thumb was that at least seven to ten miles between towns was required to gain full control of a small hinterland or "circle of trade." William Walters's examination of the survival rates among town speculations in central Illinois during the 1830s suggests that any town's chances of success rose from 1:3 to over 1:2 whenever the nearest town was seven or more miles away. The spatial requirements for towns competing on a broader regional scale were less obvious. A later observer in Livingston County, Illinois, stated that "it will be noticed that as general thing while towns established at a distance of ten to twelve miles have flourished, those lying between have invariably been less successful."[12] As towns grew larger, many merchants came to believe that the minimal cordon of safety around a town expanded. Among subregional competitors evidence indicates that often as much as sixty miles between towns was necessary to support either one.

On a regional level, William Darby argued that two or more entrepôts could exist in one region but that they needed hundreds of miles between them for both to survive. For instance, he predicted, in 1820, that the trade of Cincinnati and Pittsburgh would remain exclusive and therefore both would prosper. At a later date, another writer scoffed at the notion that Dubuque and Keokuk competed with each other, stating that, given their range of trade, they were too far apart and that, in any case, there was plenty of trade for both of

10 Edmund Dana, *Geographical sketches on the western country: designed for emigrants and settlers... including a particular description of unsold public lands, collected from a variety of authentic sources. Also, a list of the principal roads* (Cincinnati, 1819), 74–80, 113, 123, 115, 117.

11 Dana, *A description of the bounty lands in the state of Illinois*, 26–8; Woods, *Two Years Residence on the English Prairie*, 215, 102.

12 William D. Walters. Jr., "The Fanciful Geography of 1836," *The Old Northwest* 9 (Winter 1983–4): 331–43. *The History of Livingston County, Illinois* (Chicago, 1878), 373

them.[13] Finally, Charles Cist, in the 1850s, formulated a "theory of circles," which, he argued, governed the systemic spatial relationships among urban units. Anticipating central place theory, Cist argued that a region was settled by numerous small places that initially developed independently of each other. After each had evolved to a certain point, they began to expand their trade and contacts, forcing numerous towns into competition with each other. The towns that emerged from these local competitions would continue to grow and broaden their range of activity, leading to broader-scale contests between ever-larger towns. These cities would, he argued, have drawn all of the smaller cities and towns across a region into their spheres or circles of influence.[14]

It was with ideas like these that some boosters, observing the pattern of urbanization at any given time, began to try to anticipate which areas in the West were prime locations for new urban development. Using our own sense of locational and spatial factors to determine whether an area boded well for urban development, and combining these perceptions with those better understood locational factors outlined by Edmund Dana, we can sketch out the average investor's or speculator's cognitive map of the early urban West and thus indirectly discern some of the spatial–locational forces that shaped the evolving urban system.[15]

Between 1815 and 1830 the Boonslick country in Missouri, the western edge of the Military Tract near the site of Quincy, Illinois, the environs of the lower rapids, the vicinity of the upper rapids, and perhaps the Sangamon plain were considered to combine excellent spatial credentials along with promising environmental and location characteristics. Almost every town developer assumed that in each of these areas an important town would evolve. Less attractive to investors but still offering the prospects of a successful effort in town building were the immediate vicinity of the base of Lake Michigan, the center of the Illinois River valley, northeastern Iowa along the river, and, finally, the American Bottom. In contrast, the short-term prospects of the Lead Region were based on its mineral resources, but its thin soil, inconvenient location via river and road routes, and disadvantageous spatial position did not bode well for long-term urban development. So too, much interest centered on the confluence of the Ohio and Mississippi rivers. From as early as William Byrd's warehouse investments of the 1810s, to the Rothschild and Illinois Central speculations of the late 1850s, many contemporaries were convinced that the site held considerable promise for the creation of a great metropolis. Its proximity to St. Louis was apparently disregarded,

13 Dana, *A description of the bounty lands, in the state of Illinois*, 26–8; William Darby, *The emigrant's guide to the western and southwestern states and territories comprising a geographical and statistical description of the states* (New York, 1818), 216, 226.
14 Charles Cist, *Cincinnati in 1851* (Cincinnati, 1851), 310–312.
15 See Table 2.1.

although the inconvenience of its wharf facing the Ohio for St. Louis boats should have indicated a problem. Less easy to ignore was the tendency for the bend of Cairo to disappear under water every spring, thus retarding the growth of a town. In addition, the land in its immediate hinterland was of only second-rate quality and unlikely to support a large population.[16] The American Bottom was equally popular with speculators. but the probable effect of its proximity to St. Louis was clearly evident in the sluggish growth of Alton, a town that had struggled and failed to get out from under its shadow.

Both general data and more detailed evidence of the density of urban settlement across the region indicate that such general perceptions did, in fact, have an impact in shaping the pattern of regional economic and urban development. One historian has argued that many investors were shrewd analysts of the factors affecting the prospects of a town's development and invested accordingly.[17] At first glance, the data seem to indicate only a very broad pattern. For example, among the 320 towns in Ohio noted by Dana in 1819, 166 were clustered on the west bank of the upper Ohio, west beyond Zanesville and across the Pickaway Plain and in the Miami River valley north of Cincinnati. That is 52 percent of the towns located in only 27 percent of the state's counties at the time. In contrast, southern Ohio, between the river counties and the prairie counties across the central part of the state, was relatively lightly urbanized and would remain so. In Illinois, on the other hand, almost half of the 500 plus towns that John Reps notes were platted out in the 1830s were located in highly desirable zones within the Military Tract.[18] A survey of those towns that had survived to be included on the detailed 1852 state map by John M. Peck and John Messinger (which, as Walter notes, was in his test area about 70 percent of the towns originally settled) indicates a higher density of successful town settlements in areas where contemporaries expected an important town to develop.[19]

Such figures may, however, reflect the unevenness in the size of counties, or the uneven distribution of population as it spread across the region. To eliminate the former effect one can divide the area of each county by the number of towns in it to get an idea of how much space each town controlled. Although the significance of such a figure, given our lack of knowledge of the functions of each of the towns in the county, is unclear, it should at least be

16 Zadoc Cramer, *The Navigator*, Cincinnati (1806): 38–9; ibid. (1814): 142.
17 John Denis Haeger, *The Investment Frontier: New York Businessmen and the Economic Development of the Old Northwest* (Albany, N. Y, 1981), 48, 61–71, 96–9, 103–4.
18 Dana, *Geographical sketches on the western country*, 72–3; John Reps, *The Making of Urban America: A History of City Planning in the United States* (Princeton, N. J., 1965), 361.
19 Walters, "Fanciful Geography," 332; and John M. Peck and John Messinger, *New Sectional Map of the State of Illinois Compiled from the United States Surveys* (New York, 1853) (all maps cited are from the Geography and Map Division of the Library of Congress).

apparent that the larger the number the less dense the pattern of town settlement in any county was. This can perhaps be grasped more easily by finding the radius of the average area controlled by towns in each county and multiplying it by two to estimate the average distance between towns within any county. [20]

The pattern of town development in Illinois and Iowa in the 1830s and 1840s was established further east in Ohio, the state from which a majority of settlers, town developers, and speculators had come. There, the density of urban settlement, measured by average town hinterland areas per county, varied from a low of 24 square miles per town in Jefferson County, behind Steubenville, and 37 square miles in Hamilton County, Cincinnati's adjacent hinterland, to a high of 173 square miles in some of the prairie counties to the north of the glacial moraine that cuts across central Ohio. As hoped, such a measure eliminates differences caused by county size. For example, Jefferson County, Ohio, had fewer towns than both Trumbull and Columbiana counties to its north and as many towns as Fairfield County. But each of these counties were from two to four times the size of Jefferson County and had less dense spacing of towns. In the middle range of town density were Muskingum County, and the two counties on the Pickaway Plain, Pickaway County and its southern neighbor, Ross County. [21]

By 1844 the number of counties with average town hinterlands of fifty square miles or less, the point at which the average distance between towns drops beneath the crucial competitive threshold of seven miles, had significantly increased. Most of the counties across the northeastern third of the state had fairly dense spacing of towns, with highest density shifting to the lake shore in Lake and Cuyahoga counties. In Jefferson and Muskingum counties, meanwhile, the number of towns had decreased, suggesting the success of fewer, more efficient towns, or a decline in population. A similar decline in the density of urban settlement was apparent across the Pickaway Plain. Meanwhile, the density of Hamilton County continued to increase slowly, while there was a considerable increase in the density of town settlement in adjacent counties. By 1855 the low threshold of below thirty square miles per town, which translates into an average distance between towns of six miles, had spread back across the center of the state, from Jefferson to Fairfield counties, and north around the hinterlands of Cincinnati.

20 See Appendixes A and B.
21 Darby, *The emigrant's guide to the western and southwestern states and territories*, 828–85; Dana, *Geographical sketches on the western country*, 72–82; William Creese Pelham, "Ohio" (map), 1817, 1818, in *The Mapping of Ohio*, by Thomas H. Smith (Kent, Ohio, 1977), 169–71; John Kilbourn, *The Ohio Gazetteer, or topographical dictionary, containing a description of the several counties, towns, villages, settlements, roads, rivers, lakes, springs, mines, and etc., in the state of Ohio* (Columbus, Ohio, 1819).

The lower figures for almost all counties (except those in the northeast), however, reflect the rapid urbanization resulting from the construction of railroad lines across the state between 1844 and 1855. [22]

Further west, such variations in the density of town placement (which should not be taken necessarily as a measure of "urbanization," but rather as a figure measuring the number of towns designated or occupied in any county and thus having a potential for stimulating urbanization) were equally apparent. In an 1852 map of the upper Mississippi, St. Louis County, Missouri, had the most crowded pattern of town settlement, while the lower central portion of the Military Tract in Illinois, extending across the river to the Salt River country in Missouri, the hinterland of Peoria, and the southwestern corner of Iowa, had as many towns as several counties beyond the reach of the larger cities of central Ohio. [23]

It remains unclear, however, whether the uneven spacing and number of towns from county to county really constitutes a higher or lower density of urban settlement or if the number of towns in any county was proportionally related to the county population, or the amount of market activity, or favorable topography or locational criteria. A comparison of town-density figures with population does seem to indicate a rough correlation between the two. In Ohio, in 1820, each of the more densely platted counties were within the band of higher population density that stretched across Ohio from Steubenville to Cincinnati. Moreover, the two counties most crowded with towns were also the two most populous counties. Twenty years later, the shift of population north and west is reflected in the increasing density of town development. Likewise, along the upper Mississippi River, each of the most densely populated counties was among those with the smallest areal extent of town hinterlands. [24]

But the relationship between population and town settlement is not as straightforward as it may appear. The simple observation that some counties in the Mississippi River valley had as many towns as several counties in Ohio in the mid-1850s, while still having lower population densities, suggests the weakness of any numerical relationship. Some have suggested, and it remains widely assumed, that as population grew in certain intervals, towns were naturally established to meet local demand. For instance, one demographer has suggested that two hundred people could support a blacksmith, six hundred

---

22 Towns are counted from maps of the period. Those that show the greatest detail and are most reliable are David H. Barr, *Ohio* (Cincinnati, 1844); H. Anderson, *Ohio* (St. Clairsville, Ohio, 1854); E. Mendenhall and Company, *New Map of the State of Ohio from the Latest and Best Authorities* (Cincinnati, 1853). The latter map was almost too detailed for practical use.

23 John M. Peck and John Messinger, *New Sectional Map of the State of Illinois Compiled from United States Surveys* (New York, 1853); *Colton's New Map of Missouri* (New York, 1851); *Colton's Township Map of Iowa Compiled from U. S. Surveys* (New York, 1852).

24 Ibid.

people a merchant, and perhaps eight hundred people a lawyer. Therefore, as local population reached eight hundred, one would expect a town to evolve. [25] As population increased and enough people moved beyond the range of the first town's control, one would expect that another town, as soon as population at that distance from the first town reached the threshold, would then be founded. Because this town supported eight hundred people and the other, no doubt, supported more, having attracted more people in the meantime, the average number of people per town, having risen sharply as population grew with only the old town in place, would decline slightly and then slowly advance toward its old level before demand pressure would encourage investors to establish yet another town. Viewed chronologically, the population and town history of any county would move in a kind of push-and-pull pattern, with population rising to a certain point, a new town being founded to serve it, further population growth bringing forth another town, and so on. All the while the average number of people per town would waver back and forth on a downward-moving trend until reaching that point at which the numbers of towns became relatively fixed and continued general population growth began to require that each town in the county accommodate more people.

A detailed examination of settlement in Pike County, Illinois, indicates that just such a pattern, with variations for local effects, does seem to have occurred. In that county, the first town was not settled until there were over two thousand people residing there. But once it was settled, several towns were founded, causing a sharp drop in the average number of people per town (Table 4.1). Between 1836 and 1855, however, continued population growth, combined with slower town settlement, caused a steady rise in the number of people per town until, when population itself leveled off, the average number of people per town also decreased. All during this time, the rate of decline of the average number of square miles per town and the average distance between towns decreased, indicating that if there was a self-correcting mechanism that limited town settlement it was the spacing among towns, not the number of people that each town served. The development of other counties across the region such as Muskingum County, Ohio, and Van Buren and Lee counties, Iowa, exhibits a similar tendency for the spacing of towns and population to approach equilibrium.

A clearer demonstration that space, and not population, is the controlling factor in town development can be seen in the interaction between the number of towns and population in any county in which population growth continued unabated. In Hamilton County, Ohio, for example, the average number of people in the eleven towns in 1820 was already 2,888, and increased to 6,274 in spite of the doubling of the number of towns by 1844. By 1855 the population

25 James E. Davis, *Frontier America, 1800–1840: A Comparative Demographic Analysis of the Settlement Process* (Glendale, Calif., 1977), 140.

Table 4.1. *County population growth and urban settlement, Pike County, Illinois, 1830–60*

| Year | Towns | Population | | | Square miles per town | Average miles between towns |
		Total	Per square mile	Per town		
1830	1	2,396	3.9	2,396	615 [a]	25 +
1835	6	3,507	5.8	584.5	102.5	11.4
1836	24	6,037	9.8	251.5	25.6	5.7
1840	29	11,728	19.0	404.4	24	5.5
1845	30	14,000	22.8	466.6	20.5	5.1
1850	32	18,819	30.6	588	19.2	4.9
1855	34	19,000	30.9	558.8	18	4.8
1860	35	19,680	32	562.3	17.5	4.7

[a] square miles of Pike County since 1830 has been 615.
Sources: Julliet E. K. Walker, "Entrepreneurial Ventures in the Origins of Nineteenth Century Agricultural Towns, Pike County, 1823–1880," *Illinois Historical Journal* 78 (Spring 1985): 45–64. J. M. Peck and John Messinger, *New Sectional Map of the State of Illinois Compiled from the United States Surveys* (New York, 1853).

per town declined slightly to around 4,700. In such a situation, urbanization defined as an increasing proportion of the population living in towns or cities is, indirectly, being measured, because only through the development of more efficient mechanisms could any town absorb more people. Indeed, when the average number of people per town rose to about 1,200, it is probably more valid to measure urbanization as a percent of population living in towns, rather than by an average population per town because as urbanization advanced and town functions became differentiated, the differences in the sizes of towns and cities would increase, eventually reducing the value of an average-size measurement in indicating urban complexity and development. [26]

Nevertheless, for the early stages of county population growth and settlement, such a measurement allows us to examine whether there was any demand-and-supply interaction between population and town creation. Moreover, by noting the range of variation in this measurement from county to county, it becomes evident that, rather than a fixed proportional relationship existing between population and town development, there were from the start counties that had more towns, given their population, than others. Such

26 Walker, "Pike County," 45–64.

Table 4.2. *Mean population growth and the density of urban settlement in Ohio, Illinois, and Iowa, 1820–60*

Population per square mile threshold	Number of cases	Population per square mile	Number of towns	Square miles per town	Population per town	Average miles between towns
0–2	3	1.1	2	411	505	22.6
3–6	7	4.8	7	219.5	989	15.2
10–14	18	10.8	9	77.5	1189	9.4
20–24	12	20.6	10	73.7	1519	9.2
30–35	18	31.4	13	72.9	2265	8.9
45–50	12	47.7	10	52	2439	8.1

Source: See Appendix B.

overurbanization could indicate speculation, or simply too many towns being set near each other too quickly, a sure sign that supply and demand were not interacting in any systemic way. The opposite phenomenon – fewer towns than normal for a certain population – may have reflected the indifference of residents to market forces and a low demand for urban functions.

Perhaps the most effective way to identify overurbanized or under-urbanized counties is to compare the level of urbanization of all the counties examined grouped according to population density (Table 4.2). [27] The figures indicate that there was no mechanical formula of town establishment per number of people in any county. Among the counties passing through the threshold of about four to five people per square mile, and thus coming out of the frontier, the range of the degree of urbanization was broad. Scott County, Iowa, and Athens County, Ohio, in their respective periods of passage through this population threshold, both had fewer towns than many other counties at that stage. We know that each of these towns was nothing more than a river-boat stop or a county seat with a few stores, yet each was compelled to serve over one thousand people. The extreme case was Pike County, Illinois, where one town served the entire county. The norm was Henry County, Illinois, where the average town controlled about three hundred people spread thinly across sixty-nine square miles. In sharp contrast, Clark County, Missouri, in 1844 with a population density of just over five per square mile, had many more towns than it could handle, each controlling a minimal twenty-three square

27 Ibid.

miles, a figure similar to heavily populated counties back East (see Appendix B).

As different counties passed subsequent population thresholds, the range in variation narrowed, indicating the stabilization of the population-per-town rate until real urbanization took off. By focusing on the counties with unusual patterns between 1820 and 1850, one can therefore measure where the speculation occurred. Among those counties achieving a population density of ten per square mile, Pike County, Illinois, by 1836 was overplatted with towns, indicating speculation, while the legacy of Clark County, Missouri's, earlier speculation in the 1840s, still had an impact on its urban arrangements in the 1850s. In contrast, Lee County, Iowa, in 1840 and Tuscarawas County, Ohio, in 1820 had fewer towns than they could have supported. In the 1830s, Clark and Ralls counties, Missouri, and Pike and Brown counties, Illinois, and perhaps Peoria County, Illinois, were oversupplied with towns. By the 1840s, Muscatine, Van Buren, and Lee counties, Iowa, joined the list. These were the counties that were actively sought after by investors and speculators. Not surprisingly, each lay within the areas previously cited as attractive to investors. It is also curious how little apparent speculation or oversettlement of towns there was in Ohio as compared with the situation in Illinois, eastern Iowa, and northeastern Missouri, these three states having many more towns per both population and area at a much earlier date than did Ohio.[28] These concentrations of investors' interests, reflected in the number of towns platted over a very short period of time and in no apparent spatial pattern, are, for us, indicators of contemporaries' sense of the larger framework of an evolving system.

For example, towns that gained early importance and counties in which there was considerable town speculation or overdevelopment in the Mississippi valley were all directly adjacent to the major rivers. In Ralls County, Missouri, several prospective towns were established along the river in the late 1830s and early 1840s. In Clark County, Missouri, at least ten towns were crowded along the south bank of the Des Moines River at intervals of less than a mile. Across the river in Van Buren County, Iowa, nine towns, with such varied names as Farmington, Palestine, Lexington, Bentonport, Columbia, Rochester, Keosauqua, Rising Sun, and Philadelphia (names that reflect regional investment interests) lined the riverbanks. To the north a string of towns stretched along the Mississippi River between Davenport and Muscatine, several of the towns spaced less than a mile apart. The speculators and investors knew what everyone seems to have taken for granted – that rivers were major channels of regional trade, a stimulus to economic growth, and a source of wealth. To

---

28 See Appendix B.

locate a town away from the river was to accept more limited prospects. [29]
Significantly, the pattern of urban settlement in the interior was much more orderly than that along the river. As settlers moved out onto the prairies, roads and eventually railroads were required to maintain their contacts with riverside markets. Each of these roads required stopover points, shipping depots, or small market centers to facilitate contacts between interior farmers and the regional market. Across the southern Military Tract, towns were strung along the important roads between Quincy and Naples, Peoria and Hancock County, Peoria and Galena, and Beardstown and Rock Island. Within a few years similar lines following the railroads would be laid out across large areas of the West from Ohio to Iowa. The geometric pattern of interior town settlement indicates the influence of economic or transportation planning at work. It also reflects their secondary, local role in a larger structure. Neatness, as is often the case, reflects a general plan, limited speculative activity, and economic order. Speculation, in contrast, was messy and inexact, proceeding by trial and error. On contemporary maps, speculative boom areas showed up as too many towns clustered too close together in no particular pattern. Such was the case around the upper and lower rapids on the Mississippi or across the central Illinois valley. [30]

Each town within these clusters aspired, at one time, to become a regional or subregional trading center. To do so, it was increasingly understood that a town had to connect itself to the developing regional transport system and begin trading between the interior and the entrepôt downriver. The considerable effort and capital required to achieve even this goal, however, insured that competitive free-for-alls among several towns were short-lived. Once a generally favorable area had been determined, and competitors rushed into it, the specific locations with the locational or topographical advantages necessary for success became quickly apparent. Therefore, within a few years, the hit-and-miss aspect of the initial town competitions narrowed down into head-to-head contests between two or three towns in one or two counties. The competitions among these successful central places would continue well into the steamboat era and ultimately be determined by the ability of the respective towns to develop an ever-larger role in the regional economy. The decisions made and strategies taken by the competing river towns played a significant role in shaping the structure of the regional transportation network, economy, and urban system.

---

29 Peck and Messinger, *Sectional Map of Illinois;* Jesse Williams, *Map of the Surveyed Part of Iowa: Exhibiting the Sections, Townships, and Ranges Complied from U. S. Surveys* (New York, 1840); Edward Huttawa, *Sectional Map of the State of Missouri Compiled from U. S. Surveys and Other Sources* (St. Louis, 1844).
30 Note the clusters on Walters's maps, in Walters, "Fanciful Geography," 334–5; Huttawa, *Sectional Map of Missouri.*

Among these intensive competitions, the most crowded and best documented were those for the development of the secondary entrepôts that
everyone assumed must develop around both the lower and upper rapids.
Some thirty town sites were established in the counties adjacent to either the
lower or upper rapids between 1825 and 1860. In each case, the progression of
the competition followed the pattern suggested previously. Initially, for
example, town founders, usually from just across the river, located new towns
at a variety of locations above and below the rapids. At the upper rapids, early
settlers simply followed the lead of George Davenport, who had a trading post
on Rock Island itself. Established in 1816, this post became the central depot
of a broad but not very intensive itinerant outpost trading network on the
upper river.[31] The men involved in this trading network had a considerable
role in founding the first towns on both banks of the upper river. In 1826
Russell Farnham, a trader at Fort Armstrong, crossed the river to found the
town of Stephenson (later Rock Island). The next year John Vanatta, another
employee at the fort, founded Keithsburg, Illinois, and began to sell lumber to
the steamboats that were increasing in number between St. Louis and
Galena – the latter being yet another site in which a Davenport post employee
had a role in founding. Five years later, when the Iowa side of the river was
opened by the Black Hawk purchase, Davenport himself platted a town site
just south of the future site of Davenport's downtown. That area was,
coincidentaly,platted about the same time by Antoine LeClaire, a French
interpreter at the post. A couple of years later Russell Farnham joined his
former associates by leaving Rock Island to found the town of Muscatine. And
when, in 1836, Farnham died, his efforts were taken over and expanded by
another trading post alumnus who had tried his hand at town founding in
Illinois a few years before, John Vanatta of Keithsburg. The same year, other
Davenport associates established towns sites at LeClaire and Rockingham,
nearby to both the Davenport and the LeClaire holdings.[32]

Amidst this rather intensive settlement radiating from a strategically located
trading post, others less directly connected to the fort, or to the region, filled in
the gaps. Preceding the extension of the trading post system to the shores
opposite, Dr. Samuel Muir, a physican at Fort Edwards, settled in 1820 near

31 Williams, *Map of the surveyed part of Iowa;* Peck and Messinger, *Sectional map of Illinois;*
   Franc B. Wilkie, *Davenport, past and present: including the early history and personal and
   anecdotal reminiscences of Davenport* (Davenport, Iowa, 1858), 155.
32 William V. Pooley, "The Settlement of Illinois, from 1830 to 1850," *Bulletin of the University
   of Wisconsin,* History Series 1 (May 1908): 423; *A History of Mercer County, Illinois* (Chicago,
   1882), 46; Wilkie, *Davenport, past and present,* 167–8, 161–2; Alfred T. Andreas, *A. T.
   Andreas' Illustrated historical atlas of the state of Iowa* (Chicago, 1875; reprint, Iowa City,
   1970), 426 449, 466; *History of Scott County* (Chicago, 1882), 82, 269; Sylvester W.
   McMaster, *60 years on the upper Mississippi. My life and experiences* (Rock Island, Ill., 1893),
   90.

the site of Keokuk, then still in Indian territory. A year later John Woods, a New York speculator, heeded Edmund Dana's advice and platted the town of Quincy; during the next season a group of Cincinnatians, led by Moses Meeker, barged north to establish the town of Galena. In 1827, Dr. Isaac Galland founded the town of Oquawka on the river in Mercer County. [33] In three out of four cases, choices followed the general impressions of locations considered to have promise for a town development, although curiously it was the outsiders who often made the shrewdest choices.

This filling-in process dramatically accelerated in the next decade and was taken out of local hands. Those with experience in the region initially played a significant role. Isaac Galland, founder of Oquawka, crossed the river about 1830 and settled Nashville, Iowa, but when the venture seemed stillborn, he occupied the vacant site of Keokuk. Likewise, Benjamin Clarke, one of the early settlers of Andulasia, Illinois, established a ferry across the river and settled the town of Buffalo, Iowa, at its far end. But as the 1830s progressed, newcomers into the region played an increasingly dominant role. [34] Burlington and Fort Madison were both founded by outsiders. So too were the new town settlements of Geneva, Wyoming, Salem, Montpelier, and Iowa, all in Iowa and approximately two, six, seven, eight, and nine miles east of Bloomington. Further north, the new towns of Elizabeth and Berlin were platted north of Davenport and across the river from Port Byron. The establishment of Sabula, Lyons, and New York, Iowa, all followed in close proximity across the same area (Figure 4.1). [35]

As choice locations were increasingly taken, subsequent town founders clustered around the original settlements, resulting in the speculation to which we have already referred. Indeed, by 1840 one observer reported, perhaps exaggerating (but not by much), that between 1835 and 1840 along the Great Bend in the river below the upper rapids, "every spot of ground along the river above the high water mark, and some below, was surveyed, platted, pictured, and named." In many cases the names are simply that, representing paper towns on contemporary maps, but not real towns. Among these, around both the upper and lower rapids, were Parkhurst, Churchville, and Huron, Iowa,

33 Andreas, *Andreas' Illustrated historical atlas of the state of Iowa*, 481, 481–2; Bernhard H. Schockel, "The Settlement and Development of Jo Daviess County, Illinois," in *The Geology and Geography of the Galena and Elizabeth Quadrangle*, ed. Arthur C. Trowbridge and Eugene Wesley Shaw (Urbana, Ill. 1916), 184; Park, "Land Speculation in Western Illinois," 121–2; Robert P. Sutton, *Rivers, Railways and Roads: A History of Henderson County* (Raritan, Ill. 1988), 11–12.
34 *History of Dubuque County* (Chicago 1880), 166–7; Andreas, *Andreas' Illustrated historical atlas of the state of Iowa*, 426.
35 Ronald Rayman, "The Black Hawk Purchase: Stimulus to Settlement of Iowa, 1832–51," *Western Illinois Regional Studies* 3 (Fall 1980): 141–53; Andreas, *Andreas' Illustrated historical atlas of the state of Iowa*, 482, 506, 426; Nelson Roberts, ed., *The Story of Lee County, Iowa* (Chicago, 1914), 107.

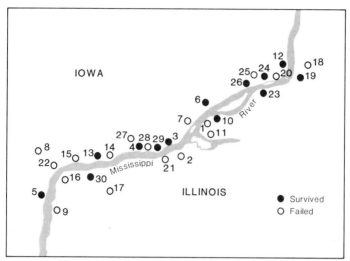

Figure 4.1. Town speculation along the Great Bend of the upper Mississippi River, 1826–42. 1, Stephenson, Ill., 1826; 2, Andalusia, Ill., 1832; 3, Buffalo, Iowa, 1833–4; 4, Montpelier, Iowa, 1834; 5, Muscatine, Iowa, 1834; 6, Davenport, Iowa, 1832; 7, Rockingham, Iowa, 1834; 8, Moscow, Iowa, 1836; 9, Phillip's Landing, Ill., 1836; 10, Rock Island, Ill., 1836; 11, Farnhamsville, Ill., 1836; 12, LeClaire, Iowa, 1836; 13, Fairport, Iowa, 1836; 14, Salem, Iowa, 1836; 15, Wyoming, Iowa, 1836; 16, Drury's Landing, Ill., 1836; 17, Illinois City, Ill., 1836; 18, Canaan, Ill., 1836; 19, Port Byron, Ill., 1836; 20, Parkhurst, Iowa, 1836; 21, Rockport, Iowa, 1836; 22, Geneva, Iowa, 1837; 23, Milan, Ill., 1838; 24, Walnut Grove, Iowa, 1838; 25, Berlin, Iowa, 1838; 26, Elizabeth, Iowa, 1838; 27, Iowa, Iowa, 1839; 28, Albany, Iowa, 1838; 29, Troy, Iowa, 1838; 30, Edgington, Ill., 1838. Dates indicate year founded or platted, whichever occurred first.

and Venus, Phillips Landing, Commerce, Camden, Rockport, Montebello, Pontoosuc, and Hancock City, Illinois.[36]

It was within this larger regional context that the local competition among towns was decided on the basis of environmental, topographical, or locational factors. But given the precision with which some choices were made, it should not come as a surprise that these contests were usually decided quickly in one town or another's favor. Often, the initial choice of a location was so good that subsequent town founders would find it difficult, if not impossible, to

36 Wilkie, *Davenport, past and present*, 220. A number of these towns are only recorded on early state maps. See Jesse Williams, "Map of Iowa," in *Home Missionary* 14 (1841); John B. Newhall, *Newhall's Map of Iowa* (New York, 1841); Henn, Williams and Company, *A Township Map of the State of Iowa* (Burlington, 1851); *Colton Township Map of Iowa Compiled from U. S. Surveys* (New York, 1852); Peck and Messinger, *Sectional map of Illinois* (1853).

counteract the advantages drawn from such a shrewd choice. Where competition was a little more evenly matched, personalities and the strategies taken by different groups in the respective towns could often account for success or failure. In such cases, a few towns remained in the running for a decade or so, until a county-seat fight or a contest for control of an important ferry service or for access to the steamboat system would decide the issue in favor of one town over another.

In the competition for the role of subregional depot at the upper rapids, Antoine LeClaire, the founder of Davenport, used the power of an extensive land grant that he had received for his services during the Black Hawk War to control the location of the ferry crossing and draw it away from his strongest competitors at Rockingham. But before ousting Rockingham's immediate threat, LeClaire and some of his new friends (merchants who had settled there) launched an all-out effort to secure the county seat. The other major contender was Buffalo, Iowa, a town closer to the center of Scott County that was established downriver a few years earlier. The centrality of Buffalo, given the contemporary expectation that county seats should lie near the center of a county, seemed to weigh heavily in its favor. To counteract this advantage, LeClaire, unable to change the location of his town, and unwilling to start another elsewhere (on account of Davenport's locational advantages), sought to "relocate" Davenport in the center of the county by having the county lines shifted upriver. As it happened, LeClaire's interest corresponded with those of one Dr. Reynolds, a legislator from Muscatine County who, as the founder of Geneva, Iowa, had a very similar problem in a similar county-seat fight with Bloomington. Like Davenport, Reynolds's new town was too near the eastern county line to become the county seat. Therefore, Reynolds, like LeClaire, thought that if the county line on the river could be shifted east by two or three townships, his town would then be located in a more central position in the newly arranged county. LeClaire and Reynolds, no doubt, found each other and pooled their resources and power to call a meeting in 1837 to discuss the placement of the county line between Muscatine and Scott counties. Not surprisingly, supporters of Reynolds and LeClaire outnumbered those from Buffalo, and the county line was moved upriver. Buffalo, therefore, was shifted toward the new western county line and Davenport pushed more toward the center of the county. [37]

As a result of these maneuvers, the contest soon focused on Rockingham and Davenport, the former remaining the larger town until 1838. Elections for the county seat were marred by repeated efforts by both sides to stuff ballot boxes by bringing in invalid voters from across the river to vote one way or another, followed by several demands for recounts. One election came down in

37 Andreas, *Andreas' Illustrated historical atlas of the state of Iowa*, 426–7.

Rockingham's favor; a recount was demanded and, after a purge of the invalid votes, ended in Davenport's favor by two votes. Protests from the Rockingham side resulted in yet another recount, which gave the election back to Rockingham by a narrow margin. Finally, the territorial legislature intervened and called a new election. But by this time, economic geography and LeClaire's control of the ferry across to Illinois were already deciding the outcome and Davenport, the larger town by 1839, carried the vote. James Burrows remarked that while charge and countercharge flew back and forth for two years, Davenport had simply passed Rockingham by in "both population and capital," even causing some Rockingham residents actually to "desert her in favor of the enemy." With rising expectations of commercial development, Davenport could also offer to build a substantial courthouse "just like the one across the river in Stephenson, Illinois." Thus Davenport "carried the day," and soon after connected itself to the regional channels of trade and secured an important functional role in the regional economy. Meanwhile, Rockingham stagnated and fell into the position of a dependent market town vis-à-vis Davenport in the county's economic and social life. [38]

In this case, personalities and local factors did play a role in deciding the fate of each town. Initially a single factor, a political boundary, affected two or more places in much the same way. Beyond that point some other factor would differentiate the performance of the two, which in turn would cause each to respond by eliminating the disadvantage, or seeking to capitalize on the advantage by developing it further. By the time a town had overcome two or three challenges, it was, quite naturally, acquiring countywide importance and would seek further functional advantages on an even larger scale by establishing contacts with the regional market and plugging into the developing regional transportation network. On the basis of such broader market access, the survivor of local contests would begin to function as a subregional depot and further enhance its advantages over its immediate neighbors. From this point, its economic future would be shaped by the regional movements of settlement, agricultural production, and transport services. Ironically, to continue to prosper in the broader, more competitive system required ever more sustained efforts to specialize one's function or to integrate it within some regional process. This could be done by oneself, by attracting outsiders to locate in one's town, or by encouraging entrepreneurs to invest in the town's development. Either way, growth required a continued response to the changing patterns of regional economic activity. As a result, the course of economic development in such towns was often discontinuous, uncertain, short-term oriented, and never entirely hopeless.

38 Ibid.; James M. D. Burrows, "Fifty Years in Iowa: Being the Personal Reminiscences of J. M. D. Burrows," in *The Early Day of Rock Island and Davenport: The Narratives of J. W. Spencer and J. M. D. Burrows*, ed. Milo Quaife (Chicago, 1942), 121–2.

The uncertainty of the outcome among competing towns in a region was often reflected in the populations of the towns in relation to each other as well as to the population of their hinterlands. By 1850, for example, the larger towns along the upper river were just becoming apparent as distinctive clusters of population within the region. St. Louis, of course, was the densest cluster; but Adams, Rock Island, and Jo Daviess counties in Illinois and Lee, Des Moines, Scott, and Dubuque counties in Iowa were also considerably more heavily populated than surrounding areas. At the center of each of these clusters were hinterland depots – middle-sized urban places such as Galena, Dubuque, Davenport, Fort Madison, Burlington, and Quincy – each of which was connected to an increasingly integrated regional system and supported by a distinctive specialized local economy.

In contrast to what one might expect, given hierarchical system models of urban growth, the relative sizes among these towns seemed to change unevenly and seemingly without pattern. Initially, St. Louis, Galena, and Alton were the largest towns on the river, St. Louis being much larger than the other two. Through 1850 most of the towns on the Illinois side were larger than those on the Iowa side of the river. But as settlement surged west, and trade began to come in from that direction, towns on the Iowa side along the river began to grow more rapidly than those in Illinois. As a result, by the mid-1850s six of the largest river towns were all about the same size, and had similar functions. The size of each of these towns relative to the population of their hinterlands was, however, strikingly different. Keokuk, for example, lagged far behind the advanced demographic profile of Lee County, Iowa. Perhaps this was due to the rampant town speculation along the Des Moines River, which may have spread out the county's urban population. Dubuque, however, was comparatively larger at an early date, but rather than continuing to increase faster than its hinterland's population, its relative size declined during the 1850s. Quincy, meanwhile, remained much smaller in relation to its hinterland population than most other towns upriver, perhaps due to a combination of an extra-large county around it and a dearth of other urban sites nearby. In any case, to explain such a general equity of size among several towns across a broad area, as well as to explain the different relationships between size of town and population of the various adjacent counties, we need more than a general model of urban development. These differences were more than anomalies. Rather, they reflect in an imprecise way the interaction of different urban units with the forces of regional change as affected by the timing of their development and their location. An understanding of diverse local reality lies rooted in the shifting forces of regional change (Table 4.3). [39]

39 U. S. Census Office, *Statistical view of the United States... being a compendium of the seventh census...* (Washington, D. C., 1854), 218–41, 344, 350–1, 354, 355, 377.

Table 4.3. Comparison of town and county population in the upper Mississippi River valley, 1840–60

	1840 population	(%)	1850 population	(%)	1860 population	(%)
Quincy/Adams	2,500/14,470	(17)	5,800/26,508	(21)	16,000/41,144	(38)
Keokuk/Lee	500/6,093	(08)	2,478/18,783	(13)	15,000/29,232	(51)
Davenport/Scott	600/2,142	(28)	2,200/5,986	(36)	14,000/25,959	(53)
Dubuque/Dubuque	1,000/3,059	(33)	4,071/7,210	(56)	14,000/31,164	(45)
Galena/JoDaviess	2,000/6,180	(33)	7,000/18,604	(38)	13,500/27,147	(49)

Source: U.S. Department of Commerce, Bureau of the Census, *Sixth census of the United States, 1840, Population* (Washington, D.C. 1841); *Eighth census of the United States, 1860, Population* (Washington, D.C. 1864). For city population figures, see Appendix C.

River routes

Evidence that speculators and investors considered locations at certain intervals along the river more valuable than others suggests that the movement of traffic along the river was, even before many towns were founded, a major factor in considering the prospects of any river town. Moreover, the fact that the crowded local competition among paper towns usually hinged upon which town could draw steamboats to its rudimentary wharf, and thus become the local drop-off point for through boats carrying immigrants or a pick-up point for mail or wood before markets evolved, indicates how quickly early townspeople became aware of the necessity of plugging their town into the evolving transportation network. Soon after a town secured the local wharf, it began to build roads across the interior to draw trade to that wharf, a sign that early merchants were keenly aware of the timeless dictum that the size and complexity of a town's economic function are based on the extent and variety of its transportation contacts with other places in the region.

The expansion of the steamboat system of the Ohio and lower Mississippi rivers, which had only become organized in 1817, followed early trappers, traders, military personnel, and, most important, lead miners up the river after about a two- or three-year lag. In 1820, to cut the cost and time of transporting supplies to the posts and forts upriver, a Cincinnati merchant hired the steamboat *Western Enterprise* to make the arduous journey to Fort Edwards. During its trip, the boat also stopped at Keokuk and Quincy and then returned to St. Louis. The next summer, another Cincinnati boat "commanded by Captain Newman," steamed north from St. Louis. Two years later a Pittsburgh boat, the *Virginia*, journeyed north with a load of supplies for Fort Snelling (near the site of St. Paul). On its return in June 1823, it carried south the very first load of lead mined by Americans and brought by steamboat to St. Louis. In doing so, it traced what would become the dominant steamboat route on the upper river from the 1830s through the late 1850s.[40]

The advantages gained from such navigation were so evident, that by 1825 two boats, the *Magnet* and the *Brown*, began regular trading on the upper river, stopping at every post or fort between St. Louis and the lead mines in northwestern Illinois. One of the boats was the first from the Ohio River to make St. Louis its base of operations, staying there even through the low-water season, a reflection, no doubt, of the owner's perceptions of the advantage gained by arriving upriver as soon as possible after the rise in the

40 *History of Hancock County, Illinois* (Chicago, 1880), 209; Henry Asbury, *Reminiscences of Quincy, Illinois* (Quincy, Ill., 1882), 34; John Thomas Scharf, *A History of St. Louis city and county*, 2 vols. (Philadelphia, 1883), 1105.

water in late summer.[41] Nevertheless, through 1826 most of the Ohio River boats, still short and blunt, with rounded hulls, small wheels, and even smaller "wheelhouses barely rising above the level of the floor," operated out of Cincinnati and steamed north of St. Louis only when immigrant traffic warranted it. Among these "not one was solely in the lead trade, a combination of fort supply and lead mine business being necessary to support their operation."[42]

The revival of trade in 1826 provided the impetus to dramatically alter this situation. By early in the season, a sharp increase in production enabled several boats profitably to steam north to pick up cargo and return with it to St. Louis. In the middle of the 1826 season, a St. Louis newspaper reported: "The immense trade which has been opened between this place and the Fever River employs, besides a number of keelboats, six steamboats: the *Indiana*, (which had been in the trade since 1825), the *Shamrock*, the *Hamilton*, the *Muskingum*, the *Mexico*, and the *Mechanic*."[43]

In addition to these 6 boats, seven others were running "fairly regular" between St. Louis and Galena, as the new town was called, in 1827. That season alone there were over 50 steamboat arrivals at the so-called Lead City. The next year various reports indicate an increase from 50 to 100 percent, peaking at over 300 arrivals in 1829.[44] Although the Black Hawk War and a slight decline in production led to a decrease in arrivals to around 120 in 1832, as many as 9 or 10 regular boats still steamed between there and St. Louis in the early 1830s. By 1835, according to Owen's reports, the number of regular boats had increased to at least 11.[45] In either case, a line of steamboats running between St. Louis and Galena was in place by the mid-1830s and ready to exert a strong rivercentric influence on the great in-migration of 1834–7.

During that rush of immigration, increasing numbers of settlers   and investors arrived at their upriver destinations by steamboat – thus reinforcing its central importance in the development of the upper river valley. Whenever a steamboat halted while on its way north or south, it was considered an event of importance by early settlers. In 1830, the steamboat *Warrior*, plying between St. Louis and Galena, stopped at "Hannibal, Quincy, and the Des Moines river," on its way north.[46] Another boat landed at Buffalo, Iowa, in 1833, "then the most important point between Burlington and Dubuque." We

41 William Petersen, *Steamboating on the Upper Mississippi* (Iowa City, 1973), 198.
42 Scharf, *St. Louis*, 1102; Petersen, *Steamboating*, 213.
43 Scharf, *St. Louis*, 1102.
44 David Dale Owen, *Report of a geological exploration of part of Iowa, Wisconsin, and Illinois*, (Washington, D. C., 1844).
45 *The History of Jo Daviess County, Illinois* (Chicago, 1878), 258.
46 Andreas, *Andreas' Illustrated historical atlas of the state of Iowa*, 423–4; Petersen, *Steamboating*, 287.

know that a steamboat arrived in Davenport in 1835 because Ebenezer Cook's family arrived on one early that season. Further north, settlers at Keithsburg and New Boston, Illinois, sold wood to passing steamboats as early as 1827 and both became regular stops on the upriver route by the mid-1830s. [47]

In a similar way, town after town, emerging from a local contest among paper towns for local dominance, drew a steamboat to their wharf, at first to drop off or pick up passengers and mail and then, somewhat later, to handle freight. By 1839, boats stopped regularly, often one a day, at Stephenson, Illinois, and "then continued up to Galena." Likewise, Quincy, Warsaw, Muscatine, Davenport, and Dubuque had become regular passenger and mail stops along the lead route. [48] The picking up of cargo from towns other than Galena, from where lead had been shipped since 1825, occurred somewhat later. Alton began shipping goods to St. Louis by about 1834. Quincy's first shipment of hogs and wheat into the St. Louis market occurred in 1837. J. M. D. Burrows sent the first shipment from Davenport up to Fort Crawford and Fort Snelling in 1841 and then south to St. Louis two seasons later. The same year several merchants at Keithsburg also hailed a southbound steamboat and shipped out a load of produce to the regional market. In each case, settlers up and down the river diverted the increasingly frequent passage of St. Louis–Galena boats to their port and thus tied themselves into a coherent system of trade and transport. [49]

Of course the great majority of the freight in both directions was intially related to the trade between St. Louis and the Lead Region. Until about 1845, when lead exports reached their peak and the number of boats on the river had increased to 30, traffic multiplied in almost direct proportion to the increase in lead exports. As a greater variety of freight began to reach the river during the mid-1840s, however, the relationship between the two became less direct. In spite of the considerable decline in the lead trade between 1845 and 1849, for example, the number of boats operating on the upper river only decreased to 28 in 1849 and 25 in 1850. [50] Thereafter, as short-line packets began to carry more downriver freight, the number of boats on the St. Louis–Galena line again became more directly related to the fate of the lead trade. By 1851 the number of boats running between St. Louis and Galena had dropped to 17.

47 Andreas, *Andreas' Illustrated historical atlas of the state of Iowa*, 426; *A History of Mercer County*, 46.
48 *Peoria Register and Northwestern Gazette*, September 19, 1839.
49 William T. Norton, ed., *Centennial History of Madison County, Illinois, and Its People* (Chicago, 1912), 91–1; Burrows, "Fifty Years in Iowa," 149–51, 176; *A History of Mercer County*, 127–8, 134.
50 St. Louis Chamber of Commerce, *Report of the committee appointed by the chamber of commerce, upon the trade, commerce, and manufactures of St. Louis, embracing a period of several years* (St. Louis, 1852), 42–4; *Annual Review, The commercial statistics and history of St. Louis* (St. Louis, 1854), 42–3.

Two years later only 15 boats were in the trade. A strong recovery in 1854, however, drew several more boats out onto the old lead-route line, leaving at least 20 boats on the St. Louis–Galena route through the 1857 season.[51]

In the course of thirty years, therefore, the Galena–St. Louis steamboat route extended a thin line out from the entrepôt, and then gradually grew in density and importance as the central artery of St. Louis's northern hinterland. It reached its peak between 1844 and 1846, thereafter stagnating in both numbers of boats in service and the frequency of their trips, before its precipitous decline as an artery of regional freight or passenger traffic. The causes of this growth and decline lie in the nature of the river environment, the shifting patterns of regional production, and, of course, competition from alternative routes and means of transport. But it also lies within the dynamics of its own success. By the mid-1840s the volume of freight and passengers and the increased demands for more intensive communications gradually overburdened such an extensive system spread so thinly across the region. Residents downriver were increasingly unwilling to await the daily arrival of the Galena–St. Louis boat, only to find it full of freight and passengers picked up on its way south. Likewise, those traveling north found overloaded boats, requiring long layovers to unload freight or delays resulting from limited maneuverability in all but the highest waters. Increasingly, smaller packet boats, running more regular schedules on shorter routes, were put into service to alleviate the frustrations of relying solely on a long-distance boat for one's travel and transport needs.

Between 1832 and 1838 the initiation of several packets accounted for a large share of the increase in the number of boats operating out of St. Louis from 82 to 132. As early as 1834 a daily packet, the *Tishilwa*, plied between Alton and St. Louis. Within three years, 7 such daily packets connected the two ports.[52] Quincy's sole reliance on the St. Louis–Galena line ended during the 1837 season, when it became a regular stop on a new packet running between the lower rapids and St. Louis.[53] This early packet line was formalized in 1843, after a discontinuance of service during the slump of 1837 through 1842, when a group of St. Louis entrepreneurs financed a new packet line between St. Louis and Keokuk. So successful was the line, contrary to the expectations of many merchants, that by 1845 a competing line went into operation along the same route. In the freight war that followed, 6 boats plied between St. Louis, Alton, Quincy, Hannibal, Warsaw, and Keokuk, drawing a

51 *Annual Review*, 42–3 *Lloyd's Steamboat and Railroad Directory* (Philadelphia, 1856); *Galena Steamboat Register*, 1855, Galena Public Library, Galena Ill.
52 Norton, *Centennial History*, 91–2; John M. Peck, *A Gazetteer of Illinois* (Philadelphia, 1837), 149.
53 Theodore Carlson, *The Illinois Military Tract: A Study of Land Occupation, Utilization and Tenure*, Illinois Studies in the Social Sciences vol. 32, no. 2 (Urbana, Ill. 1951), 89.

record amount of produce into the buoyant regional markets. In 1847 the competition finally ended with the St. Louis and Keokuk Packet Company buying out its competitor and expanding its service to 5 boats running at daily intervals. [54]

Indeed, wherever local trade increased at a rate faster than the lead-trade boats were able to handle, small local packets were put into service. In spring 1852, the St. Louis–Keokuk line extended its parket operations to Rock Island, thus connecting the upper and low rapids with regular local service. In the early 1850s, Keokuk was also the home port of another irregular packet line that ran up the Des Moines River, when water allowed it. Another packet seems to have been in operation in 1855 between Rock Island and Galena. [55] Further north, packets were used not only to provide more intensive local service but also to extend the coverage of the regular line beyond the current route. Boats from the regular lead-trade line had, of course, been making occasional excursions north to Fort Crawford and Fort Snelling since 1823. And as the number of boats running the St. Louis–Galena line increased, the number of boats that went further north during slack times downriver also increased. Yet as late as 1851 only three St. Louis–Galena boats apparently made any trips up to St. Paul.

To fill in this void, and convinced that they possessed a geographic advantage in trying to control the trade with the northern frontier, a group of Galena merchants and capitalists organized a company in 1847 to provide regular service to St. Paul. The next year, the Minnestota Packet Company began running two boats on a regular schedule between the Lead City, Dubuque, and points north to St. Paul. Within two years, three to five boats were in regular service along the upper river and, as happened further south, were trying to extend their service during high-water season up major tributaries. One Minnesota Packet Company boat steamed as far north and east up the Wisconsin River as Portage, Wisconsin. The success of this line naturally attracted competitors from the south. In 1852 one of the Galena–St. Louis line boats was diverted north on a regular basis. As trade continued to stagnate further south, they increased this coverage to one boat a day by the 1853 season. [56] As the size of the Galena fleet increased from three to eight to seventeen boats between 1850 and 1855, St. Louis competitors responded in kind. [57] Finally, in 1854 they organized the Northern Line Packet Company

54 Scharf, *St. Louis*, 1116; William Petersen, "The St. Louis and Galena Packet Company," *Iowa Journal of Politics and History* 50 (1952): 194, 198–9; Petersen, *Steamboating*, 237; Steamboat Passage Book, June 9, 1847, Galena Public Library, Galena, Ill.
55 *Galena Daily Advertiser*, June 9, 1847; Scharf, *St. Louis*, 1106.
56 Scharf, *St. Louis*, 1106.
57 Robert C. Toole, "Competition and Consolidation: The Galena Packet Company, 1847–1863," *Journal of the Illinois State Historical Society* 7 (Autumn 1964): 229–48.

and began sending eight boats on an entire circuit of the river between St. Louis and St. Paul.[58]

The local intensive purpose of such shorter packet lines within the interstices of a more extensive network is even more apparent in the timing between the shifting patterns of local packet service and the arrival of railroads at various river towns. Soon after the Chicago and Rock Island Railroad reached Rock Island, a new packet line, the Rock Island Mail Line, was put into service between Galena and the railroad terminus. In 1855, when another rail line reached Fulton, Illinois, the line extended its service to that terminal as well. The year after that, after the Rock Island had bridged the river and moved its railhead to Davenport, that town became the primary depot of the route. In 1855, when the Illinois Central Railroad advanced through Galena and reached its railhead at Dunleith, Illinois, across the river from Dubuque, the Minnesota Packet Company began to stop there. Within a year the company shifted its operations to Dubuque and made that port and Dunleith the central ports of its service. By late 1856, its northern service was also redirected to provide more intensive service with the new railhead west of Milwaukee at Prairie du Chien.[59] Further south, an "Express Mail Line" was established between Keokuk and Quincy, while Quincy merchants set up a special direct line between their port and St. Louis so as to avoid the incovenience of having to wait for boats to turn around at Keokuk before returning south. In each case, these express lines also provided direct service between nearby points and the new Chicago, Burlington, and Quincy Railroad line, which reached Quincy on the last day of 1856.[60]

The impact of this proliferation of local lines on the general structure of the system, as measured by the frequency of steamboat arrivals, can be discerned from the few surviving records of steamboat arrivals and departures at various ports on the upper river (Table 4.4). Early on, the rough equality in arrivals at Galena and St. Louis and the dearth of data for ports in between suggest the dominance of the Galena–St. Louis route. Most boats arriving at either place had come from the other. By the mid-1840s the thirty boats in this line accounted for about three hundred arrivals at each place, or most of the traffic on the river. Within such a system, ports in between would, of course, record double the number of arrivals and departures, since each boat on the line, while running a round trip between St. Louis and Galena, arrived and departed at each intermediate port both on its way upriver and downriver –

58 Scharf, *St. Louis*, 1106; Petersen, *Steamboating*, 206–7.
59 Galena Steamboat Register, 1855, Galena Public Library, Galena Ill., Toole, "Competition," 230–5.
60 *Quincy Whig*, April 10, 1857.

Table 4.4. Steamboat arrivals at ports along the upper Mississippi River 1840–60

Year	St. Louis[a]	Galena	St. Paul	Dubuque	Davenport	Burlington	Quincy
1840		300					
1841	143	350 (141)					218 +
1842	195	195			188		1,000
1843	247	244	26				
1844		308	30				
1845	547		29			208	
1846	663	333	41		523	581	
1847	717	284 (268)				524	
1848	697	(268)	104				
1849	806	(270)	119				
1850	635	180 (332)	171				
1851	639		229	351			
1852	705			418			
1853				496			
1854				672	780		
1855		1,388	1,076	846	556		1,076
1856				908		487	1,480
1857		590		1,000	793 (512)		1,280
1858							
1859							
1860							

Notes: Numbers in parentheses are estimates from other sources. [a] Arrivals from upper Mississippi River only.
Source: Chapter 4, see n. 61.

hence, the apparently heavier traffic at Davenport and Burlington in the late 1840s than at Galena.[61]

During this period, however, the numbers of arrivals at St. Louis and Galena began to diverge significantly. In the south, the sudden rise in arrivals at St. Louis to over five hundred seems most likely attributable to the increased frequency of service provided by the St. Louis–Galena packet company. At Quincy, where boats on both lines were double-counted, arrivals surged past one thousand per year. Meanwhile, the initiation of service from

61 These figures are either from complete steamboat registers, or from registers reported in the local newspapers. Estimates were not made from incomplete data. Figures from secondary literature were accepted only if reported in at least two different places. Because such figures are surprisingly difficult to find, the sources for each steamboat-arrival figure in Table 4.4 are listed below.

St. Louis: (1841–6) Delegates to the Chicago Harbor and River Convention, *The commerce and navigation of the valley of the Mississippi and also that appertaining to the city of St. Louis considered, with reference to the improvement, by the general government, of the Mississippi River and its principal tributaries* (St. Louis, 1847) 19–20; (1845–8) Petersen, *Steamboating*, 22; (1845–52) Louis C. Hunter, *Steamboating on Western Waters* (Cambridge, Mass., 1949), 49, 661.

Galena: (1840–2) *Northwest Gazette and Galena Advertiser*, December 30, 1842; (1843–6) Delegates to the Chicago Harbor and River Convention, *The commerce and navigation of the valley of the Mississippi*, 20; (1847–50) *Galena Gazette and Advertiser*, January 6, 1851; (1855) Galena Steamboat Register, 1855, Galena Public Library; (1857) *The Galena city directory containing also advertisements of the principal merchants* (Galena, Ill., 1858), 133.

St. Paul: (1843–6) *Galena Gazette and Advertiser*, March 17, 1848; (1850–3) *Galena Gazette and Advertiser*, November 21, 1853; (1857) Hunter, *Steamboating on Western Waters*, 646.

Dubuque: (1837) I. S. Semper, *Dubuque through the Eyes of Visitors* (Dubuque, Iowa 1954), 32; (1851–7) *Commercial advertiser and directory for the city of Dubuque to which is added a business directory, 1858–9* (Dubuque, Iowa 1858), 68; (1854) *Chicago Tribune*, January 20, 1855.

Davenport: (1842) *Davenport Gazette*, January 5, 1843; (1846) *Davenport Gazette*, June 10, 1847; (1854) *Twin cities directory* (Davenport, Iowa, 1856), xxxvi; Harry E. Downer, *Early Davenport* (Davenport, Iowa, 1931), 8; (1855) *Directory for the city of Davenport for 1856*, 57 (Davenport, Iowa, 1856), 57; (1857) Wilkie, *Davenport, Past and Present*, 274; *History of Scott County*, 478.

Burlington: (1845) Delegates to the Chicago Harbor and River Convention, *The commerce and navigation of the valley of the Mississippi*, 19–20; *Burlington Hawkeye*, August 14, 1845; (1846) *Burlington Hawkeye*, Weekly Steamboat Register; (1847) Delegates to the Chicago Harbor and River Convention, *The commerce and navigation of the valley of the Mississippi*, 19–20; *History of Des Moines County, Iowa* (Chicago, 1881), 482; (1856) *The first annual directory, of the city of Burlington for 1859*, comp., Watson Bowron (Burlington, Iowa, 1859), 8; August M. Antrobus, ed., *History of Des Moines County, Iowa* (Chicago, 1915), 118.

Keokuk: (1855) Orion Clemens, *The City of Keokuk in 1856* (Keokuk, Iowa, 1856), 19; William Rees, *Rees' Description of Keokuk, the "Gate City", Lee County, Iowa* (Keokuk, Iowa, 1855), 18.

Warsaw: (1841) *The Warsaw Signal*, Weekly Steamboat Register.

Quincy: (1837) S. Augustus Mitchell, *Illinois in 1837* (Philadelphia, 1837), 128; (1841) *Illinois state gazetteer and business directory for 1858 and 1859* (Chicago, 1858), 178 (I suspect that the figure of one thousand arrivals may be a misprint). Carlson, *The Illinois Military Tract*, 89; John Tilson, *A History of Quincy* (Quincy, Ill. n.d.), 41; (1856) Joseph T. Holmes, *Quincy in 1857* (Quincy, Ill., 1857), 19.

Galena to St. Paul during the same period seems to have caused a similar increase in arrivals at Galena, although it is poorly documented. Nevertheless, by the mid-1850s, arrivals of northern boats at St. Louis and Galena were again about equal, but this time not because of some intensive system between the two ports but due to an intensification of local service, unconnected to each other, around each port. When the Minnesota Packet Company shifted its operations to Dubuque, however, arrivals at Galena again quickly fell off. In any case, the general pattern seems to have been that of a single, integrated, extensive transport system, being gradually covered over by two more intensive local networks on the northern and upper parts of the river, above and below the rapids. In between these areas, river towns continued to rely on the older, more extensive system, the ports of Davenport, Burlington, Fort Madison, and Muscatine experiencing little increase in steamboat arrivals in spite of considerable economic development during the 1850s. Moreover, what packet service they did receive to meet local needs was, through the period, seasonal and sporadic. [62]

Because the range of boat sizes able to navigate the upper river was limited, translating these arrival figures into tonnages does not substantially change the pattern of relative volume. Although by 1851 the average Mississippi boat had increased in size from 85 to 168 tons, the mean size from port to port and route to route north of St. Louis did not vary significantly. The sizes of well-known boats on the upper river ranged from 118 tons in the small class (the *Uncle Toby*), to about 140 to 501 tons in the intermediate class (the *Wisconsin* and the famous *Bon Accord*), to about 200 tons, the maximum size for boats capable of regularly navigating the channel north of Keokuk. [63] Although in general packet boats were smaller than main-line boats, the latter often hired smaller boats during low water and the packet lines often hired larger boats during high water, an arrangement that balanced out any significant differences of tonnage due to average size of boat.

Not until one reached St. Louis's harbor did the size of the riverboats increase dramatically. Between 1839 and 1846 the average tonnage of the arriving boats rose from 144 to 194 tons, or at somewhat less than the rate of size increase among all boats on the upper river. [64] At some point between 1848 and 1854, however, the average size of steamboats at St. Louis's wharf

---

62 At ports in between St. Louis and Galena, or between St. Louis and Keokuk, one arrival at the end point of a line was double-counted, each boat arriving on its journey north and south in the course of a single trip. This fact may account for the rapid rise in arrivals at Quincy after 1850.

63 St. Louis Chamber of Commerce, *Report of the committee appointed by the chamber of commerce* 42–4; Delegates to the Chicago Harbor and River Convention, *The commerce and navigation of the valley of the Mississippi,* 6, 20.

64 Delegates to the Chicago Harbor and River Convention, *The commerce and navigation of the valley of the Mississippi,* 22.

jumped to above 250 tons. Clearly the more frequent arrivals of northern boats were being outweighed by the arrivals of ever larger boats that ran between St. Louis and New Orleans. These "floating palaces," reflecting in their size both the wealth of the trade and the size and power of the southern river, began at about 220 tons, averaged 300 to 400 tons, and often went up to over 500 tons in weight. For such boats to venture north of St. Louis into the narrow turbulent river below the Missouri and beyond into the narrower river below the rapids was increasingly unprofitable and dangerous. And, of course, there was never any question of getting over the rapids. Likewise, the smaller northern boats could hardly expect to compete economically with boats able to carry passengers in such comfort and freight in such volume. As a result, St. Louis's wharf became a kind of natural breakpoint at which northern and southern boats met, but did not compete. [65]

This fact should make it apparent that the differentiation of the system into divergent pools of activity was not so much a reflection of the relative economic power or the rate of capital investment in various towns, or even the rate of economic growth along different stretches along the river. Rather, it seems that these configurations can be most clearly tied to similar, less dramatic limitations on the navigation of different boats in different areas on the upper river. A few surviving steamboat registers from ports on the upper river clearly demonstrate how one's location, in relation to the rapids, could affect the number of arrivals.

At Galena, Illinois, in 1855, for example, boats from the south edged their way north with the spring thaw, coming in just ahead or alongside of boats that had wintered at nearby ports. About ten days later boats from St. Paul came down and arrived at the wharf. From early in the season, boats from three different lines arrived in varying frequencies. The long-distance boats connected to the lead trade arrived in great numbers for a month, but after the middle of May dropped off to between three and five boats a week. Soon thereafter, low water made it increasingly difficult for St. Louis boats to reach Galena, and as freights rose and business declined, the number of weekly arrivals dropped to less than two a week for most of the summer. The fall recovery was, in contrast to the spring upsurge, gradual. In the meantime, the number of boats arriving from the local packet lines as well as from Minnesota remained fairly regular throughout the season. Therefore, while another port without the local packet traffic of the northern river may have seen its rate of arrivals drop to nothing, Galena's wharf remained busy, at least statistically (Figure 4.2). [66]

65 *Annual Review*, 42–3; *Lloyd's Steamboat and Railroad Directory*, 267–73.
66 Galena Steamboat Register, 1855, Galena Public Library.

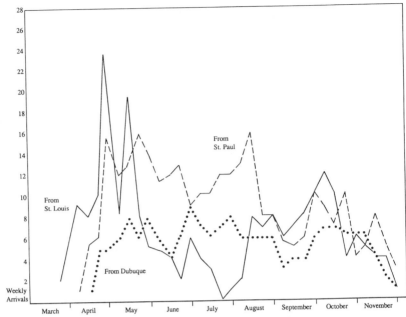

Figure 4.2. Steamboat arrivals at Galena, Illinois, 1855.

In between the rapids, where few packets made regular local connections on account of the proximity of the rapids, the midsummer break brought a complete cessation of traffic arriving at the wharf. At Burlington, if one discounts the double-counting factor, the number of arrivals was far below that at Galena. South of the rapids, however, the local packets would begin to have an effect on traffic records (Figure 4.3). At Warsaw, Illinois, in 1841, early high water brought in a number of arrivals from considerable distances (Figure 4.4). By the second week of May, however, two boats from New Orleans turned around at the rapids, signaling the end of the traffic increase caused by the presence of free-lance boats. Boats on the Galena–St. Louis line became the dominant carrier of local trade through July. In August, however, the decline of the water level blocked the rapids. Blocked from the northern river, Galena–St. Louis boats temporarily prefigured the Keokuk–St. Louis packet line and steamed between the rapids and southern ports.[67] Several years later, of course, the regular operations of the Keokuk packet would further support and increase arrival figures below the rapids. This similar

---

67 *Burlington Hawkeye and Iowa Patriot*, March 1–December 15, 1846; *Warsaw Signal*, February 15–December 15, 1841.

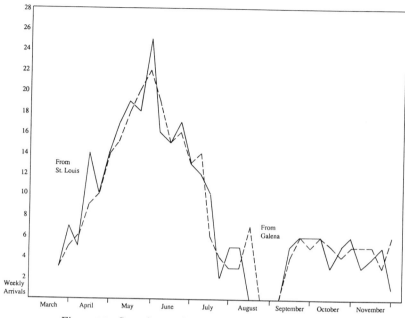

Figure 4.3. Steamboat arrivals at Burlington, Iowa, 1846.

effect is apparent in the strong arrival figures from upriver at St. Louis in 1845, in spite of a drop in the water after the spring flood.

It was the rise and fall of the river that ultimately shaped the different structural arrangements of the steamboat system. At different times of the year, the river really was divided into different spheres of influence. The imbalance in traffic figures from the north to south was also reinforced by the wanderings of free-lance boats through the system, a few of which were noted in wharfmaster records at both Galena in 1855 and Warsaw in 1841.[68] The fact that captains, in response to a drop in the water or a decline in business, set off across the river system in search of freights indicates to what extent these disruptions hurt their operations economically. A boat paid for and expected to generate freights was, during low water, simply being wasted. As a result, many Ohio River boats would move up the Mississippi, while other upriver boats, if they were large enough, would temporarily seek trade on the Missouri or the lower Mississippi above Memphis. Long-distance routes were further plagued by the uncertainties of water levels, delays in operations, or seasons of varying length. As remunerative ventures, therefore, it is no wonder that operating packets was considerably more popular than investing in a

68 St. Louis Harbormaster's Report, (1845), in Scharf, St. Louis, 1126.

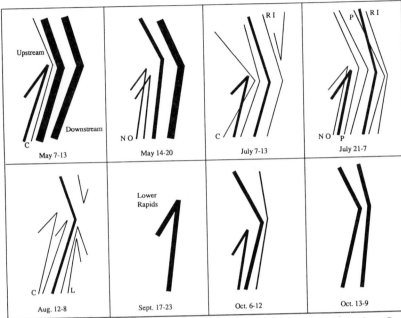

Figure 4.4. Steamboat traffic at Warsaw, Illinois, 1841. All upstream arrivals from St. Louis and all downstream arrivals from Galena unless otherwise noted: C = Cincinnati; L = Louisville; NO = New Orleans; P = Pittsburgh; RI = Rock Island.

long-distance route. To integrate fully a long-distance system and to reduce the chance and risk would require far more capital than even St. Louis merchants had or were willing to invest. But if a long-distance route did not continue to maintain its coverage across a region with a growing population and rising demand for transport, inefficiency, inroads from competition, and fragmentation seemed almost inevitable.

Unlike this geographical explanation, the only other possible explanation – one that views traffic as a reflection of relative economic power and investment among various towns operating across an area – seems to have had, with few exceptions, almost no basis at all on the upper river. Although it would be attractive to view the proliferation of local packets as evidence of the rising wealth and autonomy of St. Louis's hinterland river towns, the fact is that, from a very early point, St. Louis merchants and capitalists controlled the lion's share of the upriver boats and maintained most of that control over the course of a generation. Within such a context, towns along the upper river could view the operations of the steamboat system only from a consumer's point of view. With the exception of Galena, there was little chance for them to begin operating their own boats. Few of the towns had sufficient capital or the economic functional support to launch a competitive steamboat line. As a result, they were forced to rely on the St. Louis system and focus on trying to make a service oriented to St. Louis more amenable to their specific interests and goals. Not surprisingly, St. Louis merchants hardly bent over backward to help secondary towns maximize their growth and shape the system to their local advantage, perhaps out of concern that their competition might eventually erode St. Louis's control.

The St. Louis control of upriver steamboating began with the opening of the lead trade. As early as 1826, George Collier, a St. Louis entrepreneur, began buying Ohio River boats and sending them north to Galena. In 1829, Collier was involved in the construction of the first steamboat at St. Louis, the *Globe*. A year later, however, in order to insure sufficient return freight for his boats, Collier began to "engage largely in the purchase and shipment of lead" from Galena to St. Louis, from where he then shipped it, via New Orleans, to a correspondent in the East, Thomas Fassit of Philadelphia, who then sold it to eastern factories. As an encouragement to other merchants in the Lead Region to ship on his boats, Collier also began to offer cheaper freights on northbound goods in exchange for contracts to carry off lead in return. By undercutting the competition, he hoped to force all but his own boats off the upper river, at which time he could then raise rates to their old level. Although the paucity of details concerning this strategy makes any assessment as to its outcome difficult, it is noteworthy that between 1835 and 1845 he controlled "ten or more boats" running on the St. Louis–Galena line. [69]

The only serious competition Collier received before 1845 seems to have come from another St. Louis entrepreneur, Captain Joseph Throckmorton. During his twenty years on the upper Mississippi, it is said that he commanded "twenty boats and had financial interests in as many more." In general, Throckmorton purchased his boats on the Ohio and joined with other St. Louis merchants to finance their upriver operations. The *Burlington,* for example, served in the lead trade between 1832 and 1837. The vessel was an old Ohio River boat owned jointly by Throckmorton, Pierre Chouteau, and the firm of Hempstead and Beebe, a company with strong Galena connections. [70] Throckmorton also ran the *General Brooke*, built in 1842 and owned jointly with John Sharply, John Sanford, and Kenneth MacKenzie, all of St. Louis, and Henry Dousman of Prairie du Chien in Wisconsin territory. Until its destruction in the great St. Louis fire of 1849, the *General* was one of the workhorses of the trade, making fifteen or more round trips to the mines every

69 Scharf, *St. Louis*, 1256.
70 Petersen, *Steamboating*, 391, 393–404, 542.

season. But Throckmorton was never able to control a large number of boats at a single time and in later years he moved his smaller boats first into the Minnesota trade, and then west onto the Missouri, where, in 1855, he sold most of his boating interests. [71]

Early on, St. Louis's control of steamboating received at least some challenge from a few upriver merchants. Henry Dousman of Wisconsin was, as noted, involved with Throckmorton in at least one boat's operations. Another boat in St. Louis was partly owned by William Hempstead, a former St. Louis merchant who had taken up residence in Galena. But most of the upriver interests were held by Galenan Daniel Smith Harris, and his three steamboat captain brothers, Scribe, Meeker, and Richard. In 1828, the Harrises financed construction of the first boat on the Fever River and called it the *Jo Daviess*. This small boat, weighing only twenty-six tons, was active for two years. From 1835 to 1840, the Harrises owned a series of boats, including the *Otter*, another workhorse boat that made between twelve and fifteen runs a year in 1841 and 1842. [72] In the mid-1830s, therefore, Galenans controlled two of the seven boats regularly navigating the upper river. But their early attempt to acquire some control of the mechanism of the system faltered after the financial panic of 1837. By 1842, the Galenans still seem to have owned only two boats, while the size of the St. Louis fleet had doubled to ten, representing 84 percent of the shipping between St. Louis and Galena. [73]

Other competitors were even less successful in challenging St. Louis's developing hegemony on the river. In 1835, for example, the merchants of Alton attempted to wrest control of the lead trade from St. Louis boats. The disastrous consequences of their effort is told in detail by Thomas Ford in his *History of Illinois:*

> In 1835 a strong desire was felt by many to create a commercial emporium in our state; and it was hoped that Alton would be the place. As yet, however, nearly the whole trade of Illinois, Wisconsin, and the Upper Mississippi was concentrated at St. Louis. All the lead of the upper and lower mines was shipped from or on account of merchants in St. Louis. Exchange on the East to any amount could only be purchased in St. Louis....
>
> The state bank sought to break up this course of things and divert these advantages to Alton. Godfrey, Gilman and Company were supplied with about $800,000 to begin in the lead business. By their agents they made

71 Ibid., 402, 543; *Lloyd's Steamboat and Railroad Directory*, 262–4.
72 St. Louis Chamber of Commerce, *Proceedings of the St. Louis chamber of commerce, in relation to the improvement of the navigation of the Mississippi River and its principal tributaries and the St. Louis harbor* (St. Louis, 1842), 26–8; *History of Jo Daviess County, Illinois*, 259; Petersen, *Steamboating*, 414.
73 St. Louis Chamber of Commerce, *Proceedings of the St. Louis chamber of commerce*, 27–8.

heavy purchases of lead and had it shipped to Alton [their agent was Horatio H. Gear]. The designs of this party were, of course, not accomplished. The St. Louis merchants had more capital. They were intimately connected, either as owners or agents, in all the steamboats running on the Illinois and Upper Mississippi. These boats required an upriver as well as a downriver freight. The upriver freight could be gotten only in St. Louis and would not be furnished to boats known to be engaged in the Alton conspiracy. The merchants in Galena and throughout the upper Mississippi were connected in trade with St. Louis merchants, many of whom owing balances not convenient to be paid and enjoying standing credits which could not be dispensed with.[74]

By this counterboycott, made possible by St. Louis's almost complete control over the system, the merchants there thus deprived Alton boats of upriver freights and forced them out of the system. Even worse, extensive purchases of lead by Alton merchants and speculators had artificially forced up prices. As soon as the Alton merchants tried to sell their holdings, prices plummeted and they were forced to liquidate their stocks at ruinous losses. The venture ended in complete failure and severely damaged the regional aspirations of the town's economy, as well as its internal health, until well into the 1850s.[75] Needless to say, other towns and merchants soberly considered Alton's foolhardy venture and were discouraged from any further assaults on St. Louis's control.

Indeed, when the movement toward packet lines developed in the 1840s, it represented not the challenge of upriver towns to St. Louis hegemony but, with one exception, a further intensification of that geo-economic control. Of the twenty-eight boats regularly in the lead trade between 1843 and 1850, for example, only four were owned outside St. Louis. Burlington merchants had launched two short-distance boats, while the Harrises of Galena still owned but two boats. Of the two, the *War Eagle* was the most famous. Built in Cincinnati from new designs, it broke every speed record between St. Louis and Galena during the 1845 and 1849 seasons. But around this famous Galena boat, other lines filled in to broaden St. Louis control. The St. Louis and Keokuk Packet Company was entirely St. Louis-owned. So too, were the boats that occasionally ran between Rock Island and Galena.[76]

This hegemony, which in some years after 1845 amounted almost to a monopoly, seems to have reached its peak between 1850 and 1852, however. Between then and 1857, entrepreneurs in a number of smaller river towns entered the steamboating business and tried, if only locally, to challenge St.

74 John M. Peck, *A gazetteer of Illinois*, 45; Mitchell, *Illinois in 1837*, 114. Thomas Ford, *A History of Illinois* (Chicago, 1854), 176–7.
75 Petersen, *Steamboating*, 218, 417.
76 *Burlington Hawkeye*, January 15, 1846; Petersen, *Steamboating*, 420, 423; Toole, "Competition," 230–1.

Louis dominance. An 1856 register of western boats, for instance, documents thirteen upriver boats built at St. Louis but, what is more significant, two at Fulton, Illinois, and one each at Rockingham and Keokuk, Iowa, and Rock Island, Illinois. Curiously, there is no record of other boats owned out of Quincy, Fort Madison, Muscatine, or even Davenport. [77]

The most serious challenge was, as mentioned, launched from Galena and made on the river between the Lead City and St. Paul. Initially, however, Galenans had to come to some agreement among themselves before they could hope to counteract successfully the St. Louis challenge on the upper river. In 1849, two years after the Minnesota Packet Company began sending boats regularly to St. Paul, Daniel Harris, recognizing the potential of the Minnesota trade, pulled his two boats out of the St. Louis–Galena line and independently sent them north to St. Paul. For two years, the Harris boats and those of the packet line engaged in a "ruinous" internecine struggle for control. [78] The immediate result of Harris's decision was to end Galena's role in the St. Louis–Galena trade and thus, over the short term, further strengthen St. Louis's power. The sudden extension of operations of the St. Louis and Keokuk Packet Company north to Galena and St. Paul can, perhaps, be read as a manifestation of this new vigor. Nevertheless, it was in the face of this formidable challenge from the south that the feuding parties in Galena finally put aside their differences. In 1853, Daniel Harris was installed as director of the reorganized Galena and Minnesota Packet Company and played an active role in buying boats for the Minnesota trade and expanding its operations.

By 1855, Galena's interests had shifted almost entirely upriver and proved sufficiently powerful to counteract St. Louis's drive for control on that part of the river. But the consequences of its decision to concentrate on developing its function within the regional infrastructure entirely in the northern trade was to isolate the town's function from its former contacts in the south. As a result, when the railroads moved across its hinterland from east to west a year later, and shifted the transshipping point from Galena to the river at Dunleith, there was no support from St. Louis to reinforce the old arrangements. The company moved its offices to Dubuque, renamed itself the Galena, Dunleith, and Minnesota Packet Company, and, after a brief competition with the fledgling Dubuque and St. Paul Packet Company owned by Jesse P. Farley, Caleb Booth, and Lucius and Solon Langworthy in 1857, began to draw in Dubuque and upriver capital to support its operations. Galena merchants still owned seventeen boats (remarkable when compared with the two boats owned

77 *Lloyd's Steamboat Directory*, 267–73.
7̂ *The Galena city directory containing also advertisements of the principal merchants* (Galena, Ill., 1855), 55–6; Toole, "Competition," 230; *Galena Daily Advertiser*, May 22, 1852; *Annual Review*, 41; Petersen, *Steamboating*, 420, 423.

just a decade before) and a majority of the stock in the company, but neither was still working for the direct benefit of Galena's functional development. [79]

There is little validity, therefore, to a geo-economic interpretation of the proliferation of packets on the upper river between 1845 and 1858. Despite the heavier traffic, and its greater diversity, evidence indicates that St. Louis retained much of its financial control over the steamboat system. Challenges from upriver towns were, with the exception of Galena, almost nonexistent. But if the proliferation of traffic does not constitute an increase in competition among various towns, what explains its development?

Most likely, the proliferation of packet traffic simply reflected the declining ability of long-distance boats to meet hinterland demands for steamboat service. Being limited by the rise and fall of the water, and by the distances and travel times between places, the reach of any transport system inevitably wore thin. St. Louis boats, whether involved in long-distance trade or packet lines, could adequately keep up with the expansion of trade in the area immediately adjacent to the entrepôt, but their ability to do so declined in direct proportion to their distance from the center. The simple fact that the river was not expandable made for an extremely linear system with little capacity to expand laterally. [80] As a result, the further a line was extended into the hinterland or, as in this case, along the river, the greater the disproportion between its operations and the size of the area to be provided with transport services. Where topography or environment intervened, the limits to the system's coverage were even more apparent.

Economic strategy at the entrepôt seems to have reinforced these limitations. A survey of a few complete registers of "steamboats owned at St. Louis" indicates that at no time between 1840 and 1860 did the tonnages of upriver boats amount to more than one-fifth of the city's other investment in the floating palaces of the south. [81] In the 1850s, when upriver towns sought to redress their grievances about inadequate service, St. Louis merchants appear to have been unresponsive. With boats going northwest up the Missouri, southwest down the Mississippi and tributaries in Arkansas and Oklahoma, and east on the Ohio, St. Louis's ability or willingness to concentrate its efforts on one part of its vast system was considerably weakened. As a result, St. Louis merchants seem, given the relative wealth of the various trades, to have chosen to consolidate their trade below the rapids and provide only limited extensive service further north. The result, by providing relatively inefficient services, was to alienate towns north of the rapids from St. Louis, and leave

79 Toole, "Competition," 230–1; *The Galena City Directory* (1858), 133.
80 Sam Bass Warner, *Streetcar Suburbs, The Process of Growth in Boston, 1830–1900* (New York, 1973).
81 St. Louis Chamber of Commerce, *Report of the committee appointed by the chamber of commerce*, 42–4; *Annual Review*, 42–3; *Lloyd's Steamboat and Railroad Directory*, 267–73.

the entire northern hinterland disaffected from southern loyalties and thus economically porous and open to infiltration from Chicago.

There is an ironic note to these developments. As the steamboat spread its influence upriver in the 1820s and 1830s, it rearranged the systemic geography of the region. Settlement and farming, trade and urbanization were drawn back to the rivers, leaving vast interior areas outside the reach of the system. But at the same time, the unnavigability of most of the major tributaries in the region severely limited the spatial reach of the boats, confronting the system rather soon after its development with the prospects of diminishing returns. As settlers continued to move into the interior, the ever-more-apparent inadequacies of the river-based system became a source of friction in the regional economy. Thus, the very geographic features that had created the system were structurally unable to expand with it, and contained within their usage the seeds of the system's dissolution. The character of the rivers, ironically, was the primary factor that eventually shifted regional economic activities back to the land.

The roads: rivers on land

With a few exceptions, most of the river towns along the upper Mississippi were unable to compete with the St. Louis-dominated steamboat system and thus had to accept and adjust local economic strategies to the frequency and pattern of the service offered. Given these circumstances, the construction of roads provided these towns both a psychological release and a chance to change their function in the system. On the one hand, individual river towns could attempt to control their own economic destinies by extending roads deeper into the interior and broadening their control over nearby areas and towns. On the other hand, road construction would facilitate the development of a produce market which, in turn would encourage steamboats going to St. Louis to stop more regularly. In this way, local entrepreneurs would gradually be given more say in setting the schedules of the St. Louis steamboats from season to season. At some future date, increased gains from market activity might encourage some local entrepreneurs to launch their own steamboat line with their specific needs and interests in mind.

Roads thus served both to reinforce and to undermine the steamboat system. Before the arrival of the steamboat, roads actually competed with the rivers, running parallel to them along the bluffs, as well as across the prairies. But as the speed and carrying capacity of steamboats began to outpace land conveyances, the roads were drawn toward the rivers, becoming "tributaries" on land by which interior residents reached the nearest navigable river. Thus, the construction of roads played an important role in extending the development of the regional system. In time, however, the traffic along these land routes increased to such an extent that they attracted further development and began to compete with the steamboat system in the transport of passengers, goods, and services. The regional pattern of road building reflects these gradual but important shifts in their regional function.

As we have seen, the heaviest concentration of population and steamboat traffic moved northeast into the lower Illinois River valley a decade or so before a continuous strip of settlement along the upper valley reached Galena and the Lead Region. Not surprisingly, the earliest construction of roads emanated from the lower Illinois River valley and extended north and west across the Military Tract toward the mining district. These roads, of course, served as extensions of the network of roads that cut across southern Illinois toward the American Bottom and St. Louis. As early as 1825, a road was built between Beardstown and Rushville, both of which had been platted the year before. Soon afterward, a local road was built to connect Havanna, on the east bank of the river, with the newly founded town of Lewiston. With the opening of the Lead Region after 1825, hundreds of individuals and groups set out from positions within this network of towns and roads across the open prairies to the north and west. [82]

By 1827 most of the traffic to the Lead Region concentrated on three important trails, each of which had been upgraded to the status of a state road. The first of these was the famous Lewiston Trail, surveyed across the high ground of Fulton and Knox counties, crossing the Spoon River southeast of Knoxville and the Rock River at Prophetstown, and continuing on a route parallel to the Mississippi River through Whiteside and Carroll counties up to Galena. The trail was laid out by Ossian Rush, the founder of (and ferry keeper at) Havanna–Havanna itself being connected by a road to Springfield in 1827. Another road, the Old Galena Trail, ran northwest from Peoria and crossed the Spoon River at Maquon, continued north across the present site of Henderson where it turned north to Rock Island, from which point it followed the east bank of the Mississippi River to the Lead City. In its day, the route was considered "long and difficult." [83] A third major route to the Lead Region was laid out in June 1827 when John Dixon and Charles Boyd passed through what is now Bureau County on their way from Springfield to Galena, their only guide being the wagon tracks made a few days before by a party that had come down from Galena to Peoria. This route, the Peoria–Dixon–Galena road, became by the early 1830s the most heavily traveled of the three,

82 *Combined History of Schuyler and Brown Counties, Illinois* (Philadelphia, 1882), 86.
83 *History of Whiteside County* (Morrison, Ill., 1877), 58; *Brevet's Illinois State Historical Markers and Sites* (Sioux Falls, S. D., 1976), 116, 184; *History of Knox County, Illinois* (Galesburg, Ill., 1878), 191.

Figure 4.5. Major roads across the Military Tract, 1825–50.

boasting six taverns along its length, as well as an interior trading post at Dixon's town. (Figure 4.5). [84]

During the same period, the first two roads were consolidated into one of the first state roads in Illinois. This state road ran from Beardstown to Rushville in Schuyler County, then to Knoxville and Henderson in Knox County, and then followed the old trail north to Prophetstown, from which point it crossed over to Savannah and ran along the river to Galena. By 1840, however, this circuitous route was being overshadowed by a new state road

84 *History of Bureau County, Illinois* (Chicago, 1885), 79, 113; Abner D. Jones, *Illinois and the West* (Boston, 1838), 175; Peck, *Gazetteer of Illinois*, 191; Pooley, "Settlement of Illinois," 178; James H. Buckingham, *Illinois as Lincoln Knew It, or a Boston Reporter's Record of a Trip Made in 1847*, ed. Harry Pratt (Springfield, Ill., 1983), 75; Tanner, *Illinois and Missouri* (1836).

that ran due north from Rushville to Rock Island, via Macomb and Monmouth, and then followed the river to the Fever River. This road was the Rushville–Galena Stage route of the early 1840s. The Peoria–Dixon road, meanwhile, maintained its important role as a major artery and stage route until about 1850. As early as 1833 another road from Peoria was built to Princeton, and from there extended on to Chicago. A year or two later a Chicago–Dixon road was connected to the Galena road at Dixon to form a continuous route between Galena and Chicago. This road complemented the other Galena–Chicago road, which, going by way of Freeport, had been laid out in 1832. [85]

After 1835 the roads extending across the Military Tract became even more important. As interior areas on the tract were settled and crops planted and sent to market, the demand for adequate roads and stages increased. Soon after river towns along the Illinois were platted out, roads were sent out across the tract toward towns on the Mississippi River. In between, Carthage and Monmouth (founded in 1831) and Macomb and Pittsfield (founded in 1832) became important post towns about halfway between the sets of parallel river towns (Peoria and Rock Island or Oquawka, Havanna and Burlington or Keokuk, and Beardstown and Quincy). The first state road was laid out between Rushville and Quincy in 1835. As early as 1839 a stage connected the two towns and extended east toward Beardstown and Springfield. About the same time Rushville also became a stop on a road from Beardstown to Burlington, then the territorial capital of Iowa, via Macomb and Shokoken. Meanwhile, the Peoria–Knoxville road was extended to Monmouth (where it was incorporated into the town plat as early as 1831) and on to Burlington via Oquawka. In later years this became the regular, and much traveled, Peoria–Burlington line. [86]

By 1840 three major additions had been made to this first generation of roads across the Military Tract. Two of the new roads went from Jacksonville to Quincy by different routes. The southern road ran southwest from Naples or Griggsville and then on to Quincy along a meandering route through such forgotten places as Liberty and Beverly, Illinois. As Juliet Walker notes, this road became an important artery in Pike County in the years that followed. A second line acted as a spur connecting Jacksonville to the original Rushville–

85 *History of Whiteside County*, 58; James Colton, *Western tourist's and emigrant's guide* (New York, 1846), 116; Nathan Fish Moore, *A Journey from New York to the falls of St. Anthony in 1845* (Chicago, 1946), 12; Owen, *Report of a Geological Exploration*, 137; Tanner, *Illinois and Missouri* (1841).

86 Tanner, *Illinois and Missouri* (1836); Peck and Messinger, *Map of Illinois*, (1840); Colton, *Guide* (1840), 116–18; Colton, *Guide* (1851), 74–77; *Historical and biographical record of Monmouth and Warren county, Illinois*, ed. Luther E. Robinson (Chicago, 1927), 33–37. Robert P. Sutton, *Rivers, Railways, and Roads: A History of Henderson County* (Raritan, Ill., 1988) 37–39.

Quincy road. From Meredosia that stage went to Mount Sterling, where it followed the main line west to Quincy via Clayton. Further north, yet another route emanated from the Beardstown–Rushville axis, heading northwest toward Keokuk via Augusta, Carthage, and Warsaw with detours to obscure places, even then, like Huntsville, Plymouth, and St. Mary's. A spur line was also laid out from Carthage to Appanoose, across the river from Fort Madison, Iowa. It was along each of these roads, but especially on those between Beardstown and Quincy and Burlington and Peoria, that merchants from respective river towns competed township by township to extend the range of their markets. [87]

In Iowa, the lack of water courses parallel to the Mississippi, which could, therefore, be used as detours when the main channel of the river was blocked, lessened the importance of roads in general and gave roads that did run parallel to the river relatively more importance. For most of the period, stage lines connected each of the towns along the river. As early as 1850 common roads connected Keokuk and Burlington, Muscatine and Davenport, and Davenport and Dubuque. There was also a stage line that crossed the river just south of Keokuk and ran south along the east bluff of the river, via Lima, Illinois, to Quincy. The major roads running due west from the river seem to have been the Keokuk–Fort Des Moines road that passed through the settlements of Ottumwa and Red Rock, the Davenport–Muscatine City road along which so many paper towns had been established, the Military Road from Iowa City to Dubuque via Anamoosa, and the Davenport–Dubuque road across the interior of Scott and Clinton counties via Dewitt, Iowa. In addition to these stage routes, Iowans by 1850 had built a few plank roads extending west from some of the major riverside towns. The plank road behind Burlington ended at Mount Pleasant, the seat of Henry County. Another formed a strong channel of trade between the riches of Cedar County, centered at Tipton, and Muscatine. Elsewhere, farmers got to the river along local trails or ungraded roads as best they could. [88]

Data about the volume of traffic, either passenger or freight, on any of these roads are almost nonexistent. The only document yet found records that between August 1, 1851, and July 30, 1852, there were 397 arrivals and 368 departures of stage coaches at Rockford on the Frink line between Chicago and Galena. [89] A comparison of the number of stages per week from town to

87 Peck and Messinger, *Map of Illinois* (1840); Tanner, *Illinois and Missouri* (1841); Colton, *Guide* (1851–1854), 74, 76, 77.
88 Jesse Williams, *Map of the Surveyed Part of Iowa, Exhibiting the Sections, Townships, and Ranges, Compiled from U. S. Surveys (New York, 1840); Colton Township Map of Iowa, Compiled from U. S. Surveys* (New York, 1852); *Township Map of the State of Iowa,* (Philadelphia, 1855).
89 *Galena Daily Advertiser,* August 6, 1852; Pooley, "Settlement of Illinois," 74; McMaster, "60 Years," 74.

town can, in lieu of such specific data for other routes, provide some measure of the volume of traffic, and thus of the relative importance of the road as a line of transport. In the 1850s, for instance, there were sixteen stage lines that originated in Galena. Quincy had seven lines, Rock Island six, Peoria five, and Burlington and Davenport two or three each. If, like most important stages, these ran three times weekly, there would have been over 1,000 arrivals a year in Quincy, 2,400 in Rock Island, 780 in Peoria, and over 900 in Davenport and Burlington. Galena, with several daily coaches in addition to the thrice weekly lines, would have recorded at least 3,000 stage arrivals per year at the Main Street stage office. At 6 people per stage, such a rate represents some 20,000 people arriving for business, pleasure, travel, or even immigration.[90] Nearby, the ferry between Dunleith and Dubuque, which would include numerous round trips between Dubuque and Galena, recorded 30,000 passenger crossings in 1855. A few years before it had recorded only 6,200 crossings. Further south, similar passenger quotations were made. John Reynolds observed that nine stages, containing about 100 people, made the journey between Belleville, Illinois, and St. Louis every day, or, if one does not include Sundays, about 30,000 passenger trips per year.[91] Likewise, other ferries recorded crowds of people crossing the river in the mid-1850s. From the population data, which show increases of more than 20,000 per year in the 1850s in east central Iowa, one can assume that much of the cross-river traffic consisted of emigrants moving west. William Oliver, as early as 1841, when taking the road east from St. Louis to Terre Haute, encountered "several parties" in the course of the day. Estimating that "parties" include about 10 people each, this represented at least 40 people, which would translate into about 12,000 people moving west along the National Road during a year – a rough figure that would certainly double in the next decade.[92]

But of course, stagecoach or passenger traffic was but a small and relatively unimportant fraction of the land traffic actually moving into any town along the river during the 1850s. More important in affecting a town's economic growth and development was the amount of freight being brought into the city for local processing and distribution or export to St. Louis. Unfortunately, the evidence of the volume and frequency of such traffic is especially sparse. Nevertheless, with some imagination we can gain a rough estimate of the volume of land traffic by extrapolating freight figures from local production and trade data. One Galenan claimed, for instance, that "fifty wagons a day left for Mineral Point and arrived each day."[93] Such a statement can be easily corroborated by dividing the amount of lead received in Galena by the average

90 Colton, *Guide* (1851), 77, 83.
91 *Dubuque city directory and annual advertiser*, (Dubuque, Iowa, 1856), 34, 135.
92 Oliver, *Eight months in Illinois*, 100–1.
93 *Galena Daily Advertiser*, November 14, 1849.

carrying capacity of a wagon to determine just how many trips were necessary
to bring that much lead to Galena's wharf. In 1850, 39,801,320 pounds of lead
were hauled into Galena and exported south. To carry such an amount to
market would have taken, if one assumes wagons had an average capacity of
one ton, about 19,000 trips; which translates to 1,658 trips a month, or about
55 arrivals a day, a figure not far from the contemporary figure referred to
previously.

More important, such traffic volume seems to substantiate contemporary
reports of traffic jams and enormous shortages of storage space near the
Galena wharf during the spring and early fall. Fifty-five wagons arriving every
day meant that, if traffic flowed smoothly, 5 or 6 would arrive every hour, or 1
wagon about every ten minutes or so. At such a rate, any decision on any
particular day – given the state of the roads, the weather forecast, or the level
of the market – to delay shipment, and thus back up the shipments of two days
into one, could easily cause a crush of traffic on the three roads into town. In
usual traffic conditions, Galena's wharf was hardly sufficient in size to
accommodate more than two or three days' worth of shipments. Therefore, if a
few steamboats were delayed in carrying away the lead, pigs of lead would
begin to pile up on the wharf. In the spring rush of 1849, for example,
Benjamin Felt found that there was "little room on the landing." Later on,
S. W. McMaster reported that almost every spring the levee would be "so
thickly covered with piles of pigs of lead that it was often difficult to find a
place." When the roads improved after a few rainy days in the spring, and the
cost of land freight dropped slightly as a result, a rush of traffic into town
would regularly cause a backup of wagons from the wharf up Main Street. [94]

Referring back to our rough traffic calculations, one can easily figure how
such traffic jams could develop in a smaller town so long ago. With 1 wagon
arriving every ten minutes on an average day, and perhaps as many as 3
arriving every ten minutes on a very busy day, a delay of three or four hours in
waiting to unload one's wagon could cause, at the very least, a backup of from
50 to 100 wagons on Main Street. At about 15 feet per wagon, such a jam
would easily extend from 750 to as long as 2,250 feet back up from the wharf,
or from about a fifth of to a half a mile, not an inconsiderable traffic jam given
the area of the town. The cost of such traffic jams became, in later years, a
point of several complaints and some entrepreneurs argued that the wharf
should be expanded or the appropriate warehouse should be built to absorb
such a rush.

Further south, we can estimate that the Quincy market received some
950,000 bushels of wheat in 1847. Being three and a half times larger than
receipts at Galena, it is no surprise that traffic was on average four times

94 Diary of Benjamin F. Felt, March 26, April 14, April 23, August 28, 1849, Galena Public
   Library; *Galena Daily Advertiser*, May 25, 1852; McMaster, *60 Years*, 108.

heavier in the Gem City, as a result of the wheat trade, than it was in Galena. To carry such an amount of wheat to market in one-ton-capacity wagons would have required 28,788 shipments. If one assumes that most of these were made during the harvest season, that would compute to 288 arrivals a day in season, or about 29 per hour all day long for three months. The fact that there were six major roads into the city decreased somewhat the crush of traffic in town, but congestion must have still been a problem near the wharf and around the five or six mills located between the wharf and the town square. At Davenport, in comparison, where receipts of wheat lay between the extremes of Galena and Quincy, about 107 wagons loaded with wheat rolled into town each day in season. Once, during a typical rush, James Burrows reported that a long line of farmers' wagons had formed near his mill and continued to grow in length until well past dark. [95]

Again, when the estimated number of farmers in a hinterland is compared to the amount of wheat hauled to market in a season and the number of trips needed to haul such an amount of wheat, one is struck by the relatively small size of each farmer's marketable surplus and the brief duration of his market activity. Even in Quincy's heavily populated agricultural hinterland, each farmer produced, per capita, only about 80 bushels of wheat for the market, which would have required about three trips into town in order to sell it. Around Galena only one or two trips per season seem to have been necessary to dispose of one's marketable surplus. Of course, the fact that many farmers specialized in one crop or another, or combined one's wheat shipments with other business in town, complicates such calculations. For example, among miners, it was a fairly regular strategy to farm on the side and carry a little along with one while hauling lead to market. Therefore, some farmers may have made considerably more trips into market. Nevertheless, the random diary of a contemporary farmer from Peoria County, which recorded in detail a farmer's hauling schedule into town over the course of a year, indicates that he made only two or three trips into Peoria to market his small surplus of 60 to 80 bushels of wheat. [96]

Corn, on the other hand, was mostly fed to one's hogs before they were driven to market in the early winter. Therefore, one held back marketing of the crop until the hog production season was at an end. Moreover, the fact that corn could stand in the field for a longer time and endure a longer storage period enabled farmers effectively to hold it out of the market for a longer time, and to await higher prices in late winter, than they could with wheat. As a result, corn shipments to market often were spread across several months.

95 U. S. Census office, *The seventh census of the United States: 1850* (Washington, D.C., 1853), 728–35.
96 Diary of Edward Henry Ingraham, Peoria County, Ill., 1852, Illinois State Historical Society, Springfield, Ill.

This strategy is apparent in the marketing schedule of Edward Ingraham of Peoria County, Illinois, in 1852–3. As shown, Ingraham intentionally stretched out the marketing of his corn surplus of 650 bushels over several months, encompassing some twenty-nine trips into Peoria. He made his first corn shipment in mid-October, along with his few wheat shipments (Table 4.5). From then through January, however, he brought in only three loads of corn of about 20 bushels each (less than one ton or the capacity of the average wagon) a month. In February he began to market his crop actively. Between February 10 and February 26, he and his son made seven trips into the distilleries and mills in Peoria to sell corn at slightly higher prices. Thereafter, however, he returned to his incidental strategy, bringing no corn into market in March (perhaps on account of bad roads) and making only two shipments in April, one specifically to raise money "to pay taxes," another to acquire some hardware. Only with the approach of the planting season did Ingraham decide to sell off the rest of his stored corn, bringing in 70 bushels in the first week of May. From then on until the next harvest, his trips into town were minimal.[97] Data of receipts at St. Louis in 1852 and 1853 indicate that, if we allow for variation in shipping due to water levels, receipts tended to follow the same pattern there. Being further south and having an earlier harvest, more grain reached the market in the wake of the harvest, but the ascending rate of shipments through the late winter is still quite obvious.

Using the same methods, but dividing the total of shipments by eight months rather than three will, therefore, provide a rough approximation of the flow of traffic in the corn trade into any town. The key question, however, remains: How much of the crop went into hog consumption and how much encompassed the "residual" that was shipped to market? In 1854 a traveler in Ohio thought that almost half of the crop was a "surplus" over local needs. Given the fact that about 1 bushel per improved acre was retained for seed, and that one could produce more than twice the hogs' consumption needs, even in such a hog-oriented area as central Ohio in 1854, I will assume that about 20 percent of corn produced reached the river-town markets, and that less than half of that actually found its way downriver to St. Louis.[98] In 1850 corn production was 4,825,521 bushels in Adams, Pike, and Hancock counties, Illinois, and Marion County, Missouri, the approximate range of Quincy's hinterland. Of that, therefore, about 965,104 bushels of corn may have been the surplus and the amount that was shipped into Quincy. It would take a rather surprising number of 38,604 trips among the 12,000 farmers in the

97 Ibid. The estimate of one ton per load as full capacity for a wagon is based upon lead-trade data. Ingraham's shipments indicate that, at seventy pounds per bushel, he was able to carry about one ton in his wagon as well.

98 *Cincinnati, Columbus, and Cleveland railroad guide* (Cleveland, 1854), 65.

Table 4.5. *A farmer's schedule of hauling the corn crop into market at Peoria, Illinois, 1852–3*

Date	July	August	September	October	November	December	January	February	March	April	May	June
1												
2	20											
3												
4							20					
5											3	
6												
7											25	
8											18	
9												
10												
11								37		52	15	
12								22			7	
13								23				
14												6
15						19						
16					18							
17												

Table 4.5 (cont.)

18											26
19	3										
20			24	15	20		23		58		
21			21				27				
22											
23											
24							33				
25				25			31				
26						17					
27											
28											
29											
30					26	7					
31							7				
per month											
Trips	2	0	2	3	3	3	7	0	2	5	2
Bushels	23	0	45	58	65	44	196	0	110	68	32

Note: Totals for 1852–3 are 29 trips and 641 bushels.
Source: Edward Ingraham Diary, Illinois State Historical Society, Springfield.

Table 4.6. *Estimate of land traffic at Galena, Illinois, by month in 1850*

		Average daily arrivals			Totals	
	Lead	Wheat	Corn	Business/Social	Freight	All
January	25	0	29	52	54	106
February	25	0	29	52	54	106
March	100	0	29	52	129	181
April	50	0	29	52	79	131
May	50	0	29	52	79	131
June	50	0	0	52	50	102
July	50	0	0	52	50	102
August	50	0	0	52	50	102
September	50	88	0	52	138	190
October	50	88	29	52	167	219
November	50	88	29	52	167	219
December	50	0	29	52	79	131

Note: Mean freight arrivals per day equals 91. Estimated annual land freight (if one assumes 26 working days a month, 310 a year): 91 × 310 = 28, 313, or 40% of the total. Estimated annual water freight: 256 arrivals average × 168 tons on average per boat = 43,008, or 60% of the total.

hinterland (or at least 5 full-capacity trips per farmer) to haul the crop surplus into town. Between October and July that would translate into 7,238 trips a month or about 241 loads a day. At Galena, around which corn production was only about 742,000 bushels, traffic was much lighter, the residual of that crop amounting only to 148,400 bushels and requiring only 29 trips a day.[99]

Combining these estimated daily shipments of wheat, corn, and lead into each of the river towns enables us to gain a rough estimate of the amount of land freight arriving in each town. Going one step further, by adding in an estimate of the number of social or business trips into town per year, at about 1 every two months, as well as the known stage traffic in operation into each town, we can gain a sense of the total traffic volume into a town (Table 4.6). In Quincy freight receipts averaged 186 wagons a day through most of the winter and early spring, then probably fell off to almost no freight traffic during the summer, only to rise again in the fall as various crops entered the market. October and November probably experienced the heaviest traffic (Table 4.7).

At Quincy it was the intensity of the corn-trade traffic that sustained the level of land freights through most of the year. In Galena, where there was little contribution to traffic from the marketing of corn, only 29 wagons a day,

99 John Reynolds, *Sketches of the country, on the northern route from Belleville, Illinois, to the city of New York* (Belleville, Ill., 1854), 71.

Table 4.7. *Estimate of land traffic at Quincy, Illinois, by month in 1850*

	Trips per day			Totals	
	Wheat	Corn	Business/Social	Freight	All
January	0	186	74[a]	186	260
February	0	186	74	186	260
March	0	186	74	186	260
April	0	186	74	186	260
May	0	186	74	186	260
June	0	0	74	0	74
July	0	0	74	0	74
August	0	0	74	0	74
September	288	0	74	288	362
October	288	186	74	474	548
November	288	186	74	474	548
December		186	74	186	260

Note: Mean trips per day per month equals 196. Estimated annual land freight (if one assumes 26 work days a month, 310 a year): 196 tons a day × 310 days = 61,000 tons, or 37% of total. Estimated annual water freight: 635 annual arrivals × 168 tons (capacity of steamboats)-106,680 tons, or 63% of total.

[a] It is assumed from diaries that farmers made a purely social or business trip about once every eight weeks, or one-half trip per farmer per month. In Adams County there were approximately 4,418 farmers, which gives 2,209 trips per month, or about 74 per day.

the sustaining power was provided by the lead trade. Peaking in March, but averaging about 50 wagons a day through the year, Galena never did experience the dramatic slowdown of traffic as occurred in Quincy during the dog days of summer before the harvest. But then, given the relatively limited scale of the wheat trade, it also did not experience the dramatic fall surge in traffic. On an average fall day in Galena, traffic was about 20 percent heavier than it had been in the spring. At Quincy, in contrast, daily fall traffic volume was probably twice the volume of spring traffic. Moreover, Quincy's harvest rush was estimated to have been three times heavier than the busiest month in Galena, while Galena's busiest days in the spring and in October and November were more like spring days in Quincy that were slightly less busy than average. Although the relative value of the freights may have lessened the disparity, there was clearly more traffic pressure on Quincy, as early as 1850, than there was on Galena.

By averaging out these monthly figures and computing an annual daily average, we can compare these figures with an occasional contemporary record of traffic volume or frequency. Quincy, on average, received 196 wagons per day. Galena could only muster a figure of 91 wagons a day. John Reynolds reported in 1854 that at Springfield, Illinois, "about 75 wagons a day" entered the town – a reasonable figure for an interior town, given our estimates. At St. Louis one would expect daily figures far greater than those at Quincy, whereas at Alton and Davenport arrivals by land in the early 1850s were probably more in line with arrivals in Galena. Indeed, the further away one went from the river town and from its usual network of intersecting roads (e.g. three at Galena and Davenport, six at Quincy), the more quickly traffic volume would probably decrease. Beyond the range of river-town markets, in fact, most traffic would be primarily local, aside from the movement of long-distance stages through an area.

Such an awareness reminds us that, in spite of the seasonal pressure on the towns and reports of roads choked with traffic, across much of the system beyond the direct reach of the markets most roads were still lightly traveled. If one journeyed out from a river town in a stagecoach, one would encounter most of the traffic intending to reach the town by early afternoon (at three miles per hour, one would be twenty-four miles from town by midafternoon, assuming a 7:00 A.M. departure). At such a distance few farmers could hope to reach town profitably, leaving the roads primarily to longer-distance teamsters carrying wheat. Further out one would encounter only other stages and travelers. Stages ran every few hours in some areas, but often did not pass through an interior district for days. Likewise, by most accounts, travelers were widely dispersed along the interior roads. In 1852, 6,200 people may have crossed the ferry at Dubuque, but that translates into only 1 person every forty minutes or if, as is likely, people traveled in groups, one group of people every few hours, depending on its size. [100] William Oliver, while traveling east from St. Louis on the National Road in 1841, encountered only "several parties" (making special note of them) in the course of one long day, or about one party an hour through the day. Later in the day and into the early evening he often went hours without encountering a soul. Out on the open road, time was still measured in hours. [101]

Such roughly estimated arrival figures can help us estimate, for the 1850s, the relative balance in the entire system between land and river freight. By annualizing the figures, it seems that 196 wagons a day would total approximately 61,000 tons of land freight per year. In comparison, the estimated 635 steamboat arrivals (if one assumes Quincy arrivals were similar to those in St. Louis in 1850) had an average capacity of 106,680 tons if they were at full capacity. Thus, land freight may have already amounted to as

100 *Dubuque city directory* (1856), 34, 135.
101 Oliver, *Eight months in Illinois*, 100–1.

much as 37 percent of the river freight arriving in town. Similar calculations for Galena reinforce this impression. There 30,070 tons of land freight compared with an estimated 43,008 tons of steamboat freight, breaking into a 4 : 6 ratio.[102] In each case, the estimates are much more precise for Galena because the capacity of the steamboats was much higher in both directions. On both the northern and the southern river, therefore, the steamboat still dominated the system's general traffic patterns, but the rising tide of land freights entering the river towns seemed to foreshadow a shifting pattern of trade in the years to come.

Such a change, however, would require considerably more road development in the 1850s. Physically most roads as late as the 1850s were still mere traces, trails, or "beeline" roads across the sod bottoms, deep grass, and soft soil of the prairies. In contrast to the roads through forests, which were often marked by blazes on trees, early roads on the open prairies were unmarked, often with little more than a beaten track left by those who had gone before to lead one's way. The first road north of Peoria, for example, was laid out by men following the "tracks of a wagon that had passed that way a few days before." Another traveler wrote that the "highways heading west were little more than wheel ruts cut into the soil."[103] These obscure paths were often impossible to find through the maze of Indian trails that, until the early 1830s, crisscrossed the prairies, and traces of such roads were, after a prairie fire, all but obliterated.

By the 1840s, however, travelers began to report on the posting of signs and markers that somewhat facilitated travel. William Oliver, again on the road from St. Louis, noted the curious, but in terms of the future landscape of roadside America, predictable appearance of "huge signs" that could be "discerned a long way." These prototype billboards were often just large boards on which the names of nearby establishments were crudely painted, letters of the name, as Oliver noted, often squeezed up to the right edge of the sign. More inventive were a kind of oversized pub sign sticking out above the tall prairie grass. In one case, Oliver noted a large parrot-shaped sign. In another, a large jug in the distance.[104] In 1851 such painted "sign boards on poles" were still unusual enough on the roads outside of towns to prompt one observer to remark on the advertising tactics of a Peoria merchant, William Grigg. To make his presence known, he placed such a sign on "every public house for miles around" and "along the principal roads leading into the city,"

102 See Table 4.6.
103 *The Old Settler Telegraph* (Springfield, Ill.), March 1882; Bayard Rush Hall, *The new purchase; or early years in the far West* (New Albany, Ind., 1855), 71; *History of Bureau County, Illinois*, 79; Jacob Ferris, *The States and Territories of the Great West* (Buffalo, N. Y., 1856), 18.
104 Oliver, *Eight months in Illinois*, 107–8.

advertising his "cheapest goods in town." Likewise, while traveling across the interior of Ohio, Charles Lyell observed, with curiosity, a similar use of small empty wooden buildings along the road on the side of which the word "movers house" had been inscribed, "intending to encourage migrants to spend the night for a small sum." Nevertheless, until late in the period, many roads across the region remained, in the words of one writer, "blind." [105]

Indeed, in the 1850s, the only major road that appears to have been built on a foundation was the National Road. In the 1830s the first macadamized road in the area was built from St. Louis to Belleville. However, most other roads and most of the streets in the towns, except in those towns on sloping dry sites near the river – Cincinnati, St. Louis and Davenport, for example – were simply packed earth that softened with the first rains and could quickly become a quagmire. In the spring, one travel writer quipped, "traveling on land became, of course, traveling on water, or both mixed mud and water." [106] One stage driver on the road from Mineral Point to Janesville, Wisconsin, took a three-mile detour just to avoid an enormous "puddle." Mrs. Steele, on crossing a western prairie, in what James Burrows would have called a "regular old mud stage," reported an occasion when the coach stopped in the middle of the night and the "coachman took out a lamp and began searching for something on the ground. 'What have you lost sir,'[she asked,]'Only my road maam!'" [he replied]. [107]

So prevalent was the impact of mud on human movement that a kind of folklore of tall tales developed about adventure on muddy roads, akin to the modern topic of delays in traveling by airplane. One characteristic story from St. Clair County, Illinois, went as follows:

> Before the road was built from Belleville to St. Louis it had, at times, been almost impossible to reach the river on account of the mud and the mire. A story was accustomed to be told in those days to the effect that a man on his way to St. Louis saw in the American Bottom a hat on top of the ground. He got off his horse to pick up the hat but found a man's head under it. The man under the hat said that "under him was a wagon and four horses, mired in the mud, that he was safe, but that he supposed that the horses and the wagon were in a mighty bad fix."

105 Charles Lyell, *Travels in North America* (New York 1845; reprint, New York, 1978), 2: 62; Hall, *The new purchase; or Early years in the far West*, 75; Ferris, *The Great West*, 16. Illinois credit report ledgers, CDXXIII, R. G. Dun and Company Collection, Baker Library, Harvard Graduate School of Business Administration, Cambridge, Mass.
106 Hall, *The new purchase; or Early years in the far West*, 46–7.
107 Daniel S. Curtiss, *Western portraiture, and emigrant's Guide* (New York, 1852), 341; W. W. David, "A Trip From Pennsylvania to Illinois in 1851," *Illinois State Historical Society Transactions* 5 (1904): 198–204; Eliza Steele, *A Summer Journey in the West* (New York, 1841), 124; Burrows, "Fifty Years," in Quaife, *Early Day*, 221. Letters of Horatio Newhall, Galena, Ill. to his wife, May 15, 1846, Horatio Newhall Letters, Illinois State Historical Society, Springfield, Ill., Charles Dickens, *American Notes*, 2 vols. (London, 1842), 2 : 11.

Such stories, however exaggerated (and many were not), do document the preoccupations of people who lived in an environment with no drainage, no roadbeds, and deep mud and mire for months at a time. [108]

Such conditions, varying with precipitation patterns, tended to create seasons of road travel just as real and significant as those on the river. When roads were goods, or finally dried up in the spring, pent-up demand to go somewhere, or to bring goods to market, or to acquire supplies in the river town, would lead to a rush of movement toward the towns from the interior. Likewise, after a period of heavy rain, which prevented travel in any season, a similar rush would also occur. Or when the river went dry, sometimes the roads drew off much of its normal traffic. Such was the case around Keokuk when a blockage of the rapids would force merchants to lighter goods by wagon around the rapids to the north, thus causing a crush of traffic on the riverside road above town. But often such travel, at the height of summer, would encounter dust and insects, which, if not precluding travel, certainly made it extremely difficult and uncomfortable. [109]

Ironically, each of these surges of land travel was exacerbated by the fact that what was good for the river (rain) was bad for the road, and vice versa. Therefore, when steamboat navigation was at its easiest and cheapest, thousands of farmers and traders were unable to get to the river to take advantage. This situation further intensified the use of the roads during the few weeks after the roads had dried but before the river fell to low water, which usually occurred in June. Conversely, when road travel was at its best, from September through mid-November, the river was often so low that, for interior farmers, the advantages gained by getting one's crop to market were often lost by higher freight rates or, in the worst-case scenario, when no boats reached the wharf, by the cost of storing one's produce, which merchants deducted from local prices. For the rivers and the roads to complement each other and facilitate the most efficient transport of the crop to market was, over the years, a relatively unusual and much appreciated circumstance. But to understand how these conditions affected the cycles of business and thus the larger patterns of development, we must take a closer look at the spatial and economic limits that they imposed on the region's economic geography.

108 *History of St. Clair County, Illinois* (Philadelphia, 1881), 61; *Chicago Tribune*, January 25, 1857; Mabel McIlvaine, *Reminiscences of Chicago during the forties and fifties* (Chicago, 1913), 15–17.

109 *Keokuk Gate City*, April 26, 1858; Oliver, *Eight months in Illinois*, 91.

5

The system takes shape: an economic geography

On the rivers, the steamboat had caused a revolution in time. Between 1821 and 1827, for example, replacement of northbound keelboats by steamboats cut the journey to Galena from over two months to less than a week. In the next decade, as speeds increased, given the improved technological adaptability of western-style boats to the rivers, the journey was shortened even more. By the 1840s, the average-sized boat could travel at 12 miles an hour downstream and 6 miles an hour upstream, speeds that reflected more the need for restraint in navigating the treacherous waters of the West than the capacity of the technology (considerably higher speeds could be achieved during the "races").

In contrast, travel across the Mississippi valley by land remained, until the early 1850s, in the age of horse and oxen. Indeed, the soft bottoms of the Illinois prairies seem to have actually caused a worsening in land-transport speed and cost in the West compared with that in the East. Canals, which cut the cost but did not necessarily improve transport times, were by that time actively used in Ohio and a few had been opened across Illinois. The railroad, meanwhile, remained for most merchants a decade or more in the future. Consequently 30 miles a day, or about 3 miles an hour in a stage, cart, or wagon was considered a good speed. When the roads were muddy, 1 or 2 miles per hour was more likely to be attained. By horse one could travel faster, and farther, but to do so cost considerably more. For this reason, the stage and wagon, continued to bear the brunt of the land-transport burden. [1]

Taking each of these speeds as averages compiled from various accounts of trips made across the region by stage, wagon, or steamboat, one can construct a general isochronous map showing areas to which it took about the same time, using the fastest conveyances, to travel from St. Louis. The voyage from St. Louis to Galena averaged about seventy-five hours, even though sixty-five hours was routinely advertised as the expected time of travel in local newspapers – an average speed of 5 miles per hour. Downriver, the same trip

---

1 For a detailed record of the data used to draw the isochronic lines across the region see Appendix D.

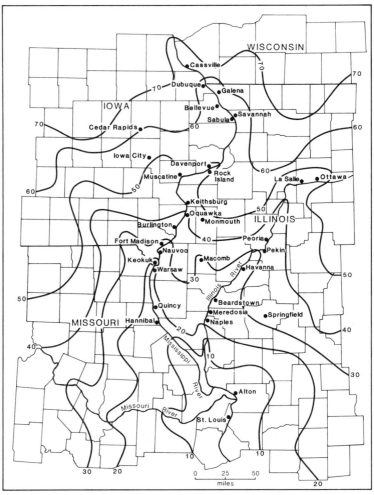

Figure 5.1. Isochronous map of travel times in hours from St. Louis by fastest means, 1840–55 (see Appendix D).

could be covered in under forty-five hours. In both directions, but especially upstream, a disproportionate period of the travel time was spent between the rapids. The effect of the rapids is evident on the map (Figure 5.1). Although Keokuk was closer to Davenport (117 miles) than it was to St. Louis (183 miles), one could, from Keokuk's wharf, reach the latter in twenty hours (9 miles an hour) while taking almost thirty hours to make it to the former (4 miles an hour), the difference being accounted for by both the current and the rapids. In general, it took a full day to clear both the lower and upper rapids,

usually consuming almost twenty-four of the forty-four hours of the northbound trip from St. Louis to Galena, even though the distance between the
open water south and north of the rapids encompassed only 113 miles of the
400-mile trip. In short, it took almost half the travel time of the trip to cover
only a third of its distance.

Of the two rapids, the lower rapids caused the greater delays. Burlington,
only 39 miles north of Keokuk, was sixteen hours away from Keokuk by
steamer. In the other direction, Quincy, lying 37 miles south of Keokuk, was
only four hours away by boat. Further north along the river, it took five hours
longer to cover the 80 miles of river between Davenport and Burlington than it
did to travel the 95 miles upstream to Galena from Davenport. The general
pattern, therefore, was one of quick transport above and below the rapids,
facilitated by the development of packet lines, and relatively slow, delay-prone,
inefficient transport in between. On the time – distance map, the isochronous
lines in the middle part of the river are compressed together, whereas those
north and south of the rapids are stretched out. Or, if one imagined the river
by travel times, river towns would be settled at close intervals in between the
rapids, and spread out from each other above and below the rapids. [2]

Slow though such times may seem to us, to contemporaries accustomed to
land travel they often seemed to verge on "annihilating time and space."
Coming to the banks of a river, after traveling across a prairie, was to arrive at
a kind of time warp where one could suddenly go much faster and much
farther than had been thought possible. Traveling in the opposite direction,
from the river to the land, one suddenly became mired in a density of space
through which it took much longer to reach one's destination, even if that
destination was a shorter distance away. For example, a traveler who came
north on the *Lucy Betram* from St. Louis to Keokuk in a record time of
eighteen hours and forty-five minutes in 1850, took almost twice that time to
travel the last 50 miles inland to his farm, his speed dropping to one-fourth of
his previous pace. Roads west out of Davenport were equally bad. Generally it
took farmers the whole day and into the evening to come into town from Cedar
County (twelve hours for 20 miles, or about 1.6 miles per hour. [3] The journey
by wagon from Galena to Chicago was half the distance of the steamboat trip
from Galena to St. Louis, but the former trip took forty-five hours whereas
the latter took only thirty. Meanwhile, from Mineral Point, Wisconsin,
Benjamin Felt took eleven hours by stage to reach Galena, or about 3.4 miles

2 Ibid.
3 William Prescott Smith, *The book of the great railway celebration of 1857* (New York, 1858), 3;
  Keokuk Whig and Register, August 22, 1850; James D. Burrows, "Fifty Years in Iowa: Being
  the Personal Reminiscences of J. M. D. Burrows," in *The Early Day of Rock Island and
  Davenport: The Narratives of J. W Spencer and J. M. D. Burrows*, ed. Milo Quaife (Chicago,
  1942), 200–1.

per hour. Stages from Chicago to Davenport ran on a thirty-three-hour schedule; in reality, however, if often took much longer. Orville Browning, a Quincy lawyer and legislator with regular business in Springfield, kept a record of his progress as he traveled through southern Illinois. Naples, Illinois, for example, was usually a fifteen-hour ride from Quincy (3.3 miles per hour). On one trip he made the "good time" of only ten hours to Rushville (5 miles per hour). Springfield, meanwhile, 100 miles east on the Quincy – Naples road, could be reached in about twenty-four hours (4 miles per hour). Further south, the stage from St. Louis to Vandalia was usually seventeen hours on the road to its destination (4 miles per hour). Charles Dickens, while on an excursion into the interior in 1842, splashed through the American Bottom at a speed of 2 miles per hour. [4]

Within such a context, river towns were much closer together and easier to get to than any town or place in the interior. North of St. Louis, therefore, the river stretched like a zone of preferential access, especially below and above the rapids, amid vast impenetrable space. Contemporary travelers would go out of their way to avoid having to cross the prairies, or at least try to minimize the distance they had to travel across them. One would, as result, be more likely to take a boat from Burlington to either St. Louis or Galena to take care of one's business or shopping needs, rather than to cross the Military Tract by horse or wagon to Peoria. Likewise, the preferred route from St. Louis to Chicago in the steamboat era was going north to Galena by boat and then across the relatively shorter prairies in northern Illinois, rather than taking a slow boat ride up the Illinois and then perhaps, on account of low water, a stage via Lewiston or Peoria to the north. [5]

The temporal dimensions of these travel and freight times approximated, in a world of face-to-face interaction, the time it took for the mails, and news and information, to move through the system. One could occasionally use an express-mail packet or even an express-mail stage line, but the gain in time, given the extra cost, was usually not worth it. The letter file of George M. Davis, an Alton attorney who in 1837 dealt mostly in the collecting of bills and prosecuting debtors for eastern clients, reflects the dimensions of the mail system. Comparing the postmark of origin with the date of receipt as noted by

4 The diary of Benjamin F. Felt, March 10, 1849, Galena Public Library, Galena, Ill.; John M. Peck, *A gazetteer of Illinois* (Philadelphia, 1837); William V. Pooley, "The Settlement of Illinois from 1830 to 1850," *Bulletin of the University of Wisconsin, History Series*, 1 (May 1908); 74, 132; Diary of Orville Hickman Browning, ed. Theodore C. Pease and James. G. Randall, Collections of the Illinois State Historical Library, vols. 20 and 22 (Springfield, Ill., 1925), March 12–13, 1851; January 16, April 25, 1852; December 13, 1853; June 16, 1854; James H. Buckingham, *Illinois as Lincoln Knew It, or a Boston Reporter's Record of a Trip Made in 1847*, ed. Harry Pratt (Springfield, Ill., 1938), 26; Charles Dickens, *American Notes*, 2 vols. (London, 1842), 2: 11.
5 Burrows, "Fifty Years," in Quaife, *Early Day*, 197–8.

Davis on the outside of each letter before he filed it, in the vertical fashion of
the time, enables us to estimate the time it took the letter to reach Alton from
its place of origin. Not surprisingly, St. Louis and other nearby places were
less than a day away. From Galena, about four hundred miles north by river,
mail usually arrived with the fastest steamboats in about two days. For some
reason, mails from towns between the rapids often took a day longer to arrive,
whereas it took four days for the few letters from Peoria and the lower Illinois
River valley to reach Davis's office. [6]

The arrival of mail from points beyond the immediate transport system
became less dependable and regular. Chicago mail reached Alton, on average,
in about six days. Letters from the Boonslick region of Missouri were usually
five days in transit to Alton. It took about the same time for the arrival of the
mails from Louisville and vicinity. Curiously, letters Davis received from
Cincinnati reached him in twelve days, while one letter from Pittsburgh
arrived in eleven. From the East, mail was routinely two weeks in transit,
ranging from an average of fifteen days from Baltimore, seventeen days from
Philadelphia and New York, to three weeks from Boston.

These greater distances increased not only the time it took to reach Alton
but also the irregularity of the mails: The longer one's letter was carried along
the roads or rivers, the better chance it had of encountering problems. When
the system worked, a letter from New York could arrive in two weeks. But
inclement weather, and winter in general, added four full days on average to
this transport time. One letter in the file arrived in twenty-eight days, and yet
another, postmarked in New York on January 14, did not reach Alton until
April 6, 1837.

Although such delays were common throughout the country, Westerners
seemed to believe that these problems imposed an especially heavy burden on
regional development. The frequency of complaints about the roads and rivers
and the delay of the mails is so prevalent in extant letters from the period that
they indicate, if not a regional obsession, certainly considerable frustration.
This frustration was especially intense in letters written by correspondents
seeking to maintain close personal ties broken by emigration with relatives
back East. In correspondence between relatives and close friends, the exchange
of information and ideas was often highly emotionally charged. Characteristic
was one Galenan's lament: "We are now shut off from all intercourse with the
outside world, until the river opens again the spring." Another "bid good-bye
to foreigners and foreign things for a while" on the occasion of the same event
in 1851. [7] Indeed, in the exchange of letters with the East, all dialogue seems to

6 G. M. Davis letter book, 1837, Missouri Historical Society, St. Louis.
7 *The History of Jo Daviess County, Illinois* (Chicago, 1878), 253; letter from James Bailey to
   Edward Wade, November 23, 1851, Edward Wade Papers, Missouri Historical Society, St.
   Louis.

have halted once the major lines were closed. As a result, rather than letting unsendable letters pile up and become outdated, many trapped correspondents put down their pens until the approach of spring navigation.

The letter file of Horatio Newhall, a druggist in Galena, is interesting for what it reveals about these emotional tensions involving correspondence. Once he dated a letter December, but admitted to not finishing it until the end of February, at which time navigation briefly reopened and he was able to mail it. In the other direction, he recorded the frustration felt waiting for the first mails of the spring, when he wrote about Gustav, one of his relations, who in March 1833 was so anxious about receiving mail from the East that he had decided that, having written so many letters and received, as yet, no response, "he will not write again until he received one from Massachusetts." But once letters arrived, or navigation opened, there was a surge of letter writing. Moreover, in order to make the news in one's letter as fresh as possible, one would often wait to finish it until just before the boat left or, if one was traveling, even write it while on board. Newhall, for example, wrote numerous letters in such a rush. In the 1830s he admitted to the rushed nature of many of his letters "because all my letters are written immediately preceding the departure of the mail, which leaves this place once a week." On other occasions, his haste was complicated by difficult writing conditions. On April 24, 1838, he wrote: "The boat is shaking so much that I do not know as you can read my writing." In another, he apologized again: "My hands tremble so much from the continued jolting of the wagon which I have travelled so long that I do not know if you can read my letter." And again, "I write on my portfolio on my knees and, of course, can but write badly." Only in one instance was he forced to stop writing a letter: On May 6, 1838, he restarted a delayed letter remarking "I thought I should have been able to have written you on the boat, but the boats have so little freight that they are rendered so unsteady that it is impossible to write on them." Though only the comments of a single, indefatigable correspondent, and thus difficult to interpret, they do, as a random sample, express the frustration and urgency involved in long-distance communication at the time. [8]

Although people sought to maintain the same dynamic between each other through correspondence as they could face to face, it was logistically impossible. Consequently, different rules, first to clarify and second to be able to qualify everything said, had to govern such long-distance correspondence. In both personal and business letters, one usually had to state the specific letter being answered. In addition, one spoke more generally about larger issues, and

8 Letter from Horatio Newhall to Isaac Lynn, December 11, 1840; Horatio Newhall to unknown, February 16, 1833; April 24, June 22, 1838; March 14, 1846; May 6, 1838; Horatio Newhall Letters, Illinois State Historical Society, Springfield, Ill.

spoke in a larger time frame than one did in conversation. Indeed, given the long distances involved, many letters from the period often have the tone of the writer talking to himself or herself, uncertain if the intended reader would ever see the letter or if a specific reply would ever be received in turn. Letters at closer quarters, in contrast, ask more specific questions, refer to recent events, and anticipate a direct response. Often, news from a great distance or old news was interpreted more skeptically, resulting in confusion and mis-understanding between correspondents. [9]

Among merchants, all of these anxieties and problems, were exacerbated by their economic import. In business, answers to specific questions were often the basis of critical marketing decisions. Merchants actively involved in buying produce or selling merchandise would routinely spend hours a day answering and writing letters concerning business conditions – the market, the crop, the level of the water. A letter file of a Galena merchant, a Mr. Mappa, documents the specific nature of the language of much of this correspondence. [10] Corre-spondence was the lifeline to information, and hence to more calculated and reasoned market actions, upon which the success of one's business often depended.

Within a two- or three-day range of information flow up and down the river, however, it was not so much the time of travel or shipment but its cost, and thus its effect on profits, that concerned merchants. One acted primarily in response to news that could affect either the price of goods in the market, or the cost of freight. News on the crops, on the state of the economy, on the supplies of wholesalers in St. Louis or back East, and on the current rates for credit influenced the former, while the state of the river, the volume of trade taking place, and the ability of steamboat companies to combine and set rates affected the latter. From such information, farmers, merchants, and busi-nessmen would all take actions that, in any year, shaped the market and the system. By exploring the dynamics of this information gathering and decision making, we can, in a general way, understand some of the spatial – economic factors that shaped the urban economic system along the river.

In 1845, the average cost of freight per mile by river for a bushel of wheat was one-tenth of a cent. By land, the transport cost per mile by wagon of the same bushel was on average about a half a cent, or five times the steamboat rate. Given these two figures, farmers and merchants would reckon their shipment strategy according to the price level in the target market, minus the cost of transport, minus the average cost of production or purchase of a bushel

---

9 Letter from Symon Ryder to J. R. Stanford, February 1845, J. R. Stanford Papers, Missouri Historical Society, St. Louis; also see Stephen Stowe, *Intimacy and Power in the Old South* (Baltimore, 1987).
10 C. W. Mappa, n.d., C. W. Mappa Papers, Chicago Historical Society, Chicago.

of wheat. If, for example, wheat cost about thirty cents to plant one bushel (an average throughout the period),[11] a farmer who lived fifty miles from the river and who thus had a minimum of twenty-two and a half cents per bushel of transport costs to get to the market, would need a market price in the river town of at least fifty-three cents to break even. The higher the price in the target market, the more quickly farmers would decide to ship. High prices bought fast action not only because farmers wanted to take advantage of a good thing, but they also knew that everyone else was thinking the same thing and would rush into the market, quickly causing a glut and forcing prices back down. In addition, the increasing prospect of rain in the fall encouraged early shipment into the wheat markets. Delays in the harvest, in the hiring of wagons, and in the marketing of the crop could therefore cost a farmer potential profits. As in so many other things, time was money. This was especially so if one was paying someone to haul one's wheat. A delay could often require another night on the road and the cost of lodging or food, as well as a higher freight rate. A delay of an hour could often cost a penny a bushel in transport cost. A longer delay of half a day could often mean the difference between profit and loss. Consequently, farmers and teamsters were careful to haul the crop when it looked like the weather would hold, because it would often take a full day to haul wheat less than twenty-five miles into town.[12]

Farmers, in general, did not correspond much about market conditions. Their source of information was the town newspaper, town merchants, and each other, as well as travelers from up and down the river; information was often acquired in preharvest trips into town to hire extra laborers for the approaching harvest work. Of course, for many farmers in the vicinity of a town, such information was, to a considerable degree, irrelevant. Whether the price was high or low, the weather good or bad, they were compelled by geography and economics to trade in the nearby town as soon as their crop was in. Only those farmers further in the interior, having options in perhaps one or two towns in which to trade, benefited from such an effort to acquire market information. As the harvest approached, therefore, information about the

11 Freight rates can be approximated by variance in local prices upriver, divided by the distance between towns. *William Rees, Rees Description of the city of Keokuk, Lee county, Iowa* (Keokuk, Iowa, 1854), 6; *Annual Review, the commercial statistics and history of St. Louis* (St. Louis, 1854), 31; Thomas S. Berry, *Western Prices before 1861: A Study of the Cincinnati Market* (Cambridge, Mass., 1943) 61–2, 551–7. For land carriage rates, see Elmer Riley, *The Development of Chicago As a Manufacturing Center* (Chicago, 1912), 94; William Oliver, *Eight months in Illinois; with information to emigrants* (Newcastle-upon-Tyne, 1843), 135. The cost of production is calculated from Oliver, *Eight months in Illinois*, 134–6; Thomas Ford, *A History of Illinois* (Chicago, 1854), 99–101; Burrows, "Fifty Years," in Quaife, *Early Day*, 169; John G. Thompson, "The Rise and Decline of the Wheat Growing Industry in Wisconsin," *Bulletin of the University of Wisconsin* 292 (1909): 35, 128.

12 Allan Bogue, *From Prairie to Corn Belt* (Chicago, 1962), 123; John Clark, *The Grain Trade of the Old Northwest* (Urbana, Ill., 1966), 151; David E. Schob, *Hired Hands and Plow Boys* (Urbana, Ill., 1975), 3.

relative level of different town markets quickly moved into the interior. The speed of its movement was also propelled by merchants advertising their anticipated prices so as to draw as many farmers as possible to their store or mill.

For the river-town grain or livestock merchant, it was not the cost of production, but rather the price paid for interior wheat, measured against the price in the entrepôt market, minus the cost of transport between the two points that directed their strategies. In general, local prices were set directly in relation to reported entrepôt prices, minus the cost of transport. With average freights as quoted previously, for example, the local price of wheat being paid to farmers from the interior would decline by about ten cents for every hundred miles further distant from St. Louis. On the upper Mississippi, an average price of seventy cents at St. Louis in the 1840s translated into local prices upriver decreasing to the break-even point of about thirty cents some four hundred miles north of St. Louis. Within this broader context, grain merchants along the river would actively compete for receipts from the interior.

The degree of competition is evident in the narrow profit margin on most buying and selling of wheat across the region. The fact that local prices often equaled the target entrepôt price minus the current cost of transport indicates how little profit local merchants were expecting from each bushel purchased. Profit was often squeezed out in a better freight rate for bulk shipment, or in a favorable change in the market conditons after one's purchase of the grain from the farmers. The search for a bulk freight was an obvious incentive behind grain merchants' desire to purchase maximum quantities of wheat. Merchants probably were willing to settle for minimal profits, however, because the dynamics of the market, and freight rates, naturally tended unfavorably against a strategy of holding on to grain. Earlier in the season prices were higher, and one had to pay more for farmers' grain, but the costs of transport were likely to be relatively low given the usual rise in the river in September and October. Hence, in an early marketing strategy one might purchase local wheat at one price, find that at the point of shipment the market in the entrepôt had actually risen a bit, and that in transit the river also rose, lowering anticipated freight costs. But such favorable conditions were short-lived. Far more routine was a decline in the market price, with wheat being rushed into the market, boats filling with freight, and a river beginning to decline, so that the market price would be lower and the transport costs higher than anticipated. The narrow margin between profit and loss in most years and the tendency for market dynamics, in all but the first week or so of the harvest, to favor the latter rather than the former indicate the need for recent information, and quick decisions. [13]

13 Burrows, "Fifty Years," in Quaife, *Early Day*, 192–5, 188–9.

The difficulty in precisely gauging freight rates is evident in one of the few available detailed records of the movement of rates in one season. In 1853, the freight rate for a ninety-six-pound barrel of flour between Galena and St. Louis fell from between $.35 and $.50 in January to as low as $.20 in May and June, or less than half the seasonally adjusted average of $.55. Late in July rates pushed back above $.40. During early September, at the beginning of the harvest, rates hovered around $.50. By the end of the month they had risen to $.70. Four weeks later the average freight rate jumped to about $1.00 and continued upward, hitting a peak of $1.10 in late November, or twice the adjusted average. Thereafter, freights fell rapidly back toward the average. The following year, a drought year, low water caused rates to soar, but the soaring market, on account of the demand for wheat from abroad, tended to counteract the effect of high rates and those merchants who had wheat to ship did very well.[14]

Each year, different river conditions brought a new freight-rate situation, and thus the need by upriver merchants to rethink their marketing strategies. Changes in freight rates from year to year are evident in the widening and narrowing range of prices paid for wheat at the various towns along the river throughout the period (see Figure 6.3). In July 1842, for example, a bushel of wheat brought $.25 less in Davenport that it did in St. Louis. The next year, the difference had shrunk to about $.10, while in mid-1845 only $.17 separated the two markets. But in 1847, while a bushel of wheat received $.95 in St. Louis, a farmer outside of Davenport only got $.45. The wide difference narrowed in the following year as only $.20 separated the Quincy prices from those offered at Galena, with only another $.05 differentiating the Quincy and St. Louis markets. This minimal range of $.25 between St. Louis and Galena, no doubt aided by prosperity and high water, widened slightly to about $.35 the following year and then, as indicated, remained fairly constant between the 1849 and 1854 seasons, a constancy that may reflect some kind of rate-fixing arrangement. Only in 1854, under the pressure of a drought, did rates rise again, increasing the difference in prices to about $.50.[15]

The difficulty of maneuvering amid such shifting market conditions, which often changed faster than news of their having changed was available, is documented in the frequent references in contemporary letters, records, and memoirs of misadventures, disappointments, or surprises in playing the produce markets. On rare occasions, delay and increased freight costs could work in one's favor. Such was the experience of H. B. Brown, an Alton merchant who in the 1830s shipped a load of produce into a declining market rather than see his produce spoil. But after his boat hit a snag, which seemed to ruin any chance for a favorable outcome, news arrived of a wheat shortage in

14 *Annual Review*, 31; Berry, *Western Prices*, Appendix 8, 551–7, 61–62.
15 See Figure 6.3.

the East and the market surged before his wheat arrived. The result, in spite of the higher freight costs, was an unexpected profit. James Burrows had similar good fortune in 1845 when he bought produce early in the season only to have the market soar before he was able to sell it to entrepôt merchants. By his delay, he increased his profits 200 to 300 percent. [16]

More commonplace, however, were the delays, higher than expected freights, or deteriorating river conditions that ended up costing more than anticipated and depriving one of expected profits. One of Charles Brewster's business correspondents told of one typical and often repeated misadventure:

> I found that after I got started that it was a mistake about there being a rise coming down the river and consequently I was a litle bothered that I decided to ship. [The freight rate was sixty cents] from Fort Madison. Cole told me he could ship on the *Excel* at fifty cents. I told him that if he could ship the light articles at that to ship them through, if not, ship to Keokuk. There will not be much difference for it is twenty cents to Keokuk. [17]

More risky but potentially remunerative were those attempts to trade in produce or merchandise just before the end of the navigation season. In 1843, for instance, James Burrows of Davenport caught the last boat north of St. Louis with a stock of goods but got stuck in the ice at Keokuk. Rather than hire a team to haul his goods the rest of the way to Davenport, however, Burrows hired Joseph Smith's (of Mormon fame) *Nauvoo* and, after reinforcing the hull, used it to break through the ice to bring his goods to Davenport. In another episode he was stopped by the ice at Warsaw and, at considerable expense, hauled his cache of goods via Carthage, Monmouth, and Rock Island across to Davenport. [18] Horatio Newhall reported in 1832 a similar costly miscalculation: "The box of clothing did not arrive in St. Louis in time for the boat to Galena and after the river was frozen, I endeavored to have it brought by stage. But the stage driver would not bring them even though I offered him $19.00, the price of a passenger." [19] In such cases the decline of freight rates late in the season, combined with the potential of extraordinary profits if one succeeded, provided the incentive for many merchants to take such risks.

---

16 H. B. Brown, "Memoirs," in *The Centennial History of Madison County, Illinois, and Its People*, ed. William T. Norton (Chicago, 1912), 92; Burrows, "Fifty Years," in Quaife, *Early Day*, 193–4.

17 Burrows, "Fifty Years," in Quaife, *Early Day*, 182–3, 188–9; letter from R. Bullock to Charles Brewster, Keokuk, Iowa, 1855, Charles Brewster Letters, Iowa State Historical Society, Iowa City.

18 Burrows, "Fifty Years," in Quaife, *Early Day*, 176–80, 197–9.

19 Letter from Horatio Newhall to unknown, March 17, 1833, Horatio Newhall letters, Illinois State Historical Society, Springfield, Ill.

Table 5.1. *Economic–geographic model of upper Mississippi River grain trade,*
1840s

Miles north	Local price[a]	Plus or minus/ $.30[b]	Size of hinterland[c]	Town near center of competition zone (distance in miles)[d]
480	$.22	− $.08	Local	
440	.26	− .04	Local	Dubuque, Iowa (400)
400	.30	.00	Local	Galena, Ill. (395)
360	.34	.04	9	Savannah, Ill. (357)
320	.38	.08	18	
280	.42	.12	27	Davenport, Iowa (302)
240	.46	.16	36	Burlington, Iowa (225)
200	.50	.20	45	
160	.54	.24	54	Quincy, Ill. (148)
120	.58	.28	62	
80	.62	.32	71	
40	.66	.36	80	
St. Louis	.70	.40	89	St. Louis

[a] Local price equals St. Louis price minus the distance from the entrepôt times .10 of a cent per mile.
[b] For cost of production estimate, see chapter 5, n. 11.
[c] Size of hinterland equals local price minus break-even price divided by .45 of a cent.
[d] No listing indicates no town of importance in area.

The general trading pattern resulting from the collective decisions and actions of thousands of people formed the underlying structure of the urban economic system. To a certain extent, however, the ability of some towns to outcompete nearby towns, to attract more business, and to become secondary grain depots in the regional system was determined more by impersonal economic–geographic forces than by the actions of town merchants (Table 5.1). For example the fact that local prices theoretically decreased ten cents for every 100 miles north along the river does not mean that towns would simply line the river in spaced intervals, each taking their local share of the regional trade. Rather, the establishment of one hinterland for trading in grain along the river would preclude the development of any other depot within its range. Only at a distance beyond the reach of this market, with an areal cushion in which another grain depot could develop its own complete hinterland, would one expect a strong market town to develop. For instance, around St. Louis, farmers from as far away as 80 miles could, in an average year, haul wheat to St. Louis. Consequently, no town could hope to develop an independent position within this 80-mile range. Likewise, towns just beyond the 80-mile range would still find much of their southern hinterland eroded by St. Louis's influence. Not until one reached a point 150 miles upriver from St. Louis did any town have the room to develop a full hinterland beyond St. Louis's reach. One would, therefore, expect a significant market town to develop there. By similar reckoning other centers of independent zones of competition free from the interference of the nearest major town to the south would lie 240, 280, 320, 360, and 400 miles north of St. Louis on the river. Logically, as local prices decreased as one went north, the distance from which farmers could profitably carry wheat to market decreased. Therefore, the area that each town could control decreased and the distance between the centers of these zones of competition declined. Significantly, important wheat-trading centers developed in the 1840s very near to each of the centers of each of these exclusive zones of competition: Quincy, Burlington, Muscatine or Davenport, Savannah, Galena, and Dubuque. The only place clearly not fitting the pattern is Alton, although its relative decline in later years only proved the rule (Figure 5.2).

Overcoming unfavorable economic–geographic locations was very difficult, as the histories of Alton, Hannibal, and Keokuk demonstrate. Yet the presence of favorable underlying economic forces did not insure success. Those towns with such advantages still had to compete actively for customers, combat the ever-changing structure of freight rates, and aggressively try to expand their hinterland at the expense of their neighbors. Sometimes a change in freight rates could significantly alter the competitive balance between two towns. Such was the case in 1845 when a "steamboat combination" decided to cut rates from St. Louis to Keokuk to six cents while maintaining the regular rate of twenty-five cents to Burlington from St. Louis. The effect was to weaken dramatically the ability of places just above the rapids to attract farmers into their markets, the higher prices at Keokuk drawing most of the trade in that direction. Burlington merchants, who had to pay an extra nineteen cents in freight for a mere forty miles further, were especially concerned about the effect of such monopoly freight rates on the economic life of their town. The editor of the *Burlington Hawkeye* went so far as to claim that the rapids cost farmers to the north up to a quarter of the value of their wheat in the market and thus were a serious drag on economic development in the region. The effect of this was to encourage farmers from just above the rapids to carry their wheat to Keokuk.[20] As one observer noted in 1850: "the farmers of the Des Moines valley won't cross the hills and ferry the Skunk River with their wheat

20 *Burlington Hawkeye*, June 5, 1845; Delegates to the Chicago Harbor and River Convention, *The commerce and navigation of the valley of the Mississippi; and also that appertaining to the City of St. Louis; considered, with reference to the improvement, by the general government, of the Mississippi River and its principal tributaries* (St. Louis, 1847), 18–22; Rees, *Rees' Description of the city of Keokuk, Lee County, Iowa*, 4.

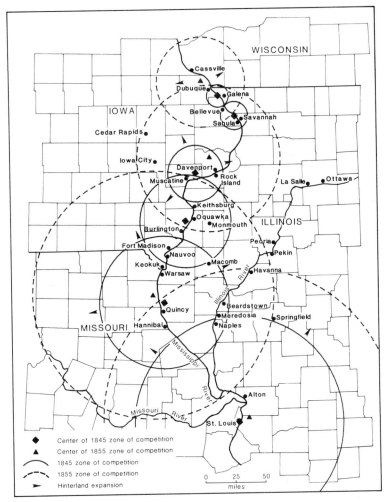

Figure 5.2. Town hinterlands in the wheat trade, 1845 and 1855.

to get 65 cents, when they can get 75 cents in Keokuk with better roads, a shorter distance, and no ferriage fees." Likewise farmers from around Burlington could haul their wheat forty miles to Keokuk, bearing the cost of land transport gladly to receive a few more cents profit per bushel than they would have received at Burlington.[21] Ironically, this northward bias in Keokuk's favor drew its trade north, leaving much of its immediate southern hinterland open to Warsaw and Quincy traders.

21 *Keokuk Whig and Register*, September 27, 1849.

Further north, Davenport, located at the foot of the upper rapids, enjoyed a similar cost locational advantage. As early as 1842, when Davenport was the northernmost place on the river that shipped grain to St. Louis, local merchants acquired supplies in Clinton, Rock Island, Savannah, Galena, and Dubuque. In 1853 the economic advantages of this early trade enabled James Burrows to pay two cents more per bushel for wheat than places just to the north. [22] In 1850, a Dubuque editor complained that "last season Davenport and Muscatine drew off a large proportion of the wheat of the upper country just because the proprietors of these establishments paid better prices for the grain than could be received here." And again, in 1854 and 1855 high local prices offered at Davenport drew in farmers from Cedar and Linn counties. [23] Located on a great east-to-west bend in the river, Davenport was more accessible to a wide area of the interior than other places upriver; as a result, farmers began routinely to ship their produce south to Davenport rather than to the nearest riverside depots.

By such thinking, Muscatine merchants harbored the belief that they had an advantage over Davenport. But Muscatine was located just far enough south to have some of its hinterlands in Louisa and Henry counties infiltrated by merchants from Keokuk and even Quincy. Davenport, meanwhile, lay beyond the reach of these southern competitors and thus did not have to expend its energy in protecting an already established trading region, while actively expanding its contacts to the north and west.

On a broader scale, Davenport also lay near the point at which the Chicago market began to attract shipments from river-town merchants away from St. Louis. To the south of the rapids, merchants had little choice but to send their wheat to St. Louis, in spite of the generally higher prices in the Chicago market. Their distance from Chicago almost certainly assured that by the time Iowa wheat reached the market it "would have been already glutted by wheat from the nearer hinterlands of Chicago in Wisconsin, Michigan, Indiana, and Illinois" and thus find prices no higher, and perhaps even a little lower, than those in nearby St. Louis. [24] Proximity to St. Louis, therefore, gave merchants in southeastern Iowa below the upper rapids almost a certain market there.

Further north along the river, however, the relative balance between the cost of transport and distance between Chicago and St. Louis shifted gradually in Chicago's favor. By 1850, a Galena merchant was already able to comment on the erosion of loyalty to the St. Louis market, "if both markets, Galena and Chicago, were equal, the dividing line between them would be eighty-five

22 Burrows, "Fifty Years," in Quaife, *Early Day*, 166–7, 187, 190, 200, 211, 266–7.
23 *Dubuque Miner's Express*, December 19, 1848, November 14, 1849; Burrows, "Fifty Years" in Quaife, *Early Day*, 200.
24 *Keokuk Whig and Register*, February 28, 1850.

miles west of Chicago. In fact, farmers from over one hundred miles west of Chicago carry their wheat in that direction."[25] This erosion of trade to the east, a trend that gathered force with the westward construction of the Galena and Chicago Union Railroad between 1845 and 1854, compelled the Lead City grain merchants to look north and west for their supplies and business. Already having a strong local economy and good milling capacity, town merchants could offer lower prices and thus undercut nearby competitors. A Dubuque merchant in 1851 remarked on these advantages:

> Farmers within eight miles of Dubuque are taking their grain to Galena! It is fair to estimate that four thousand loaded teams cross the river from the Iowa side to Galena and return in a year. As corroborative of this the Galena merchant will tell you that he buys a great deal of wheat from Iowa. The large steam mill at the city draws largely on Iowa for its supplies.... Merchants and millers are sending runners into Iowa to induce farmers to come to their town.[26]

Other Galena wheat supplies were also drawn from upriver. Not only Galena's proximity but also its distance from either entrepôt reinforced its control of southwestern Wisconsin. As one Galenan noted in 1849, "after paying Wisconsin river freights, its price was generally too high to pay the shipping to a lower market" and the wheat was probably sold locally.[27]

Back to the south of the rapids, Quincy's power as a shipping point was drawn from its locational advantages vis-à-vis the Military Tract. Its distance from St. Louis – close enough to have intensive contacts and high local prices but sufficiently far away to avoid direct competition for farmers – combined with its relatively open harbor and elevated position on a fertile plain to provide it with considerable competitive advantages. The fact that the Illinois River tended to fall earlier in the summer than the Mississippi further enforced its advantage by dropping local prices in the Illinois River markets, driving products from the eastern part of the Military Tract west in search of higher prices. In the southern Military Tract, Quincy became the focal point of this pressure. In 1845, for example, a low river in late summer and high freight rates drove prices down at Meredosia, Beardstown, and Naples. As a result, many farmers from the immediate vicinities of those towns hauled their wheat to Quincy or Alton. East of the Illinois River farmers tended more often to choose Alton as their depot, as it was accessible without crossing the river, whereas to the west of the river, most of the farmers across Pike, Brown, and Schuyler counties chose to trade, in such years, at Quincy.[28]

25 *Galena Daily Advertiser*, February 6, 1850; May 24, 1849.
26 *Galena Gazette and Advertiser*, July 25, 1851; November 8, 1849.
27 *Galena Daily Advertiser*, May 24, 1849.
28 Schob, *Plow Boys*, 56; *Alton Telegraph*, October 15, 1845; *Quincy Whig*, December 24, 1845.

To the north of Quincy's reach on the Illinois River, even earlier low water further depressed prices in the late 1840s. Wheat from that far north heading for St. Louis often was diverted across the Military Tract to Quincy, or arrived in St. Louis so late that profits were rare. Increasingly, farmers above Peoria began to turn to the Chicago market. As already noted, some farmers from Knox and Peoria counties began hauling grain northeast to Chicago rather than bring it to the river. [29]

So long as this weakness in the Illinois River valley market remained, Quincy had almost a monopoly control over the trade of the Military Tract. Once the canal opened, however, prices rose all along the river, drawing wheat and corn from much further south back to the river towns and north to Peoria and Chicago and away from Quincy. The end result seems to have limited the extent of the expansion of Quincy's hinterland to the east and sent its traders scurrying north and west for new markets – an area that was controlled by Davenport and therefore difficult to penetrate. In fact, by later in the 1850s, Davenport was able to make up considerable ground as a wheat market on Quincy.

The changing general price level of the market could have similar, though more short-term, effects on trading patterns across the region. In general high market prices broadened each town's hinterland, by enabling farmers from a greater distance to trade, but also increased the intersection among hinterland territories and thus the competition among towns for grain supplies. In 1841, for example, Chicago's strong market relative to St. Louis drew in farmers from as far away as Maquon, Illinois, a town in Peoria County on the road between Peoria and Knoxville. Four years later, Davenport merchants reported receipts from further in the interior than ever before. In 1850, we are told, high prices in Muscatine attracted farmers from as far away as the vicinity of Dubuque. Meanwhile, the boundaries of the trading territories around Warsaw and Quincy regularly intersected during the 1840s. Conversely, in low-price years trading regions contracted, localizing trade and isolating competitors. In such years, farmers within the reach of a market in normal years might find themselves beyond the range of profitable shipping. In describing market conditions in the late 1830s, for example, Thomas Ford noted that "in low price years I have known whole crops to rot in the fields while farmers waited for a rise in the price." [30]

Although most of these changes were short-term and had the effect of merely disrupting the normal trading patterns for a season or two, a sustained change in the price structure of the market could, in fact, restructure the

29 *Peoria Register and Northwestern Gazette*, September 14, 1841.
30 Ibid., October 8, 1841; Burrows, "Fifty Years," in Quaife, *Early Day*, 200; *Dubuque Miner's Express*, July 25, 1850; *Quincy Whig*, March 29, 1853; December 24, 1845; *Warsaw Signal*, August 18, September 29, 1841; Ford, *History of Illinois*, 99–101.

economic power of towns within the system. Such was the case of the price rise of the mid-1850s, which lasted for more than three years. In that time, the temporary shifts of the first season were subsequently reinforced, enabling those towns that had gained most from the expansion of the hinterlands to acquire permanent control over their neighbors. In St. Louis, one observer reported, "remunerative prices justify extensive land carriage and sections remote from navigable rivers, under this influence, contribute larger than normal additions to the market."[31] Within two years the regular hinterland of St. Louis had shifted north and west by almost fifty miles. In reaction to this northward intrusion into its territory by St. Louis, Quincy was also forced to move north to attract farmers into its markets, cutting dramatically into the once exclusive trading territories of Keokuk, Burlington, and Hannibal.

North of the rapids, where closely spaced towns had previously traded in harmony, each town, in response to Quincy's growing attractiveness, sought to attract more farmers from nearby areas. Only Davenport, located far enough away to avoid completely an incursion from Quincy, and having, as noted, a price structure reinforced by its new proximity to Chicago, was able to expand its trading territory successfully. By 1856, farmers from the south and west of Muscatine and from east of Rock Island were carrying their grain to Davenport, signaling the locational advantages of the town and reflecting its growing economic supremacy between the rapids. Likewise, during the same price boom, farmers outside of Dubuque began to bypass the nearby town for Galena, a fact that had earlier irked Dubuque merchants, as we have seen. (The end result of the several-year change in the price structure was the rearrangement of trading patterns as shown in Figure 5.2). Such changes in grain-trading patterns resulting from either altered freight-rate schedules or shifts in the level of regional markets formed the underlying context in which towns defined their economic function, and differentiated themselves from other towns. For us, it provides a sensitive record of the shifting patterns of economic activity throughout the region.[32]

Other trades had their own geographic patterns, but for various reasons they tended to be more narrowly defined by environmental and economic factors and thus much less likely to change. In the lead trade, for example, most of the lead mined in northwestern Illinois and southwestern Wisconsin was shipped from Galena. From the late 1820s until the mid-1840s as much as 98 percent of the lead mined in the region was exported south on steamboats to St. Louis. In 1853, with the approach of the Galena and Chicago Union Railroad, about 3 percent of the total lead production was sent east toward Chicago. By 1854 that amount had increased to a 20 percent share. But it was only in 1859 that

---

31 *Annual Review*, 32.
32 Ibid., 31.

the railroads built west from Chicago were able to draw off more than half of the lead produced.

In contrast to the wheat trade, almost all the produce shipped into the regional market faced the same general freight-rate costs and price levels. As a result, one's specific location vis-à-vis the entrepôt market was considerably less important in affecting where one shipped from. Instead it was the timing of one's participation in the market in relation to one's competitors, both in hauling lead to Galena and in shipping it from Galena to St. Louis, that became the crucial determinant of one's relative market return. A maximum-return scenario required that one haul lead to Galena as soon as navigation was open and sell it to a merchant able to ship it on the first boat going south. On a high river, and arriving early in the market, such lead usually brought high returns. As the amount of lead entering the market increased, of course, the price received declined. In addition, an excess of lead over the carrying capacity of steamboats during the rush period often required merchants to lower prices to pay for wharf-storage fees. Later in the spring, as freight rates began to inch upward with the declining water level on the northern part of the river and prices began to soften, market returns also tended downward. Summer low water, needless to say, made freights for a heavy item like lead very high. Only a fall rise and a rebounding of market prices would draw more lead south from the mines at a rate comparable with the spring surge.

One could follow this cycle of spring surge, summer lull, and fall rebound from year to year. In general, annual differences tended to follow the river level and the closely related freight costs. A detailed record of monthly shipments in the early 1840s, for instance, clearly indicates the strong relationship between freight rates and the amount of lead shipped. In each year, the largest shipment of lead occurred in the first month after the opening of river navigation. Almost half of the annual total of lead shipments was made in March, April, or May. Later records of receipts at St. Louis in 1853 show a similar pattern of low freights and heavy receipts in the first month of the season, and declining receipts after the passage of the rise upriver in mid-May.[33]

The nature of this dynamic resulted in a kind of "spring rush" in which thousands of miners and teamsters flooded the city after the roads had dried. We have already noted comments to the effect that whenever the roads were good in the spring, they were jammed with teams carrying lead, sometimes backing up the entire length of Main Street and, if the boats had yet to arrive, piling up great stacks of pigs of lead on the wharf. In such a market timing was of the essence. If one arrived too early, the length of storage or the cost of

---

33 *Galena Gazette and Advertiser*, January 9, 1844; *Annual Review*, 27.

delayed carting might prove too long and cut into one's potential profit margins. To arrive late was to bring lead into a market fully supplied by the spring rush. The optimum scenario lay somewhere in between. One aimed to arrive at Galena when boats had been hauling away lead for a few days and space on the wharf and on southbound boats had become available. The difficulty with this strategy was that early in the spring many roads were still "unnavigable." Some sought to avoid this by carting their lead to Galena when the ground was still frozen in late February. Others found themselves delayed until the roads had time to firm up by mid-April, explaining, to some extent, why the heaviest rush seems to have followed the opening of navigation by a few weeks.

The only impact that the market price had on this mechanism was to raise or lower the general break-even point and thus encourage more or less lead to seek out a market or be mined in one year than not in another. In a report of 1846 Stephen Langworthy of Dubuque reported that it cost a little over three dollars per hundred-weight to mine and smelt lead into pigs and another thirteen to fifteen cents per hundred weight to ship it from the Lead Region to St. Louis. By usual reckoning, therefore, a market price around three dollars at Galena and a half dollar more at St. Louis would not offer much of a prospect for producers and shippers, resulting in a relatively light volume of shipments. But given the narrowness of options in the industry during the 1840s, and the tendency toward a glutted market, lead still seems to have been shipped with some regularity.[34] Nevertheless, it was only the price rise of the early 1850s that drew in lead from regular producers and free-lance producers alike and provided strong profits over production costs. In such a year the precision of one's market strategy was less critical than when the market hovered around the break-even point. In a high-price year, what was lost by bad timing in the market was simply a larger return than one would receive anyway. But in low-price years, such as those of the late 1830s and early 1840s, poor timing meant the clear difference between profit and loss.

In contrast to the wheat trade, therefore, the dynamics of the lead trade and its arrangement across the region had little to do with differentiation of economic space. The environment determined where the product could be acquired. The topography established the natural routes to the most conveniently located river port. And all shipments from the river port faced the same general market and freight dynamics. Deciding to ship in another direction and to shift one's pattern of economic activity only became an option with the arrival of the railroad. And then, given the glut of lead in the St.

---

34 *Annual Review*, 31. "Report of Stephen Langworthy," in "Walker Tariff Report" in *Tariff Proceedings and Documentation, 1839–57*, 10: 2028.

Louis market, and the relative high cost of freight, the shipment of lead to Chicago by railroad quickly became the preferred strategy.

Further south along the river, the interaction between space, the cost of transport, and the timing of one's activity had a rather different effect on farmers' strategies and, therefore, on the functional development of nearby towns. In contrast to wheat, which can bear a rather extensive land carriage, corn was generally too heavy to profitably haul more than ten miles or so. Therefore, most corn was shipped locally and milled into feed or, especially around Peoria, Illinois, distilled into whiskey. From time immemorial in market economies, the best way to market one's corn production was to feed it to livestock and then to drive the animals to market. In general, livestock increased one's return on wheat by 400 or 500 percent, thus adding to the incentive to employ one's corn, grown on more expensive land nearer the entrepôt, in fattening livestock and then having it provide its own relatively cheap transport to market. The major drawback, however, lay in the fact that the packing houses toward which hogs would be driven could only operate after the average daytime temperatures dropped below freezing, but still required access to the river during the packing season. Thus they were optimally located in that zone where the temperature dropped to near freezing but not low enough to freeze the river. On the Mississippi, most places north of the rapids found it difficult, until the age of refrigerated railroad cars, to operate very efficiently or on a very large scale. But Alton, St. Louis, Louisville, and Cincinnati were all located in the zone of optimum environmental conditions for maximization of hog-packing operations.[35]

This geographical limitation served to constrict the range of livestock production because hogs could be driven only so far to market before they began to loose the weight they had acquired. Not surprisingly, therefore, production of both livestock and corn concentrated in the southern Military Tract and across the Sangamon plain for most of the period.[36] Within this relatively narrow area, the relative cost of driving one's cattle or hogs on late-autumn roads to the river market town was essentially unimportant. One could usually get to St. Louis as easily as to Alton. Only upriver, beyond the range of the entrepôt market did the distances between farms and the entrepôt reinforce local trade. Nevertheless, the relative unimportance of transport costs on the value of one's product tended to focus attention on the level of the market and, indirectly, on the infrastructural advantages such as ready capital,

35 Robert Leslie Jones, *History of Agriculture in Ohio* (Kent, Ohio, 1983), 120–35; Margaret Walsh, "Pork Packing as the Leading Edge of Midwestern Industry, 1835–75," *Agricultural History* 51 (1977): 702–17; Margaret Walsh, "The Spatial Evolution of the Midwestern Pork Packing Industry, 1835–75," *Journal of Historical Geography* 4 (Spring 1978): 1–22; Burrows, "Fifty Years," in Quaife, *Early Day*, 223.
36 Bogue, *Corn Belt*, 225–6.

a large transient work force, and adequate steamboating during the winter, all of which allowed larger firms to offer higher prices than smaller ones. The result was to encourage further the centralization of the industry at the regional entrepôts of Cincinnati and St. Louis. [37]

The composite of these different spatial, economic, and temporal dynamics served to shape the general structure of the regional urban economy. Individually, however, the staggered timing of each of these major produce trades gradually imposed a spatially selective economic – financial cycle on the life of the river valley. During the late winter economic activity surged forward in the Lead Region hinterland as miners and teamsters sought to haul the year's production to market before the opening of navigation and the softening of the roads. When navigation opened, most of the southbound freights came from the north, there being little reciprocal trade from the towns downriver, aside perhaps from some late-season pork production. In return, Galenans, on the basis of lead sales, were in the strongest position to pay back debts contracted for the spring goods moving north on the river. Consequently, Galena merchants could often settle an account within the same season and, on that basis, encourage eastern merchants to extend them more credit in the late autumn for new orders for next year's spring goods.

Further downriver, some merchants could take advantage of the spring harvest of winter wheat, some of which was being grown further north in the valley as early as the 1840s, but most had to await the late-summer harvest before the flow of capital began to move back in their direction and bills could begin to be paid off. For those towns between the rapids, therefore, the healthiest economic season, when goods were being received in return for produce sold, was early autumn. Further south, the delay of the livestock drives until late autumn tended to extend the period of economic return and reinforce the ability of local economies to clear up last years's bills before the anticipated arrival of the spring goods.

The significance of these varying cycles of economic activity from north to south, which curiously paralleled the configuration of high- and low-water periodizations – brief and frenetic in the north, later and often more extended at midriver, and extending often to ten or eleven months of the year south of the Missouri – lay in the timing in which the different towns in the valley, in a world of face-to-face communication and environmentally limited transport, were able to balance their books and plan economic strategies from year to year. But this timing was tied not to the timing of the return from local production – spring in Galena, late summer around midriver, and, in smaller amounts, from midsummer to midwinter south of the rapids – but rather to the timing involved in ordering goods from the East, having them shipped, and then selling them in local or regional markets.

At this level of economic interaction, the slowness of long-distance communication and shipments, combined with the regional reliance on the East for both manufactured goods and capital, established a cycle of economic activity that almost amounted to an economic structure. As one analyst wrote, "we had in those days no banks or capitalists and the transmission of funds to the East, either by lawyers or merchants, who had collected off them, was very difficult. Money was sometimes idle for considerable lengths of time waiting for a means of transmission."[38] This fact was reflected in the lengthy terms of western bills of exchange written against eastern houses and used in the West. From the 1837 letter book of William Morrow of Alton we have a fairly complete listing of over one hundred bills he had negotiated during the year. Among the forty-five bills from New York and several others from Providence, the average term was 320 days (Table 5.2). St. Louis and Cincinnati banks would pay on an Alton note in about 120 days. Local bills, meanwhile, were usually negotiable in six months, whereas some of the notes from upriver were payable in 60 days. What such terms meant is that instead of using funds from the recent selling season to replenish one's stock, most merchants had to buy local bills of exchange and send them off to New York or St. Louis months before their due date. In turn, bills of exchange on eastern houses circulating in the West could only be exchanged among a few merchants before being sent back East to meet some obligation.[39]

The dynamics of the buying and selling seasons, combined with the timing of paying off one's debts by bills of exchange, gave to the business year a distinctive cycle with clearly delineated periods of more and less financial pressure. Because it took so long for money to be transmitted from the East to the West and vice versa, most business had to be done on credit. But because it also took some two to four months to receive shipments from the East, merchants in the West had to anticipate their seasonal needs several months in advance. Therefore, debts were contracted long before goods were received and sold. The result was to put considerable pressure on the merchant to receive his goods early in the spring season and sell them quickly in order to have sufficient funds to transport a bill of exchange back East early enough to meet payment deadlines. The dynamics of competition in each town, which determined successful from unsuccessful merchants within a few weeks in the spring, made it rather clear who would be able to meet his obligations by the end of the average 320-day term (which, if one reckons his orders made in November or December, would be due in the following October, requiring

38 Charles Ballance, *The History of Peoria, Illinois* (Peoria, Ill., 1870), 31.
39 Letter and Record Book of William Morrow, Alton, Ill., 1837, Missouri Historical Society, St. Louis.

Table 5.2. *Terms of bills of exchange, Alton, Illinois, June–October 1837*

City of bill	Number of bills	Days of term
Quincy, Ill.	2	155
Naples, Ill.	4	60
Meredosia, Ill.	2	60
Jacksonville, Ill.	2	100
Alton, Ill.	50	180
St. Louis, Mo.	4	127
Booneville, Mo.	2	120
Louisville, Ky.	4	319
Cincinnati, Ohio	3	120
New Orleans, La.	1	180
Philadelphia, Pa.	4	180
New York, N.Y.	45	320
Providence, R.I.	4	320

Source: Letter and Record Book of William Morrow, Alton, Illinois, 1837, Missouri Historical Society, St. Louis.

transmission by midsummer). If one was late in transmitting funds east and had, in addition, gone ahead and purchased more goods on credit for the fall season, the potential pressure could be exacerbated. Moreover, if one's debts from the previous autumn had not been paid in full by midautumn, the actual due dates from the August before would begin to come due just as one needed to get orders out for the follwing spring, adding further to the carly-summer pressure the following year.

Distance and the slow transmission of funds, therefore, imposed on regional life a cycle of credit, sales, repayment, or default that any merchant who hoped to be successful had to master. [40] But the cursory evidence from credit ledgers and business records indicates that few merchants ever did. Only the very richest merchants in the West, able to travel east and buy for cash and to accompany their own purchases back west, seem to have been immune from the vagaries of the slow-motion credit transmission and transport system. In the words of one observer, so difficult was mastering this cycle that "it required a merchant of more than ordinary firmness and judgement to buy and sell goods on the western market. Unfortunately we have, especially in the smaller towns, a class of merchants utterly inexperienced in business who are led into serious errors in buying, and in selling on letters (with) insufficient security." [41] The consequence of this was a seasonal cycle of expectation and

40 Burrows, "Fifty Years," in Quaife, *Early Day*, 162.
41 *Dubuque Express Herald*, October 23, 1857.

failure that haunted western mercantile experience to such an extent that one could call it part of the "mentalité" of those unstable times.

The cycle would begin with unsold goods still on one's shelves in the late spring and a drawer full of unpaid notes, overdue, or soon to become overdue, along with the notes taken out against the goods on the shelves, which would come due in the fall. As the notes from the previous autumn fell due, the merchant would inevitably receive letters from creditors reminding him of this fact. If a merchant was confident of future success, he would request an extension. When, for example, D. G. S. Hogan of Alton was hard-pressed in July 1849, he "went East during the pressure and got extensions because it was realized, by eastern creditors, that in the absence of country collections it was impossible (for western merchants) to meet their paper." If such nonpayments from farmers continued, whether because of an epidemic, as in 1849, or a drought, as in 1854–6, merchants were inevitably faced with having to pay up or default. In 1857, Alton merchants were horrified when they heard that a "good collector went into the country last week with $8000 in accounts and came back with about $500 collected."[42]

Soon after such initial communications with the merchants, letters of complaint would be directed to the local lawyer, who would then be instructed to take the appropriate action to insure that the creditors' demands were satisfied. For a merchant in trouble, the end of direct correspondence with his creditor was an ominous sign. At first such letters would be cordial in tone. Wepson and Trask of New York, for example, sent to a lawyer named Krum in Alton the following letter in late spring 1837:

> Enclosed we hand you a note versus Darman and Salter payable at the bank in your place on the 15th of May for $188.28. It is at present difficult to make collections from that section. We presume that they will pay at maturity and will please remit to us by mail or cheque on this city or some neighboring city and much obliged.[43]

A more direct request that legal action be taken meant that the note was officially protested:

> We wish you would inform us at what time we may expect to receive the amount of the Manfield and Company debt. And if you have not already taken active measures to collect the amount we would wish you to do so without delay.

As payment was delayed even longer, the pressure on the merchant increased proportionally:

42 Illinois credit report ledgers, CXXXIX, R. G. Dun and Company Collection, Baker Library, Harvard University Graduate School of Business Administration, Cambridge, Mass.
43 Wepson and Trask, New York to Davis and Krum, Alton, Ill., April 10, 1837, Papers of George T. M. Davis, Alton, Ill., Missouri Historical Society, St. Louis.

> I must request that you will see Mr. Bostwick and unless he can either pay you or give you a satisfactory draft I wish to proceed and foreclose his mortgage and hold onto the property to the coming term of court of Madison County. P.S. a draft of longer sight than thirty days will be of no service to me.

William Ruppell wrote an angrier letter to George M. Davis of Alton in August 1839 reflecting the frayed tempers at this stage of litigation:

> Please date, sign, and enclose for me the above receipt and bring suit immediately against Spauling on the enclosed note. I have another on him for near $300 that I will also sue before the next term of court. It may be enough to enquire before you bring suit if he is still in the country – for if he has run away it would be useless to sue – if he has not (and I fear he has) sue immediately, the villain has by one lie or another been suing me for years. [44]

Although such a scenario could unfold during any season, it seems on a general level to have followed the business cycle. A survey of seventy-two cases of failures reported in the R. G. Dun credit report ledgers for Alton, Peoria, Dubuque, Galena, and St. Louis between 1845 and 1858 shows that more than two-thirds of the failures or "embarrassments" occurred in May, June, and July (Table 5.3). A random survey of Galena court records shows a similar annual cycle in the pattern of suits for unpaid debts. Notes went to protest most often between April and June, then fell off in frequency during the summer months, and increased again in the fall. What made the spring especially volatile was the long lead time for orders combined with the depleted supply of profits from the previous fall's crop there to meet the acquired goods. As a result, merchants, no matter how much they sold, may have taken credit as payment and thus come to the end of the selling season having little more than the expectations of the next fall's crop to meet their eastern demands. During the fall, in contrast, orders could be planned at a shorter range and sales often met the crop coming into the market, providing ready funds to pay off some of their notes. The pressure put on river-town merchants in the late spring and early summer was also facilitated for collectors by the easier communications and the resumption of court sessions. In contrast, it was hard to prosecute a debtor in the late fall and winter. Distance, obstructed lines of communication and transport, and dull business protected the average merchant. [45]

---

44 Lynch and Trask, St. Louis, to Davis and Krum, Alton, Ill., May 18, 1837; J. S. Lane, New York, to ibid., April 22, 1837; William Ruppell, St. Louis, to ibid., August 19, 1839; Papers of George T. M. Davis, Alton, Ill., Missouri Historical Society, St. Louis.

45 Illinois credit report ledgers, XCVIII, CXXXIX, CLXXVIII; Iowa credit report ledgers, XVI, XXXI, XLVII; and Missouri credit report ledgers, XXXVI, XXXVII, R. G. Dun and Company Collection.

Table 5.3. *Reported business failures and "embarrassments" per month in Galena, Dubuque, Alton, Peoria, and St. Louis, 1845-55*

	Embarrassments	Failures	Both	% of total
January	3	1	4	5
February	1	1	2	3
March	0	1	1	1
April	1	4	5	7
May	7	4	11	15
June	5	10	15	21
July	8	13	21	29
August	2	3	5	7
September	1	4	5	7
October	1	2	3	4
November	0	1	1	1
December	0	1	0	0
Totals	29	44	73	

Sources: Illinois credit report ledgers CXXXIX, XCVIII, XLXXIII; Missouri credit report ledger, XXVI; Iowa credit report ledger, XXXI; R. G. Dun and Company Collection, Baker Library, Harvard Graduate School of Business Administration, Cambridge, Mass.

Given this reality, it is not surprising that summer, in general, was a time during which less than honest men often slipped out of town by a late steamer and into the anonymity of the broader system, in the hopes of avoiding their creditors. Such was the case of a certain Dr. Hunt of Alton who, deep in debt and under pressure, "sold out for a song and took a boat for St. Louis." Those more honest merchants would stay in town and "face the music," first by letting their stock run down and then, eventually, by allowing it to be seized and sold at auction. As a new sales season approached, local merchants would often be on the lookout for auctions at which they could acquire decent goods at rock-bottom prices. Such was the intention of Benjamin Felt when, in January 1849, he "attended the auction of Nathaniel Sleeper's goods." In any case, when the pressure was on, reputations were at stake, and men had to choose sides in petty disputes. As a result, the level of social tension in town inevitably rose, often giving to late summer and early autumn a mood of grim determination. [46]

The dimensions of transportation and communication, therefore, not only imposed a time-and-space economic map on the system and affected the

---

[46] Illinois credit report ledgers, CXXXIX, R. G. Dun and Company Collection; Diary of Benjamin F. Felt, January 20, 1849, Galena Public Library, Galena, Ill.

patterns of interaction and trade, but also established seasonal rhythms of activity distinctive to that system.[47] These rhythms penetrated every aspect of regional life, both economically and socially. A farmer's year was, of course, rooted in the seasons. A merchant's schedule, however, was less directly related to the planting and harvesting schedules of the farming population than it was to the rise and fall of the water.[48]

The rhythm of local economic activity was based on the interplay between these two similar and yet not entirely simultaneous cycles, as we have seen. Each of these local rhythms existed within a broader cycle of business involving the slow movement of goods and services across the region and beyond that – by way of the time leads needed for orders, the lag in shipment of goods, and the delays in information and transmission of funds – put uneven pressure on western merchants from season to season. In each case, the seasonal or business cycle-related rhythms inposed limitations on action, which when translated to the general collective level tended to define the limits of what was and was not possible for that town economy to achieve in the course of its competitive struggle to maintain a regionally oriented function. More often than not, it seemed as if merchants were too often embroiled in their own problems deriving from the temptations of an overly expansive and competitive system to offer much aid in more community-oriented, long-term development programs or strategies.

The impact of these spatially and economically derived cycles on the social and economic life of the river towns was even further enhanced by their effect on the lives of workers and laborers and their interactions with the more permanent town populations along the rivers. The number of steamboatmen entering any town, for example, varied in direct proportion to the amount of steamboat traffic on the wharf. On an average spring day that meant that some 160 to 240 men, reckoning at about 20 boatmen on each of the eight to twelve boats entering Galena on peak days in the spring, would disembark to work and to patronize saloons, gaming halls, eating establishments, and places of entertainment, creating brief but often tense confrontations between locals and these transient outsiders near the wharf.[49]

The friction derived from the widely perceived depravity of the steamboatman's working life, and thus of his lack of morals and social conscience. Travelers and townsmen regularly remarked on the rough, antisocial behavior of the poorly paid, undereducated foreign or black

47 David Wishart, *The Fur Trade of the American West: A Geographical Synthesis* (Lincoln, Neb., 1979), 177.

48 John Mack Faragher, *Women and Men on the Overland Trail* (New Haven, 1979), 45–9.

49 Delegates to the Chicago Harbor and River Convention, *The commerce and navigation of the valley of the Mississippi*, 7; *Niles Weekly Register*, vol. 20 (November 1848); *Appleton's Western Tourist Guide* (New York, 1852), 36.

riverboat laborers. James Thompson, traveling upriver in 1852, described them in some detail:

> The deckhands on the boat are commonly Irish or Americans of the lowest class, interspersed with Negroes. Their dress and fare are coarse. Their sleeping bunks miserably furnished, and their whole physical condition exceedingly uncomfortable. As many of these boats consume several days on their regular trips, in the course of which they often stop for wood, and at every town land to take in freight, they usually have two sets of hands to alternate at intervals of four hours. The resting hours are spent in sleeping, lounging, smoking, drinking, swearing, carousing, and the habits of profaneness and intemperance grow fearfully. [50]

The staggered work schedules of these crews meant that at almost any hour of the day or night some men were on their "four-hour breaks." As a result, raucous and carousing crewmen, either on the boat or on the wharf, became a regular source of annoyance and disorder along the river. The indefatigable traveler, Mrs. Steele, while stuck in St. Louis wrote that "we were obliged to spend the night in our hot narrow berths among the mosquitoes listening to the noise and profane converse of the crews of the boats around us." Stephen Hanks, a captain on the northern river who called Albany, Illinois, his home, remarked that the deckhands "were almost all addicted to drink and many generally had liquor with them most of the time. Wherever the opportunity was given, they would make for the nearest saloons and dives where drinking, card playing, and worse, were the chief amusements." [51]

Saloons, gambling houses, and brothels, catering to the rougher sort of deckhand or raftsman from the river, were located along the edges of nearly every major wharf. Gangs of rivermen were especially active in those areas during the evening and, given their proximity, were viewed by townsmen as a source of evil and disorder that threatened the integrity and morals of the hard-working mechanics, laborers, and other youth of the city, by "infecting them with vulgar instincts." [52]

This general public impression was often reinforced by outbreaks of violence among deckhands or between crew members and passengers, again with a seasonal occurrence. In April 1846, for example, the *Daily Gazette* of Galena reported a series of events that lead to a near riot on the Galena wharf between onshore steamboat workers and the captain of the boat. On the way north, it seems that the captain had allegedly whipped and beaten an Irish deckhand and forced him to get off the boat at Bellevue, Iowa. The deckhand, incensed at the treatment he had received, traveled ahead of the boat to Galena

50 Daniel S. Curtiss, *Western portraiture, and emigrant's guide* (New York, 1852), 336.
51 Eliza Steele, *A summer journey in the west* (New York, 1841), 200; Autobiography of Stephen Hanks, Manuscript in sixty installments, no. 38, Putnam Museum, Davenport, Iowa.
52 *Iowa State Democrat* (Davenport), May 27, 1857.

and incited a group of Irishmen to meet it. Upon its arrival there, the boat was attacked and the captain beaten and "dangerously wounded." [53] In May 1852, another "terrible affray" occurred between the crew of one boat and some of its passengers over the alleged attempt by one of the crew to molest ("commit an outrage upon") a passenger's wife. Four were killed and several wounded seriously, when the deckhand attacked the passengers who had roughed him up at night. Likewise, Stephen Hanks reported on a row between two factions of Irishmen that "erupted into a general melee on the Galena wharf" in the spring of 1856. Davenport, Iowa, was also the scene of a serious wharfside riot in 1858 between steamboat hands and local police, in which two policemen were wounded. But unlike the others this incident occurred in late summer, not spring. [54]

Contemporaries were well aware of both the spatial and temporal aspects of this problem. Most of the reported incidents occurred along the wharf and during the late spring. As a result some towns beefed up their security and often cordoned off rivermen from the life of the town by restricting their movement up Main Street during the spring months, while encouraging their citizens not to go down to the wharf after dark. A notorious confirmation of these fears, which reflected the evolution of a social–spatial perception in various river towns, was the Richter murder in Galena in June 1854. Again the details fit the seasonal and spatial pattern. Eduard Richter's body was found floating in the river near the wharf. The last anyone had seen of him was when he left the Louisville House hotel on the south side of the wharf with a boy and then, near Peck's building, "fell in with company with several men whose conduct was such as to induce" the witness to leave. [55] This shocking event followed an alarming incident earlier in the spring in which a group of intoxicated boatmen left a saloon near the wharf and wandered up Main Street where they were "arrested at the corner of Main and Warren while trying to stone a hotel." This event, and others like it, no doubt reminded some older residents of the time in March 1848 when a "desperado" paraded up Main Street from the wharf "in the daytime, with two loaded pistols and terrorized the townspeople, and did defiance to anyone who might arrest him." [56]

The occasional, impressionistic nature of such evidence is corroborated in more public records of disorder. In the "City of Galena Justice of the Peace Court Record" between 1849 and 1851, the highest number of arrests for "drunk and disorderly conduct," occasionally described as "quarreling, fighting, and disturbing the peace and quiet of Main Street," or even as "fighting in the

53 *Galena Daily Advertiser*, April 26, 1846.
54 Ibid., May 25, 1852; Hanks, Autobiography, manuscript, installment no. 39; Harry E. Downer, *Davenport and History of Scott County, Iowa* (Chicago, 1910), 985.
55 *Galena Daily Advertiser*, June 10, 1854.
56 *Galena Gazette and Advertiser*, January 13, 1854; March 15, 1848.

streets, or "public drunkenness," or "indecent or profane speech or activities in public" occurred in April and May, during the peak of the navigation season. Most of those arrests for which locations were given were made on the wharf and lower Main Street. In 1850, for instance, there were ten arrests in March, sixteen in April, fourteen in May, six in June, and one in July. A similar pattern also reappeared in 1849 and 1851. Although such figures hardly represent public disorder, they do trace the seasonal patterns of activity, and thus document the extent to which life followed those cycles of the economy. [57]

Each in their different way, all the people of the valley were somehow constrained, limited, or redirected in their economic strategies and social interactions by the spatial and economic dimensions of the system in which they lived. Such dimensions played an important role in shaping the structure, setting the volume, and determining the dynamics of growth in the regional economy and thus directly affecting the pattern of regional urbanization. Indeed, in some cases, the economics of transportation explain the patterns of local participation in regional life. By differentiating locational perceptions, these dimensions also shaped the patterns of social activity among and within towns, and thus played an important role in forming the character of regional society. Where the dimensions of time and space brought people together and enabled them to interact for some time, social development could occur in a straightforward manner. But where the economic location of a town was in flux, or its nodal force insufficient to sustain year-round activity, social contacts were less intensive, and thus liable to sudden dissolution, the result being a limited self-awareness of the people there as a distinctive local "society." But the most direct impact of the temporal and spatial dimensions of western life were most directly translated into the pattern of economic development and the urban system that evolved from that activity.

---

57 Justice of the Peace Court Records, City of Galena, March 10, 1848, through January 12, 1851, Chicago Historical Society, Chicago.

6

The structure of the regional economy

In their struggles against time and space to produce and exchange goods and services across the breadth of the upper Mississippi River valley, merchants, farmers, miners, and entrepreneurs forged the structure of a regional economic system. Fernand Braudel reminds us that such systems are not simply impersonal structures in space. They are composed of living, working, interacting groups of people among whom the actions of any member elicits a response from the other members. The existence and character of such interactions are easily discerned in diaries, record books, newspaper reports, and steamboat-traffic data, as we have already seen. But the actual impact of such activity on improving regional life was most directly and clearly translated to the lives of the people and the towns they lived in by the efficiencies and development they triggered in the economy. The shifting patterns of production, the volume of goods brought to market, and, stimulated by specialization, the amount and range of trade such market activity encouraged, directly affected the well-being of town life and generated significant forces of change. It follows, therefore, that the structure of the regional urban system, defined primarily by the actions of merchants, can most directly be explained by analyzing the structure of and the dynamic forces of change within the regional economic system.

Patterns of production

The pattern of production of each of the region's major export products resulted from an interplay between the nature of the product and the environment, climate, and marketplace. Of these, the geographical pattern of lead production was most directly determined by geological and environmental factors. Lead was formed in crevices of limestone beneath extensive areas of the Midwest but, given contemporary technology, was only accessible where those strata of limestone were close to the surface. As a result, mining was practical only in the nonglaciated areas of the region, in particular, north central Missouri and extreme northwestern Illinois and southwestern Wisconsin.

Of the two areas, mines in the latter were far richer and more extensive.[1] Consequently, the pattern of production was fixed, and any market had to accept that fixed base of operations and organize itself, given the contemporary channels of trade, on that basis. Wheat, on the other hand, could be produced across a wide range of soil and climatic conditions. As Edmund Dana argued, all it needed for reasonable yields was good to very good soil, somewhat less than twenty inches of rain a year, with a growing season of around 120 days. In the Midwest, these requirements eliminated only the very richest bottom soils and the area south of St. Louis, where summer was usually too wet and humid for premium wheat production. Conveniently, such conditions, as they declined for wheat growing, approached optimum conditions for corn production. In general, however, good corn yields could be had far north into the area best for wheat conditions, only declining significantly in Minnesota and west of the Missouri, where a shortened growing season or overly dry summers limited production.[2] Livestock and hogs tended to follow corn production patterns, although before refrigeration the need for packing plants to be within a rather narrow zone between the river freeze line and areas with an average winter temperature below forty degrees tended to limit hog production to the fringes of the Ohio River valley. Superimposed on the environmental limitations, the full extent of which contemporaries discovered only by trial and error, were market factors, which, given the product's price in regional markets and the cost of transportation, often reinforced environmental factors in geographically differentiating production patterns.

On higher-priced land near the center of the regional economy, farmers had to farm more intensively to generate returns sufficient to cover costs. Because wheat had a high market value and could bear considerable transport, the wheat market soon became chronically oversupplied and prices fell to near break-even levels. This encouraged farmers nearer to the regional entrepôt to specialize in the production of goods that could not bear extensive transport, thus limiting their competition. For some, this meant planting orchards, vegetables, and garden products for town and city markets. For most others, planting corn and feeding it to hogs, which were then driven to market, could multiply returns more than four times over mere extensive grain production. And, for farmers close to the marketplace, excess corn could be hauled into

---

1 David Dale Owen, *Report of a geological exploration of part of Iowa, Wisconsin, and Illinois,* (Washington, D.C., 1844); Edmund Dana, *Geographical sketches on the western country: designed for emigrants and settlers... Including a particular description of unsold public lands, collected from a variety of authentic sources. Also, a list of the principal roads* (Cincinnati, 1819).
2 Timothy Flint, *The history and geography of the Mississippi Valley* (Cincinnati, 1832).

local distilleries as well. In the southern Midwest especially, these market factors reinforced the environmental factors already mentioned. [3]

Beyond certain distances, however, the hauling of corn and then the droving of hogs became impractical, and farmers turned to planting wheat and smaller grains that could bear more extensive carriage. In addition, on lower-priced land, average yields became sufficient to meet general costs, thus encouraging farmers to plant and work extensively, rather than intensively. Further out, beyond the range of profitable carriage of wheat to market, grasses and cattle, produced initially for local markets but soon after connected by railroads to a regional market, gradually replaced grain culture. Across the upper Mississippi River valley between 1830 and 1860, the interaction between these environmental and market factors led to the gradual development of distinct rings or zones of different production around the regional entrepôt at St. Louis. Hypothesized by von Thünen a generation before, the appearance of such rings on a regional scale provides significant evidence of regional-scale interaction among farmers in a systemic marketplace. [4]

Ninety percent of the lead received at St. Louis between 1820 and 1860 was mined and exported from the Lead Region. As a result, the economic ups and downs of the market in lead affected the existence of one or two ports and small groups of miners and entrepreneurs throughout the period. In sharp contrast, the grain and livestock markets, following the pattern of settlement, responding to environmental and market variables, and sensitive to outside economic forces, involved most of the rest of the people living in the region throughout the period. Moreover, the broad shifts in patterns of agricultural production selectively supported and abandoned different areas and thus different towns over time. As a result, the underlying patterns of agricultural production, by means of the capital they drew into differing local economies, played an important role in shaping the functional structure of the regional urban system. Decennial production figures from the agricultural census report indicate the significance of these shifts between 1830 and 1860. [5] In

3 Margaret Walsh, "The Spatial Evolution of Midwestern Pork Packing Industry, 1835–75," *Journal of Historical Geography* 4 (Spring 1978): 1–22.
4 Johann Heinrich von Thünen, *Der isolierte Staat* (Darmstadt, 1966); see also Johann Heinrich von Thünen, *The Isolated State*, ed. Carla M. Wartenberg (Oxford, 1966). Among the applications of this analysis to modern conditions, see J. Richard Peet, "A Spatial Expansion of Commercial Agriculture in the Nineteenth Century: A Von Thünen Interpretation," *Economic Geography* 45, no.4 (October 1969); Diane Lindstrom, *Economic Development in the Philadelphia Region, 1810–1850* (New York, 1978), 141; James Lemon, *The Best Poor Man's Country* (Baltimore, 1972), 189–97.
5 U.S. Census office, *Sixth census or enumeration of the inhabitants of the United States* (Washington, D.C., 1841), 298–301, 311–13, 348–9; U. S. Census office, *The seventh census of the United States: 1850* (Washington, D.C. 1853), 675–82, 728–35, 956–9; U.S. Department of the Interior, U.S. Census Office, *Agriculture of the United States in 1860: compiled from the original returns of the eighth census* (Washington, D.C. 1864), 30–7, 46–53, 88–95.

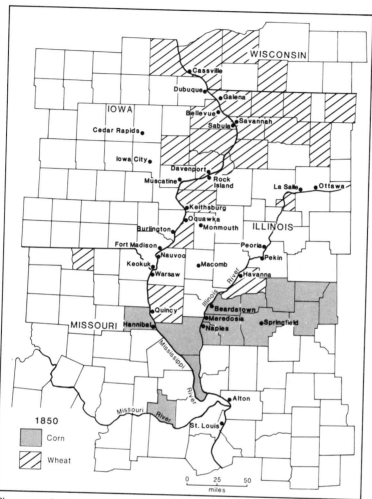

Figure 6.1. Agricultural specialization in St. Louis's northern hinterland, 1850 (see Appendix E.2).

each case, the observed shifts can be clearly explained by a mix of environmental, population, and market factors.

Indeed, even before 1840, the geographic pattern of lead production had been established and would remain unchanged during the period. In contrast, no clearly differentiated pattern of wheat or corn production had yet developed. In 1839 there was some clustering of hog and corn production around the larger towns in the southern part of the valley, especially around Hannibal and Quincy, and along the American Bottom opposite St. Louis, but in general, production tended to follow population proportionally from south to north and from the river into the interior. The fact that wheat production followed the same pattern, with small clusters of heavier production around the larger towns, further indicates that most farmers planted according to their own needs and not in response to a regional market.

Between 1840 and 1850, however, a market-related pattern of production began to emerge from this population-oriented pattern (Figure 6.1). The most notable development was the explosion in corn production in a broad band across the lower Illinois River from Calhoun County east into Sangamon and Logan counties. Rather than simply reflecting more production in proportion to the number of new farmers, this band of heavier corn production clearly reflected a decision by many farmers to change from mixed self-sufficient production strategies and to produce a more intensive, specialized crop for sale in a regional market. A z-score test of all Illinois counties documents a specialization in corn production across this broad band. Furthermore, the shift of this area away from the immediate core around the entrepôt into an immediate area beyond is reflected in the stagnating production figures around St. Louis and Alton. In addition, in each of these counties in which corn production was on the rise, wheat production declined significantly. During the same decade wheat production began to center around Quincy, Illinois, in the southern Military Tract, as well as show signs of shifting north along the river. The few settlers then in Henderson and Mercer counties, Illinois, heavily specialized in wheat production over corn and produced significant surpluses. Hog production, meanwhile, increased in all the river counties within the Military Tract, but especially in those along the river north of St. Louis and into the lower Illinois River valley – again evidence of some more general response to regional market factors. This same area, and especially in the counties adjacent to St. Louis, Alton, and Quincy (as well as around Galena, Peoria, and even Springfield) showed significant increases in vegetable and fruit production, an obvious response to locational advantages near market towns (see Appendix E). [6]

By 1859 each of these tendencies had become more pronounced, though by no means fixed. The "corn belt" had, during the 1850s, crossed the Shelbyville moraine and centered itself near Galesburg, extending in a broad arc from Shelby County, Illinois, on the southeast, through Peoria and Fulton counties and then across the river toward south central Iowa (Figure 6.2). Meanwhile the area just to the north had become a zone of highly specialized wheat production extending from LaSalle County, Illinois, on the east and the

---

6 U.S. Census office, *Sixth census*, 298–301, 311–13, 348–9; U.S. Census office, *Seventh census of the United States*, 675–82, 728–35, 956–9; for z-score methodology, see Lindstrom, *Economic Development in the Philadelphia Region*, 141. For calculations on specialization, see Appendix E.

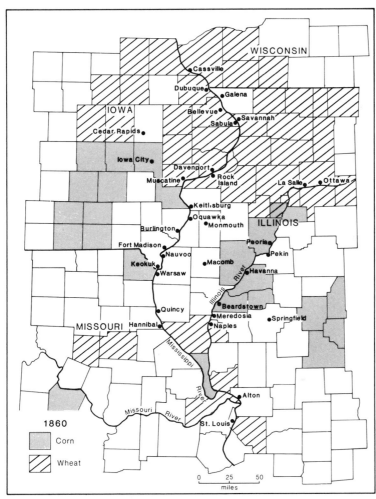

Figure 6.2. Agricultural specialization in St. Louis's northern hinterland, 1860 (see Appendix E.3).

Lead Region on the north, west across the Mississippi into most of northeastern Iowa. Even as these distinct production zones seemed to be solidifying, however, rising corn produ   ction alongside of wheat production in the counties along the southern edge of the wheat area suggests an imminent northward push of the corn belt and a further retreat of the wheat-producing area to the north and west in the years to come. Meanwhile, hog production clustered heavily along the river north of St. Louis and along the lower Illinois River valley, though again a northward movement seemed apparent. The doubling of hog production in many areas of eastern Iowa and in Henry, Mercer, Rock Island, Whiteside, Lee, and Bureau counties during the same period suggests a closer alignment of hog production to that of corn. Indeed, by the 1870s, the Rock River valley would become one of the heaviest hog-producing areas in the entire region. In contrast to these shifting patterns, orchard and vegetable production continued to concentrate exclusively around the larger towns and cities in the region. [7]

It was within the context of the shifting areal coverage of production that producers in each of these markets sought out channels to regional markets through nearby towns and cities. From this activity, the structure of market interactions or the "shape of the market" developed.

The shape of the market

The spatial organization of the lead trade hinged upon the fact that both the locus of its production and the primary source of its demand were relatively fixed in place. Most of the demand for lead for use in paint and glass was centered in the East while the newly opened mines in the West were the only American source. As a result of this distance between supply and demand, a premium was placed on efficient transportation and effective marketing. This tended to encourage the creation, by a few companies that both marketed the product and owned and operated the boats, of a highly integrated outpost system in which profits were made at the shipping point and at the entrepôt. The tightness of this system is evident in the trade figures kept at the ports of St. Louis and Galena, Illinois, which because of its location, became the primary entrepôt of the Lead Region. A comparison of the widely available figures of "lead shipped from the port of Galena" and the "total production of the upper Mississippi River mines received at St. Louis" shows Galena's exclusiveness as the only point from which lead was shipped to St. Louis. Between 1842 and 1853 the two figures of shipments from Galena and receipts at St. Louis were nearly equal (Table 6.1). [8] Such figures suggest an economy apart, connected by a near monopoly control of shipping, and organized and operated for the benefit of a very few. Furthermore, the close alignment between shipping figures from St. Louis and receipts and reshipments from New Orleans throughout the 1840s suggests a strong eastern control over this

7 U.S. Census Office, *Agriculture of the United States in 1860*, 46–53; Allan G. Bogue, *From Prairie to Corn Belt: Farming on the Illinois and Iowa Prairies in the Nineteenth Century* (Chicago, 1963), 217–20, 225–6.
8 *Annual Review: The commercial statistics and history of St. Louis* (St. Louis, 1854), 31; *The History of Jo Daviess County, Illinois* (Chicago, 1878), 273; St. Louis Chamber of Commerce, *Report of the committee appointed by the chamber of commerce upon the trade, commerce and manufacturers of St. Louis, embracing a period of several years* (St. Louis, 1852), 22.

Table 6.1. *Comparison of St. Louis lead receipts from upper Mississippi and Galena, Illinois, shipments of lead, 1842–57*

	Total product of upper mines received at St. Louis (lbs.)	Galena lead shipments (lbs.)	Difference between total product and lead shipments
1842	33,158,930	31,353,630	+ 1,805,300
1843	40,889,170	39,148,270	+ 1,740,900
1844	43,722,070	43,727,040	− 4,970
1845	54,492,200	54,494,860	− 2,660
1846	52,668,210	51,268,210	+ 1,400,000
1847	56,185,920	54,085,920	+ 2,100,000
1848	47,737,830	47,737,830	0
1849	43,789,340	44,035,380	− 236,040
1850	39,724,720	39,801,230	− 76,510
1851	35,262,570	33,188,050	− 2,074,520
1852	28,651,980	28,603,960	+ 48,020
1853	30,955,260	29,806,980	+ 1,148,280
1854	21,470,890	26,654,000	− 5,183,110
1855	22,097,390	30,126,000	− 8,028,610
1856	15,356,880	30,496,000	− 15,139,120
1857	14,028,140	34,164,000	− 20,135,860

Note: One "pig" of lead equals approximately seventy pounds.
Sources: St. Louis Chamber of Commerce, *Report of the committee appointed by the chamber of commerce, upon the trade, commerce and manufactures of St. Louis, embracing a period of several years* (St. Louis, 1852), 22; *Annual Review, The commercial statistics and history of St. Louis* (St. Louis, 1854), 31; *The History of Jo Daviess County, Illinois* (Chicago, 1879), 273; *Galena Gazette and Advertiser,* January 3 1851; "The Lead Trade in the West," *De Bow's Review* (New Orleans) 7 (1858): 211.

system. In 1839, for example, 80 percent of St. Louis receipts were transshipped to New Orleans. A year later the share had risen to nearly 90 percent, and a year after that to 99 percent.[9] This suggests that by 1842 the flow between Galena via St. Louis to the East was almost completely without interruption or diversion.

Because the structure of the lead trade was based on a steamboat monopoly, its continuation was dependent on maintaining control over the means of

9 St. Louis Chamber of Commerce, *Proceedings of the St. Louis chamber of commerce, in relation to the improvement of the navigation of the Mississippi River, and its principal tributaries and the St. Louis harbor* (St. Louis, 1842), 14.

transport between the source of the raw material and the market. Inevitably, however, the frustrations of other producers and shippers, combined with shifting patterns of demand for lead, began to erode such a centralized marketing system. For example, after river towns to the north of Galena began to develop, there was no particular economic reason, other than the tradition of following entrenched patterns, why lead from the northern fringes of the producing area should continue to be hauled overland to the Lead City rather than find a more direct and convenient outlet to the south. Five times before 1853 – in 1832, 1842, 1846, 1847, and 1851 – an excess of St. Louis receipts from the Lead Region over shipments from Galena received at St. Louis suggests some erosion in Galen's control over regional production. In each case, the erosion did not amount to more than 5 percent of total exports from the region, it is true, but such figures suggest some dissatisfaction with the dominant structure of the market.[10] In 1851, the share of total export that found another outlet besides Galena rose to 12 percent. This reflected the presence of merchants other than those involved directly in the lead trade on the upper river, allowing some producers to bypass the regional entrepôt. It also suggests some competition as a shipping point from Dubuque, Iowa. By 1853, merchants in Cassville, Wisconsin, and Dubuque exported about 10 percent of the region's total exports, leaving Galena only a 75 percent share of the shipping trade. Within another two years Dubuque would claim shipments of almost ten million pounds of lead, or about one-third of Galena's total shipments. Even so, most of this lead still went to St. Louis. This erosion of Galena's control of its hinterland reminded contemporaries that, in spite of appearances, the dominance of one route of trade over another was primarily a matter of transport costs between the Lead Region and any entrepôt.

If a new line of transportation into the region could be opened and provide service at competitive cost, there was no real reason why local producers would remain loyal to the old lines of activity. Given this realization, fears of the impact of the continuing railroad construction between Chicago and the Lead Region appeared at an early date. In 1846 a Burlington editor seemed certain that "if the proposed Chicago – Galena railroad goes through, the lead trade will go east to the lakes instead of via New Orleans. Not a pig [of lead] will find its way to St. Louis."[11] To most observers the comparative economics seemed to assure a rapid shift. The difficulty of transport on the upper Mississippi, though not a factor when all the lead went south on the river, would quickly

10 *Annual Review*, 31; *Dubuque city directory and annual advertiser, 1856–57* (Dubuque, Iowa, 1856), 35; Berhard H. Schockel, "Settlement and Development of Jo Daviess County," in *The Geology and Geography of the Galena and Elizabeth Quadrangle*, ed. Arthur C. Trowbridge and Eugene Wesley Shaw (Urbana, Ill., 1916), 190–2.
11 *The Burlington Hawkeye*, January 15, 1846.

become an important disincentive to continue shipping south, as opposed to using the rail line going east. In an average year in the 1850s, the rapids increased transport charges and insurance by at least a million dollars, while the delays and vagaries of river travel made market activity more volatile and risky. Thus, when in 1851 the construction of the Galena and Chicago Union Railroad began to move west, reaching Belvedere, Illinois, by year's end, the fears of St. Louisans turned into openly expressed alarm. Note this local comment: "In the course of two or three years, the railroad, connecting Galena with Chicago, will in all probability be completed, when, unless the obstructions at the rapids shall have been removed, we will find the lead trade diverted through a new channel, lost to us forever." [12]

In fact, the drift to the east was already well underway by that time. In 1851, a limited amount of 20,000 pigs of lead found its way to Chicago. In August 1852, lead merchants Stillman and Rood caused comment when they "opened a new current of trade" by choosing to ship their lead east in wagons to rendezvous with the end point of the railroad in Rockford. The freight from Galena to Rockford was forty cents per hundred weight, and to Chicago was another ten cents, and though still over twice the cost of transport to St. Louis, the difference was compensated for by higher prices on the Chicago market. But until the railroad got closer to Galena no more than 3 or 4 percent of the total shipped from the Lead City followed this route. [13]

In October 1852, however, the arrival of the Chicago and Galena Union Railroad in Freeport, Illinois, only fifty miles from Galena, opened the floodgates for the next season. In 1853 shipments to Chicago increased to 23, 471 pigs of lead, or over 1.5 million pounds, about 5 percent of regional exports. Although we do not have accurate figures for 1854, Table 6.1 does show a sharp drop in receipts at St. Louis as compared with total shipments from Galena. Within a single season, as much as 20 percent of the region's lead exports were diverted east. Of this total, 582,081 pounds were shipped on the Galena and Chicago Union Railroad, while the rest probably was shipped on the Illinois Central, which, after buying out the line, had a banner year (Table 6.2). [14]

The speed of the shift anticipated the effect of the railroad's actual arrival in Galena on June 12, 1855, and its subsequent continuation on to Dunleith, Illinois, on the east bank of the Mississippi opposite Dubuque by summer's

12 St. Louis Chamber of Commerce, *Report of the committee appointed by the chamber of commerce*, 21.
13 *Galena Daily Advertiser*, August 13, 1852; Elmer A. Riley, "The Development of Chicago and Vicinity as a Manufacturing Center Prior to 1880" (Ph.D. dissertation, University of Chicago, 1911), 81, 92.
14 Galena and Chicago Union Railroad, *Annual Report* (title varies) (Chicago, 1851–8); *Report and accompanying documents of the Illinois Central Railroad Company, made by order of the stockholders at their annual meeting* (New York, 1856), 9, 24, appendix K.

Table 6.2. *Chicago receipts and shipments of lead, 1856–70*

	Production in lead region	Receipts (in lbs.) in Chicago	Receipts in Chicago production	Forwarded to East	Forwarded East receipts in Chicago
1856	30,496,000	6,627,506	.21	4,257,936	.64
1857	34,164,000	4,256,207	.12	2,214,308	.52
1858	30,000,000	8,670,028	.29	8,449,870	.97
1859	27,500,000	14,351,179	.52	8,725,747	.61
1860	24,000,000	12,315,260	.51	8,392,066	.68
1861	27,750,000	18,477,939	.66	16,852,698	.91
1862	30,000,000	14,329,719	.48	6,516,796	.45
1863	34,000,000	16,412,302	.48	11,607,713	.71
1864	32,000,000	10,699,078	.33	6,853,633	.64
1865	30,000,000[a]	6,935,433	.23	6,371,703	.91
1866	27,000,000[a]	8,426,730	.32	6,433,218	.76
1867	25,000,000[a]	11,236,957	.45	4,162,074	.37
1868	23,000,000[a]	11,543,917	.50	7,974,740	.69
1869	20,000,000[a]				
1870	20,000,000[a]	13,845,100	.70	5,994,751	.43

[a] Estimated figures.

Sources: Chicago Board of Trade, *Annual statement of the trade and commerce of Chicago* (Chicago, 1856-70). Bernhard H. Schockel, "The Settlement and Development of Jo Daviess Country, Illinois" in *The Geology and Geography of the Elizabeth and Galena Quadrangle*, ed. Arthur C. Trowbridge and Eugene Wesley Shaw (Urbana, Ill., 1916), 192.

end. In 1856, the first full season of operation under the new economic arrangements, half the region's lead output was shipped to Chicago rather than St. Louis. By the end of the next season receipts in Chicago exceeded those in St. Louis. By 1860 almost 70 percent of the lead produced went to Chicago. At St. Louis, meanwhile, arrivals dropped, business plummeted, and wharfside warehouses went out of business. Further south, the ripple effect cut off New Orleans from its northwest trade. Receipts of lead dropped from 785,000 in 1846, to 210,287 in 1853, to a mere 18,291 in 1851. Although some lead continued to move along the old route, the predictions of a decade before had proved essentially correct.[15]

Yet, to a certain extent, the new trading arrangements, though geographically changed, maintained the old characteristics of the trade. The Illinois Central simply replaced the St. Louis steamboats as the transport

15 Chicago Board of Trade, *Annual statement of the trade and commerce of Chicago* (Chicago, 1856–9), 37; ibid. (1859), 71; ibid. (1861),53.

monoply and Dubuque replaced Galena as the entrepôt at the end of the line –
until, that is, business as a whole faltered from low production and competition
from better sources of lead further west after the Civil War. Within the Lead
Region, the impact of the railroad was to spread out the point of shipment and,
to certain extent, disperse the concentrated forces of urban development that
had supported Galena's growth. Even during the steamboat period, Galena's
export monopoly, which regularly amounted to about 99 percent of the
region's lead exports between the 1820s and the 1840s, had begun to erode.
The establishment of Dubuque as the headquarters of the Minnesota Packet
Company reinforced Dubuque's desire to have a say in the matter, and further
encouraged river towns up in Wisconsin to ship local supplies directly to
Dubuque rather than overland to Galena. By 1854, as a result, Galena's export
amounted to only 70 percent of all lead shipped from the region. As an
accounting of railroad shipments in the first year of operation along the Illinois
Central indicates, further erosion was to be expected from small market towns.
Within a year less than half of the region's lead actually found its way to
Galena's wharf or depot, and this share continued to decline as production as a
whole fell off in later years. [16]

In sharp contrast to the lead trade, which as an outpost economy channeled
market activity along a narrow corridor between the supply outpost and the
entrepôt, the structure of the grain trade was organized and reorganized across
a wide area of the region. As a result, it was the arrangement of the wheat trade
in particular that ultimately had the most important effect in shaping the
pattern of urban development across the region. To demonstrate this, one
must determine and explain the geographic movement of grain production
across the region over time.

It may surprise one, given our previous comments about the relative fertility
of western soil, but recently settled areas often experienced several years of
grain shortages before achieving self-sufficiency and then a surplus. Evidence
suggests that long before western farmers were sending their wheat east, via
St. Louis or Cincinnati, into national markets, they were able to dispose of
much of their surpluses by shipping it west toward the recently opened
frontier. By comparing production figures with population, and reckoning
subsistence at 5 bushels per person per year, we can estimate the geographic
pattern of this early market activity. [17]

In 1839, for example, wheat production in Illinois totaled 3.5 million
bushels, or a margin of 2 bushels per person over the subsistence level of per

16 *Report and accompanying documents of the Illinois Central Railroad Company*, appendix K.
17 James Mak, "Intraregional Trade in the Antebellum West, Ohio: A Case Study," *Agricultural History* 46 (October 1972): 489–97; *Galena Gazette and Advertiser*, May 16, 1845; "Wheat Crop in the United States," *De Bow's Review* 24 (1858): 574–6.

capita production. The greater part of this production clustered around the towns of St. Louis, Alton, Quincy, Lewiston, Peoria, and LaSalle, requiring, therefore, some shipment of surpluses from near the rivers out into the sparsely inhabited hinterlands to relieve local deficits. Such was the case across the river in Iowa, where new settlers had produced only 154,963 bushels of wheat, representing a shortfall of some 50,000 bushels. Some of this deficit was filled by the production surplus of Scott County, Iowa (the only Iowa surplus producer in 1839), but most of it must have been filled by surpluses from the nearby Military Tract. To the north, surpluses in Stephenson County were most likely absorbed by the strong demand for foodstuffs in the Lead Region. A more serious shortfall, which certainly drew surpluses from upriver toward the south, existed in the St. Louis area. St. Louis County, Missouri, for example, produced only 1.6 bushels per person, leaving a huge shortfall of almost 180,000 bushels for that county alone, with more added to that from the adjacent counties to the west and south. Most of these shortages were covered by the generous surpluses of St. Clair and Madison counties, Illinois, amounting, in that year, to 80,000 and 90,000 bushels of wheat respectively. But that still left a need for some 30,000 bushels in the St. Louis area. Some of this was no doubt filled by shipments from the lower Illinois valley, while the remainder can only have been acquired in the Ohio River markets to the east, either at Cincinnati or Louisville.[18]

The difficulty with assuming that surpluses just naturally flowed toward demand, however, is that as the volume of production rose, one must also consider the milling capacities of the surplus areas, and thus the local ability to supply flour directly to the local market. If there was no local mill, one must assume, given the volume of production with which we are dealing, that local merchants had to export wheat to some milling center and then reimport flour for local use. As strange as this circumstance seems, such appears to have been the case in Galena until well into the 1840s. In 1839 seven mills produced 17,700 barrels of flour. At 5 bushels of wheat per barrel of milled flour, such production required receipts of 88,500 bushels of wheat, or most of the wheat production from Ogle, Carroll, and Winnebago counties. But such production only met 65 percent of the area's demand for flour (reckoned at 1 barrel per person per year) while leaving 150,000 bushels of unmilled wheat. Given the minimal evidence of milling activity, we must assume that most of the surplus wheat was exported to St. Louis or even further east to the Ohio and that enough flour was imported to fill local needs. In fact, it seems that throughout the upper valley milling capacities were inadequate to meet local flour needs and that much of the region's surplus wheat, before supplying local shortfalls,

18 U.S. Census office, *Sixth census*, 298–301, 311–13, 348–9.

must have been exported to the Ohio River, and then reimported as flour to supply consumption needs.[19]

Regional shortages were even more pervasive. The Illinois River valley was unable to meet its flour needs in 1839. Although valley wheat production topped 400,000 bushels, the seven mills in Cass, Scott, and Jersey counties combined could absorb only 50,000 bushels, producing a mere 10,000 barrels of flour. As a result, 300,000 bushels of wheat had to travel to Ohio River mills and, on its return, be joined by more than 30,000 additional barrels of Ohio River flour to feed the region's 108,000 people. Add to this wheat movement that from the Mississippi, amounting to about 480,000 bushels, and it seems one must conclude that nearly 800,000 bushels of wheat moved from north to south in search of milling during the 1839–40 season. This was just about enough to meet the 180,000 barrels of flour needed to supply valley residents with proper sustenance. Therefore, while the region quickly approached self-sufficiency in producing its wheat needs, it fell far short in turning that wheat into flour and thus had to rely on extensive and redundant trading activity to acquire it.[20]

Where did the imported flour come from? Apparently it did not come from the lower valley around St. Louis. There, an impressive milling surplus of 46,000 barrels at Alton was quickly bought up by the serious shortfall noted in the vicinity of St. Louis. St. Louis county alone needed more than 22,000 barrels of flour to meet its annual needs. The nearest surpluses outside of the region were those along the Ohio, suggesting, in spite of strong trade evidence, that as much as three-fourths of the region's flour needs were supplied by Cincinnati and Louisville merchants.[21]

However silent the record before 1840, after that time the improvement in clarity and details of wheat-trade statistics gives us a much clearer notion of the shifting patterns of the market. For example, the St. Louis report for the 1841 season records that Alton and St. Louis together shipped 174,000 barrels of flour; 150,000 went east to New York, the rest north toward the frontier or east into the Ohio. In addition, 237,000 bushels of wheat were exported, most of which "went to the Ohio." Given these figures, and the fact that local flour needs stood at 60,000 barrels, and that 10,000 barrels of flour were supplied from mills at Belleville, Illinois, it stands that total flour production in the two

19 Manuscript Manufacturing Schedule, Jo Daviess County, Ill., Sixth Census of the United States, 1840; U.S. Census office, *Sixth census*, 298–301.
20 Manuscript Manufacturing Schedule, Madison County, Ill., Sixth Census of the United States, 1840; U.S. Census Office, *Sixth census*, 298–301, 348–9; *Quincy Whig*, January 24, 27, 1857.
21 St. Louis Chamber of Commerce, *Proceedings of the St. Louis chamber of commerce*, 18; *Northwest Gazette and Galena Advertiser*, January 13, 1842; *Peoria Register and Northwest Gazette*, March 26, 1841; A.D. Jones, *Illinois and the West* (Boston, 1838), 187.

towns may have been as high as 215,000 barrels, more than three times the 1839 total. To produce so much flour, local mills required 1,015,000 bushels of wheat, which, taken together with local wheat exports, means that total combined receipts at the two towns were near 1.3 million bushels. St. Louis's share was 900,000 bushels, a slight increase from 1839. The big difference, therefore, was not so much wheat production, but suddenly increased milling capacity. [22]

These new mills, combined with more efficient steamboat connections, continued to expand St. Louis's wheat trade in the coming years. By 1842 receipts topped 1 million bushels. More significant was the increase in receipts of flour to over 80,000 barrels, a certain indicator of new excess capacity upriver. A slight dip in receipts in 1845 to 900,000 was made up for in the next few years by marked increases, rising to a high of 2.2 million bushels in 1848 (see Appendix F). [23] Flour imports continued to rise as well, exceeding 250,000 barrels by 1846.

With such dramatic increases in receipts of both wheat and flour, combined with increases in their own milling capacity, it is apparent that exports from St. Louis to various points – New York, the Ohio, west and north toward the frontier – continued to rise. Our concern is to determine just how much the towns of the upper Mississippi River contributed to this boom and how that contribution was distributed among the various river towns. Curiously, however, it seems that rather than increasing in proportion to the increase in St. Louis, wheat exports from towns upriver were declining. The most optimistic combination of export figures from the major ports of Quincy, Alton, Burlington, Davenport, Galena, and Dubuque, in an average year between 1845 and 1849, totaled about 1 million bushels. Of that, as much as 50 percent came from Quincy, and another 20 percent from Alton. Clearly, rising wheat receipts at St. Louis must have been generated from another area. As much as 20 percent might have come from the Illinois River valley, but after the opening of the Illinois and Michigan canal even this amount began to decrease significantly [24]

In fact, the relative decline in upriver wheat exports seems to have been due to the increased milling capacity of a number of river towns, which absorbed much of the wheat surpluses. Almost every town along the river constructed a mill and ended the local importation of flour between 1840 and 1845. As early as 1842 Platteville, Wisconsin, and Galena produced flour and pushed St.

22 St. Louis Chamber of Commerce, *Proceedings of the St. Louis chamber of commerce*, 18, 30.
23 John Thomas Scharf, *The History of St. Louis city and county*, 2 vols. (Philadelphia, 1883), 1126; W. D. Skidman, *The western metropolis* (St. Louis, 1846), 82.
24 John Clark, *The Grain Trade in the Old Northwest* (Urbana, Ill., 1966), 474–5; U.S. Census Office, *Sixth census*, 298–301, 311–13, 348–9; U.S. Census Office, *Seventh census of the United States*, 675–82, 728–35, 956–59.

Louis imports out of northern markets. About the same time, the opening of the Pratt and Manson Rockdale Mills in Dubuque County cut St. Louis flour completely out of the Lead Region trade. [25]

In Quincy, eight mills were reported in the city by 1848, although only four were listed in the 1850 census. There were also mills in Davenport, Keokuk, Burlington, and Muscatine by this time. [26] Various estimates indicate that in the late 1840s these mills exported about 230,000 barrels of flour after local consumption (Table 6.3). Another source suggests that the amount of flour shipped on the upper river may have been nearly double that figure. In flour exports as in wheat, Quincy led the way. However, Quincy's dominance was soon to be challenged by both Burlington and Davenport. Likewise, although some of the surplus at Galena and Dubuque may have gone north, most of it was shipped south to the entrepôt. The 220,454 barrels of flour received at St. Louis in 1846 approximates the total amount shipped from all towns on the upper Mississippi. By 1848, therefore, it is apparent that the river towns had become supply depots that processed and supplied both wheat and flour for St. Louis's regional and national market trade.

Ironically, however, the northward expansion of the wheat belt above the rapids underscored the inefficiency of St. Louis's steamboat connections with Burlington, Muscatine, and Davenport, and thus intensified the pressures that threatened to undermine the system. As wheat receipts increased at the river towns above the rapids, the profits lost in the cost of lightering goods over the rapids rose, and a search for alternative markets broadened. Meanwhile, as the wheat belt moved north, it became a more powerful attraction to Chicago railroad entrepreneurs who sought to broaden that city's trading territory. Financially supported by bond issues voted at a number of towns in eastern Iowa, the railroad began construction and reached the river at Rock Island in 1854. A year later the Illinois Central reached Dunleith, Illinois. And within two more years, other railroads had established contact with Burlington, Muscatine, and Quincy. Almost immediately, wheat and flour flowed east seeking the generally higher-priced Chicago market. A large share of river exports was, within a very short time, irrevocably lost to the railroads. Therefore, even though combined exports by river and rail at Davenport surged ahead of Quincy in 1856, Quincy retained the supremacy in the river

25 *History of Dubuque County, Iowa* (Chicago, 1880), 474–5.
26 Pat H. Redmond, *A History of Quincy and its men of mark* (Quincy, Ill., 1869), 14; *Quincy Whig*, December 24, 1845; John Tilson, *A History of Quincy* (Chicago, n.d.), 107; Manuscript Manufacturing Schedule, Adams County, Illinois, Sixth Census of the United States, 1840; ibid., Seventh Census of the United States, 1850; J. M. D. Burrows, "Fifty Years in Iowa: Being the Personal Reminiscences of J. M. D. Burrows," in *Early Day of Rock Island and Davenport: The Narratives of J. W. Spencer and J. M. D. Burrows,* ed. Milo Quaife (Chicago, 1942), 208–14; Jacob A. Swisher, *Iowa: Land of Many Mills* (Iowa City, 1940), 245–70.

Table 6.3. *Flour exports from river towns on the upper Mississippi River, 1844–9*

Town and year	Surplus/exports (in bbls.)	Annual average	% of total
Dubuque, 1848	40,000	40,000	17
Galena, 1847	10,000	10,000	4
Davenport, 1847	40,000		
Davenport, 1849	30,200	35,000	15
Burlington, 1846	32,821		
Burlington, 1849	39,500	36,100	15
Quincy, 1846	70,000		
Quincy, 1848	60,000	65,000	28
Alton, 1840s	20,000	20,000	9
Muscatine 1840s		10,000	4
Rock Island, 1840s		10,000	4
Warsaw, Ill. 1840s		5,000	2
Oquawka, Ill., 1840s		3,500	2
Total estimate		234,600	100

Source: See Appendix F.

trade that it had had since the 1840s. Its wheat export accounted for one-third of all upriver shipments to St. Louis by the late 1850s (Table 6.4) [27]

Nevertheless, discounting in which direction the wheat or flour was shipped, the fact remains that both wheat and flour exports from the hinterland to the entrepôts had not risen significantly during the 1850s, and this in the face of soaring production figures and receipts at most ports above the rapids. We know, for example, that while production behind Quincy leveled off by 1855 and receipts there rose only slightly during the 1850s, huge increases in production behind Davenport and Dubuque inundated the town with over a million bushels of wheat a year by 1857. Yet exports remained stable just when one would have expected them to increase dramatically (Table 6.5). [28]

In part this may have been due to a series of fires at mills in Quincy, Keokuk, and Hannibal between 1849 and 1851 that, because they were not

27 See Appendix F. Frank Dixon, *A Traffic History of the Mississippi River System* (Washington, D.C., 1907), 21; St. Louis Chamber of Commerce, *Report of the committee appointed by the chamber of commerce*, 12.
28 Scharf, *St. Louis*, 1126; Wyatt Belcher, *The Rivalry between St. Louis and Chicago, 1850–1880* (New York, 1947), 191; Harry E. Downer, *History of Davenport and Scott County, Iowa* (Chicago, 1910), 276; Willard Barrows, *The Annals of Iowa* (Iowa City, 1964), 199.

Table 6.4. *Wheat shipments to St. Louis and Chicago from upper Mississippi River ports, 1850–8*

Town and year	Exports (bu.)	Annual average (bu.)	% of total
By river to St. Louis			
Dubuque, 1854	29,300		
Dubuque,1855	17,820	23,560	4
Galena, 1854	19,384		
Galena, 1855	35,840		
Galena, 1857	74,580[a]	43,268	7
Davenport, 1855	15,000[a]		
Davenport, 1857	30,072	22,536	4
Oquawka, 1851	107,416[a]		
Oquawka, 1854	177,705[a]		
Oquawka, 1856	270,727	185,282	29
Burlington, 1855	33,375		
Burlington, 1856	17,000		
Burlington, 1858	10,000	20,125	3
Keokuk, 1857			
Quincy, 1854	22,294		
Quincy, 1856	370,000	196,147	31
Alton, 1853	84,780		
Alton, 1854	192,849	138,815	22
Totals		629,733	100
By railroad to Chicago			
Galena, 1854	1,300		
Galena, 1855	60,352		
Galena, 1857	149,160[a]	70,270	19
Davenport, 1855	15,000[a]		
Davenport, 1857	51,936	33,468	9
Burlington, 1855	233,625		
Burlington, 1856	187,000		
Burlington, 1858	187,500	202,708	55
Keokuk, 1857	60,000	60,000	17
Totals		366,446	100
Combined totals			
By river		629,733	63
By rail		366,446	37
		996,179	100

[a] Estimated figures.

Source: See Appendix F.

Table 6.5. *Flour shipments to St. Louis and Chicago from upper Mississippi River ports, 1850–8*

Town and year	Exports (bbls)	Annual average (bbls)	% of total
By river to St. Louis			
Dubuque, 1854	3,780	3,780	2
Galena, 1854	28,894		
Galena, 1855	3,891		
Galena, 1857	40,025	24,270	14
Davenport, 1855	20,150[a]		
Davenport, 1857	19,819	19,985	11
Burlington, 1856	1,683		
Burlington, 1857	2,738	2,233	1
Muscatine, 1854	10,000[a]	10,000	6
Rock Island, 1855	10,000[a]	10,000	6
Quincy, 1854	48,000		
Quincy, 1856	60,000[a]		
Quincy, 1857	70,000[a]	59,333	33
Alton, 1850	60,000		
Alton, 1853	27,003		
Alton, 1854	58,800	48,601	27
Total		178,202	100
By railroad to Chicago			
Galena, 1854	10,427		
Galena, 1855	5,600		
Galena, 1857	5,600	7,209	10
Davenport, 1854	10,000[a]		
Davenport, 1857	86,509	48,254	66
Burlington, 1855	19,162		
Burlington, 1856	17,017	18,089	24
Quincy, 1857			
Alton, 1857			
Total		73,552	100
Totals			
By river		178,202	71
By rail		73,552	29
Combined		251,754	100

[a] Estimated figures.

Source: See Appendix F.

replaced in the ensuing years, severely cut back on the milling capacity of the upper river.[29] But if this were the only cause, one would have expected a considerable increase in wheat exports to the entrepôt, which did not happen. It seems more probable that most of the increase in wheat and flour production went to feed the rising population of the area. In regional terms, therefore, the intensification of local production to meet increasing local demands meant that relatively less wheat and flour were being exported to either St. Louis or Chicago during the mid-1850s. In the St. Louis market, this decline was especially sharp. In the 1840s at least half the wheat grown in the upper valley found its way to St. Louis. By 1850 only 1 bushel in 4 was exported south. From another perspective, the percentage of wheat received at St. Louis that came from the upper valley was also declining. In the 1850s, St. Louis received 600,000 bushels of wheat from the upper Mississippi, less than one-fourth of its total wheat receipts. This was down significantly from a 42 percent figure in 1842. St. Louis was losing its produce trading contacts with the upper river, a development that implies a similar loss in trade as well.[30]

There was, quite frankly, little St. Louis could do about it. Part of the decline was due to factors over which its hinterland towns had full control. If both local production and local demand were soaring, then local merchants, without interference from the entrepôt, would naturally have the advantage and gain the most. For the first time in more than two decades, hinterland merchants possessed relative freedom where and with whom to trade because their profits were not based on credit arrangements with the entrepôt. What is interesting about this recent settlement-demand effect, therefore, is the independence and sense of centrality that it seems to have given hinterland towns. Controlling a regional trading network based on the receipt, milling, and resale of wheat and flour to a regional population, river-town merchants felt they were now in a position to pick their economic arrangements rather than have them dictated by the entrepôt. The overtures made to Chicago and New York can be seen in this light. Whatever the cause, however, and whatever its impact on merchandising and the arrangement of urban function, it should also be noted that within a decade the same towns, in another system, returned to their secondary functional role as collectors and transshippers of flour and wheat between the country and the entrepôt.

In contrast to the northward spread and "filling in" of the hinterland in the grain trade, the marketing and processing of hogs for regional markets became, for a variety of economic reasons, more concentrated around St. Louis.

29 Tilson, *History of Quincy*, 107; Joseph T. Holmes, *Quincy in 1857. Or, facts and figures exhibiting its advantages, resources, manufactures and commerce* (Quincy, Ill. 1857), 29.
30 U.S. Census office, *Sixth census*; Scharf, *St. Louis*, 1126.

Initially, in the 1830s Alton, Illinois, took advantage of its direct contacts with the Ohio River and its proximity to corn and hog production in the southern part of the valley to become the largest producer of pork products in the valley. In 1837 Alton packing houses prepared enough pork to supply local needs, drive down area prices, and halt the importation of that commodity from Cincinnati. Four years later Alton packed 47,000 hogs and shipped out more than "8000 tons of pork in various stages of preparation to St. Louis and beyond."[31] By that time, however, new towns to the north were doing to Alton's trade what it had been able to do to Cincinnati's trade only a few years before – replacing imports with locally produced goods. By 1841 and 1842 pork packing had become widespread throughout the Illinois River valley. In Peoria, for example, 10,000 hogs were packed during the 1841 season. During the same period, production in Quincy rose from 400 hogs in 1834, to 500 in 1837, and to 10,500 by 1841. A major packing house had been built there between 1838 and 1841, making Quincy another important local supplier of pork for the river trade.[32]

The most important development of the early 1840s was the entrance of St. Louis into the packing business. From 1843 through 1845, 13,000 to 16,000 hogs were packed there each winter. Most of the swine were raised in adjacent Missouri counties. But it was in 1845–6, when over 30,000 hogs were packed in town plants, that "the business of cutting and curing meat for distant markets commenced." Within two years production doubled again to 69,000 hogs packed, and by 1850–1 as many as 200,000 hogs were packed in St. Louis. Many of these hogs came from the lower Illinois River valley.[33]

The impact of this great increase in production on nearby packing towns is evident in the stagnation of business at both Alton and Quincy. While St. Louis production rose from 16,000 to 200,000 hogs packed between 1843 and 1851, Alton production slumped from 37,000 to less than 20,000 packed.[34] At Springfield, where hog packing in the surrounding hinterland was so heavy, the number of hogs packed remained at between 3,000 and 9,000. At Pekin, Peoria, and Beardstown, about 25,000 hogs were packed annually between 1847 and 1851, but little increase was reported in subsequent years.[35] Within

31 St. Louis Chamber of Commerce, *Proceedings of the St. Louis chamber of commerce*, 17.
32 S. W. Augustus Mitchell, *Illinois in 1838* (Philadelphia, 1838), 116; Henry Asbury, *Reminiscences of Quincy* (Quincy, Ill., 1882), 113; Tilson, *History of Quincy*, 157; Holmes, *Quincy in 1857. Or facts and figures*, 12; *Quincy Whig*, February 28, 1854.
33 St. Louis Chamber of Commerce, *Report of the committee appointed by the chamber of commerce*, 9–11.
34 *American Quarterly Register and Magazine 1* (May 1848): 128–9; *Galena Gazette and Advertiser*, March 13, 1846.
35 *Peoria Weekly Republican*, January 23, 1852.

four years, the amount of packing at St. Louis equaled almost all the packing done at ports along the Illinois. Such a pattern seems to document the local production of pork, with small surpluses sent downriver, while a considerable number of live hogs must have been shipped to the St. Louis markets for processing export to the south.

While production at Alton fell from above 40,000 in the mid-1840s to less than 20,000 by 1854, the number of hogs packed at Quincy rose steadily from about 20,000 to near 40,000 per year.[36] However, it was even further north beyond the controlling influence of St. Louis that the largest gains were made. In 1847–48 each of the smaller ports below the rapids produced about 5,000 hogs. Above the rapids, however, Keokuk and Fort Madison packed 10,000 hogs each, Burlington 15,000, and Bloomington (Muscatine) 19,000. Although capital was in short supply that far north on the river, local markets were apparently strong enough to support such production. During the 1850 season, production at Keokuk rose to 30,000 hogs packed, but thereafter declined, due in part to short crops in the early 1850s. Only in 1854 did Keokuk packing houses regain 1851 production levels. In 1855, Burlington surged ahead of Keokuk with 50,000 hogs packed. But this surge seems to have been due to anomalous local circumstances because the next season production at both towns was again about the same. Farther north, Davenport, Dubuque, and Galena remained local centers of production, each having less than two packing plants during the period.[37] Not until the use of refrigerated cars and the reorientation of the entire meat production system toward Chicago did these northern river towns find local niches in the broader supply and product-ion system.

Although the financial needs of packing triggered such rapid centralization of the industry to the disadvantage of hinterland depots, the pattern of agricultural production around St. Louis reinforced the centralizing forces at work. Because of heavy competition in the smaller grains, many farmers on the adjacent high-priced ground went into corn and livestock production. As a result, an enormous pool of livestock was available nearby and easily drawn into St. Louis. This fact made it difficult for towns further out to acquire any supply of hogs for packing. Consequently, in sharp contrast to the wheat trade, the production and preparation of hogs tended to reinforce centralizing forces of mercantile activity. For towns like Alton that had lost control of their grain trade as the corn and wheat belts shifted north, therefore, there was little hope that they could regain what they had lost by specializing in hog production.[38]

36 *American Quarterly Register and Magazine* 1 (May 1848): 128–9.
37 H. McCarthy and C. W. Thompson, *Meat Packing in Iowa* (Iowa City, 1933), 9–27, 124–6.
38 Margaret Walsh, "Pork Packing as the Leading Edge of Midwestern Industry, 1835–75," *Agricultural History* 51 (1977): 702–17; Walsh, "Spatial Evolution" 1–22.

The measure of the market

The mechanism that ultimately decided the expansion and contraction of production, the breadth and extent of trade, and its geographic pattern across the region was a product's market price. It was in their response to market prices that the towns and cities of the region were tied to the farmer, and each to one another as part of an integrated market system. So too did the rise and fall of prices, as affected by forces far away, tie local and regional to national reality. Finally, it was the timing of the impact of positive or negative external effects on local or regional development that, to a considerable extent, determined the geographic dispersion of the benefits or detriments caused by such interaction on local revenues, profits, and accumulated capital and thus on the future course of investment and development. In the rise and fall of the general price level of respective markets, therefore, one can discern the underlying forces that helped shape, both synchronically and diachronically, the structure of the regional urban economic system.

For example, the history of the rise and fall of Galena and the adjacent Lead Region can be traced to the internal mechanisms of the lead market. Initially, the high price of lead in the early nineteenth century provided the impetus to trigger a boom in production between 1819 and 1827. [39] In the latter year, as prices continued to rise, miners pushed north into Wisconsin and discovered new rich mineral lodes around Shullsburg and Mineral Point. As a result of such price encouragement, production surged beyond five million pounds, a volume of lead that, upon reaching the East, triggered the market's supply-and-demand mechanisms for the first time. The result was a slight drop in prices. Slow to respond in a burgeoning "rush" investment climate, production continued to increase for two more years, exerting an ever stronger downward pressure on prices. By mid-1829, however, the market had become so glutted and prices were dropping so steadily that creditors cut back on the expansion of the industry and called in loans. The inevitable shake-out and recession followed, resulting in widespread work stoppages and an industry-wide slump that lasted for several years (Table 6.6).

This lead-industry slump persisted even while other sectors of the economy enjoyed prosperous growth, indicating that there had been a serious over-extension and overproduction only in this line of activity. Aware of this problem, Congress intervened to support the market by passing a high tariff against imported English lead, which accelerated the absorption of over-

39 Schockel, "The Settlement and Development of Jo Daviess County, Illinois," 192; *Annual Review*, 31; *Chicago Tribune*, February 7, 1854; Kenneth Owens, *Galena, Grant, and the Fortunes of War* (Rockford, Ill., 1964), 18.

Table 6.6. *The lead trade: production and gross income, 1825–65*

Year	Lead (lbs.)	Average price for 100 lbs. at Galena	Estimated gross income
1825	664,530		
1826	958,842		
1827	5,182,180		
1828	11,105,810		
1829	13,343,150		
1830	7,500,000[a]		
1831	6,000,000[a]		
1832	5,000,000[a]		
1833	7,250,000		
1834	7,750,000		
1835	8,125,000[a]	$2.00	$ 110,000
1836	13,000,000	4.00	520,000
1837	15,000,000		600,000
1838	14,000,000	2.50	351,000
1839	15,000,000		375,000
1840	22,000,000		550,000
1841	30,000,000		750,000
1842	31,353,630	2.24	700,000
1843	39,148,270	2.34	900,000
1844	43,727,040	2.80	1,200,000
1845	54,494,860	2.96	1,613,050
1846	51,268,210	2.89	1,481,650
1847	54,085,920	3.17	1,714,525
1848	47,737,830	3.24	1,546,700
1849	44,025,830	3.67	1,615,730
1850	39,801,230	4.20	1,671,650
1851	33,188,050	4.08	1,354,070
1852	28,603,960	4.12	1,178,485
1853	29,806,980	5.50	1,639,390
1854	26,654,000	5.75[a]	1,532,600
1855	30,126,000	5.90	1,777,435
1856	30,496,000	5.50	1,677,280
1857	34,164,000		
1858			
1859			
1860			
1861	8,136,000		
1862	7,062,517		
1863	16,000,000		
1864			
1865			

Table 6.6 *(cont.)*

ª Estimated figures.
Sources: Bernhard Schockel, "The Settlement and Development of Jo Daviess County, Illinois" in *Geology and Geography of the Galena and Elizabeth Quadrangles,* ed. Arthur C. Trowbridge and Evgene Wesley Shaw (Urbana, Ill., 1916), 192; *Galena Daily Advertiser,* January 11, 1835; *Annual Review, The commercial statistics and history of St. Louis* (St. Louis, 1854), 31; *Chicago Tribune,* February 7, 1854; *Galena Gazette and Advertiser,* January 12, 1861, January 14, 1862; Kenneth Owens, *Galena., Grant, and the Fortunes of War* (Rockford, Ill., 1964), 18.

production. But before the tariff really could have any significant effect, a more general slump in the American economy limited importation and thus, paradoxically, supported the lead market. Eventually, by 1839, demand for lead began to rise beyond the market glut and entrepreneurs were again encouraged to produce lead for a steady-price market.

Unfortunately, with demand so sluggish, it took less than two years for the new wave of production to again approach an oversupply. Again in 1842 prices turned downward. Again Congress sought to halt the decline by restricting foreign imports, this time imposing a stiffer tariff, which all but cut off European imports and provided American producers with a near monopoly in the eastern market. This adjustment, along with a general economic revival after 1843 set the industry back on the road to recovery. Indeed, after 1845 lead producers faced the best scenario the market could offer: readily available capital to invest, increasing demand, rising prices, and the ability to meet that demand with increased production. By 1846 production surged toward record levels, never to be realized again, with strong prices. For Galena and the Lead Region these were the very best of times [40]

But beneath the buoyancy of the late 1840s, the dictates of the growth curve began to make themselves felt. As production increased, so too did competition, and prices began to falter. Moreover, as production continued at record amounts, drawn forth by high prices, miners had to begin to go deeper and deeper in search of new lodes. During the boom of the late 1840s production costs began to rise toward the market price per unit, narrowing profit margins and placing many entrepreneurs under financial pressure. In 1846 Stephen Langworthy of Dubuque estimated that, in spite of the active

[40] James E. Wright, *The Galena Lead District: Federal Policy and Practice* (Madison, Wis., 1966), 100–1, 98; "Walker Tariff Report," in *Tariff Proceedings and Documentation, 1839–57,* 10 vols. Senate Document no.72, 62nd Congress, First Session, (Washington, D.C., 1911) 10: 2028; *Galena Gazette and Advertiser,* August 14, 1846; Schockel, "The Settlement and Development of Jo Daviess County, Illinois," 192.

market, the middling producer was no longer making a profit.[41] And because
there were only limited economies of scale in mining and smelting of lead,
larger producers were only getting by on the strength of previous accumulated
capital resources. Thus, in spite of high demand, high prices, and record
production, there was a growing feeling among producers in the Lead Region
that the limit of expansion had been met and that some kind of shake out was
impending.

It is in this context that the dramatic, even catastrophic, impact of the
Mexican War and then the California Gold Rush on regional production can
best be understood. Lead mining had become a solid and respectable way to
make a small profit each year, but it was no longer a "strike-it-rich" industry.
Therefore, numerous peripheral miners and smelters welcomed the challenge
to give it up and go to war, while many more in 1849–50 compared what they
had heard about financial returns in California and easily decided to leave the
old mined-out shafts that scarred the hills between Galena and Mineral Point.
As a result, thousands of entrepreneurs and miners left the region and hundreds
of mines were left vacant and unworked, open to flooding and cave-ins.
Production, to no one's surprise, plummeted.

In fact, between 1849 and 1853 production fell off by almost 40 percent,
dropping in the latter year to levels of production before the boom. Ironically,
however, as this happened, again the rest of the economy enjoyed prosperity
and the rapid urbanization of the 1850s caused a steady rise in the demand for
lead. This fact, combined with continuing restraints on foreign imports of lead,
supported a rise in market prices and, for those who remained, a return to
good times. But this time, in contrast to the situation in the 1840s, the
production capacity of the industry was simply unable to keep up with rising
domestic demand. As a result, prices stayed ahead of rising production,
resulting in record returns and, for Galena and the Lead Region, a kind of
Indian summer of prosperity.[42] The "positive effects" of this revival were
everywhere to be seen. Those mines that "had been abandoned as too
unproductive to be remunerative" were reopened. High prices in 1853 created
a frenzy of excitement in Galena: "Scarce a man," we are told, "in town was
idle; merchants, lawyers, mechanics, and day laborers with pick and axe and
spade are prospecting almost everywhere."[43] It should be noted, however, that

41 "Report of Stephen Langworthy," in "Walker Tariff Report" in *Tariff Proceedings and Documentation, 1839–57*, 10: 2028.
42 *Galena Daily Advertiser*, July 6, 1847; *Galena Gazette and Advertiser*, September 29, 1848; *History of Jo Daviess County*, 274; St. Louis Chamber of Commerce, *Report of the committee appointed by the chamber of commerce*, 20–21; *History of Dubuque County, Iowa*, 523–5; Schockel, "The Settlement and Development of Jo Daviess County, Illinois," 192–4; *Annual Review*, 31.
43 Letter from James Bailey, Galena, Ill., to Edward Wade, Alton, Ill., March 6, 1853; Edward Wade Papers, Missouri Historical Society, St. Louis.

this revival was primarily among old-timers. Few newcomers or outsiders invested in the revival. Few new mines were opened and there does not seem to have been any improvement in technology or the scale of operations. It was simply a case of using short-term resources to acquire whatever, with minimal effort and investment, could be mined for market. It was a boom of amateurs, not serious investors; short-term, not long; and, ironically, it set the stage for the final collapse of the industry once these mines had been completely worked out. When that happened during the Civil War, the lead market had, so to speak, come apart. Prices and demand remained high, but the industry was unable to respond to the demand. The market, as a working mechanism, had ceased to operate. Production fell off to a thirty-year low in 1865 and continued to decline until almost no lead at all was produced by 1870. [44]

This scenario of the lead market reinforces the image of its autonomous, sui generis existence within the regional economy. The rise and fall of lead prices followed its own dynamics related to supply and demand for lead. The rising production of the 1840s began its ascent during a recession, and then collapsed during a general period of economic prosperity. Likewise, as the rest of the economy sizzled in the mid-1850s, driven on by new waves of technological innovation and development, the lead trade returned artificial short-term gains before collapsing. In terms of wealth the best years of the 1850s equaled those of the 1840s, with production valued at $1.6 million reaching the market in both 1847 and 1855. Indeed, on a pure dollars-and-cents level the $1.7 million revenue in 1857 was the highest annual return in the industry – a fact that reminds one that current wealth often obscures the reality of the structure beneath. [45]

In contrast to the complex interplay between supply and demand in the lead market, the ever-rising tide of wheat and corn and hog production quickly pushed western prices and costs of production into alignment with those in the East, minus the cost of transport with some margin for the better quality of western wheat. As a result, production became extremely sensitive to demand, as reflected in the market price, at a rather early date. This sensitivity was augmented by a general glut in the market caused by the opening of the West, which forced prices even lower toward the break-even level. Indeed, by 1845, the American grain markets already relied on demand from abroad to give prices some buoyancy and to raise farmer's incomes. This was especially true in the West, where in many low-price years, transport costs precluded extensive market activity – a sluggish condition that penned up market expectations for years at a time. As a result, when prices did rise to levels sufficient to encourage western farmers to produce large surpluses, farms were planted

44 Schockel, "The Settlement and Development of Jo Daviess County, Illinois," 193–6.
45 Ibid.

fence row to fence row, vast areas of new land were opened for production, and immigrants streamed into the region, setting in motion brief dramatic booms until corrected by a decline in the price to usual levels. A combination of potential abundance and distance from national markets intertwined to create a volatile regional agricultural economy.

The movement of grain prices before the Civil War is well known and need only be referred to here (Figure 6.3). Break-even market prices, ranging from $.30 to $.50 at St. Louis, a price level that barely enabled Westerners to market wheat beyond the region, tended to move up and down with the general movements of the domestic economy. In the 1830s and 1850s prices tended to be high, whereas prices fell in the late 1830s and early 1840s, for a brief period in the early 1850s, and then again later that same decade. [46] The first external stimulus to this price curve came when the specter of famine in Ireland and Germany in 1845–46 and then the disruptions of the revolutions of 1848 significantly increased European demand for American wheat. [47] In each case, however, huge overproduction from frustrated farmers quickly satisfied the new international demand, which eventually dissipated in any case, and prices returned to their previous level. The fortuitous outbreak of the Crimean War, combined with severe crop failures in western Europe between 1853 and 1856, provided the next stimulus to the sluggish American market, one that was far larger and more important. The fact that this rise in demand occurred simultaneously with a more general prosperity, spurred by a combination of speculation in real estate, land, railroads, and stocks, as well as a major new wave of immigration, gave buoyancy to the market and fueled an inflationary pressure that caused an unprecedented and rarely to be repeated run-up in agricultural prices. [48] In response to the first reports of war, prices jumped from $.90 to $1.50 in St. Louis in early 1853. The large harvest that responded to this price rise pushed prices back down in the fall. But more pressure from war, and the growing renewed threat of famine caused an even greater price rise in the first six months of 1855. Between February and late May, prices at St. Louis soared from just under $1.00 per bushel of wheat to a record $2.19 on June 1. Not surprisingly, a record harvest flooded the market in the fall, pushing prices back toward $1.50 but still providing impressive returns in comparison to the recent past. Indeed, only the collapse of the inflationary pressure that supported such high prices in the crash of 1857

46 Thomas Berry, *Western Prices before 1861* (Cambridge, Mass., 1943), chap. 5; Douglass North, *The Economic Growth of the United States* (New York, 1961), 144–8.

47 Burrows, "Fifty Years," in Quaife, *Early Day,* 187–9, 264–8.

48 Data on prices were recorded every week in the local newspapers: *Galena Gazette and Advertiser* (1837–62), *Quincy Whig* (1843–52); *Alton Telegraph* (1838–45); *Davenport Gazette* (1842–60); *Burlington Hawkeye* (1852–8); *Keokuk Gate City* (1850–5); *Dubuque Express Herald* (1852–8); *Iowa State Democrat* (1840–4); *St. Louis Republican* (1842–52); and *Chicago Tribune* (1850–61).

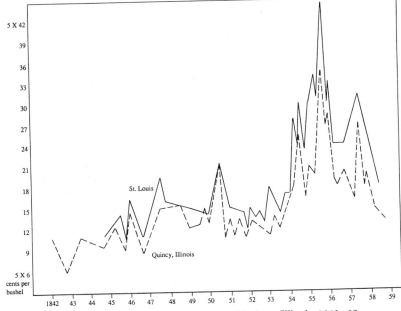

Figure 6.3. Wheat prices at St. Louis and Quincy, Illinois, 1842–60.

finally "corrected" prices, bringing them back to their traditional level. By mid-1858, wheat prices and the prices of other farm products that were pegged to them had returned to $.80, thus ending the decade about where they had begun it.

Given these market-price trends, the economic impact of the shifting patterns of production on the currents of trade becomes more comprehensible. The northward and westward shift of the wheat belt coincided, for example, with the boom in wheat prices, thus rapidly increasing the profits to be made in the center of the valley and focusing trade in that direction. Likewise, towns in the path of this inflated production boom were certain to experience a kind of exaggerated economic expansion. Moreover, the higher prices encouraged longer-distance trading patterns, which increased competition among towns for hinterland control and thus encouraged a more rapid differentiation among urban functions in that area. That the great pool of wealth created by the simultaneous rise in wheat prices, a shift in the wheat belt, rapid in-migration and land sales, and dramatic urban growth should have attracted the interest of outside railroad entrepreneurs should, of course, come as no surprise.

A perhaps more important consequence was the relative shift in the financial support, in the form of accumulated profits, that economic activity in different areas of the valley received, and, secondarily, how the timing of the boom at certain places deepened its effects. Profit margins among farmers varied, and thus any cumulative figure would require numerous diverse calculations, if the data existed. As a substitute, rather crude gross-income figures will suffice to compare the relative gains accrued to the economy in different areas and thus provide the basis of assessing their prospects. The figures show that in the 1840s the strongest gains were being made among the farmers in the southern part of the valley, providing towns in that area with stronger growth. In the mid-1850s, the financial dominance of St. Louis was still apparent, but impressive gains had been made by Quincy and especially by Davenport and Dubuque.

A composite of these figures for the wheat trade, as well as the hog and lead trades, presents a broader picture of relative financial support among the towns on the upper river between 1830 and 1860. In the 1830s wheat brought in negligible returns across the valley. Therefore, Galena, with its income from the lead trade, was clearly the second city behind St. Louis on the upper river. By the mid-1840s the early development of a wheat and grain market had enabled Quincy to reach about 50 percent of Galena's wealth. But it was not until the wheat boom of the mid-1850s that other river towns began to challenge Galena's economic hegemony in the valley. Davenport, for example, achieved 75 percent of Galena's total in 1855 and surpassed the Lead City a few years after that. Dubuque, meanwhile, was right behind. And yet, Galena, with an impressive pool of capital, continued until as late as 1859 to make significant economic decisions in the valley. Of further interest is the speed with which both of these towns also made up relative ground on St. Louis in the mid-1850s, the effect of which has already been suggested. It is important to recognize these locally defined pools of wealth, because it was on the basis of such calculations, though often using different figures and criteria, that contemporaries ultimately based their perception of the relative power among towns and formulated their strategies for action. In a world of still rather simplistic local mercantilist assumptions, profitable trading and the fastest return on one's investment were assumed to be located where there was the greatest amount of productive wealth coming from the hinterland. The extent to which the merchandising activities of valley merchants actually correlated to these shifts in gross income, or developed according to other criteria and concerns, is the primary focus of the next chapter.

PART III

The regional urban system

7

The currents of trade and regional urbanization

Mercantile activity across the upper Mississippi valley developed from the predisposition of settlers toward market farming. Before outsiders began to establish towns with mercantile activity in mind, barter and peddling activity had spread across the southern part of the region. At first, bartering developed because different farmers, having different skills, were unable or unwilling to maintain a self-sufficient existence. Those unable to meet their needs in one area sought out those able to produce more than they needed, and offered something they produced well, which the other farmer needed, in return. As barter activity increased, one or two farmers inevitably perceived the advantages of someone acting as a middleman between the various household demand and supply curves in the neighborhood. Soon thereafter, one of these prototype merchants relocated at some central site and thus established the beginnings of the town market.

Yet most of these local merchants remained isolated from the outside. Therefore, peddlers, perceiving the rising demand for goods, began to move through the region selling those goods that the locals could not make themselves: fine cloth, pots and pans, chinaware, sewing materials, belts and buckles, buttons, brooms, cordage, furniture, and, of course, clocks. By one account, the roads of southern Illinois were full of peddlers during the 1820s. We also know that peddlers out of Cincinnati continued to ply between river wharfs along the Ohio until after 1830. A similar peddling barge did business between St. Louis and the lower rapids, stopping at ports in between, during the 1820s.[1] But it was not until a permanent merchant arrived that the reciprocal relationship developed between agricultural and urban development. The settled merchant was different from the peddler or local merchant in that he purchased his goods on credit from a wholesaler back East or at the nearest entrepôt and, therefore, was under some compulsion to sell goods on credit or in exchange for produce to local farmers. In initiating such activity, he not only triggered the local market and thus connected the well-being of his town to

---

1 Thomas Ford, *A History of Illinois* (Chicago, 1854), 97; John Tilson, *A History of Quincy* (Quincy, Ill., n.d.), 25–6; Lewis Atherton, *The Pioneer Merchant in Mid-America* (Columbia, Mo., 1971), 45.

agricultural production and marketing but also plugged the local economy into the regional market at St. Louis. Wherever and whenever first merchants established themselves – in and around Alton in 1815, Quincy about 1825, Galena in 1827, Rock Island by 1835, and Dubuque and Davenport after 1840 – grain and livestock rushed into market in return for mercantile goods. Increasing mercantile sales, in turn, triggered more rural specialization and set in motion the dynamic forces upon which urban development depended. [2]

The early reciprocity between the two activities is evident in the relationship between the dominant market crop and the spatial pattern of urban development. As we have already seen, the number of towns established in most counties continued to increase until the average distance between towns was down to about seven to nine miles or, in less populated counties where extensive farming dominated, about ten to twelve miles. The former distance is about the furthest extent that a load of corn could be carried to market and a profit made, whereas the latter, at a slightly further distance, represented the average range, given normal prices, of the portability of wheat. Of these two markets, the wheat market tended to be more active and thus create more dynamic urban centers. The buoyant wheat market, combined with the need to get wheat into market quickly, compelled most farmers to carry their crop to the nearest merchant for sale. There the merchants could, by buying in bulk, take advantage of limited economies of scale, and ship wheat to the market at a lower rate than a farmer could have gotten by himself. Thus the middleman provided the farmer with an extra margin of profit by shortening the distance that he had to carry his crop. In return, the farmer purchased what he needed for the coming season. [3]

In a corn-growing district the relatively limited external demand for corn encouraged many farmers to feed their corn to hogs and then drive them to some more distant packing town on the river, reinforcing the centralization in the industry that has already been noted. Hence, many towns in the interior did not necessarily command the loyalty of nearby farmers. Likewise, when they did, the pattern of trade was often considerably more spread out across the year, as corn farmers marketed their crop over the course of the winter after the harvest. Therefore, not only were towns closer together in the southern regions of the valley, but they also tended to be less vigorous, a fact

---

2 William V. Pooley, "The Settlement of Illinois, 1830 to 1850" *Bulletin of the University of Wisconsin*, History Series 1 (May 1908): 320; Tilson, *History of Quincy*, 25–56; Bernhard Schockel, "The Settlement and Development of Jo Daviess County, Illinois," in *The Geology and Geography of the Galena and Elizabeth Quadrangle*, ed. Arthur C. Trowbridge and Eugene Wesley Shaw (Urbana, Ill., 1916), 184; J. M. D. Burrows, "Fifty Years in Iowa. Being the Personal Reminiscences of J. M. D. Burrows," in *Early Days of Rock Island and Davenport:The Narratives of J. W. Spencer and J. M. D. Burrows*, ed. Milo Quaife (Chicago, 1942) 150, 176–7.

3 Morton Rothstein, "Antebellum Wheat and Cotton Exports: Contrasting Marketing and Organization," *Agricultural History* 40 (April 1966): 91–100.

that enabled one or two towns to control far more towns in their hinterland than was generally the case further north. [4] In addition, many of the towns further south in the valley had been established when wheat was the major market crop there, and then left to languish in the slightly different spatial arrangements of the corn and hog trades. That this distance is just about how far the average farmer could haul a load of wheat on his own should be no surprise. Likewise, as we have seen, the further from the entrepôt, the closer together these secondary shipping points were located, until one reaches the distance from market at which only local market towns providing local exchange services exist somewhat more widely spaced from one another. And yet, in spite of varying spatial economics, towns in each area continued to grow so long as the agricultural production and trade expanded.

At some point in this process, however, those towns along the river that transshipped goods from and distributed goods to interior market towns became more specialized wholesaling centers between the hinterland and the regional entrepôt. Rather than being directly related to the volume of produce receipts, such activity depended on the number of towns to which it could provide those services. The wholesale merchants thus became one step removed from the direct reciprocal relationship between local agricultural production and merchandising. The degree of specialization within these wholesaling towns, and the urban market for goods and services within them, quite apart from the rural demand for the same services, further insulated these towns from the direct impact of the rural economy. And as this happened, town merchants, rather than passively accepting their role as mere middlemen between the rural population and St. Louis wholesalers, began to encourage economic development actively and to broaden their markets, and their regional function, by competing against other towns within the system. This could involve upgrading local merchandising to include forwarding and commissioning services, which often meant bypassing the entrepôt and acquiring the goods elsewhere, or launching an initiative to gain a new trading territory by means of novel merchandising techniques or the support of railroad construction or river improvement. [5]

Between 1840 and 1850, therefore, a flood of merchants entered the upper valley. They reinforced the divergence from the produce markets and, by encouraging more merchants to specialize, reoriented the concerns of other people in towns away from the hinterland. In the first place, specialized merchants never experienced the reciprocal relationship between local trade and hinterland production the way that earlier, more general merchants had. They could no longer estimate next year's needs on the concrete basis of this

4 Johann Heinrich von Thünen, *The Isolated State.*, ed. Carla M. Wartenberg (Oxford 1966).
5 This discussion is informed by Allan Pred, *Urban Growth and City Systems in the United States, 1840–60* (Cambridge, Mass., 1980), 48–65.

year's business in return for a certain volume of produce. The greater competition among merchants for both the farmers' produce and other townsmen's and interior merchants' dollars compelled them to become much more efficient in their trading practices, both in the selection and timing of the receipt of their goods. To sell, goods had to be of better quality, bought from St. Louis or from the East, and in the store early enough to meet the seasonal shopping rushes. [6]

As a result, orders had to be out months in advance, sometimes even before the current year's final returns were in. Often a merchant would leave on a buying trip uncertain exactly of the final tally on a season's business. It became, under such circumstances, more and more difficult to estimate the next year's needs on the basis of this year's business. The extension of credit to farmers, to enable them to purchase goods year round, placed one more time lag between production, monetary returns, and future market strategies. In the face of such a balancing act, and amid such competition, it is no wonder that merchants began to focus not so much on the returns of production (which they knew did not equal the amount of goods being offered by all local merchants) but rather on providing the most attractive and useful goods so as to assure getting at least one's fair share of that local return. What mattered was the ability of local merchants to play with these outside merchants, or even, as we will see, to compete directly with them. It was in this way that a town prospered and gained the potential to broaden its economic function within the regional system. [7]

As merchants focused more on broadening their trade, so too did they work on upgrading the local infrastructure and deepening the local economy. Some invested in industrial activity, focusing on those lines of production for which some supply advantage existed. Not only would such industry increase local profits, it also would create more jobs, and thus increase local demand for goods and services upon which local specialized merchants depended for further expansion of business. Capital investment, further mercantile special-ization, and nascent industrial activity would, in turn, draw more farmers into

6 John Beauchamp Jones (Luke Shortfield), *The western merchant. A narrative* (Philadelphia, 1849), 47–9, 214. Also see Timothy R. Mahoney, "Urban History in a Regional Context: River Towns on the Upper Mississippi, 1840–60" *Journal of American History* 72 (September 1985): 318–39, table 1, 330–1.

7 This discussion is derived from a wide variety of contemporary mercantile records. Illinois credit report ledgers, XCVIII, CXXXIX, CLXXIII; Iowa credit report ledgers, XVI, XXXI, XLVII; and Missouri credit report ledgers, XXXVI, XXXVII; R. G. Dun and Company Collection, Baker Library, Harvard University Graduate School of Business Administration, Cambridge, Mass.; Burrows, "Fifty Years," in Quaife, *Early Day*, 162; Augustus Chetlain, *Recollections of seventy years* (Galena, Ill., 1899), 47; Allan Pred, *City Systems in Advanced Economies: Past Growth, Present Processes and Future Development Options* (New York, 1977), 16–20, 66–70.

town both to sell produce and to buy goods and services. Town economic development became the catalytic force in regional economic development. Indeed, so important did the policy of stimulating town growth became on the local agenda that local merchants began to loose sight of the actual functional position that their town played within the broader urban system and began to argue, parochially, that each town could develop along lines parallel to the development of the entrepôt. Although the interaction between the town and country never ceased and continued to generate economic development, it became a secondary force, the foundation of the local market. To establish a role within the regional system of trade and to connect local progress to regional mechanisms of urban development became the agreed-upon strategy for success. To survive and prosper, a town had to rise above the web of local trade and exchange.

Such efforts to connect themselves to broader economic interactions, whether in the produce market or, more practically, in merchandising, are evident both in the lack of any smooth, upward-moving progression in specializing from retailing to wholesaling or forwarding and commissioning merchandising, as well as in the rather clear evidence of nonhierarchical contacts and interactions. The former indicate that outsiders often arrived with the intent of placing a town in the context of some regional framework of trade and exchange, regardless of its previous local development, whereas the latter indicates that towns, both from the center toward the fringe and from the fringe toward the nearest or even outside entrepôts, did not accept the constraints of a rigid, functional hierarchical structure among towns and cities. The fact that in time, as entrepôts became the overwhelmingly dominant centers of regional trade, many towns and cities did settle into set relationships does not mean that such interactions were the symptoms of a period of turbulent changes in the structure of regional systems. Rather, they reflect an openness, porosity, and ever-changing arrangement based on a search for a comparative advantage in one function, or one critical variable that would give them the edge in a function, over time. This dynamic is characteristic of all urban systems but, given the unsettled reality, the abundance of space that, as Robert Wiebe has suggested, encouraged competitors to try to outflank actors near the center by successfully gaining a foothold on the fringe and then returning to the core to compete, it is especially characteristic of American urban systems. [8]

The shifting patterns of merchandising among the towns along the upper river demonstrate this characteristic well. In the mid-1830s both St. Louis and Alton merchants were vying for control of the trade of the upper valley. That trade, as noted, had begun almost fifteen years before and had gradually

8 Mahoney, "Urban History in a Regional Context," 318–39; Robert Wiebe, *The Opening of American Society* (New York, 1984), 287–90.

developed into an outpost monopoly between St. Louis merchants and retailers in Galena. St. Louis's advantage was based on its recently having broken free of purchasing arrangements in Cincinnati and shifting the location of its wholesaling purchases. Their relative proximity to New Orleans compared with that of Cincinnati merchants gave them a natural locational advantage for trade further west. Initially, St. Louis merchants seem to have purchased predominantly in Philadelphia, but the rise of New York as a wholesaling center after the opening of the Erie Canal and the establishment of more efficient contacts with English exporters drew St. Louis merchants to New York as well. Tying into New York's deepening contacts with New Orleans, St. Louis rapidly developed as the entrepôt of the upper Mississippi and trans-Mississippi West. By 1837 there were ninety merchants located at St. Louis, at least a third of whom were more specialized forwarding and commissioning or wholesaling merchants, both activities reflecting the towns growing entrepôt status.[9]

St. Louis's early lead did not, however, go unchallenged. Indeed, much of St. Louis's advantage in bringing trade in from the East was based on its merchants' control of the lead trade, which they maintained, as we have seen, by monopolizing the shipping lines between St. Louis and Galena. By shipping lead south and east, most St. Louis merchants had direct access to a captive demand that by itself was sufficient to provide a considerable return. Across the rest of the region, its merchants' control was considerably less impressive. In the southern valley the web of contacts between places like Alton, Beardstown, Peoria, and Cincinnati remained intact. And in most cases it seems that this was trade that literally passed right in front of St. Louis's wharf without St. Louis merchants being able to step in between upriver retailers and wholesalers and their traditional Cincinnati contacts. The strength of this resistance to St. Louis's regional hegemony is evident in the disposition of specialized merchants along the Mississippi and lower Illinois: seventy-two merchants in Alton, eleven in Quincy, thirty in Peoria. Of these, the *Peck Gazette* of 1837 indicates that two merchants each in Peoria, Beardstown, and Pekin and twenty in Alton were wholesalers. The merchants of Alton, we are told, "had a heavy trade with New Orleans" and also purchased directly from Philadelphia and New York.[10] A letter book of William Morrow (see Chapter 5) indicates that gradually their eastern connections were, as in St. Louis, shifting to New York. In his case, of the sixty-three interregional bills he negotiated, forty-five (71 percent) were from

---

9 Mahoney, "Urban History in a Regional Context,," 328
10 John M. Peck, *A gazetteer of Illinois* (Philadelphia, 1837), 149; *Alton city directory and business mirror, for 1858* (Alton, Ill., 1858), 20; Augustus S. Mitchell, *Illinois in 1837* (Philadelphia, 1837), 114; William T. Norton, ed., *The Centennial History of Madison County, Illinois, and Its People* (Chicago, 1912), 91–2.

New York. [11] Alton's role as a wholesaling center, in the words of John Peck, map maker and gazetteer, "commanded a large portion of the upper Mississippi and Illinois rivers and the interior country for a hundred miles." [12]

This is not to say, however, that even secondary towns like Peoria, Pekin, or Galena received all their goods via Alton's wharf and passively accepted secondary roles. In fact, Alton had as much trouble controlling its hinterland trade as St. Louis had in infiltrating Alton's trade. St. Louis's problem seems to have been due to the fact that "prices in St. Louis were higher than the cost between Philadelphia and St. Louis warranted." As a result, hinterland merchants were encouraged to bypass St. Louis and either trade with Alton or buy their own goods directly from the East. In Galena, for example, mention was made as early as 1828 of merchants "who bought goods at Philadelphia, New York, and other markets, and had them shipped via New Orleans to Main Street." About the same time, Horatio Newhall, a Galena druggist, purchased his supplies in Philadelphia on a buying trip that he recorded in a series of letters home. The Corwiths, meanwhile, seem to have divided their purchases between St. Louis and New York, whereas Moses Meeker supplied his outpost trade from Cincinnati. [13]

Further south, Cincinnati contacts became more widespread. We know from contemporary credit reports that Peoria had direct contacts with Cincinnati, a connection reinforced by the operations of an Illinois River steamboat that ran from Peoria to Alton to Cincinnati, bypassing St. Louis. [14] Even a St. Louis observer conceded, before 1850, that "merchants throughout the western portion of Illinois and even Missouri purchased many kinds of goods in Cincinnati and Louisville and brought them around here for sale." Among these merchants was the first permanent merchant at Davenport, Iowa, James Burrows, who was supplied by his uncle, a prominent Cincinnati wholesaler. So too supplies for several of the upriver forts were, throughout the 1840s, acquired at Cincinnati rather than at St. Louis. [15]

Around 1840, therefore, only a rough outline of an integrated urban mercantile system was apparent on the upper river. St. Louis's evolving role in the hinterland shadow of Cincinnati was based primarily on its control of a lucrative export trade. Gradually, it would use the economic advantages it accrued from that trade to stave off challengers, to undercut competitors, and

11 Letter Book and Record of William Morrow, Alton, Ill., 1837, Missouri Historical Society, St. Louis.
12 Peck, *A gazetteer of Illinois*, 149.
13 Atherton, *The Pioneer Merchant in Mid-America*, 67–9; *The History of Jo Daviess County* (Chicago, 1879), 305, 241–2; letters of Horatio Newhall, Illinois State Historical Society, Springfield, Ill.
14 Illinois credit report ledgers, XCVIII, CXXXIX, CLXXIII, R. G. Dun and Company Collection; Peck, *A gazetteer of Illinois*, 147–9, 153, 251, 259.
15 John Hogan, *Thoughts about the city of St. Louis, her commerce and manufactures, railroads and Etc.* (St. Louis, 1854), 1; Burrows, "Fifty Years," in Quaife, *Early Day*, 137, 141–4.

to draw more and more hinterland merchandising trade to its wharf. In the meantime, the bypassing of the entrepôt by upriver towns to buy in Cincinnati or in the East was rampant and widespread. Once received at the larger mercantile towns in the southern part of the valley, these goods were then sold to the few wholesalers and retailers who had settled at nascent interior towns.

So long as these networks were primarily organized to ship goods into a region, which were then exchanged locally for some produce or currency, such bypassing was relatively easy to achieve and to maintain. But as merchandising became tied to sales on credit or for crops sold in the developing regional market, hinterland merchants, relying increasingly on the ability to sell local supplies to St. Louis merchants and acquire credit from them, found it easier and more convenient simply to acquire their goods in return for those credits. Therefore, as the grain and livestock markets became more integrated around St. Louis, its merchants were gradually able to gain control of the wholesaling trade in their neighborhood. A St. Louis observer made a direct connection between the developing produce trade and St. Louis's improved position as the primary source of eastern goods for hinterland merchants. In 1852, he wrote that "the great amounts of produce in the West passing through the city, are drawn against by bankers in the interior of Missouri, Illinois, and Iowa." By tying new merchants arriving in the West to credit arrangements in St. Louis, the banks thus encouraged merchants to do their business there in order to facilitate the settling of accounts. Moreover, a general lowering of prices for eastern goods, as the volume of goods arriving in St. Louis rose, also encouraged more and more hinterland merchants to choose St. Louis over the East. In 1852 one local writer remarked that the notion that prices were higher in St. Louis than warranted due to the cost of transport from the East was, by them, "fallacious," and that the "eastern cities offer [the western merchant] no inducements superior to those constantly held forth" in the St. Louis market. The result was to turn much of the western wholesaling business "that was previously transacted in Eastern cities" to St. Louis. [16]

To some extent, this shift may have been reinforced by the growing number of hinterland merchants and the increased competition among them for lower prices on better-quality goods. Given their smaller profit margin, fewer merchants may have been wealthy enough to incur the cost and risks of buying their own goods. Likewise, one suspects that St. Louis's domination of the steamboat system after 1840 may have given local merchants shipping-rate preferences. In either case, the effect on regional merchants was the same. Around Alton, J. R. Kimball reported that after 1840 "the country all around Alton depended chiefly on St. Louis for goods." Likewise, in the mid-1840s, a

16 The St. Louis Chamber of Commerce, *Report of the committee appointed by the chamber of commerce, upon the trade, commerce and manufactures of St. Louis, embracing a period of several years* (St. Louis, 1852), 27–9.

Davenport editor noted that "our merchants are in receipt of their goods, while others are in St. Louis purchasing." A closer look at the connections between Davenport and St. Louis as recorded by R. G. Dun and Company confirms this impression of trade having shifted from Cincinnati to St. Louis in a matter of just a few years. [17]

Even at Galena, a town that had been buying in the East from the beginning of trade there, and continued to do so in spite of the strong lead-trade connection with St. Louis, the general trend was clearly in St. Louis's favor. Of the fourteen merchants whose places of purchase were listed in credit reports during the 1850s, seven (50 percent) bought in St. Louis, two in Chicago, and only one in Cincinnati. The rest bought in New York. [18]

This filling in of the mercantile system and its shift to the west side of the river are evident in the numbers of merchants who had located at various river towns by the mid-1850s. Between 1850 and 1855, while the number of forwarding and commissioning merchants remained stable at Galena, Rock Island, and Quincy, their numbers at Davenport, Dubuque, Keokuk, and, to a lesser extent, Fort Madison and Burlington steadily increased. The first such specialized merchants only seem to have crossed the river in the 1851 or 1852 season. But as more people crossed the river, and the productive base of western trade shifted north and west, outside merchants were drawn into eastern Iowa. [19]

The effect of this movement was to heighten the impact of the inefficiencies of the transport system above St. Louis by making its spatial–economic biases more apparent. Nowhere were the burdens of having to bear excessive short-distance transport costs heavier than in the vicinity of the rapids on the upper river. As noted, merchants in both Keokuk and Davenport had sought to alleviate these cost burdens as early as 1840. In 1847 Burlington was singled out in the offical report of the Chicago River and Harbor Convention as a town single-handedly suffering the impact of the high cost of crossing the rapids. [20] The year before a similar convention at Rock Island had called for the improvement of the rapids as a prerequisite for continued local development both there and at Davenport. But the selective impact of such costs, combined with jealousies based on the anticipated functional arrangement among towns resulting from such improvements, thwarted any unified movement. For

17 John M. Reynolds, *Sketches of the country on the northern route from Belleville, Illinois, to the city of New York* (Belleville, Ill., 1854), 64; *Davenport Gazette*, April 29, 1847; Iowa credit report ledger, XLVII, R. G. Dun and Company Collection.
18 Illinois credit report ledger, XCVIII, R. G. Dun and Company Collection.
19 Mahoney, "Urban History in a Regional Context," 330–1.
20 Delegates to the Chicago River and Harbor Convention, *The commerce and navigation of the valley of the Mississippi; and also that appertaining to the City of St. Louis; considered, with reference to the improvement, by the general government, of the Mississippi River and its principal tributaries* (St. Louis, 1847), 16–20.

example, those towns further north realized that their distance from St. Louis would preclude the possibility of their becoming secondary entrepôts. For them, improvement of the rapids seemed like a fine way to encourage more trade to bypass them. Likewise, Keokuk merchants realized that their locational advantage was to a considerable extent based on their position just below the rapids, a natural location for a break of bulk and transshipping place. Towns in between such as Burlington or Fort Madison found themselves torn between diverging local interests on both their south and north.

As trade into Iowa increased, this divergence in interest became more apparent and operative in explaining the different local strategies for acquiring a regionally oriented economic function. When a regional conference on the issue of river improvement was held in St. Louis in 1849, these differences became public. Apparently, delegates from Davenport and Keokuk got into a heated argument over whose perspective ought to represent the general Iowa position at the conference proceedings. The dispute quickly spilled into local papers when the editor of the *Davenport Gazette* openly took issue with the Keokuk editor's assumption that Keokuk's interests and those of the rest of the state were parallel. He argued that Keokuk's interests favoring St. Louis encouraged town merchants, for obvious reasons, to advocate only limited river improvements. The necessity of stopping at Keokuk was, after all, what gave the town its purpose. And that purpose was set firmly against the interests of towns to its north. [21]

In response to this exchange, Davenport merchants organized another convention to be held locally in October 1849. The conference was heavily attended only by merchants from the Davenport and nearby area. The delegates advocated establishing railroad connections with Chicago and resolved to begin planning to achieve this end. At first, interest focused on a plan to build a railroad between Peoria and Burlington. But Burlington merchants were unable to interest enough people and raise the money needed to encourage a railroad company to begin construction. [22] It was this effort that Davenport merchants quickly took over and within a year, after they agreed with Chicago investors that any road would run from Chicago to Davenport, a public bond issue was authorized and a sale campaign begun. Key to the impetus behind this effort was the Chicago support, and it was clear that if Chicago investors were going to put down money on such a project, the railroad would have to come directly to that city. A similar effort was launched further north, but as noted, Chicago merchants were unable to gain the support of Galena's steamboat-based mercantile elite. As a result, they offered the opportunity to merchants in Dubuque who, in spite of their role in the

21 Ibid.; *Davenport Gazette*, August 11, September 13, October 11, November 1, 1849; *St. Louis Republican*, October 7–14, 1849.
22 *Davenport Gazette*, November 8, December 13, 1849.

steamboat company to the north, eagerly gave their support. Therefore, during the very years that population and production were shifting north, and the mercantile contacts between St. Louis and its upriver hinterland were deepening, forces were at work that, within a season or two, would totally unravel those hard-fought-for connections.

The speed and finality of those shifting trading patterns are reflected in the changing numbers and specialized activities of different merchants at the towns along the upper valley after 1853. While Galena lost three forwarding and commissioning merchants and their numbers remained the same at Rock Island and Quincy between 1854 and 1856, seven new forwarding merchants each settled in Davenport and Keokuk, eight in Burlington, and ten established themselves in Dubuque, across from the railhead of the Chicago and Galena Union Railroad at Dunleith. The locational choices of these merchants were still rather provisional, as it was not yet certain how much traffic would be moving along each of the major railroad lines west of Chicago. Within two years, this pattern became clear, as did the new mercantile arrangements. While Dubuque added eight and Davenport two forwarding merchants to their local establishments, Burlington and Keokuk had lost all but two or three each. Only one forwarding merchant remained in Galena, while seven hung on in Quincy, encouraged perhaps by the possible impact of the newly opened Hannibal and St. Joseph Railroad, which gave Chicago wholesalers access to the trans-Mississippi West via the Gem City. [23]

The close correlation in the timing of these moves, the construction of the railroads, and the demonstrated shifts in production patterns between 1854 and 1858 should not, however, be taken as evidence that one integrated regional urban economic system centered at a new entrepôt (Chicago) simply moved in and replaced the old system. Such a description would oversimplify the economic confusion caused by such intersections. Alongside Chicago merchants in the towns along the upper river were also merchants from Cincinnati, New York, and even Boston, each trying to establish for their cities a foothold in a market in which they once had, or would like to have, direct contacts. Such interest inevitably increased the supply of goods reaching these disputed areas and dramatically heightened competition among an excess of merchants. [24]

The towns within the target region, wanting to be in on the subsequent development of any new arrangement, added to this volatility by openly courting such contacts and directly trading with nonentrepôt cities. The ability to succeed in such an effort depended, of course, on the state of the local economy and its prospects for growth. For example, Chicago entrepreneurs,

23 D. A. Barrows, *Annals of Iowa*, (Iowa City, 1863; reprint, 1970), 118–21; Mahoney, "Urban History in a Regional Context," 333–4, 330–1.
24 Mahoney, "Urban History in a Regional Context," 329–32.

when searching for a railhead site in eastern Iowa or western Illinois, seem to have become aware of the northward shift of both the wheat- and corn-producing areas near St. Louis as immigrants poured into the middle part of the valley. This perception worked in Davenport's favor and against that of Galena or, at least over the short term, Quincy.[25]

Unfortunately, the decision-making process in such matters was undermined by a clear divergence between locals and outsiders as to what constituted the best interests of the town. To the outsider, a town's attractiveness was based entirely on its economic location vis-à-vis the existing transport system controlled by the entrepôt, its spatial position in relation to other towns already functioning within that system, and its proximity to the center of agricultural production and to the main currents of in-migration. The willingness of town merchants and politicans to support financially their end of the construction project seems to have been a secondary factor that may have tipped a close decision in favor of one town or another. But, in reality, no town deserved any special treatment, or meant anything more to the decision makers than any other. The railroad, no matter what towns it ran through, would provide growth and development for the entrepôt and expand the range of its hinterland control.

For town merchants and entrepreneurs, however, considerably more was at stake. Where there was only one railroad through an area, access to that railroad was the sine qua non of future economic development – hence, the almost desperate ends to which locals would go to entice a railroad company to run its survey through town limits. But we should not overestimate the receptiveness of local entrepreneurs. It is also clear that many entrepreneurs placed the maximization of the town's economic development ahead of any other criteria and that sometimes the railroad, or the current arrangement being promoted, might not offer the best avenue to economic growth. This hesitation was due to the end that locals had in mind, which usually was at odds with the role outsiders perceived the town would be pleased to play.[26]

It is no wonder, given the different intent of these strategies, that when two regional systems intersected, more outsiders penetrated the region and more regional entrepreneurs went in search of new outside contacts. The former sought to wrest some of the trade away before the nearest entrepôt with locational and transport advantages gained control, whereas the latter sought to use the relative freedom of such a period to establish potentially fruitful contacts for later in its economic development. Of these two phenomena, the first is easier to document. From credit reports, newspaper accounts, and shipping information, we know that several of the newcomers into Davenport

25 Ibid.
26 Ibid., 338.

and Dubuque were indeed New Yorkers or New Englanders who sought to establish new trading contacts with the West. Further south, the extension of the Baltimore and Ohio to St. Louis in 1857 encouraged Cincinnati merchants to try to reestablish some contacts in its old western hinterland.[27] Allan Pred has argued, using a survey of place names mentioned in Cincinnati newspaper advertisements between 1850 and 1860 as evidence, that Cincinnati definitely reasserted its presence in the upper valley after 1854. To some extent it sought to do this through rather than around Chicago. In the course of the decade, its contacts with Chicago increased ninefold. Less impressive was the reestablishment of trading contacts directly with St. Louis, the number doubling in the late 1850s. In any case, Cincinnati merchants reestablished a wholesaling presence where they had been absent for more than a decade, in towns such as Quincy, Hannibal, Keokuk, Fort Madison, Rock Island, Muscatine, Galena, and even Cassville, Wisconsin. Noteworthy is the absence of Davenport or Dubuque in this list; Cincinnati merchants probably conceded both towns, given their strong railroad connections, to Chicago.[28]

In the other direction, upriver merchants actively set out across the East to establish new contacts. For example, a number of merchants who were part of the transshipping boom at Keokuk in the middle year of the decade traded directly with New York. Likewise, there is cursory evidence that other towns along the river initially "settled towards New York" rather than buy goods in the Windy City. Before they went out of business, Galena merchants still boasted of " buying in the markets of the world." At Quincy in 1857, it was reported that "our merchants purchase their stocks in the East to as good advantage as at Chicago or St. Louis houses." Another Quincy merchant went so far as to claim direct importing from Europe via New Orleans during this period. Merchants in Burlington also seem to have been involved in similar bypassing activities.[29] These attempts should be seen as efforts to give each town more leverage and flexibility in dealing with the dominant nearby entrepôt and to establish a broader economic functional basis for the future.

The cumulative effect of these contacts, in combination with those more directly tied with the produce trade between the river towns and either Chicago and St. Louis, was to flood the region with merchandise between 1854 and 1857. The high price of grain, the rising value of land, and the surge of immigration, of course, further inflated the overtrading caused by the confusion in traditional trading arrangements. The extent to which this trade had surpassed current production is evident in the very rough figures we have comparing the amount of imports from the East with regional agricultural and

27 Ibid., 326–7, 329
28 Pred, *City Systems in Advanced Economies*, 161–3.
29 Daniel S. Curtiss, *Western portraiture, and emigrant's guide* (New York, 1852), 330.

mineral production figures (Table 7.1). At the focal points of the rush to expand trade, imports exceeded exports by three to five times in the late 1850s.[30] Very clearly, to enable that volume of trade to be maintained, western merchants and, indirectly, western farmers who borrowed from the merchants to increase their standard of living were mortgaging their futures for the sake of current investment. The obvious hope was that continuing population and production growth, combined with increased productivity made possible by these material investments on credit, would increase regional capital and enable these debts to be paid off. As yet Westerners had no idea of the fragility of the production base and the market on which they were pinning such hopes.

To many contemporaries, running such debts was a prescription for a kind of colonial dependence under the heel of eastern creditors – merchants, manufacturers, and especially bankers. To those who believed that each town had the potential to create its own centralized independent economy, which could generate genuine economic development on a level with that in older entrepôts, such imbalances of imports over exports reflected an impatience, an overexcitement beyond the capacity of the local economy, and thus an effort by outsiders to distort, and eventually to take control of, the linear course of local development. To grow in a healthy manner required that one advance slowly, gradually, surely, with credit used only as a means to expand the economy into the next year. Given the rapid growth of population and the immediate needs for buildings, housing, streets, and wharves, some imbalance was accepted as normal – perhaps as much as 2 or 3:1. But hard work, propriety, and self-reliance would, it was hoped, quickly pay off those debts and set the economy on a surplus basis. More economic growth and development would eventually enable the local economy to draw other local economies actively under its control.[31]

The sudden and alarming increase in imbalances, however, drew concern from both local and regional commentators. Under the pressure of increased immigration, increased production, and rampant speculation, imports into Keokuk soared by 1857 to almost six times annual exports. Davenport's deficit rose briefly to 6:1. And even Galena, away from the speculative frenzy in eastern Iowa, saw its imports quadruple over annual exports, which as we have

30 Iowa credit report ledger, XXXI, R. G. Dun and Company Collection; *Galena Daily Advertiser*, May 10, 1852; *Business directory and review of trade, commerce, and manufactures of the city of Burlington, Iowa for the year ending May 1, 1856* (Burlington, Iowa 1856), 11; Pat H. Redmond, *A History of Quincy and its men of mark* (Quincy, Ill., 1869), 111. Joseph Holmes, *Quincy in 1857. Or, facts and figures* (Quincy, Ill., 1857), 20. For a detailed acounting of the figures in Table 7.1 see Appendix G.

31 Henry C. Carey, *The Principles of political economy* (Philadelphia, 1837–40); idem., *The harmony of interests, agriculture, manufacturing, and commercial* (Philadelphia, 1851). For uses of his ideas in the western press, see *Warsaw Signal*, May 21, 1841; *Davenport Gazette*, January 13, 1843; *Galena Daily Advertiser*, June 2, June 3, 1852. Jane Jacobs, *Cities and the Wealth of Nations* (New York, 1983) Anthony Wallace, *Rockdale* (New York, 1978), 394–7.

Table 7.1. *The local balance of trade: imports versus exports in river towns,*
1841–60

Town and year	Imports	Exports	Estimated ratio: imports/exports
Dubuque			
1851	$ 1,175,207	$ 233,207	5.0
1852	1,658,450	629,140	2.6
1853	2,400,000	1,000,000	2.4
1854	4,900,000	1,500,000	3.3
1855	11,266,845	3,689,266	3.0
Galena			
1842	1,250,000	875,000	1.4
1846	3,569,795	1,852,063	1.9
1850	3,966,438	2,089,563	1.9
1851	3,966,438	1,693,338	2.4
1853	4,958,048	2,049,238	2.4
1855	6,941,267	2,221,793	3.1
1857	9,122,808	2,250,000	4.0
1860	6,742,945	1,320,000	5.0
Davenport			
1845	207,900	60,750	3.4
1848	148,500	343,800	0.6
1852	891,000	216,000	4.2
1855	3,542,670	567,000	6.2
1857	4,738,340	1,593,000	2.9
Burlington			
1847	245,440	949,328	0.3
1856	2,945,280	1,307,400	2.3
1858	3,426,923	952,000	3.6
Keokuk			
1850	882,231	382,500	2.3
1854	1,960,515	850,000	2.3
1855	2,913,653	1,275,000	2.3
1856	5,037,543	1,360,000	3.8
1857	6,045,056	1,020,000	5.9
1859	6,548,805	1,050,000	5.9
Quincy			
1841	460,620	825,000	0.6
1846	780,495	1,100,000	0.7
1850	1,010,805	1,083,333	0.9
1852	1,100,370	500,000	2.2

Table 7.1 *(cont.)*

| 1854 | 1,279,500 | 910,000 | 1.4 |
| 1859 | 2,942,850 | 933,333 | 3.2 |

Source: See Appendix G.

seen were steady during the period. A similar situation existed in Dubuque. The immediate effects of such imbalances were seen in the quality of local currency, which until 1863 continued to be issued by any bank with capital and local or state laws supporting it. Because such currency was really nothing more than a short-term loan that was negotiable among third parties more easily than a bill of credit, and could be used as currency and then redeemed at the bank or the store of the issuing merchant for its amount in specie, its actual value was determined by the perceived soundness of the issuing bank or merchant. Its value, obviously, was connected to the balance of trade of the larger economy by means of local merchants' debts to outsiders or to the local bank. The amount owed to the East determined, to a considerable extent, the ability to repay local loans, and thus indirectly affected the bank's solvency and the value of the notes it had issued. [32] If merchants got deeper into debt, and were less able to repay local loans, the bank's reserves would decline and suspicions of the redeemability of its notes would increase. The more one doubted one's ability to redeem a note if one was caught with it during a slowdown, the lower the value of the note, subsequent buyers requiring more notes per dollar prices to hedge against their uncertainty. As currency lost value, prices rose, and local issuers were compelled to print more to support it.

The weakening of the currency's value was compounded by external responses to increasing debts and declining confidence in the redeemability of local notes. In time, eastern creditors, growing concerned about being paid back or about getting full return on western bills and notes, began to demand more notes in return for each dollar of credit extended. This pressure, in drawing more currency to the East, further decreased local money supplies, thus compelling bankers in the West to issue more notes to meet local demand. Gradually, their newer notes would flood the local economy and push outside currency (the only means by which local merchants and bankers had to draw outside specie back into the local economy) into other channels of exchange. Why western banks just did not stop issuing currency is difficult to say. Some, of course, did stop. But it seems that most bankers believed to have done so would have aggravated local currency shortage, pulled down local prices, and

---

32 St. Louis Chamber of Commerce, *Annual Review. The commercial statistics and history of St. Louis* (St. Louis, 1854), 22; William Bross, "Banking, Its History and Commercial and Social Importance," *Peoria Weekly Republican*, April 30, 1852.

lessened the chance that merchant's debts, incurred at higher prices, would ever be paid back in full. The potential defaults arising from deflation would erode the solvency of western banks, and push holders of their currency closer to the panic point. It should be noted that at some point, the short-term profit derived from such currency issuing was such that it became very difficult for local banks to sit by and watch other currencies taking such gains away from them. Continuing to issue and use local currency became a matter of pride. [33]

Nevertheless, once caught in this inflationary cycle – in which the bank was sending more currency east for redemption to try to increase one's specie holdings on the one hand and yet issuing more currency against those holdings to stave off local pressure to redeem notes on the other hand – the position of the bank became precarious. For a while several banks in the valley tried to maneuver between this doubled-edged sword. But once trapped in such a bind, it was difficult, if not impossible, to get out. If, for instance, a bank stopped issuing currency, and more outside currency circulated in town to meet basic commercial needs, the increased amount of outside currency presented for exchange would force the bank to reissue many of the notes it had just retired. Likewise, they defeated their own purposes by acquiring more and more currency, the soundness of which was, with each passing day, more in doubt. Attempts to obtain specie for those notes they had exchanged for their own became less successful, causing a rundown in their specie on hand and thus further weakening their ability to support their own issue. In time, cornered by the demand to continue exchanging notes for their own, which were presented to them for redemption from both local and outside sources, and unable to acquire any specie to support that redemption, the local bank would run out of currency or cash, be forced to suspend payment on its notes, and close its doors. As the bank desperately put pressure and ultimately foreclosed on numerous local merchants and debtors, while they responded to similar pressure on loans they had received from the entrepôt or the East, the value of their extant notes would plummet. If they were unsuccessful in acquiring any assets from foreclosures, failure followed, and those holding bank notes would find them completely worthless. [34]

In a mercantilist way, therefore, contemporaries connected debts associated with excess imports to the value of their currency, reflected in exchange rates, and thus to the potential for an inflation that set in motion the pressures already described. The slightest hint of such a scenario would, they argued, discourage residents, dissuade settlers from coming to town, frustrate investors, and deepen the slump by causing people to seek out a more buoyant local economy. So too would farmers be disinclined to buy or sell in such an uncertain economy, further weakening the economy's demand structure and

33 Burrows, "Fifty Years," in Quaife, *Early Day*, 241–4, 250–83.
34 Charles Kindelberger, *Manias, Crashes, Panics* (New York, 1978), 14–51.

deepening the crisis, eventually bringing it to the breaking point. Such a course of events would weaken the town's ability to compete against neighboring towns and impede its progress toward acquiring and maintaining a function with regional importance. In short, succumbing to the temptations of expanding too fast could often, over the long run, cost the town its very existence.

What sparse evidence there is about currency circulation in the West corroborates some of these ideas. Where we know the circulating medium was strong and supported by a good supply of specie, the balance between imports and exports was relatively good. Galena, for example, supported as it was by strong exports from an early date, was known for its sound local currency. In the 1840s gold and silver circulated freely in the local economy. When the exports of lead dropped, however, the economy was required to accept some currency from St. Louis and Ohio to facilitate local exchange.[35] In contrast Keokuk in the mid-1850s, facing the burden of a flood of imports in return for normal export levels, found its economy awash in outside currency of doubtful value. The volume of debts against local businessmen sucked any money of value back East in repayment and discouraged any local banker from issuing money. With good money unable to circulate, bad money flowed in. Such "shinplasters," "wild cat," or "red dog" currency was used for local exchanges; it was spent as soon as received, gradually depreciated as its ability to be redeemed came into doubt, and caused prices to soar. Local business continued, but the pressure against local merchants increased because the currency in use was no good in meeting the demands of eastern creditors.[36] In between these two extremes, and following the scenario just described, were banks in Davenport and merchants in Dubuque. In each place overissuing of local currency forced banks to the wall when they were unable to redeem it. In Davenport the pressure was staved off by placing the home bank in Florence, Nebraska, which enabled the local bank to refuse to redeem notes for specie. Instead of facing the pressure of having to pay off notes, these banks exchanged them for others and kept their notes circulating. Nevertheless, when the pressure finally hit, the end came much as it did elsewhere. Drained of specie by demands on their notes from outside the town, and unable to

35 S. W. McMaster, *60 years on the upper Mississippi. My life and experiences* (Rock Island, Ill., 1893), 104; Alexander Leslie, "A Diary of a Journey from Scotland to Galena and Back to Chicago," Chicago Historical Society, Chicago, 25; *The Galena city directory containing also advertisements of the principal merchants* (Galena, Ill., 1855) 136.

36 *Keokuk Gate City*, June 10, September 3, September 9, August 17, 1857; "shinplasters": *Dubuque Express Herald*, October 18, 1857; "wildcat": Quincy Whig, June 14, 1853; Burrows, "Fifty Years," in Quaife, *Early Day*, 232; Charles Ballance, *The History of Peoria, Illinois* (Peoria, Ill., 1870), 259; Ford, *History of Illinois*, 175; "red dog": *History of Dubuque County* (Chicago, 1880), 383; Among other terms used were "sandstone notes": *History of Dubuque County*, 383; "rag currency": *Dubuque Miner's Express*, January 3, 1853; "stumptail currency": Redmond, *History of Quincy*, 110.

withstand the pressure to do so in town – a pressure built up by an overissue to maintain prices at their former level – these banks finally suspended operations in 1859. [37]

Of course, such concerns fail to note the other nonmercantile means by which local capital could be increased, or to recognize outside forces as the cause of local economic disaster, and thus overstate somewhat the relationship between debt and collapse of the local economy. The rising land values around a town, combined with its sale to newcomers, may in general have reduced these negative trade balances by as much as 20 percent. Likewise, construction in each town and improvement in the physical infrastructure of the town added to its value and capital base and may have provided more collateral for loans. In either case, however, such concerns clearly express the mercantilist assumptions people at the time had about the organization of local economies and their relationship to other local economies and to the broader regional economy. [38]

For example, their awareness of the relationship between the balance of trade and local economic health encouraged them to try to break the chains of credit dependency on the East. Whether imaginary or real, one could combat this predicament in ways not unlike those taken by Revolutionary colonists seventy years before: One could resist going into debt, one could abstain from consumption of eastern goods, or, because in a growing frontier economy it was so hard to do either of these, one could encourage local interests to reduce their reliance on eastern sources of supply by producing their own goods. To encourage investors to set up manufacturing operations in western towns, local entrepreneurs and politicans had to wage a strong fight against the people's accustomed reliance on eastern sources for their manufactured goods. Thus, long before there were "buy at home" or "shop Main Street" or "support your local chamber of commerce" campaigns, residents were exhorted to shop at home, even if what one could acquire was of lesser quality than what they could import. Such sacrifice encouraged local production by increasing local demand. [39]

In spite of the rhetoric, however, manufacturing drew its capital from similar sources as the merchants, and the development of specific lines of production and their relative success were strongly influenced by the patterns of agricultural production and mercantile activity we have already examined.

---

37 Burrows, "Fifty Years," in Quaife, *Early Day*, 250–83; Josiah Conzett, "My Recollections in Dubuque from 1846–90," typewritten copy, Iowa State Historical Society, Iowa City, 204–5; *History of Dubuque County*, 531–2; Diary of Solon Langworthy, handwritten manuscript, December 1858, Iowa State Historical Society, Iowa City; *Dubuque Express Herald*, October 18, October 20, October 22, November 18, December 8, December 11, 1857.

38 Robert Swierengra, *Pioneers and Profits* (Ames, Iowa, 1968), 69, 127, 203.

39 *Warsaw Signal*, May 21, 1841; Galena Daily Advertiser, June 2, 1851; *Davenport Gazette*, January 13, 1843.

Earlier, whenever and wherever merchants were unable to sell imports at a reasonably low price, local craftsmen and manufacturers were able to carve out a small market. But as transport improved, and the cost of imports declined, western manufacturers found themselves only able to compete in those lines of manufacturing in which there remained a distinct regional advantage that allowed them to operate at or near costs in the East. Either abundant local supplies of produce or raw materials, or the continued inaccessibility of goods produced in the East – for instance, in wagons, iron parts for local machines, farming equipment – tended to decide what could and could not be produced. In short, the vitality of manufacturing in any western town tended to follow its mercantile activity. Therefore, just as in merchandising, any local industrial development was prone to be disrupted by outside competition as determined by external investment locational decisions. [40]

In the 1840s, both the lack of capital and the limited market for manufactured goods retarded craft or manufacturing development in all but the largest towns. St. Louis and Galena, for example, both developed a nascent manufacturing sector. In large part, their ability to do so resulted, as Julius Rubin suggested, from the "high cost of transport," which effectively operated as a kind of natural tariff on eastern goods, enabling western producers to sell lower-quality, higher-priced goods in the neighborhood market. Even so, most furniture, leather goods, boots and shoes, cloth and clothing production faced an ever-rising tide of fine eastern goods arriving for sale to customers in merchants' stores. The majority of such firms gradually confined themselves to a very local custom or craft trade, rather than actually attempt to capture or maintain control of a subregional or regional market by producing similar goods in cost and quality. By the late 1840s, the impact of this pressure increasingly favored those manufacturers who went into fields of activity for which the West had some raw material, and hence significant cost-of-production, advantages. [41]

40 This discussion is derived from Julius Rubin, "Urban Growth and Regional Development," in *The Growth of Seaport Cities*, ed. David T. Gilchrist (Charlottesville, Va., 1967), 9–12; Margaret Walsh, *The Rise of the Midwestern Meat Packing Industry* (Lexington, Ky., 1982), 15–54; Diane Lindstrom, *Economic Development of the Philadelphia Region* (New York, 1978) 145; Carville Earle and Ronald Hoffman, "The Foundation of the Modern Economy: Agriculture and the Costs of Labor in the United States and England, 1800–1860," *American Historical Review* 85 (December 1980): 1068–73; David R. Meyer, "Emergence of the American Manufacturing Belt: An Interpretation," *Journal of Historical Geography* 9 (April 1983): 145–74; and Edward K. Muller, "Regional Urbanization and the Selective Growth of Towns in North American Regions," *Journal of Historical Geography* 3 (January 1977): 21–39.

41 Rubin, "Urban Growth and Regional Development," 9–12; Margaret Walsh, "Industrial Opportunity on the Urban Frontier," *Wisconsin Magazine of History* 57 (1974): 99–133; Manuscript Manufacturing Schedule, Jo Daviess County, Ill., Scott, Dubuque, and Des Moines Counties, Iowa, Seventh Census of the United States, 1850; Walsh, *Rise of the Midwestern Meat Packing Industry*, 15–54.

In St. Louis, for example, hog packers "drew on mercantile capital for investments in plant and materials and took advantage of the established commercial infrastructure to offer competitive prices." Locational decisions that followed the commercial infrastructure also drew on the rising demand for such processed goods that developed as agriculture became more commercial and specialized. Ronald Hoffman and Carville Earle have suggested yet another tie between the two by noting that the seasonality of rural work provided towns in heavily populated rural areas with a readily available, relatively low-cost labor force.

Galena's manufacturing sector, in contrast to the limited activity in any of the towns on the west side of the river, reflects the impact of these intertwining forces on the scale and focus of local manufacturing development. Aside from smelting lead, which evolved out of the need to ship lead to the entrepôt, the strength of Galena's manufacturing sector was in providing consumer products and prepared foodstuffs for the large local population. Plough making was the most productive line, even though still performed by hand. So too, the strong production in roping, hardware products, wagons and carriages, heavy clothing, and boots and shoes attests to the demands of the mining population. Unable to acquire such heavy goods at reasonable cost from either St. Louis or the East, local producers were able to thrive (Tables 7.2 and 7.3). [42]

In contrast, no such demand encouraged the development of small local producers in the smaller towns between Galena and Alton before 1850. Without such demand present, most investors focused their energies on exploiting the local resource base. In Dubuque, smelting and lumbering appeared early and would continue to play an important and expanding role throughout the period and beyond. Each line of activity obviously served to prepare local raw materials for export. The same could be said for the early importance of flour milling and hog packing, although before the mid-1850s local production was hardly sufficient to supply local needs. Nevertheless, with such abundant raw materials in the area, it seemed a logical step to apply manufacturing skills to turn them into consumable finished products that townspeople could buy locally rather than having to import from downriver. Similar incentives explain the beginnings of hog-packing activity at Alton, Quincy, Keokuk, and Peoria, a response to the incongruity and waste of importing a finished product from Cincinnati with so much of the raw material in one's immediate vicinity. [43]

42 Margaret Walsh, "The Spatial Evolution of the Midwestern Pork Packing Industry, 1853–75," *Journal of Historical Geography* 4 (Spring 1978): 14; Margaret Walsh, "Pork Packing as the Leading Edge of Midwestern Industry, 1835–75," *Agricultural History* 51 (1977): 708–17; Earle and Hoffman, "The Foundation of the Modern Economy: Agriculture and the Costs of; Labor in the United States and England, 1800–1860," 1068–73, Manuscript Manufacturing Schedule, Jo Daviess County, Ill., Seventh Census of the United States, 1850.
43 See Chapter 6.

Table 7.2. *Industries in selected river towns, 1850*

Industry	Firms	Total value added
Galena (population, 7,000)		
Plough making	3	$ 29,294
Meat packing	3	23,793
Breweries	7	18,970
Harnesses and saddles	5	16,340
Carriages	7	15,180
Boots and shoes	10	14,853
Blacksmithing	17	11,197
Tailoring	5	10,910
Mining	5	10,880
Flour milling	2	7,062
Total	64	158,479
Total plus all others		189,758
Total processing	17	60,705 (32%)
Dubuque (population, 4,000)		
Flour milling	6	25,194
Blacksmithing	9	17,010
Smelting	6	16,200
Meat packing	2	8,124
Lumber milling	6	7,500
Boots and shoes	4	6,208
Harnesses	1	3,000
Carriages	3	1,935
Coopering	5	1,461
Total	42	86,632
Total plus all others		90,419
Total processing	20	57,018 (63%)
Davenport (population, 2,000)		
Flour milling	3	51,030
Lumber milling	4	11,750
Plough making	1	1,534
Boots and shoes	2	1,822
Brick making	2	821
Carriages	3	463
Harnesses and saddles	1	390
Coopering	2	316
Bakeries	1	32
Iron foundries	1	14
Total	20	68,172
Total processing	7	62,780 (92%)

Table 7.2 (*cont.*)

Source: Manuscript Manufacturing Schedules: Jo Daviess County, Ill., Dubuque and Scott counties, Iowa; *Seventh Census of the United States,* 1850.

At some point, however, local production in these lines began to exceed local needs and, as a result, manufacturers, just like merchants, had to compete with producers spread across the region. This regional competition gradually determined which places would be better suited for larger-scale production. In hog packing, the high volume of production at which economies of scale began to lower per-unit costs encouraged, once this threshold had been achieved, a rather significant centralization of the industry, thus sapping the vitality of the industry in smaller towns upriver and forcing those producers to accept local market niches in the regional and national market. Furthermore, the external economies drawn from selling wastes to specialized producers such as glue makers, brush makers, soap makers, and candlemakers added to the advantage of large-scale production. So too, the need for great amounts of salt, manpower, capital on short demand, and an unfrozen river reinforced the agglomeration tendencies in the industry along the lower river and the Ohio River. [44]

Upriver, therefore, towns turned to either flour milling or smelting lead to seek some competitive advantages. In spite of rather inefficient methods, the quality of western wheat enabled millers to produce a flour in high demand and thus attract a share of the regional and national market. Only after 1858 or so would the sudden increase in milling and storage capacity at Chicago begin to draw that activity from the secondary centers to the entrepôt. [45]

In lead processing, the George Collier works at St. Louis was the only producer of white lead in the region from the early 1840s to the late 1850s. Collier, a lead merchant who owned several steamboats and had been involved in the opening of the lead trade, decided that rather than shipping lead to Philadelphia for processing and then reimporting it back to St. Louis, both capital and time could be saved by producing white lead, pipe, and perhaps even glass at home. The gradual expansion of the firm indicates that he achieved some success in this production and gained a significant portion of the slowly increasing western market. Indeed, the extent of Collier's dominance is perhaps reflected in the fact that as the western market further increased, both Galena and Dubuque began to respond to their importation of white lead, paint, glass, and related products from St. Louis in the same way

44 Edward K. Muller, "Regional Urbanization and Selective Growth of Towns in North American Regions," 34; Charles Cist, *Cincinnati in 1851* (Cincinnati, 1851).
45 See Chapter 6.

Table 7.3. *Industries in selected river towns, 1860*

Industry	Firms	Total value added
Galena (population, 10,000)		
Meat packing	8	50,020
Mining	4	33,868
Breweries	9	29,430
Printing	4	20,320
Bakery and confectioners	1	19,350
Soaps and candles	4	12,940
Boots and shoes	5	12,903
Lumber milling	3	10,650
Harnesses and saddles	6	9,337
Plough making	1	8,130
Others	34	47,466
Total	79	254,414
Total processing	24	94,538 (37%)
Dubuque (population, 13,000)		
Breweries	4	40,690
Flour milling	2	38,800
Iron foundries	3	18,865
Plough making	3	11,210
Harnesses and saddles	1	10,500
Sash and door makers	3	10,150
Tin shops	2	10,078
Marble works	2	9,450
Soaps and candles	2	7,700
Mining	1	4,950
Others	19	14,765
Total	42	177,228
Total processing	6	79,490 (44%)
Davenport (population, 11,267)		
Flour milling	3	53,943
Breweries	4	23,728
Plough making	5	21,650
Carriages	4	21,132
Lumber milling	4	16,740
Gas company	1	14,850
Furniture	7	13,250
Brickmaking	2	13,150
Iron foundries	4	12,326
Printer	1	8,040
Others	7	16,268
Total	35	215,077
Total processing	11	94,411 (44%)

Table 7.3 (cont.)

Source: Manuscript Manufacturing Schedules: Jo Daviess County, Ill., Dubuque and Scott counties, Iowa; *Eighth Census of the United States,* 1860.

that Collier had responded to eastern imports fifteen years before. [46] The import-substitution impetus in the hinterland started first with shot production, an extension of smelting, then advanced to white lead and paint, and finally to piping and glass. In 1848 John Kennet of Dubuque established the first shot tower upriver since a similar effort had been made in Galena with middling success a decade before. Within five years Kennet had "driven out all regional competitors" and carved out for himself a wide market in the upper Midwest. A Galena entrepreneur followed Kennet's lead and added a bar and sheet lead manufactory to his shot-tower operations. The reasons for this development were self-evident: "If these products can be made at home [rather than be imported from the East] we not only maintain the manufacturer's profit but also the profits of the various items which enter into production." [47]

Rather than deriving from the needs of the local economy, manufacturing had begun by the mid-1850s to follow the capital flows set in place by the mercantile system. As a result, by 1856 both the capital and the decisions were coming increasingly from the entrepôt, if not directly, then indirectly in response to what was happening there. In several lines of production agglomeration effects at the entrepôt had begun to centralize industry, leaving hinterland industries to cultivate small local markets based, as Muller notes, on "local preferences or habits," or local advantages that still persisted. Indeed, before the era of specialization, it seems that the only alternatives for an entrepreneur wanting to compete on a regional scale were to gain control of one of these local markets or to move to the entrepôt itself. Therefore, while local merchants faced heavy competition from entrepôt merchants for control of their local markets, local manufacturers faced a similar challenge from outsiders who wanted to use local markets to establish themselves in one line of manufacturing, and perhaps to develop a base from which they could compete with the growing firms of the entrepôt agglomeration. [48]

46 John Thomas Scharf, *History of St. Louis city and county,* 2 vols. (Philadelphia, 1883), 1256; Hogan, *Thoughts about the city of St. Louis, her commerce and manufactures, railroads, and Etc.,* 13–5.

47 Shockel, "Settlement and Development of Joe Daviess County," 192–3; Hogan, *Thoughts about the city of St. Louis, her commerce and manufactures, railroads and Etc.,* 60. Jacobs, *Cities and the Wealth of Nations,* 35–42; *Dubuque Express Herald,* September 20, 1856.

48 Muller, "Regional Urbanization and Selective Growth of Towns in North American Regions," 35–6.

That the selective pattern of such hinterland manufacturing activity followed the capital flows of merchandising, moving west along the railroads, should be no surprise. At Davenport, at the railhead of the Rock Island line, new manufacturing firms in the late 1850s, all but two of which were founded by newcomers, were on average about seven thousand dollars richer than the firms they deposed from the prerailroad era. In contrast, the few newcomers at all interested in choosing to locate in Galena were barely larger than the firms that had managed to survive the decline in the town's regional position. In between these two extremes was Dubuque, where more newcomers (although relatively smaller than the newcomers in Davenport compared with the size of the local survivors) posed a less considerable challenge to local manufacturing establishments. All of these firms were considerably smaller than firms developing in Chicago and St. Louis and were, therefore, meant to supply particular subregional markets within the broader hinterland markets of the entrepôt. [49]

By 1856, therefore, the pattern of manufacturing throughout the region had begun to follow the structure of the mercantile-based regional system. What mattered, increasingly, was not the supply and demand of goods and services, but rather the availability of, the cost of, and the potential return on capital and credit. Credit flows, investment decisions, interest rates, and the circulation of currency were, in a period of bank proliferation and easy money, causing economic activity and change rather than responding to it. It was a point brought home to Westerners, and to producers and consumers throughout the regional and national economy, by the general financial distress of 1857.

For merchants, bankers, manufacturers, and farmers, the panic of 1857 proved to be a bitter historical lesson in the new forces of capitalism. Indeed, it could be argued that the pattern in which the effects of the panic spread through the regional system, and the diversity of responses to those effects, represented a kind of forced integration of resisting local economies into a centralized capitalist regional and national economy. Throughout 1857 western observers, confident that the mercantile and demographic base of local development was sound, and choosing to ignore the course of much of the capital upon which that development relied, refused to acknowledge the connection between dysfunctions in the credit markets in the East, and their own economic prospects. Given the issue at hand, and the impact of its resolution on the life of the region, the nature of those responses should be examined in some detail.

Early in 1857 the decline in railroad stocks, brought on by the peak in the tide of speculation in railroad investment, caused in part by the natural

---

49 Manuscript Manufacturing Schedules, Scott County, Iowa, Jo Daviess County, Ill., Seventh Census of the United States, 1850; ibid., 1860.

exhaustion of the market but also by the less-than-expected returns on newly opened lines, seems to have set in motion a general worry about the overstimulated western economy. In the face of such concerns numerous banks in the East suddenly became cautious in their lending policies, in contrast to an almost anything-goes attitude a year before. First, they refused to extend loans.[50] Then in February, they began to limit the kinds of western currrency that they would accept as payment in return for these loans. At first this involved only raising discount rates. Later in the month, however, some Philadelphia banks began to refuse to accept Illinois currency from twenty-two state banks, given the "unhealthy and speculative climate" and an "extraordinarily high interest rate."[51]

At first, western observers scoffed at this action. One editor remarked that such a financial move would "hardly cause a ripple upon the bosom of economic life" in the West, given the wealth of the land and the continual demand for agricultural goods. In Davenport, another observer expected, in spite of dire predictions of having eventually to pay the cost of these eastern moves, "a rush of tradesmen to this city which will astonish even the most sanguine." And though the generally more cautious Galena newspaper reporter did warn against overspeculation, and thus an overvaluing of the land and tying western interests to an overvalued debt, he never doubted that some restraint would enable the local economy to continue to prosper.[52]

The refusal by eastern banks to redeem western notes and currency for specie slowed the return of hard money into the region and exacerbated the chronic outflow of specie. As a result, faith in the redeemability of western currency in general further declined, and, as it did, more and more money was needed to cover a similar transaction of a few months before. Some banks printed more money, but increasingly Westerners began to rely on the refused currency from the East – currency that, because suspect, forced exchange rates even higher. With a suddenness that seems to have caught merchants and consumers north of St. Louis off guard, local prices began to soar in June 1857. At Keokuk, there was an "alarming rise in prices." In Quincy, by early July, "the laborers, the mechanic, the clerk all complain that their money does not go as far as it used to" and found themselves required to pay "exorbitant" prices and face dramatic declines in real income. That this slowed down new purchases from town merchants, and further delayed the repayment of old debts, thus placing the merchants in a nearly impossible position in facing their obligations to the East, should be apparent. Predictably, local merchants

50 Edward Stanwood, *American Tariff Controversies of the Nineteenth Century* (Boston, 1903), 113; Amasa Walker, "The Commercial Crisis of 1857," *Hunt's Merchant Magazine* (November 1857): 532; George Van Vleck, *The Panic of 1857* (New York, 1943), 50–60; Kindelberger, *Manias, Panics, and Crashes*, 15–24.
51 *Iowa State Democrat* (Davenport), January 19, February 21, 1857.
52 Ibid; *Galena Gazette and Advertiser*, May 1, May 30, 1857.

began to call in debts and, in doing so, because the townspeople thought they were forcing them to pay for their overextensions of trade, drew the ire of locals. Nevertheless, as orders for goods from the East dried up, and merchants began to retrench, few observers were willing to connect these problems with those in New York or Philadelphia. [53]

The comments of the editor of the *Keokuk Gate City* characterize the general scoffing mood across the region:

> There is no evidence of such a visitation. We lately looked on nearly
> every town from Galena down and never saw so much improvement....
> Every city, village, and hamlet gives the appearance of activity and thrift
> in blissful ignorance of the terrible financial calamity which must have
> fallen upon it here, in order to sustain the prophecies of eastern ravens.
> Western prosperity is founded upon a surer basis than the slippery subtle
> gold and fancy stocks of Wall Street. [54]

Within two weeks this rosy Fourth of July picture was brought into relief by a rapid slowdown in land sales across Iowa. With the flow of capital from the East shut off, few were willing to pay the inflated prices. A decline in orders from the East became apparent by mid-July as commercial shipments to the West, both across the lakes and up the Mississippi, reported extremely light freights. Again, with Easterners charging more to borrow, and merchants unable to meet last year's obligations, few had the wherewithal to buy in expectation of normal sales in the fall season. One Keokuk observer passed it off as a summer slump. But the editor in Dubuque knew better; an empty land office and a road and a ferry from the East, crowded for years before on fine summer days, now only lightly traveled, indicated that a major blockage from the East had changed the patterns of economic activity. Even in Galena, "dull times" were reported in August. As luck would have it, a poor early crop added to the general reluctance to act, further depressing trade – though, of course, enabling some to point to agricultural failure as the source of their problems. [55]

Coincidentally, it was in the same last week of August that news arrived in Galena of the failure of the New York branch of the Ohio Life and Trust Company on August 24. The branch company had apparently borrowed two or three millions dollars on call from its parent company in Ohio, which it then, acting as a banker, loaned out in exchange for various stocks and bonds. The decline in the stock and bond market, however, compelled both the parent and the branch companies, on account of a reduction in collateral, to begin to

---

53 Stanwood, *American Tariff Controversies in the Nineteenth Century*, 114; *Quincy Herald*, July 2, 1857.
54 *Keokuk Gate City*, July 24, 1857.
55 *Galena Gazette and Advertiser*, August 31, 1857; *History of Dubuque County*, 531; *Galena Gazette and Advertiser*, August 25, 1857; *Keokuk Daily Post*, August 6, September 9, 1857.

reduce their loans. The weaker Ohio firm thus called in its loan, which of course the New York firm, overextended on declining security, could not repay, forcing it to default. When this happened, other New York banks holding Ohio Trust paper protected themselves by tightening money and calling in loans on mercantile houses and manufacturing establishments. But, again, the sluggish economy made it impossible for many companies to meet these "call" demands, forcing them to default and liquidate whatever was necessary to pay off. The banks, meanwhile, were unable to meet their requirements and, by September 7, a number were forced to close their doors. Within another week, a round of failures rippled through Philadelphia's economy, and more failures, or at least extreme pressure, spread to Boston and Baltimore soon thereafter, exerting a pressure on their debtors that quickly spread west. [56]

Even as these events proceeded, and the signs of a sluggish economy became undeniable, mercantilists in the West refused to accept that they were connected, and thus affected. "The fancy games of Wall Street" had little to do, they believed, with the production and consumption of goods and services in the West. One Keokuk editor was still taunting the New York "croakers" as late as September 2. A few days later, however, the first round of pressure hit western regional entrepôts. In both Chicago and St. Louis, merchants with connections to New York were severely strained by the sudden demands being made on them by New York creditors. And on September 9, this pressure began to claim casualties among weaker hinterland customers. A private letter from Keokuk reported that "among the calamities" were the failures of several important merchants, one of which "grew out of the failure of their correspondents in St. Louis." A few days later, the largest distillery and mill in Quincy was forced to the wall by its St. Louis investor, while several Davenport merchants began to feel the pressure to meet their obligations soon, or face the same consequences. But the sharpest stab to the western system came where the contacts with New York had been traditionally most direct, Galena. [57]

On September 12, 1857, the suspension of the largest bank in town, James Carter and Company, which had been supported by the Ohio Trust Company, deflated the optimism of Galenans that they would be unaffected by the troubles in the East. Elsewhere, as people became nervous about redeeming their currency, the pressure on local banks and hence on merchants continued to increase, even as all trade ground to a halt. [58]

56 Stanwood, *American Tariff Controversies in the Nineteenth Century*, 114; *Galena Gazette and Advertiser*, August 28, 1857; Van Vleck, *The Panic of 1857*, 66–70.
57 *Keokuk Daily Post*, September 1, 1857; *Quincy Herald*, September 9, 1857; letter from C. M. Reynolds to C. Throop, Keokuk, Iowa, September 9, 1857, Iowa State Historical Society, Iowa City; *Northwest Gazette and Galena Advertiser*, September 26, 1857.
58 Illinois credit report ledger, CXXXIX, Jo Daviess County, R. G. Dun and Company Collection, September 12, 18, 23, 1857.

Once it became apparent how closely western economies, at the end of a chain of debt, would follow eastern pressure, the response to that pressure quickened and spread. Within ten days, the second wave of pressure moved more quickly, and with sharper impact, from the entrepôts to their hinterland debtors. Within a few days of the failure of an important St. Louis bank, a major bank in Keokuk shut its doors, followed, on September 28, by a general panic in Quincy. An unusual Saturday afternoon run on a small bank forced it to close for good by nightfall. On Sunday, the wealthiest banker in town, making private calls through the town, pressed his debtors but found nothing to save him. When crowds gathered in the street before his bank on Monday morning, he decided not to open. That same Monday more banks went down in Chicago and Burlington, and on Tuesday another wave of failures in St. Louis toppled several correspondents in Burlington, another in Quincy, and others in towns as far north and west as Omaha.[59]

By the third week of the downward spiral, the implications of the chain of debt into which they had become intertwined were becoming clear. And some entrepreneurs, observing what made such connections work – the maintenance of confidence in the bank – began to respond in overtly capitalist ways. In Galena, a notice on October 2 reported that the Corwiths, the richest men in town and owners of a still-standing bank, received numerous deposits of specie from local merchants and residents in an effort to support the value of the local currency. The same week St. Louis merchants did essentially the same thing by deciding, in a joint meeting, to pay out Illinois currency at par, in hopes of stopping the erosion of confidence in the still-open banks and to allay the panic in the East. And, indeed, when runs on two banks were halted on October 9, some believed there were grounds for hope. In private, however, a credit reporter in Alton thought such actions too little too late: "There is not now enough specie to be had to pay maturing notes, unless good currency, perhaps can be used as specie at a good discount" – which is what the St. Louisans tried. But he saw little sound currency around and thus expected that the isolated suspensions would soon broaden into a "general suspension." The once cocky editor of the Keokuk newspaper seemed to admit the same, although his imagery seemed still rooted in mercantile conceptions of the problem: "the country merchants owe the city merchants, the farmers owe the country merchants, and neither at the western end, nor in the middle, nor in the east end of this linked chain of debt is there any money."[60]

In mid-October another round of failures swept through St. Louis's

---

59 *Keokuk Daily Post*, September 23, 1857; *Galena Gazette and Advertiser*, September 28, 1857; *Quincy Herald*, September 29, October 1, 1857.

60 *Galena Gazette and Advertiser*, October 2, October 9, 1857; Illinois credit report ledger, XCVIII, Madison County, Ill. R. G. Dun and Company Collection; *Keokuk Gate City*, October 30, 1857.

mercantile community and north through the dissolving system. This wave of pressure finally brought the anticipated general suspension in Keokuk, and claimed numerous casualties in Quincy. But further north, the economies of Davenport, Dubuque, and Galena were now able to respond in different ways to pressure both from the South and East. In Dubuque, the Langworthy Bank rather selfishly, and meanly, refused to accept the notes of other banks or merchants in town "unless backed by something else." This policy brought the next largest bank in town "to bust." Meanwhile, merchants in town tried to support their discredited script by redeeming it with their own assets. Having temporarily halted the pressure, they then used the script to buy grain from area farmers and used the grain to pay back some eastern creditors. But putting more script back in farmers' hands only drew more in to be presented for redemption, and without Langworthy support this "swapping cats" on themselves could only last a short time. A general suspension followed in mid-December, forcing scores of merchants into insolvency.[61] Galena, meanwhile, not having participated in the boom and expansion of credit like the Iowa-side towns, actually felt an easing of pressure. And though trade was stagnant, most town merchants, and the town's richest bank, had "survived and could stand another."[62]

In Davenport, the town's largest bank, Cook and Sargent, with the support of several local merchants, tried a strategy similar to that attempted in Dubuque. In a classic "swapping cats" scheme, it steadily redeemed its own notes. Because the "home" bank was in eastern Nebraska, and, as a branch bank it was not required to pay out specie, the bank simply paid out the local checks of one of the richest merchants in town in return for their own notes. The merchant, James Burrows, would then accept these notes as payment for goods and hold them as an IOU from Cook and Sargent. Likewise, because he did not constitute a bank, Burrows was under no obligation to redeem his notes for specie and, if pressed, would often just pay out Cook and Sargent notes in return, sending the customer back to the bank in much the same position he had been in before. The short-term effect was to take the pressure off the bank by using the assets of Burrows's business as security. Ethics aside, it was a policy that kept the wolf at bay for almost two years.[63]

The general pattern of the diffusion of financial pressure through the region reflects, among other things, the complexity of mercantile, and hence financial

61 *Keokuk Gate City*, October 9, 1857; Tilson, *History of Quincy*, 29; *Quincy Whig*, October 20, November 12, 1857; *Dubuque Express Herald*, December 5, December 11, 1857.
62 Illinois credit report ledger, CXXXIX, R. G. Dun and Company Collection; letter from James Bailey to Edward Wade, November 28, 1857, Edward Wade Papers, Missouri Historical Society, St. Louis.
63 Harry E. Downer, *History of Davenport and Scott County, Iowa* (Chicago, 1910) 985; Swierengra, *Pioneers and Profits*, 120–1; August Richter, "A True History of Davenport and

contacts, which had developed in the course of Chicago's move into the upper valley. Pressure from St. Louis spread north in several waves, striking hard where its connections were strongest, and then weakening where it had lost some of its trade in the previous few years. Dubuque, for example, felt some pressure from St. Louis, but little or none seems to have been felt in Galena or Davenport. When the pressure hit the former place early in the crisis, it was generated directly from New York, via some reverberations in Chicago. Likewise, when Davenport's merchants finally succumbed, it came not at the hands of merchants in Chicago or St. Louis, but rather by way of a failure of a branch operation of the local bank in Boston.[64] Indeed, Davenport's location near the intersection of the competing hinterlands seems to have weakened loyalties and connections, and thus enabled the town perhaps to resist the general pressure more effectively. Moreover, the fact that the timing, locale, and severity of suspensions seem to have correlated generally to the various debts carried, vis-à-vis local production, suggests that the security of a town's economy did depend on the nature of its contacts with outside capital markets. Outside capital, supporting local investment, is what fueled local development. But if relied on in excess, such capital could inflate local ambitions, deepen town debts, and, when the pressure came, worsen the suspension. Indeed, the ability to recover from suspension was also tied to the amount of debt owed. The deeper the debt, the longer it took for a town to recover. Unlike in older mercantile days when isolation would force prices so low that some locals would begin reinvesting and generate a revival, in a capitalist framework old debts had to be settled or refinanced before major firms in the East would resume trading, manufacturers reopen their factories, and farmers return to the fields. The energy and human capital were still there, and the resources of the land and the town's infrastructure remained, but the credit to set things moving was stifled so long as old debts hung over a town or region.

This state of things, George Van Vleck believes, slowed the recovery from the panic of 1857 throughout the West.[65] The exaggerated overextension of credit during the price, land, and immigration boom and the widespread speculation left regional affairs buried under a mountain of obligations that had to be renegotiated before economic activity could return to normal. The heavy investment in railroads further mortgaged the region to the hilt. Moreover, the scarcity of local capital forced those in search of repayment into the lowest levels of the economy, wiping out not just banks and merchants, but shopkeepers, craftsmen, workers, and bank depositors among the general

Scott County, in *Davenport Democrat*, April 11, 1920, to January 31, 1921 (Putnam Museum, Davenport, Iowa); Burrows, "Fifty Years," in Quaife, *Early Day*, 250–60.

64 Burrows, "Fifty Years," 276–83.
65 Van Vleck, *The Panic of 1857*, 84–5.

population. [66] The depth of the suspension further restrained the ability of the economy to rebound. This pervasive weakness across the hinterland perhaps helps explain why, during and after the Civil War, the entrepôts were able to draw secondary merchants so quickly into more rigid arrangements.

The disruptions of the financial crisis of 1857–8 served to replace a diverse, porous, often confusing set of urban economic arrangements with a more clearly defined regional urban system. This clarity was, after 1863, reinforced by the the use of a national currency, the enlargement of national markets, and the continued centralization of industrial activity in the largest entrepôts. The railroads also played their part, of course, in establishing more direct and one-dimensional contacts. Secondary economic functions followed the railroads into the interior of Iowa and beyond, causing such functions to disappear from the old river towns, especially at Davenport and Dubuque. By 1865 few forwarding merchants were located at either place. Manufacturers meanwhile had no choice but to follow the wheat supplies west, leaving river-town entrepreneurs to take advantage of the only resource base left, lumber from the north, while more firms in other lines found the competition from Chicago and Milwaukee harder to withstand. [67] Meanwhile, Cincinnati withdrew all of its fleeting aspirations of 1856 through 1858, while St. Louis concentrated on its trade to the west and south, having conceded the northern river valley, save for a lingering steamboat line, to Chicago interests. [68]

In terms of local capital flows, manufacturing had become, therefore, just part of the problem. More and more of what was manufactured in the hinterland was controlled by outsiders. And thus the fate of the town's economy was often dependent on impartial, purely economic decisions. At this point, many of these outsiders would, in the next generation, become the staunchest supporters of local development. We had not yet arrived at the stage of national development in which small towns and cities had to await the choices by national firms of where to locate their plants across the country. Such conditions had, however, already begun to shape local mercantile sectors. Existing as one point in broad national and regional systems, the circular feedbacks between the mercantile and manufacturing activity that stimulated development of the local economy were stretched across ever-broader systemic spaces. Furthermore, as the scale of operations to maintain a role in this system grew, so did the necessary critical mass in people, capital, and transport, leaving fewer and fewer urban units able to play significant roles in these

66 Conzett, "My Recollections in Dubuque," 204–5.
67 Agnes M. Larson, *History of the White Pine Industry in Minnesota* (Minneapolis, 1949), 105, 107, 122, 125; Walter A. Blair, *A Raft Pilot's Log: A History of the Great Rafting Industry on the Upper Mississippi, 1840–1915* (Cleveland, 1930), 256–65.
68 Pred, *City Systems in Advanced Economies*, 162–3.

economies. As this happened, their connections to the forces of change became more discontinuous, partial, indirect, and peripheral – and thus substantially different in form and character from those within local economies in the East or nearer or at the entrepôts.

On a broader theoretical level, one might label these characteristics "provincial." To be provincial is to exist within a reality in which the web of feedbacks and exchange, measured locally, appears open-ended on account of their being dependent on broad and distant regional interactions. It is a place that contributes to the center, interacts with it, but because it is not a center, rarely experiences interactions that "click" and generate local feedback mechanisms and development. Attempts at action in such places almost always dissipate, fail to get going, or are cut off in the bud. Unable to find local stimuli to respond to and relying on infrequent and distant impulses, projects and ideas in such places rarely pan out, move sluggishly along, or simply wind down in the low density of social and economic activity. And those things that do change come increasingly not from some local interpretation of events, but from the outside, imported intact. Such imports are imposed on local reality even though based on outside interests and contexts, values and ideas. All of this tends to happen as the rhetoric of local wholeness, self-reliance, and progress continues to be expressed, an evasion of reality. In the 1850s, the rise of the great metropolitan centers that would control the American economy transformed hundreds of towns, once the centers of small local worlds, into "provincial" places. This historical process, occurring in the wake of the metropolitanization of American life, had far-reaching effects on American society and culture in the second half of the nineteenth century. To ignore it is to deny the initial diversity and vitality of small-town and city life in nineteenth-century America, and to fail to discern the difficult struggle of people in countless towns and cities to evolve some new sense of identity and to achieve some sense of security in the generation or two before their children were able to connect themselves to and draw support from the all-pervasive metropolitan-centered national economy and society.

8

Town and system: local history in a regional context

To move to a new town in the West and to tie one's life and career to its destiny was to acquire, between 1830 and the Civil War, a lesson in the dynamics of power within a regional urban economy. Hoping to re-create life as it was in the East and draw the core of the national system west, Easterners poured out of the older states along the Atlantic Coast and into the Midwest. In coming west, however, they faced considerable uncertainty. As we have seen, they first had to make the difficult decision of where to settle. If they intended to settle in a town, they had to choose one in which they had the initial advantages necessary to be successful. Often, given the rapidity of settlement and speed of economic development, a settler had only one or two chances to find the right venue for his strategy. Once decided, the newcomer then had to forge his way through the thicket of intense local competition. If one survived, the next step was to establish a position that could serve as a platform for expanding one's regional activity and securing the continued success of the town. The town, therefore, gradually became the focus of one's efforts because its success or failure in the regional economy and in continuing to adapt to changes in that economy, determined the success or failure of most of the townspeople. The difficulty of pinning one's hope's on a town was that one could, given a town's environment, topography, and economic location, only do so much to insure its success. Many of the decisions on which the future of a town depended were increasingly made at the entrepôt or in the East. For Westerners, nurtured on expectations of success or failure based solely on one's own efforts, this realization was often hard to take. But it was a reality that many middle-sized towns, founded in the optimism of the 1820s and 1830s, were forced to recognize and gradually to accept in the economic expansion of the 1850s.

Consider the history of towns along the upper river during this period, and one will discern local dynamics of competition, economic and social differentiation, and institutional development that, though varying in scale and timing, followed a general pattern. But in each town, one will also find that these processes were being disrupted, redirected, altered, or even coopted by new influences from the outside. Rather than becoming more alike, the economies and societies of each river town evolved into locally specific juxtapositions in one place of different groups, associated with different regional or local activities occurring during different periods of regional and local interaction. With each change in a town's function in the regional system, a new reality superimposed itself on an old, and the two were, in one way or another, compelled to interact and come to some local compromise if the town was going to be ready to meet further challenges ahead.

The response of townspeople to regional forces varied with the demands being made or the alternatives offered. Some simply resigned themselves to the changes. Others responded defensively, feeding a deeper, self-centered parochialism. This often manifested itself in hyperboosterism rhetoric, exclusionary activity, or the development of a strong sense of local loyalty. Often this response backfired by simply making it even harder to accept the dictates of the regional economy, as well as more difficult to adjust to changes elsewhere, if one was forced to move. The development of a regional system did not, intially, homogenize life within its area and create economic order. Rather, it struggled against all sorts of local resistance; the townspeople, each in his own way, sought to preserve futures for their towns, for which the new system seemed to have no place. The dynamics of this struggle – economic, social, and cultural – constitute one of the unexplored aspects of nineteeth-century American life. One way to approach the issue is by analyzing local history in a broader regional context. This perspective enables one to articulate the character of the interactions among towns and between local and regional processes of change, and thus uncover the dynamics by which a cluster of new towns across an area became first an urban system and, after considerable struggle, an urban region.

The economic and social history of Alton, Illinois, between 1815 and 1860, for example, was unable to escape the shadow of St. Louis, being located, as it was, only twenty miles to the north. As a result, few events in town could occur independently of regional forces. As early as 1815 the first permanent merchant had established himself on the Alton wharf and began to compete with St. Louis merchants for the upriver trade. St. Louis responded within a decade by launching a steamboat trade to Galena and taking the position as the lead exporter and outpost supplier of the region. Alton, however, was sufficiently busy with supplying the tide of immigrants moving through Madison County and into the lower Illinois River valley in the 1820s that it continued to grow apace with St. Louis.[1] In fact, the earliest relevant census (1840) indicates that Madison County, Illinois, and its immediate hinterland produced a large surplus of flour and wheat and shipped it to St. Louis for

1 John M. Peck, *A gazetteer of Illinois* (Philadelphia, 1837), 146–9; William T. Norton, ed., *Centennial History of Madison County, Illinois, and Its People* (Chicago, 1912), 91–2.

local consumption due to shortfalls in the St. Louis hinterland. [2] Although such figures suggest a positive flow of trade, they are probably deceptive. By that time, Alton was already contracting its regional role to that of a depot for the lower Illinois River valley. We know its function had once been relatively more significant in the regional economy because only three years before Alton had had about the same number of merchants as St. Louis, while by 1840 its merchant community had fallen to a third the size of St. Louis's. Indeed, the peak of its regional power can be pushed back at least two more years to 1835, as it was in that year that Alton purchased several steamboats and attempted to wrest control of the lead trade away from St. Louis merchants. Their strategy to buy lead at high prices and receive merchandising contracts in return failed, however, because they were unable to break the contracts for mercantile trade that had been already made between Galena and St. Louis merchants. [3] We also know that in the mid-1830s Alton initiated several daily packets between St. Louis and the lower Illinois River, and another one or two lines directly with Cincinnati, the entrepôt marketplace from which many Alton merchants still received their goods. The number of these packets increased until 1837 and then stabilized, again indicating a relative decline of economic power in the late 1830s. Nevertheless, in 1837 Alton merchants traded directly with New Orleans, Philadelphia, and New York, as well as with Cincinnati. Clearly the town was more than a secondary central place and sought to challenge St. Louis's role by maintaining bypassing contacts with entrepôts in the East. One lawyer in town, whose account book has survived, supplemented his local business in collecting debts, with transactions for clients extending as far west as Jefferson City, Missouri, as far north as Chicago and Galena, south to New Orleans, and east to New York and Boston. In fact, 40 percent of his business was located in New York City, reflecting the business done by Alton merchants in that supply center. [4]

Between 1841 and 1845, however, the entrepôt aspirations of the town, reflected in its complex trading network, began to weaken. After St. Louis had surpassed it as the region's merchandising entrepôt, Alton diverted its capital into the pork industry (a strategy perhaps encouraged by its strong Cincinnati contacts). As more farmers moved north along the river and sent increasing amounts of wheat to river-town markets, from which surpluses were relayed to St. Louis, the regional market tended toward a chronic oversupply, forcing some farmers with locational, cost, and climatic advantages to specialize in corn and hog production. This changing production strategy occurred primarily

2 U.S. Census Office, *Sixth census or enumeration of the inhabitants of the United States* (Washington, D.C., 1841), 298–301.
3 Thomas Ford, *A History of Illinois* (Chicago, 1854), 176–7.
4 Norton, *Centennial History of Madison County*, 91–2; Peck, *A gazetteer of Illinois*, 149; the letter book of William Morrow, Alton, Ill., Missouri Historical Society, St. Louis.

nearer to the entrepôt, resulting in the familar von Thünen rings.[5] By the early 1840s hog and corn production had increased significantly in the lower valley, ending the importation of such supplies from the Ohio River. Reacting to this development, Alton, near the mouth of the Illinois River, prudently concentrated on developing a hog-packing industry. But, as noted, the profitable packing of hogs required heavy capital outlays, and thus was reliant on a strong mercantile base, as well as abundant supplies of salt, a good fleet of boats for quick transport to markets, and a large readily available labor force. So while the wheat belt shifted north toward Quincy, Illinois, Alton saw the hog trade move steadily toward St. Louis's higher market.

By 1843 Alton's once impressive production figures had fallen even with those of St. Louis. Five years later, St. Louis was clearly the region's dominant producer, Alton now left to packing hogs for only a local market along the lower river.[6] As the shifting patterns of agricultural production in the upper valley left Alton in this functional vacuum, its merchandising contracted. By the late 1840s most of its old ties with Cincinnati and its contacts in the East had been severed, while a few newcomers into town supplied themselves from St. Louis. During the 1850s, in spite of the general increase in production throughout the valley, Alton's role continued to wane. In contrast to towns to the north, imports to and exports from the town were declining, and the former more than the latter, indicating the lack of outsider investment interest in the small town.[7] By that time, the local elite, once highly specialized and with contacts throughout the country, had become ingrown, conservative, and bitter, and instead of continuing to invest in new ventures that might have drawn the town's economy out of its doldrums, purchased vacant midtown lots in a stagnant real-estate market and sat on their holdings simply as a means to consolidate their local positions.[8]

Davenport, in contrast, stood at the intersection of the St. Louis-oriented, river-based regional economy and the Chicago-centered railroad system expanding to the West. Initially, the site of Davenport lay across the river from Rock Island on which Fort Armstrong, a military outpost and trading center, was built in 1815. There, George Davenport, the Englishman who later gave

5 St. Louis Chamber of Commerce, *Report of the committee appointed by the chamber of commerce, upon the trade, commerce and manufactures of St. Louis, embracing a period of several years* (St. Louis, 1852), 10–11.
6 Margaret Walsh, "The Spatial Evolution of the Midwestern Pork Packing Industry, 1835–75," *Journal of Historical Geography* 4 (Spring 1978): 1–22; St. Louis Chamber of Commerce, *Report of the committee appointed by the chamber of commerce*, 10–11; St. Louis Chamber of Commerce, *Proceedings of the St. Louis chamber of commerce, in relation to the improvement of the navigation of the Mississippi River and its Principal tributaries and the St. Louis harbor* (St. Louis, 1842), 17, 39; *American Quarterly Register and Magazine* 1 (May 1848): 128–9.
7 *Alton Telegraph*, March 26, 1844.
8 John Reynolds, *Sketches of the country on the northern route from Belleville, Illinois, to the city of New York* (Belleville, Ill., 1854), 61–2.

the city its name, established his own trading post and soon made it the center of a system of outposts spread across the upper valley frontier. The Fort Armstrong post received its supplies by barge from St. Louis, and then Davenport distributed the goods by foot and boat to the north and west. Later, in 1821, Amos Farrar, one of Davenport's associates, was sent north to the Fever River to establish another post at the lead mines, near the site of Galena, Illinois, thus drawing the early lead trade into the frontier outpost network north of St. Louis. [9]

Although the first settlers of Davenport, Antoine LeClaire and George Davenport, simply crossed the river in 1832, the early economic history of the town was more closely tied to Cincinnati. Soon after LeClaire's establishment of the town, in 1835, several families from upstate New York and two or three merchants from Cincinnati settled there. For several years thereafter Davenport seems to have been a Cincinnati outpost, even though it was located on and indeed became a regular stopping place along the steamboat route between St. Louis and the Lead Region. [10] As the back country filled with settlers, however, the conveniences of St. Louis contacts became apparent and Davenport began to assume its role as a local central-market town at which settlers in eastern Iowa could acquire goods from St. Louis.

In 1841 this outpost connection was reciprocated when one of the town's first merchants sent a load of wheat and produce south to the regional market at St. Louis. Because there was little currency in circulation, he gave credit to interior farmers and was, in turn, given credit by St. Louis merchants. Similar developments occurred at Muscatine, Fort Madison, Burlington, and, to a lesser extent, LeClaire, by the mid-1840s. The relative independence of these towns' markets was reinforced by high transport costs, both from the back country to the river and from the local wharf to St. Louis, which lowered prices and prohibited extensive profitable movement of the crop. By the early 1850s, the heaviest areas of wheat production, which could be called a "wheat belt," moved north into eastern Iowa. Simultaneously, high prices in regional markets during the boom years of 1845–6 and again in 1853–5 caused local prices to rise, extended hinterlands, and brought the exclusive small local markets into competition for the role of subregional marketplace or even entrepôt. Given its ferry location just below the upper rapids, its distance above the cost-consuming lower rapids, as well as its distance from Quincy's formidable market competition, Davenport quickly emerged dominant. [11] The

9 *History of Scott County, Iowa* (Chicago, 1882), 600–10; Franc B. Wilkie, *Davenport, past and present: including the early history and personal and anecdotal reminiscences of Davenport* (Davenport, Iowa, 1858), 167–9, 221–3, 233.

10 J. M. D. Burrows, "Fifty years in Iowa: Being the Personal Reminiscences of J. M. D. Burrows," in *Early Day of Rock Island and Davenport: The Narratives of J. W. Spencer and J. M. D. Burrows*, ed. Milo Quaife (Chicago, 1942), 107, 109–10, 120–1, 175–7.

11 Ibid., 163–6.

increase of wheat receipts and reexports to St. Louis, encouraged local entrepreneurs to build one of the earliest steam flour mills on the upper river in 1847.[12] In response to this growing stream of produce shipments from Davenport to St. Louis, more merchants arrived in town after 1850, further drawing its economy into St. Louis's orbit. All that was lacking, in the eyes of townsmen, was a more efficient steamboat connection to the south because, in spite of the increase of trade, they still had to rely on the overtaxed St. Louis – Galena boats, receiving only seasonal help after 1852 from a competing packet on the same line and another from Keokuk to Rock Island.[13]

The limitations that such inefficient transport links to St. Louis imposed on Davenport became evident when, in 1853–4, St. Louis merchants chose Keokuk as their shipping point from which to send goods into central Iowa.[14] That town, as noted, drew its role from its location at the head of the rapids and thus at the end of efficient packet service to and from St. Louis. As more goods were transshipped through the Key City and up the Des Moines River on local packets toward the Iowa frontier, it became increasingly apparent to Davenport merchants that the cost of the rapids would preclude the town's development as an entrepôt for central Iowa. These two factors drew its attention away from St. Louis toward Chicago. There, town merchants possessed not only a locational advantage over other river towns, given their relative proximity to Chicago, but they also found more lucrative markets for their produce and lower costs on their purchased eastern goods. Thus, it took relatively little encouragement for town merchants to support railroad construction between Chicago and the riverbank opposite Davenport.

By 1854 the Rock Island Railroad had been built to Rock Island and the next year was extended across the river, thus establishing Davenport as the railhead entrepôt on the new western line. As a result, the flow of goods and services between the town economy and the river-based system dramatically shifted toward the railroad and Chicago. Within eighteen months two-thirds of the produce once sent from Davenport to St. Louis was put on railroad cars to Chicago.[15] In return, the town was flooded with Chicago and eastern capitalists, interested both in opening wholesale houses and in founding processing plants and manufacturing establishments to supply new markets,

---

12 Ibid., 186–90, 208–10; Louis Swisher, *Iowa: Land of Many Mills* (Iowa City, 1940), 242–70; Harry E. Downer, *History of Davenport and Scott County, Iowa* (Chicago, 1910), 182.

13 *Galena Daily Advertiser*, May 22, 1852; John Thomas Scharf, *A History of St. Louis city and county*, 2 vols. (Philadelphia, 1883), 1116; William Petersen, *Steamboating on the Upper Mississippi* (Iowa City, 1937), 237.

14 William Petersen, "The Keokuk Packet Company," *Iowa Journal of Politics and History* 50 (July 1852): 193–208; *Keokuk directory and business mirror for the year 1857* (Keokuk, Iowa 1857), 157.

15 D. A. Barrows, *Annals of Iowa* (Iowa City, 1863; reprint, 1970), 118–21; *Davenport city directory and advertiser* (Davenport, Iowa, 1855) xxviii, xl; Downer, *History of Davenport and Scott County, Iowa*, 276.

doubling the number of town merchants within two years. But as is the nature of such secondary relationships, local prosperity lasted only so long as the regionally oriented function persisted. When, after the Civil War, the railroads extended their lines further west, much of the railhead-associated business – processing plants, wholesalers and forwarding merchants, and hotels and taverns – moved west as well. Consequently, by the late 1860s Davenport retreated into the role of a subregional center of specialized manfacturing and trade and languished for a generation before another resurgence of hinterland manufacturing activity toward the end of the century revived the town economy.

Go north or south to another town, change the location at which a cross section of regional forces is taken, and the story line, though similar in many general features, changes in details and sequence, resulting in yet another distinctive local milieu. A similar history of Galena, for example, would emphasize the town's early development as a lead depot and merchandising outpost before much of the nearby region was settled. This early development made it the focal point of much of the steamboat traffic on the upper river, and allowed the town to gain wide influence in the North. In town, the impact of the early boom was felt in the dominance of a large porous cohort of merchants, professionals, and entrepreneurs who arrived with or just behind the first wave of development in the economic, social, and political affairs of the town. It was predominantly this group that invested in the steamboat system that was extended north into Minnesota in the late 1840s and early 1850s. And this group also, on account of its commitment to the steamboat, rejected requests for funds from the Illinois Central Railroad. All the while, the town's business shifted from supplying the sluggish lead industry, to serving as a secondary entrepôt for the northern trade for a short while in the 1850s before retrenching to a local county trade after the railroad arrived.[16]

Regional concerns directly manifested themselves in each local economy up and down the river by shifting the balance of power among merchants, altering the dynamics of Main Street competition, changing institutional structures, and even transforming a town's physical appearance. The latter evidence – whether manifested in a new wharf or railroad depot, new buildings down-town, a reorganization of land use near downtown, or the building of new residential neighborhoods for different income groups – was perhaps the most public evidence of regional forces interjecting themselves into local life. In Keokuk, for example, the Main Street was extended several blocks in from the river during the boom of the 1850s, and then, in the wake of the crash, was left underused and even vacant, a forlorn document of the boom-town experience.

16 Timothy R. Mahoney, "Urban History in a Regional Context: River Towns on the Upper Mississippi, 1840–60," *Journal of American History* 72 (September 1985): 332–4.

Upriver, the shifting pattern of land use in downtown Davenport developed less rapidly, but then unraveled in a more diffuse and unclear pattern. For example, one did not need many records to determine the simplicity of the town economy in 1845. At that time the wharf was only an extension of the road that ran from interior Scott County to the river, comprising a cluster of stores, shops, and houses where business between farmers, a few town merchants, and the passing steamboat was conducted. Opposite the steamboat landing at the northwest corner of Perry and Front streets, in 1845, stood the log-cabin store of James D. Burrows, an early observer of Davenport's growth and development whom we have met before. Near him, at adjacent street corners, were located some of his important early merchant colleagues in town. A block to the west Charles Lesslie and John Owens located their dry goods and hardware stores, respectively. In between was situated William Van Tuyl's store, a "center of attraction" in its days, according to one account. Next door were two more dry goods merchants and the Shays building in which the town doctor and the newspaper were located, across from the wharf. At this early date only a few businesses were located near or beyond Main Street. Significantly, those who had been located further west along the river, A. C. Fulton, for example, or the Davenport Hotel, had moved away from the river up to the corner of Second and Rock Island streets, perhaps to serve more effectively the business coming into town from the north rather than west. [17]

The cross streets running north from the wharf were generally occupied by tradesmen who lived above their stores. James McCarney, for instance, ran a tailor's shop just up from the wharf on Brady Street. Nearby was the boot and shoe shop of David Miller. A block west, another tailor chose to locate on Main Street just north of the river. Otherwise, the only significant functional – spatial pattern was the decision in 1838 by Antoine LeClaire, the town's founder, to build the LeClaire Hotel at the northeast corner of Main and Second streets. Initially above the town, and located somewhat higher above the riverbank to catch breezes for the comfort of the tourists for which the hotel was built, it had become by 1845 the focal point of a minor cluster. Around it were a number of novelty shops, as well as a few residences. One of the permanent boarders at the hotel was Ebenezer Cook, the lawyer turned banker, whose office was located in a small wooden building across the intersection of Main and Second from the hotel. [18]

The simple arrangement of Davenport's early Main Street through about

17 *Keokuk and business mirror for the year 1857* (1857); *Iowa State Democrat* (Davenport), 1845 advertisements; Barrows, *Annals of Iowa*, 44, 58, 67–8; *Davenport Democrat*, March 19, 1902, obituary of Patience Cook Van Tuyl.

18 Barrows, *Annals of Iowa*, 81, 111–12; Ambrose C. Fulton, *A Life's Voyage* (New York, 1898), 436–7; *History of Scott County*, 665, 925; August Richter, *Die Geschichte der Stadt Davenport und des Countys Scott* (Chicago, 1917), 261–2; Wilkie, *Davenport, Past and Present*, 27.

1850 documents the town's unchanging role as a central marketplace with a regional contact at the wharf from which subsequent development might be generated. In that year, observers still noted that it was best to cling to the wharf in locating one's business, so much so that "when a man opened a store on Second Street he was almost pitied by the wiser ones for his hazardous daring." [19] The dynamics of local competition, of which there seems to have been relatively little, still occurred within a few hundred feet of the wharf and the main wholesaling stores. Nevertheless, it was in 1850 that the first ground was broken in a new wave of capital investment in the town's infrastructure. That year the hotel district, if one may call it that, was reinforced by the construction of the Pennsylvania House hotel at the northwest corner of Second and Main, across Main Street, that is, from the LeClaire House. Meanwhile, Antoine LeClaire contracted for the enlargement of his older hotel to meet the standards established by the new one. He also had built the first of a planned row of buildings to run along the north side of Second Street between the hotel and Brady Street. Of further significance, in reflecting the changing demand for local produce, Samuel Hirschl opened the first wholesale grocery store just a few doors east of Brady Street on the wharf. [20]

More rapid development occurred in 1852, after an apparent lull in 1851. That year LeClaire contracted to complete his plans to fill in Second Street and had a four-story, block-long structure put up. On the first and second floors would be stores and offices respectively, with an extension of the hotel running through the third and fourth floors east to Brady. With the completion of the project by early 1853, other investors, responding no doubt to the rising land values created by the construction of a full block, began to cluster around the LeClaire complex. Across the intersection of Second and Brady, the Witherwax Building was put up late the same year. Right next to it, Orr's block was finished and occupied in 1853. In short, the development of Second Street touched off a wave of construction on Brady Street, thus connecting the wharf to the LeClaire Hotel by a kind of zigzag pattern. [21]

The centrality of this hotel, shopping, and meeting place was by 1853 manifested in the opening of a Literary Hall on the second floor of the Witherwax Building, and an Odd Fellows and Sons of Temperance Hall above Orr's store. Two doors south, near the wharf, the new post office further reinforced the communications and social hub created by the hall and new business blocks. Meanwhile the second-floor offices along Brady between the wharf and Second Street were occupied by the usual contingent of lawyers,

19 August Richter, "A True History of Davenport and Scott County," *Davenport Democrat*, April 11, 1920 to January 30, 1921 (Putnam Museum, Davenport, Iowa).
20 *Davenport city directory and advertiser* (Davenport, Iowa, 1854); Barrows, *Annals of Iowa*, 117–18, 121; Downer, *History of Davenport and Scott County*, 105–267.
21 Barrows, *Annals of Iowa*, 117; *Davenport City Directory* (1854).

insurance agents, physicians, and other professionals. There were seven lawyers in Witherwax's block alone, George Hubbell, James F. Parker, and James Thorington being the most pomrinent in local and state affairs. The town's first photographer, to record the professionals and businessmen in downtown, had also set up shop in Witherwax's block by 1854. [22]

The importance of the intersection of Second and Brady streets was secured by the decision of two bankers, Thomas Macklot and August Corbin to buy the first corner offices in LeClaire's Row (northwest corner of Second and Brady). Next to them William Inslee, another early merchant of some prominence, moved in. From his store to the hotel a series of luxury and specialty retail merchants quickly set up shop, creating as a result, adjacent to the town's prominent hotel, Davenport's and perhaps Iowa's first specialized shoppers' promenade, with its tall buildings, colorful windows, fine goods, and hustle and bustle–a kind of miniature "Ladies mile." Curiously, however, LeClaire also opened an iron-goods shop across from the hotel, a shop that no doubt received its goods from his foundry, which had been established in 1851 down at the corner of Scott and Front streets. To the west beyond the Pennsylvania House the German shopping district began, while a few doors to the north, along Main, one was on the edge of the town's middle-class residential district.[23]

Inevitably this growth attracted population, increased the demand for space, and drove up land values. As this happened, entrepreneurs began to choose different locations for their activities. In particular, those unable to bear central costs, began to push out along the edges of the developed commercial area, hoping, from their peripheral locations, to compete against merchants at the center. Indeed, by 1854 the spillover from the commercial core near Second and Brady and along Second Street to Main into surrounding streets was clearly underway. First, the post office moved from just above the wharf on Brady Street, to a site a half-block above Second Street. Several other businesses from the Brady Street cluster just above the wharf quickly followed, indicating, most likely, significant land-cost pressures on wharfside businesses. Indeed, a confectioner, a clothier, and a stonemason anticipated a further push northward and leapfrogged into the residential area around Fifth Street. More significant, if only for its name, "Cameron's Railroad Grocery" set up shop on Fifth Street near Perry. [24]

The arrival of the railroad into town provided the most dramatic evidence of external forces making a direct impact on the town's spatial arrangement. In 1853 Antoine LeClaire broke ground for the Davenport–Council Bluffs railroad at the corner of Rock Island and Fifth streets, to the northeast of the

22 *Davenport city directory* (1854).
23 Ibid., Barrows, *Annals of Iowa*, 116–20.
24 *Davenport city directory* (1854, 1855).

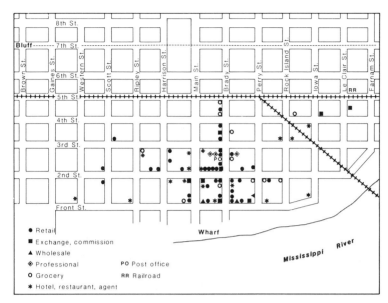

Figure 8.1. Location of businesses in Davenport, Iowa, 1856.

center of the commercial district. To the distress of many residents, Fifth Street was platted out as a railroad right-of-way and tracks were laid right down the middle of the street from the depot west beyond the edge of town. The next year the grading for tracks to be laid from the depot to the river, in anticipation of the arrival of the Rock Island by way of the Mississippi River Bridge, cut another path through the town's plat. The bridge, constructed in 1855 and 1856, entered Davenport's city limits at the corner of Third and Iowa streets and cut diagonally across Fourth and Rock Island streets to join the Fifth Street tracks at Perry Street. From this junction, trains from the east had to advance west down Fifth and then back into the depot (Figure 8.1). [25]

The town was soon flooded with travelers and businessmen from up and down the river, wishing to take the trains to the East. At first, to handle the increased traffic at the wharf and to make connections between the arriving steamboats and departing trains easier, downtown hotels organized a series of private omnibus lines to carry people the half-mile between the hotels and the station. The uncertainty of railroad schedules and the frequency of delays or premature departures or arrivals, however, made this system inefficient and unpopular with many passengers. It was easier and more comfortable to wait

25 Downer, *History of Davenport and Scott County*, 726–7; Barrows, *Annals of Iowa*, 119–20, 121–7; Alfred. T. Andreas, *A. T. Andreas' Illustrated historical atlas of the state of Iowa* (Chicago, 1875; reprint, Lowa City, 1970), 123; Wilkie, *Davenport, past and present* 114–20; *City journal, City Council proceedings* (Davenport, Iowa, 1862), September 15, 1858.

for a train to arrive or depart at the hotel, rather than taking the omnibus to the small station and waiting there. Accordingly, newcomers into the town began to construct a series of railroad hotels near the depot. First, the new Pennsylvania House located at the corner of Fourth and Iowa streets, soon followed by the City Hotel and The U.S. Hotel, which located across from each other at the corner of Third Street and Rock Island Street, one block from the railroad tracks and less than three from the station. Directly facing the tracks, which cut diagonally across the intersection of Third and Iowa streets, the Mansion House and, its name evidence of new connections, the Baltimore Hotel opened for business. In 1858 the great Burtiss Hotel was opened at the corner of Fifth and Iowa streets acorss from the depot itself. In each of these hotels patrons could wait for departing trains to arrive in the comfort of the hotel parlor and, once the train had arrived, still have sufficient time to make it to the station while the train switched up to Perry and Fifth and then backed into the station. Whether there were complaints about the noise and smoke that no doubt attended such convenience is not apparent. [26]

The extension of the hotel district to the northeast encouraged other railroad-dependent businesses to move into that part of town. Forwarding and commissioning merchants, dry goods and grocery wholesalers, sawmills, flour mills, and hog packers all moved northeast and east toward either the station or the tracks, invading the briefly exclusive residential area nearby and deflecting the cluster that had just taken shape around Third and Brady north to above Sixth Street (see Figure 8.1). Meanwhile, the outward expansion of the commercial area in the other direction stalled. The extension of the hotel districts, as well as the relocation of regional merchants to the depot vicinity, relieved land-cost pressures emanating from the wharf and thus short-circuited further encroachment by businesses into the adjacent residential areas to the north or west of Brady Street between Second and Fifth. [27]

Where external intrusions into internal arrangements were less obvious, the internal dynamic of a town's shifting spatial arrangements requires even closer analysis, revealing, not surprisingly, an even more subtle sensitivity of local events to outside forces. This was especially the case in Galena, where the basis of its local growth was established early and, until the railroad bypassed the town, no major dramatic intrusions onto Main Street or into the downtown area occurred. Nevertheless, the changes on the Lead City's Main Street between 1845 and 1858, if read correctly, can provide detailed evidence on the precise timing of the local economy's shifting role in the regional urban system.

26 *Directory for the city of Davenport for 1856, 57* (Davenport, Iowa 1856).
27 Ibid.

Galena, in this regard, is interesting because, on account of its early and rapid growth, its commercial district began to break up into specialized zones ten or more years before its neighbors. In addition, the narrow cramped river-bank on which the town's commercial district was forced to locate tended, by limiting the room to expand behind the wharf, to crowd business along a single Main Street and, by concentrating demand, to increase the intensity of land usage and raise land values. Contemporary reactions to the crowded city plat varied from picturesque to forboding, depending on one's experiences and aesthetic values. In 1845, the wharfside businesses in newly built warehouses included several forwarding and commissioning merchants, one with St. Louis and another with New Orleans connections. In the newly built Peck's building, at the north end of the wharf and on the right entering Main Street, the tenants included another forwarding merchant, William Hempstead, son of one of the town's early founders, and Charles Peck, a merchant and entre-preneur with strong St. Louis connections. In many of the wharfside buildings, the upper floors were turned over to wholesale warehouses. In the upper floors of the Peck's building the most prominent lawyers in town, among whom were Elihu Washburne, had their offices, in close proximity to the majority of their mercantile and steamboat clients. The remaining space on the wharf was reserved for the business and recreational needs of businessmen, steamboatmen, and their hired hands. The St. Anthony Coffee House, its name perhaps reflecting new northern contacts, was a center for deals and conversation. Many of the final transactions in the shipment of lead were made in the Henry Corwith Mining Office, located in the same building as his brother Nathan's dry goods establishment, which, according to one report, provisioned miners who had come in with a load of lead before they left again for the mining country to the north (Figure 8.2).[28]

As commercial activity intensified on the wharf during the middle and late 1840s, the concerns devoted to providing leisure for the workers and steamboat captains were pushed, by rising land values and rents, into the first block of Main Street north of the wharf. Travelers often remarked on this entrance into the town, a kind of "white way," crowded at all hours with single men and strangers. As one observer reported, "in the number of gambling and drinking saloons Galena betrays the influence of the foreign mining population. Yet after all, these are not so numerous as at first they appear to a stranger who meets them all at once along the river front by which he enters the city."

Up Main Street from the Peck's building but still within shouting distance of the wharf were two saloons, in 1847, and next to these a boardinghouse and an ordinary. Here one could get a bed for the night, or a meal on a daily or

28 *Galena directory and miner's annual register for 1847–48* (Chicago, 1847).

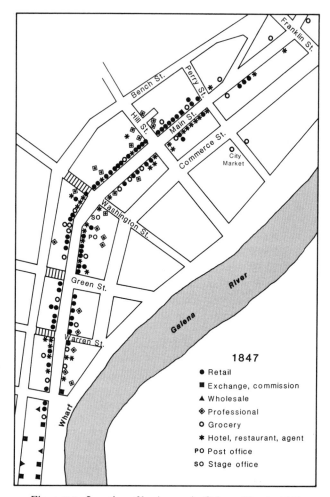

Figure 8.2. Location of businesses in Galena, Illinois, 1847.

weekly plan. Next door was a cigar shop where, inevitably, in back, strangers, vagabonds, and rivermen traded stories and gossiped. Across the street was Peter Smeler's Coffee House, which, by mention of its sign, seemed a finer sort of place. To its north stood the Washington Hotel, which had a barbershop run by a black man, Joseph Tailor. Further north, near Warren Street, was yet another boarding hotel and coffeehouse. [29]

29 Ibid.; *The History of Jo Daviess County, Illinois* (Chicago, 1878), 652–3; Illinois credit report ledger, XCVIII, R. G. Dun and Company Collection.

Beyond this wholesaling district near the wharf, one moved into an elongated zone of commerical land use that was similar to that in many towns at the time. Past the first set of stairs that connected residential areas on the bluffs above the Main Street, one moved from the transient area into a retail commercial area. A new brick block on the east side of Main north of Warren, filled with clothing merchants, and another new store up at the corner of Green Street occupied by a jeweler, attested to the rising land values and the rising demand for trade from the local population. That some of these merchants may still have attracted outsiders' trade is evidenced in the row of small wooden structures containing small stores selling everything from boots to family groceries, stores that seem still geared to the needs of travelers. North of Green Street the commercial area was solidified by the large, newly constructed Davis Block, from which A. C. Davis sold hardware, as did E. A. Collins in his impressive hardware shop next door, and which also included the harness and saddle shop of C. R. Perkins. [30]

The character of these establishments, geared toward clothing and hardware, may be explained by the location of the stage office at number 131 and the post office, also a center of information and meetings, just to the south. Around these two entryways into town clustered three boardinghouses, three saloons, a tobacco shop, two small grocery stores, two German bakeries, and a tailor shop. In the post office basement were the offices of an attorney, as well as a drugstore, a barbershop, and a dubious-sounding refectory called "The Shades." Up the street on the corner of Main and Washington two finer hotels, the St. Charles and the Napoleon, set the somewhat higher tone of this second travelers' area of Main Street. It was, after all, in the parlors, saloons, and gambling halls of these establishments that travelers going to or coming from the Lead Region waited for stages arriving or leaving town. [31]

Briefly, in the mid-1840s, the next block to the north developed its own functional distinctiveness. Until 1847 the newspaper office of the *Galena Gazette and Advertiser* was located at 141 Main. But in the next year it moved south to 91, into a new building put up just north of the Davis Block and thus drew its clustering influence back closer to the wharf, between there and the post office. Not until one almost reached Hill Street did one clearly reach the core of the town's commercial retail and hotel center. The American House Hotel, three stories high and four doors across, was an early center of town life, serving as a hotel for the finer sort of traveler as well as home for many of the town's most important young professionals and merchants. Among the occupants of "Commercial Row" along the first floor were a land agent and a saloon, obvious meeting places. "Across from the American House" were the Globe Hotel, which served a similar purpose for a slightly less elite clientele, as

30 Ibid.
31 *Galena directory and miner's annual register* (1847).

well as three important dry goods stores and the pharmacy of Horatio Newhall, the letter writer we have encountered before. Just south of the American House, on the east side of Main, L. S. Felt,s Dry Goods Store, Boyce's Drugstore, and D. A. Barrows' Confectionery, each of them steady and reliable merchants, rounded out the southern flank of this shopping area. Porter and Rood Dry Goods store on the northwest corner of Main and Hill, and an adjacent hardware store bounded the north side of this zone. Beyond lay a cluster of saloons that seemed to cater, as their names (Reaper's Hall and the Plough Inn) indicate, to the rural traffic associated with the farmers' market around the corner on Commerce Street. Further north one entered an area of light manufacturing, where a variety of manufacturers produced wagons, guns, leather goods, tin, iron and sheet-metal products, and furniture, and provided the blacksmithing services demanded by both the country and town population. [32]

Through the economic high tide of the late 1840s, each of Galena's business areas grew. In the 1848 directory, the wharf remained much as it was the year before. With the completion of buildings under construction, it now began to provide an impressive backdrop for the town's forwarding and shipping activity. Perhaps in response to the rising land values, which resulted from the limited space available, or perhaps seeking to encourage a major shift in a functional area, Nathaniel Sleeper relocated his wharfside forwarding and commission office in the heart of the commercial zone at 188 Main Street. His failure, leading to the auctioning of his goods in January 1849, was a signal to newcomers that locational demands could not be ignored in competing against one's colleagues. In the forwarding business one had to be on the wharf, or very near it, to buy and sell efficiently on commission and forward goods within a loosely scheduled and often very ad hoc business. [33]

The commercial core into which Sleeper sought to move continued, without his aid, to fill in. Smaller stores became somewhat larger, more general merchants continued to specialize, and, one assumes, the contacts between the wharf and the retailers continued to improve slightly. The cohesiveness of this area of Main and its connection to the wharf is reflected in the pattern of personal and professional contacts recorded in the 1849 diary of Benjamin Felt. Having located recently on the southern fringe of the commercial core, at 149 Main, on the east side, Felt's business remained healthy, if not buoyant, throughout the year. Of the eleven other merchants he specifically mentions, five were located within the commercial core around him, a few others were located up toward Diagonal Street, and the rest were in business on the wharf. In between, and especially in the area between the wharf and Green Street, he mentions no one and seems to have had no professional contacts or associations. In time, the relatively low land values and underuse of Main Street real estate in these transitional zones would inevitably draw on overflow from the wharf or commercial core, if space was demanded. For the time being, however, Main Street between the wharf and Warren Street remained an area of quick turnover, small wooden shanties, few successes, and few contacts with the locals or the local mercantile establishment that made its headquarters at the American House hotel. Only the recently built and commercially occupied Davis Block, on the east side of Main, suggested the possible future development of this area. [34]

That these variations seem to have been due, in part, to local dynamics was evidenced in the uneven persistence and prosperity of the businesses in the respective zones. In the prosperous late 1840s, the merchants in the wharf area and the hotel–commercial core persisted and prospered, while those in between continued to experience problems. When the merchants in the core areas also experienced difficulties, one could be certain that regionally oriented forces were at work in the local economy.

Such was the case in 1849 when the town faced rapid out-migration in the wake of the California Gold Rush and a sharp decline in local commercial business and demand for wholesaling services. Several forwarding and commission merchants soon faced severe pressure. One or two failed and left town, while others, such as George Campbell, Orrin Smith, and S. W. McMaster dissolved partnerships and retrenched in order to survive. Similar pressure was felt by a number of stable merchants in the commercial core, while numerous other smaller merchants left town. By the time the local newspaper editor published a new directory in 1854, the town's economic doldrums following the Gold Rush exodus and slump had been left behind and the lead trade faced, as we have seen, a sustained price rise. The result was a revival of business that had been already there but few new businesses or any significant functional development beyond that of the 1840s.

An initial look at the commercial district as platted out from the 1854 directory and compared with the arrangements of 1848 indicates two areas of development: the first block beyond the wharf and the stretch of Main Street across from the American House hotel on the east side below Hill. (Figure 8.3) One area was on the fringe of a core area, the other apparently right at the heart of another. Theoretically, such a pattern would suggest the expansion of one business district, simultaneous with the further development and filling in of the core of another zone. A close analysis of the newcomers in the first case indicates quite a different dynamic, however. Rather than being made up of merchants moving up from the wharf – forced out, if you will, by high rents, but still desiring peripheral locations – most of the merchants who moved into

34 Diary of Benjamin F. Felt, 1849, Galena Public Library, Galena, Ill.

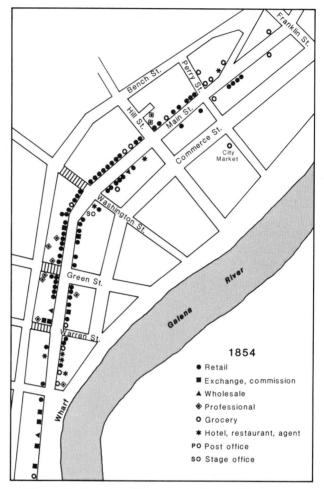

Figure 8.3. Location of businesses in Galena, Illinois, 1854.

the block just above the Peck's building came from just further up the same block. Rather than reflecting some general push outward from one core, the development of the block seems to have been carried out by businessmen from elsewhere on Main Street who grabbed up the stores and offices left vacant. Hence, rather than necessarily reflecting prosperity, this intrablock movement suggests sluggishness in the lines of trade performed here before – boarding-houses, restaurants, tea rooms, and coffeehouses. Perhaps there was a decline in the number of travelers coming to town, or in the number of steamboat personnel (a fact that can be substantiated from arrival and departure records) demanding such services. In any case, a boom in fundamental functions would have shown an outward push and the records indicate only one wharfside merchant who moved inland during the period. Business was good, but the slightly larger buildings still had enough excess capacity created in the building boom of the late 1840s to absorb the increase in trade. A similar localized dynamic of "musical chairs" was at work in the weaker blocks to the north. There, older merchants tended to move toward slightly better positions, leaving their old stands to newcomers or other smaller-scale merchants previously unable to move up into even secondary positions. [35]

More striking is the reshuffling of business activity across from the American House hotel at the center of the commercial core. Again, however, it seems that we have a situation not of strong firms being pushed out, or forced to upgrade their properties by strong competitors, but rather the filling in of a void left by a severe fire in 1851. For the urban historian the significance of fires is not just in their frequency, but how local businessmen responded to a major disruption. In this case, the destruction of a hotel and a few surrounding businesses was followed by the purchase of the land by other local merchants and the replacement of the hotel with three substantial business blocks. Perhaps the hotel had become unprofitable, or the owners sought a better location, or found the taxes too high. Whatever the case, its replacement indicates a need for more local mercantile space, and relatively less need for transient tourist or travel trade in town. By allowing this expansion of floor space to occur in the center of the district, however, the push into adjacent areas was, most likely, slowed for a number of years. [36]

A similar strategy was followed when yet another fire in May 1854 burned down the American House, a few adjacent buildings, and one or two across the street. Again, the hole in Main Street between numbers 155 and 183 was not filled in with another hotel but rather with a few more substantial brick business blocks, into which several merchants moved. In this case, the very high cost of the land, given the centrality of the hotel in the town's affairs, delayed its purchase. As a result, a buyer was not found, and contractors were not set to work until late in the year, and the new buildings were not occupied until late spring 1855. [37]

The apparent reason why, after two successive fires, the two wooden hotels were replaced by brick commercial establishments rather than by new hotels was, first of all, due to an increased demand for specialized mercantile services. Therefore, fire helped facilitate the further specialization of this area as

---

35 *The Galena city directory containing also advertisements of the principal merchants* (Galena, 1848, 1854, 1855); Illinois credit report ledger, XCVIII, R. G. Dun and Company Collection.

36 *Galena Daily Advertiser*, October 12, 1851; June 22, 1852; *Galena City Directory* (1854); City of Galena Tax Lists, 1851–4, Galena Public Library, Galena, Ill.

37 *Galena Daily Advertiser*, March 20, March 29, March 18, April 10, 1854; City of Galena Tax List, 1854.

Galena's primary shopping district. But it also seems that given the high land prices here, development was being diverted south into the lower-value transitional areas between Green and Warren streets. And in a prosperous but not developing economy, for reasons we have seen, real estate development in one area will certainly take something away from development attempted elsewhere. In 1854 A. C. Davis, the builder of Davis Block in 1846 on the east side of Main below Warren, purchased land across the street, demolished a row of shanties, and put up two other brick buildings. In one of the buildings, it was reported, he intended to build a meeting hall (which would compete against the hotels). The building was finished by late 1853, and by mid-1854 was already drawing some activity toward the south into a former shanty area of Main Street. The fact that among the new tenants were a music store, a bookstore, and an "Emporium of Fashion," owned by Mary Merrick, seemed to reflect the presence of an exhibition hall upstairs and to set a new tone for the block. [38]

About the same time, the Corwith brothers, in business on the wharf, decided to build a five-story structure at the northwest corner of Main and Warren streets. By mid-1854 they had opened the Corwith Bank on the corner and the H. P. Corwith dry goods emporium next door; a physician and a printer took two of the offices upstairs. The value of the land quickly soared, drawing further investment to this underused area and, again, no doubt drawing some of the vigor from the development of either of the two functional locational cores. This surge of impressive building, all in previously underused, lower-value areas, was completed in 1855 by the construction of the massive DeSoto House Hotel. Put up just to the south of the stage office, on the site of boardinghouses and small convenience stores, the five-story half-block-long structure transferred the nodal core of the Main Street of the 1840s to the south. Indeed, once in place, other smaller hotels filled in, and new stores moved into its first floor, enhancing the commercial and social aspects of this area of Main Street. It could be said that the location of the new hotel bore witness to the increasing role of land travel into town, as the railroad, which stopped across the river after mid-1855 and from which people crossed into Main Street by a bridge behind the DeSoto House, reoriented the function of the town economy. The new railroad hotel thus served as a new grand entrance into the old, secondary entrance into town. Meanwhile, the few listings for the block just above the wharf seem to document the further decline in the vigor of this once lively block that catered to the large population traveling along the rivers. Therefore, while the old center of Main Street filled in and lost some of its diversity, new hotel and financial centers shifted south toward the vicinity of the stage office, while ever-greater distance seemed to widen between the wharf and either of these specialized areas. [39]

Meanwhile, down on the wharf, many merchants remained where they had been a decade before. The Corwiths had left, but Mssrs. Campbell, Lorraine, and McCloskey continued to flourish in their old locations. Lorraine and Company had survived a small fire in their store in 1850 and continued to prosper, buying and selling "an extensive stock of goods." H. F. McCloskey had shifted his trade, with the steamboat interests headed by B. H. Campbell, to Minnesota. Both were now among the largest firms in town and prospering. Nearby the taverns had changed names, and a few new competitors had appeared on the wharf. In Peck's building Hempstead and Washburne were still in business, but their neighbors, Hempstead and McMaster, had dissolved their relationship – Hempstead moving to Chicago, and McMaster deciding to try his hand in the milling or pork-packing business. The wharf, therefore, remained a vital area of wholesaling and forwarding business and those merchants in that line who tried to move away from the wharf continued to fail. Nevertheless, it was clear by the mid-1850s that development along the wharf had peaked, relative to the considerable development at the new center of Main Street just a few blocks to the north

At the core of the old Main Street economy, around the old site of the American House, economic conditions were somewhat more fragile. Horatio Newhall's corner pharmacy continued to prosper and remained one of the most secure businesses in town even though Newhall himself had retired and his son ran the store. William Fiddick, a retailer nearby, "continued to draw desirable customers," something harder to do as the action moved further south. More indicative of the area's plight was A. M. Haines, who was "just getting along" and F. E. Bergman, who was only slowly recovering from the fire. Otherwise none of the burned-out businesses had reopened, and those that replaced them were not doing very well. One dry goods merchant at number 154 was about to close and go into managing the new DeSoto Hotel down the block. Newcomers from Connecticut, Merrill and Cowles, set up in a big way but failed badly soon thereafter. They were followed by Thomas Dean's budget "one price store" (always an indication of a declining shopping area) but he was unable to sustain his selling spree beyond 1855. B. F. Felt had slowed down his business for health reasons, adding to the mood of sluggishness in this area of Main Street. The confectioner John Crumbacker returned from California in 1852 to open a new bakery but failed by late 1854. And Robert Henry, who opened a clothing store in the Newhall block, had "fallen way behind in his payments" in early 1854, and sought to save his

---

39 City of Galena Tax List, 1854; *Galena Daily Advertiser*, April 9, 1855.

business by hiring a new employee Robert Cribb, but his reputation for being "an old hand at the swindling game" only further damaged Henry who, in his tardiness in meeting his credit obligations, "had seriously embarrassed his reputation for honesty." In 1856 he failed. Indeed, more than half the businesses in the old core of Main Street were in financial trouble in 1856. [40]

In spite of the relatively buoyant lead trade, therefore, Main Street Galena's economy was shifting its core and weakening at its point of interaction with the system. The focus of development had moved south to Green and Washington streets. The wharf was just maintaining itself and there were clear signs of softness at the old core around Main and Hill streets. This weakness became manifest in the wake of yet another fire that raged across Main Street north of the DeSoto Hotel beyond Washington Street in March 1856. In its wake, the fire left the last vestiges of Galena's old stage office district in ashes. The Napoleon House Hotel and the Shades, a saloon from steamboat days and a landmark of sorts, were both destroyed. Across the street, a row of mercantile establishments, all stocked with spring goods, was destroyed. Significantly, only about half of the stores, and only one on the east side of the street, had insurance, a reflection of the declining profit margins in town business. As a result, few were in a position to rebuild quickly. Particularly badly hit was James Carter who, in spite of his uninsured losses, went ahead with rebuilding and thus put himself in a perilous state to face the financial pressures of 1857, which, as we have seen, he did not survive. Few others were able or willing to risk such an effort and failed to reopen. The result was that within two months of the fire sidewalks were laid down along the empty lots covered, one surmises, by rubble. In subsequent years these lots remained undeveloped. Five years later the empty lots remained, in spite of their close proximity to the new business core. An 1885 survey of Main Street reveals the same blank space. And even today, the newer structures on this stretch of Main Street form a gap in the streets' nineteenth-century physical fabric. [41]

That so little redevelopment occurred so near to a recent boom area of building is strong evidence of a contracting local economy. The 1857 crash and the continued decline in trade did not affect the solid older merchants dramatically, but did, clearly, continue the decline in business and the decrease in demand pressure on Main Street. By mid-1858 few newcomers, other than a smattering of small, self-employed merchants worthy of a small marketplace, came to Galena at all. Businesses at the old core of Main continued to muddle along but there was little or no new building or even modernization of existing

40 Illinois credit report ledger, XCVIII, R. G. Dun and Company Collection; *Galena Daily Advertiser*, April 1, 1856; newspaper file through June 1856; *Insurance Map of Galena, Illinois* (1885), Library of the State of Illinois Department of Conservation, Galena, Ill.
41 Illinois credit report ledger, XCVIII, R. G. Dun and Company Collection.

buildings. Galena's once vibrant Main Street was gradually declining into the sleepy reality of a county central place. [42]

Nowhere was this decline more in evidence than down on the wharf. Indeed, by 1861, the next date on which the beleagured townsmen thought to issue a directory, only seven businesses still occupied the once-crowded functional area that had defined the town's economy. Among these, only four of the old vanguard of wholesalers and forwarding merchants who had expanded with the town's regional role continued to operate: R. S. Harris, S. W. McMaster, H. F. McCloskey, and James Rood. The Harris store was no longer providing local forwarding and commissioning services but rather was a branch of a chain of boat stores owned by the Harris brothers based, significantly, in Dubuque. The main offices of the St. Louis and Galena Steamboat Company had also shifted to Dubuque, following the lead of the Minnesota Packet Company, which had moved a few years before. Likewise, S. W. McMaster had tried to make a go of pork packing but ultimately failed in 1861. John Lorraine went out of business in 1861, having been on the wharf for fifteen years. So too had Benjamin Campbell. Even more surprising was the failure of George W. Campbell in May 1861. A year later H. F. McCloskey followed his lead, closing his doors and leaving his building vacant. One by one, such was the fate of many of the buildings along the wharf and in the first block of Main Street. The 1861 Directory lists no one at the address of the Peck's building.

Whatever demand had made this area of Main Street the center of Galena's local economy was clearly, without so much as referring to a single report on the shifting pattern of trade, gone. It is often said that it was the drying up of the silted-in river in 1863 that blocked steamboat traffic, closed down the wharf, and ended Galena's day as a subregional entrepôt. In fact, the bypassing of the railroad and the shift of entrepôt activities to Dubuque had resulted in, by 1861, a wave of departures and failures. In 1863 the river ran dry before a wharf that was already in decline. And when, after the Civil War, the founders of the town's economy gradually retired or died off, a wave of newcomers established a typical market-town Main Street unconnected to the wharf and only indirectly, by railroad and telegraph, connected to the larger forces of the regional economy. [43]

Economic development was, in every town, the basis on which social development proceeded. The significantly different courses of local economic development in Davenport and Galena suggest both dramatically different local social histories and histories of how their people interacted with the region. In Davenport, for instance, the town economy was controlled throughout the 1840s and 1850s by a small oligarchy of early settlers, who, in

42 Ibid.; *Galena City Directory* (1855, 1856, 1858).
43 Illinois credit report ledger, XCVIII, R. G. Dun and Company Collection.

turn, controlled the nature of economic competition on Main Street. The degree of control is suggested in inequality of wealth in town. For instance, in 1849 the top decile of taxpayers in town (twenty-one men) owned 54 percent of the town's taxable wealth. The ten richest men in town controlled 47 percent of the town's wealth, and the two richest men, Antoine LeClaire and George Davenport, owned 25 percent of all the taxable wealth in town. [44] This early, urbanlike concentration of wealth in a town that provided only a "central place" for the surrounding area derived, of course, from the early advantages that Antoine LeClaire and George Davenport had gained from being the town proprietors.

In 1832, just after the Black Hawk Purchase opened the western bank of the Mississippi to settlement and just before the arrival of the first settlers, LeClaire and his associate Davenport received large parcels of land on the site of Davenport in return for their services as traders and interpreters for the local Indian tribes. With complete control over an entire tract of land, LeClaire was able to plat a town, sell lots, control its future development, dispense land as he saw fit, or invest in its development as he felt the need. [45] His incentives, of course, lay in the fact that everything he did appreciated the value of the land and thus added to his fortune. At first, he used his holdings as collateral to get credit to buy up all the parcels of land around him. In one case he settled a land dispute by simply buying out the two litigants for a hundred dollars. Then he proceeded to sell the western portion of his holdings to the proprietors of a new town to be called Davenport. The price of two thousand dollars made LeClaire a handsome profit. But when the proprietors failed to attract settlers because, given the legal confusion involving territorial law, secure fee-simple deeds could not be guaranteed, LeClaire platted his own first addition and sold his land, with deeds, directly to newcomers. As a result, by 1839 land sales along ther river shifted to the center of LeClaire's addition between Main and Brady streets. Within a short while, LeClaire became, for all practical purposes, the owner of a newly settled town and for the next twenty or more years often acted as if he owned it, or certainly paternalistically supported it. [46]

When a wharf was needed to give the town a locational advantage, LeClaire built it. It was LeClaire who built the first hotel to attract tourists, who provided financial support for a number of the town's first wholesaling merchants, and who continued to make later additions to the town plat. In 1841 LeClaire donated a number of parcels of land to the town for school sites and two churches. And though evidence is less direct, it also seems that

44 Scott County Iowa Tax List, 1894, Iowa State Historical Society, Iowa City.
45 Barrows, *Annals of Iowa*, 58–9, 64, 68, 74–6; Wilkie, *Davenport, Past and Present*, 221–3, 233.
46 Ibid.

LeClaire built private housing as well and leased it to newcomers. To a Davenporter, LeClaire's self-interested largess "improved the city," and "elegantly memorialized his generosity."[47] A traveler from Dubuque saw it, as one might have expected, quiet differently: "Davenport contains a large number of houses – much larger than its businesses would warrant. This is owing to its being owned (or at least three fourths of it) by a Frenchman named LeClaire who is determined to have a town there. It requires, however, something besides buildings to make a place important and that something is not in Mr. LeClaire's power to bestow."[48]

As we have seen, LeClaire continued to think otherwise through the 1850s. To the LeClaire Row, which he built in 1853, he added a new post office and the Davenport Hotel down by the wharf. In 1851 he also went into the wholesaling business with George Davenport, who was also his partner in the opening of one of the area's first iron foundries that same year. More important, LeClaire played a central role in encouraging the railroads to make Davenport their railhead both on the east and west. Rather than balk at the heavy Rock Island Railroad demands, as other towns had done, LeClaire contributed the first $25,000 for the issue and encouraged or pressured other townsmen and merchants to contribute. LeClaire also was free to donate the right-of-way through the town plat as well as his own house on Fifth and Iowa streets to serve as the first temporary railroad depot.[49] Not surprisingly, when ground was broken for railroad construction, it was LeClaire who performed the honors. And when, in 1854, the first locomotive was shipped across the river and put on tracks heading west into Scott County, the townspeople could not have been surprised to learn its name, emblazoned on a front shield, the "Antoine LeClaire." Nor could they forget, of course, that such largess eventually paid off to Mr. LeClaire. Between 1853 and 1855 tax records indicate that his fortune rose from over $100,000 to over $250,000 making him one of the richest men in the West.[50]

LeClaire's economic power helps explain much of the inequality of wealth in Davenport and the tightness of the grip that such a small group had on the local economy. To a considerable extent, Antoine LeClaire picked his allies and supported their operations while excluding others. In addition to providing loans, he also dispensed contracts, demanded goods and services, initiated public-works projects that employed laborers, and supported financial ventures that sought to improve the town's infrastructure. Among his oldest associates were James Burrows, George Davenport, Henry Prettyman,

47 *History of Scott County,* 609.
48 William J. Barney diary, April 5, 1846, Iowa State Historical Society, Iowa City.
49 Barrows, *Annals of Iowa,* 345–9; Antoine LeClaire Papers, Putnam Museum, Davenport, Iowa; H. A. Porter, *Rock Island and its surroundings in 1853* (Rock Island, Ill., 1854), 27.
50 Barrows, *Annals of Iowa,* 345–9; Scott County Iowa Tax Lists, 1853, 1855.

Ebenezer Cook, and George Sargent. These last two men owned the bank previously mentioned and, with LeClaire's support, were able to survive the financial pressure of 1857 and extend their operations by means of a somewhat questionable currency-issuing scheme until late 1859. As the end approached, it was LeClaire who bailed them out but who also at last decided their fate by refusing to continue to risk his wealth in such a venture. When in December 1859 the bank failed, it was LeClaire again who repossessed the bank, and Sargent's and Cook's houses while trying to cover the losses of many other townsmen, several of whom, tied into the Cook, Sargent, and LeClaire scheme, went down with them. [51]

The strength of this group is evident in their ability to persist over a long period of time. Of the 21 members of this group listed in newspaper advertisements in 1845, 16 were still in business in 1855, among whom 6 – Burrows, Lesslie, Bowling, Van Tuyl, Cook, and Sanford – were still at the same locations. Thirteen of these merchants survived the Cook and Sargent crash and continued in business well into the 1860s, forming one-third of the larger group of merchants in business in 1856 who were still in business in 1861. Not surprisingly, 8 of the richest 10 men in town owning some 40 percent of town wealth in 1858 were in this cohort. [52]

Nevertheless, while these men continued to dominate in terms of wealth, their numbers continued to erode in the face of waves of newcomers arriving in Davenport during the 1850s. This decline in numerical control was significant because it counteracted any attempts by its members to pass on their control to others as they retired or went out of business. In the mid-1840s these men may have represented as many as half the merchants in town. By 1856 the 21 survivors of the old-settlers cohort formed, however, only 10 percent of the over 200 merchants in Davenport. Two years later, only 5 percent of the 300 merchants in town had arrived before 1845. Then, in 1859, came the failures of Cook and Sargent and of Burrows. Two years later Antoine LeClaire died, and soon thereafter other early settlers retired. As their numbers declined, so too did their presence and power, leaving the town economy and society open to the influence of the previously powerless or to newcomers for whom life in Davenport represented new opportunities. [53]

Merchants achieved such control and power not simply because, being wealthier, they were able to reinvest more in their businesses and thus outcompete newcomers. In small-town economies there was also a spatial dimension to competition that gave first comers considerable advantages over later arrivals. Back on Galena's Main Street, for example, it is noteworthy that

---

51 Burrows, "Fifty Years," in Quaife, *Early Day*, 250–9, 273–83.
52 *Iowa State Democrat*, July 1845; Scott County Tax Lists, 1849, 1853, 1854, 1858, 1860, Iowa State Historical Society, Iowa City.
53 Burrows, "Fifty Years," in Quaife, *Early Day*, 285; *History of Scott County*, 627–8.

all but four of the new brick buildings built along the wharf and at strategic corners on Main Street in the previous few years were occupied by wealthier merchants who had arrived before 1840. In contrast, all of the 65 merchant newcomers onto Main Street that year operated out of wooden structures. This was true even of newcomers with substantial capital support. The advantages of location that accrued to early arrivals becomes more apparent when one compares the persistence of merchants from block to block along Main Street between any two dates. Along the wharf and around the corner of Hill and Main, the two centers of Main Street at the time, persistence rates were significantly higher than elsewhere on Main Street. Indeed, along the west side of Main Street north of Green persistence rates in one year were only 12 percent, or a five to six times greater likelihood of failing during the year than for merchants located just a few blocks south or north. [54]

Furthermore, when, as happened after 1849, a general decline cleared some room in the older, persisting cohort, others who survived competed strenuously to move into the choice locations just vacated. Between 1848 and 1854 all but 74 of the 223 merchants operating in the former year survived. Of these survivors, only 19 stayed at the same address and in the same building. Of the 24 who stayed in the same buildings, 4 were from the 1848 cohort (i.e., newcomers in 1848), 6 were from 1844, and 14 from 1847 (including many merchants who had been in business since before 1840). Most of these merchants were in brick buildings and, as we have noted elsewhere, almost all moved toward the choicest locations in town on the wharf or near Main and Hill streets. And when, in the mid-1850s, the value of the wharf and the core around Main and Hill weakened, movement tended toward the center of Main Street between Warren and Washington streets, the result being a dramatic rise in the stability of these blocks as measured by persistence. In addition, when fires swept through Main Street in 1852, 1854, and 1856, it was always the oldest cohort that responded and rebuilt most quickly. Finally, a similar differentiation in the ability to survive between older and newer merchants was very clear in the general response to the financial distress of 1857. Of the 30 merchants reported on in 1857, 10 were from the pre-1844 cohort and only 1 of them had serious difficulties. In particular, the Corwith Bank stood through the crash and, as the reporter quipped, "could stand another." But the 1847 cohort had somewhat more problems, 2 of its members failing badly. More recent arrivals were, in general, hurt the most, only 2 of their numbers surviving the crash. Indeed, 3 out of 4 merchants who had gone into business after 1854 were wiped out. [55]

54 *Galena City Directory* (1847); Illinois credit report ledger, XCVIII, R. G. Dun and Company; *Galena City Directory* (1848).
55 *Galena Directory and miner's annual register* (1847); *Galena city directory*, (1848, 1854, 1855,

After 1858, the power of this oldest cohort began to wane, less from business failure or being forced out by the competition, than by departure to another town, retirement, and, given the average age of the members of the cohort, death. Others went off to the war. Indeed, of the 46 members of the pre-1850 cohort who survived until 1861, only 22 were still in business in 1866. But the war years were bad for all involved. Of the 216 newcomers in 1861, only 36, a disastrous 16 percent, survived the contraction in the town's economy and were replaced, in 1866, by only 70 newcomers (Table 8.1). [56]

As in Davenport, the obvious basis of such control and persistence was capital. Indeed, during the boom years of the mid-1840s, the significant increase in the capital wealth of the older cohorts enabled them to continue to control the economy, which they did, in spite of the California exodus and early 1850s slump, into the mid-1850s. It is noteworthy, for example that most wealth actually declined between 1851 and 1853. By 1854, however, the revived boom in the lead trade, combined with a general buoyancy in the regional economy, sent profits up, capital appreciated, and wealth rose dramatically. Throughout the period, older merchants added to their capital much faster than newcomers. That they used such an advantage to sell better goods at lower prices, command high-priced real estate and build impressive structures on it, and thus box out most competitors should be self-evident. [57]

The end result of this game of musical chairs, in which the advantages accrued more rapidly to those who had been there first, was their continuing domination of town economic activity, in the face of a relative decline in volume and value of trade and an atrophy in the town's functional base. Supported by the rise of the town's economy in the 1840s, these merchants continued in control until past 1860 (Table 8.1). Throughout the 1850s the pre-Gold Rush cohort included 35 to 50 percent of all the merchants on Main Street, only dropping below that after 1860. The result was that for almost every year in the 1850s, over 60 percent of the newcomers failed within a year, while none of the older merchants left town, further enhancing their control, and prompting one observer to remark: "The secret of their success lies in their fewness. They guard their market carefully and make a determined resistance to any newcomers." As a result, there was little chance for a newcomer to penetrate Main Street. It is noteworthy that not a single newcomer successfully broke onto Main Street and joined the ranks of the

1858); Illinois credit report ledger, XCVIII, R. G. Dun and Company Collection; *Galena Daily Advertiser*, April 1, 1856; Merchant Licenses Reports, 1844, 1853, Library of the State Department of Conservation, Galena, Ill.

56 *Edwards's descriptive and commercial directory of the Mississippi River* (Chicago and Milwaukee, 1866).

57 Jo Daviess County Tax List, 1845; City of Galena Tax Lists, 1852, 1854; Illinois credit report ledger, XCVIII, R. G. Dun and Company Collection.

Table 8.1. *The persistence of the 1844–5 cohort in Galena, Illinois, through 1866*

Year of arrival	Number of survivors from previous count (%)							
	1844	1847	1848	1853	1854	1855	1861	1866
1844	128	32 (25)	28 (88)	16 (57)	16 (100)	16 (100)	14 (88)	8 (57)
1847		191	120 (63)	36 (30)	36 (100)	31 (86)	26 (84)	10 (38)
1848			65	14 (22)	14 (100)	11 (79)	6 (55)	4 (66)
1853				59	38 (65)	30 (79)	14 (47)	5 (36)
1854					96	37 (39)	10 (27)	6 (60)
1855						42	10 (24)	3 (30)
1861							216	36 (17)
1866								71
Total	128	223	213	125^a	200	167	296	143
Pre-1853/total				(61)	(33)	(35)	(16)	(15)
1844/total			(13)	(13)	(8)	(10)	(5)	(6)

^{a} This figure, from Merchant Licences, may underestimate the number of merchants by at least 20%.

Sources:Galena City directory and miner's annual advertiser for 1847-48 (Chicago, 1847); The Galena City directory containing also advertisements of the principal merchants (Galena, Ill. 1854, 1855, and 1858); James Sutherland, comp., Umberhine and Justin's Galena and Dubuque classified directory and business mirror (Indianapolis, 1861); Merchant Licenses, in Northwestern Gazette and Galena Advertiser, 1844, 1853 (typewritten copy in office of State Department of Conservation, District Historian, Galena, Ill.; Edwards's descriptive gazetteer and commercial directory of the Mississippi River (St. Louis, 1866).

older cohort during the 1850s. The most spectacular attempt, that of Merrill and Cowles of Connecticut in 1854, failed within three seasons. Otherwise, the prospects of a location away from the center of trade, on the edge of Main or off on some side street, made Galena a frustrating prospect for any newcomer to the West. Galena became known as a closed town where opportunity was limited and chances of success slim. By the mid-1850s, newcomers in search of a better chance increasingly bypassed Galena (evident in their declining numbers from year to year) for towns to the north and west where trade was expanding more rapidly and early settlers had had less time to gain full control of the local economy.

This was, of course, the same group of merchants who arrived early and gained control of the lead business, established contacts with St. Louis, and invested heavily in steamboats and transformed the town's function from that of an outpost to an entrepôt serving the northern trade. It was these men as well who, deeply involved in steamboat investment, were unable or unwilling to offer similar funds to the railroads and allowed them to bypass the town, thus ending the town's regionally defined functional role. It was also members of this cohort who, having thus blundered, or at least miscalculated, were the first to follow the shifting functional arrangement of the system and move to Dubuque, Chicago, or points farther afield.[58] At every step, therefore, their efforts on Main Street interacted with, and ironically may have even been counterproductive to, their actions and strategies within the broader regional economy. That such economic centrality on Main Street, and in the decision-making process affecting the town's larger role, translated into both social and political power, should be self-evident. Within the dynamics of Main Street competition, continually ineracting with the regional system, therefore, lay the individual basis of a town's social or political history and, collectively among a variety of town experiences, the real underlying character of a region's social and political history.

58 Ibid.; Alexander Leslie, "A Diary of a Journey form Scotland to Galena and Back to Chicago," 23, Chicago Historical Society, Chicago.

Epilogue

Toward a regional social history

The regional history one writes depends, to a large degree, on the region one defines and studies. I have defined the "Great West," a region that developed across the Mississippi River valley in the middle of the nineteenth century, primarily as an economic and urban system. The patterns of settlement, urbanization, market production and consumption, and transportation and information flows were all shaped by the intersection of behavior shaped by previous experiences along the Ohio River and in the East with the environment, topography, and climate along the Mississippi River north of St. Louis. Early settlers, as we have seen, clustered along the rivers and moved slowly from south to north, and from the river into the interior, across the area between 1820 and 1850.

The exception to this was the early settlement of the Lead Region in the late 1820s and early 1830s, far ahead of the line of first settlement downriver. This island population producing a much needed resource provided the original stimulus for the economic development of the valley. By the late 1820s, Galena, Illinois, had become the primary entrepôt of the Lead Region, and a distant outpost of wholesalers, steamboatmen, and bankers in St. Louis, Missouri. This outpost economy, connected by a long-distance line of steamboats, established the foundation of the valley's transportation and, hence, its economic system. In the following two decades, as settlement moved north along the river and scores of towns were founded, a few of which became local depots, the steamboat system filled in and farmers on both sides of the river began sending enormous amounts of produce to the entrepôt in St. Louis. It was within this larger regional context that towns such as Quincy, Keokuk, Burlington, Davenport, and Dubuque developed and eventually began to compete against each other for access to the steamboat system, control of the produce trades, and ultimately the role of secondary entrepôt north of St. Louis.

We have seen how the shifting pattern of settlement to the west of the river and the northward movement of wheat production combined to shift the balance of power in the valley gradually in the favor of the towns on the west bank of the river. On the strength of these advantages, Davenport and Dubuque became the prime targets of the railroads moving west out of Chicago. Having endured a secondary status behind Quincy and Keokuk, vis-à-vis St. Louis, on account of inefficient transport and high freight rates to St. Louis, local businessmen were only too happy to accommodate the interest of Chicagoans and eastern railroad investors. Therefore, the system known as the Great West was eventually cut in half and broken up. With this invasion into the upper valley from the East, most of the ties with St. Louis were broken, the steamboat traffic declined to local and freight trade, and river towns unconnected to the new railroad system stagnated, as did all the businesses catering to the river. The system that had evolved in the mid-1820s, consolidated itself in the mid-1840s, and faced increasing pressures in the early 1850s, did, in fact, come to an end by 1860. It was eventually replaced, after several years of uncertainty, active competition, and considerable experimentation, by a new railroad-based system centered in Chicago. Such a story should remind one that, although the environment and topography may endure, different patterns of land use, and different kinds of economic activity oriented to different goals and occurring within different regional systems, ultimately define a place and establish its role in the broader forces of history.

The history of the development of any town occurred within these broad, complex regional changes. The success or failure of a town often depended on the ability of townsmen to read these trends and to respond in creative ways. More often than not, however, forces beyond the control of individual towns determined success or failure among the towns in the hinterland. Interacting with the system did not insure success, but to avoid cultivating such interactions would insure failure and stagnation. A variety of economic strategies was apparent. A town could, within the limitations of its previous history and current status, replicate the activities of another town and, by head-to-head competition, seek to replace it. A subtler strategy, drawing on some local advantage, was to try to substitute some dependence on another town or city by replacing imports with local production or specialized activity. If a town lacked the centrality to carry off such a strategy, or even attempt it, a town could simply try to fit some local specialized activity into the needs of some regional network of production or exchange.

Each of these strategies varied according to their assumptions about local growth and development. If one accepted the reality of the system, one would tend to form conservative strategies based on consolidating local advantages. If one resisted the system and denied its arrangement, one would be more likely to compete ambitiously against another town with the intention of eventually trying to overtake it. Specialization carried out under the assumption that it would replace dependence on another place, feed local centrality, and ultimately help one's town replace another city was much different than that undertaken simply to fit into the regional system. The fact that the old "parallelist" assumptions, which argued that each new town could replace old ones after competing independently from beyond the old town's range of influence, were being questioned by the realities of regional urban system development in the middle of the nineteenth century, however, makes such intepretation especially difficult.

Simultaneously some towns upriver maintained strategies reflecting the old assumptions (e.g., Galena's disinterest in the railroads), while others launched more active strategies that ironically, by whatever centrality and power they sought to achieve, still seemed to maintain the old parallelist assumptions (Keokuk's and Davenport's brief attempts to bypass both St. Louis and Chicago); still others seemed resigned to the dictates of the new reality (Dubuque's embrace of the railroad and a secondary function in a Chicago–centered system). Ultimately, however, the new systemic forces, reinforced by new assumptions about the nature of relationships between towns and cities, made themselves felt and transformed the ideology of economic activity. The result on the upper Mississippi River, therefore, was not only the emergence of a new urban arrangement, but also a system defined in new ways and supported by different assumptions.

Each of these economic concerns has a role in the writing of a regional social history. Just as in the economic analysis of a system, a regional social history should focus on interurban, lateral social activity and try to understand how such contacts affected social structures and relationships among groups within any town or city in the system. It is apparent, for instance, that if a town's role changed with the development of a new system around it, the social organization of the town would follow the economic change. As in economics, townspeople could respond to the changes around them in a variety of ways. Some responses were internal and occurred among themselves or vertically with other groups in town. Others followed regional economic interactions, responding horizontally to social developments in other towns or cities in the system. These social responses by different groups, classes, or individuals to the forces of systemic change could appear in a variety of ways: physical movement (in- and out-migration), demographic responses (changes in family work or reproduction strategies), or intellectual responses (rationalizations, defensiveness, bitterness, conservative backlash, cultural introspection, frustration, decadence, or even an active or hyperactive boosterism in which one claims that one's town can import the culture of the entrepôt and establish a similar cultural establishment).

In any case, people's social and intellectual lives in any town were constantly buffeted by outside forces and compelled to respond to ideas, actions, and attitudes of social groups that positively or negatively challenged their social identity. In short, as the system continued to grow at the entrepôts, the patterns of interurban social relationships were continually transformed. Urbanization brought a greater variety of social structures across the whole system and thus complicated issues such as social mobility and social control by confounding class identities. On a regional level, the process of urbanization increased lateral as well as vertical social frictions and accelerated in the words of Thomas Bender, "the interplay and interaction of communal and non-communal ways in the lives of all," [1] giving to later nineteenth-century regional society a particular vitality and diversity before the onslaught of homogenizing forces of the national economy and metropolitan mass markets made themselves felt in the early twentieth century.

On a general level the structure of any local society, and in particular a town's elite classes, can be explained by the functional history of the town economy in the course of its interaction with the regional system. As the contours of local history followed regional history, different groups arrived, acted and often departed in direct relation to the timing of regional interactions. At an early stage of local development, isolated early marketplaces developed slightly differentiated elites as they became more specialized than the surrounding rural economy. As the town's hinterland expanded, however, they came into contact with increasing numbers of towns, and the pool from which people sought to enter the town elite expanded. In particular, local elites competed with each other for subregional social control. Early on, such small elite groups could easily control the local economy, and thus local society as well. But as the hinterlands expanded, and the variety of directives affecting the town's economic activity increased, it became increasingly difficult for a single group to maintain control.

In fact, even as towns with advantages continued to grow and draw nearby towns into dependent relationships with them, the consequences of that victory undermined the ability of local elites to maintain social dominance. As centralization of economic activity in a few towns accelerated, more and more local merchants, finding it no longer profitable to stay in a small declining town, sought opportunities in the cities or out toward the frontier where they hoped to re-create the initial market advantages that had propelled them into the social and economic leadership of the town. Hence the irony that, at the very moment of apparent success, the process of growth that this victory set in motion drew even greater numbers of competitors into town to challenge their social hegemony.

Within these larger towns the older elites eventually had to accept that they could no longer control local society, as they once had done. But while accepting that newcomers had to be allowed entrance into "society," they still sought to exercise some control over which people would be allowed to enter.

---

1 Thomas Bender, *Community and Social Change in America* (Baltimore, 1978), 43.

Whether conscious or not, this screening process often served to articulate subtle class lines and distinctions among outsiders and locals.

The ability of an elite group to control this screening process often depended on the timing between their own length of tenure and the cycles of growth and decline in the regional economy. Obviously, the older an elite group, the more it would be forced, by sheer demographic decay, to open its ranks to newcomers and the young and thus to increase opportunity for newcomers in town. Likewise, if the economy grew too fast and the elite was unable to maintain control over this expansion, they would lose control of the screening process, the result being intense social conflict and confusion as groups with different social identities vied for places that, as soon as the economy slowed down, would stabilize in number and be controlled by only a limited number of families. If the two factors intersected, old age and rapid growth, a full elite class could be ousted or swept away almost overnight (as at Davenport between 1858 and 1860). However, if a relatively young elite persisted during a period of slow economic growth, it could maintain its position for many years and put a stranglehold on a town's prospects for opportunity almost to the complete exclusion of newcomers. Such seems to have been the case at Galena between 1849 and 1859.

From the perspective of the transient newcomer, the configuration between the experiences of a town's elite cohort and the cycles of the regional economy would, or could, significantly affect strategies on how to gain entrance to a local society. When growth was rapid and the elite relatively new and young, newcomers could gain entry-level employment, invest in some elite enterprise as a partner, or independently carry off some bold entrepreneurial action to gain a competitive edge over the slightly older and more complacent merchandising houses. Often, such an action by a newcomer could be dramatic enough to force the older elite to defend itself or to acquiesce and redefine its role and accommodate its ideas to those of the newcomers. In Chicago, the actions of Pullman, Palmer, and Armor, and in Dubuque, those of the Langworthys and Ryans, were significant enough to cause older elite members to respond by embracing the new ways. In less expansive times newcomers might pursue entry by more traditional, communally based social tactics: through intermarriage, by calling in a social debt and using a kinsmen as a contact, or by acquiring direct sponsorship from an out-of-towner known by members of the local elite. In such a case, it would probably be more common for the newcomer to identify with the values establshed by the older elite. In either case, as newcomers challenged the older elite, social tensions and frictions were increased.

Such tensions could also be felt in interactions from cities out into the hinterlands. As systems expanded their trading networks, city merchants would export city culture across the landscape, thus bringing more and more towns, which had been exporting their young for decades, in contact with the culture to which they had gone. Likewise, individuals who had moved into the cities or larger second-order towns could maintain contacts with their families, friends, and associates in their hometowns, and in doing so create a forum in which the values of two differnetiating societies and cultures clashed. By the time of the Civil War, and especially in the West, where everyone had been at one time or another an emigrant, a return to the old hometown – whether from Chicago back to Galena, or from Dubuque to Jacksonville, whether going back one, two, or even three steps in one's chain of migration, either to maintain periodic contacts with family members left behind or to reestablish, often for sentimental reasons, lost ties after a long absence – became a common ritual among city dwellers and often the denouement through which individuals and families came face to face with the impact of urbanization on their lives.

The fact that such patterns of interaction followed the increasingly complex interactions of towns within the system only complicates the analysis of such phenomena. Nevertheless, it was in the course of such social interactions across the system, as well as those within the vertical hierarchy of any town or city, that groups or classes (and particularly the elite because they tended to persist longer in different towns and cities) gained an identity and self-consciousness and articulated their local position in the context of larger regional and national entities. Yet in most elite studies scholars continue to describe rather than explain the nature of this process. To do so one must go beyond the blue-book litanies of incomes, club and association memberships, occupations, and public activities and examine their responses to newcomers into the city and to the forces at work in the regional society.

One can appreciate the complexity of local "circles" or "sets" or "social enclaves" scattered across an urban system that results from the process of regional urbanization by trying to define a general entity such as the middle class. For example, to speak of the middle class as a general social or cultural entity (as is so common) requires that one recognize all its constituent parts in various town hierarchies, living under slightly different local criteria, and therefore having somewhat different identities spread across the system. At one time or another, each of these local groups would be seeking, directly or indirectly, to establish social contacts with each other, screening each others' credentials, and, in doing so, trying to formulate a more general systemwide set of criteria for class membership in which general and objective characteristics replaced more local and subjective ones. Wherever, presumably at the entrepôt, the managerial and professional occupations had sufficiently differentiated themselves from manufacturing and merchandising, one could expect to find the most clearly defined structures of the middle class. But many others who defined themselves locally as members of a middle-class group would seek to join, or at least associate or identify with, this class. Some local elites would accept a role in the regional middle class by forming local enclaves, patterned after, but never compared directly with (in fear of rebuff), the entrepôt elite. Other elite groups would spread out across the system, planting marriage connections, kin and business contacts, and thus "influence" in a variety of local enclaves. Still others abandoned the pretext of membership from afar, on the basis of local prestige, by migrating to the entrepôt and trying to enter the relatively closed world of that elite group. Thus, within just the middle class, interurban contacts and movements could continually force one to redefine one's social position and identity as the structural context of that position changed from town to town and from city to city.

The complex patterns and experiences of such interactions within a class would be the focal point of a regional social history. The basis of those inter-actions lie rooted, however, in an understanding of the complex dynamics of economic activity and urbanization across a regional system during a certain period.

Appendixes

Appendix A: *Distribution of towns in relation to county population and area in Ohio in 1820, Illinois in 1850–2, and Iowa in 1852*

County	1	2	3	4	5	6	7
Ohio, 1820							
Adams	9	10,406	586	17.7	1,156	65.1	9.1
Ashtabula	6	7,382	828	8.9	1,230	138.0	13.2
Athens	4	6,312	1,233	5.1	1,578	308.3	19.8
Belmont	11	20,329	558	36.4	1,848	50.7	8.0
Butler	9	21,746	470	46.2	2,416	52.2	8.2
Champaign	9	8,479	887	13.1	942	98.5	11.2
Clermont	8	15,820	949	30.7	1,977	118.6	12.2
Clinton	3	8,085	410	19.7	2,695	136.6	13.2
Columbiana	17	22,033	864	25.5	1,296	50.8	8.0
Coshocton	2	7,086	1,170	6.0	3,543	585.0	27.3
Delaware	7	7,639	1,100	18.9	1,091	157.2	14.1
Gallia	12	7,098	792	8.9	592	66.0	9.2
Fairfield	15	16,633	1,010	24.8	1,108	67.3	9.3
Fayette	4	6,316	405	15.6	1,579	101.0	11.3
Franklin	8	10,292	543	18.9	1,287	67.9	9.3
Greene	6	10,529	416	25.3	1,755	69.3	9.4
Guernsey	9	9,292	1,098	8.5	1,032	122.0	12.4
Hamilton	11	31,764	421	77.0	2,888	37.5	6.9
Harrison	1	14,345	450	31.9	14,345	450.0	23.9
Highland	7	12,308	553	22.2	1,758	79.0	10.0
Jackson	2	3,746	420	8.9	1,873	210.0	16.4
Jefferson	15	18,531	360	51.5	1,235	24.0	5.5
Knox	5	8,326	864	9.6	1,665	172.8	14.8
Lawrence		3,499	450	7.7			
Licking	7	11,861	864	13.7	1,694	123.4	12.5
Madison	6	4,799	467	10.3	800	77.8	9.9
Monroe	3	4,645	576	8.0	1,548	192.0	15.6
Muskingum	11	17,824	654	29.2	1,620	59.5	8.7
Pickaway	10	13,149	503	26.1	1,315	50.3	8.0
Pike	2	4,253	443	9.6	2,127	70.5	16.7
Preble	7	10,237	432	23.7	1,462	61.7	8.9
Ross	16	20,619	692	29.8	1,289	43.3	7.4
Scioto	9	5,750	576	9.9	639	64.0	9.0
Trumbull	19	15,556	1,440	10.8	818	75.7	9.8
Tuscarawas	6	8,328	864	9.6	1,388	144.0	13.5
Warren	5	17,837	403	48.2	3,567	80.6	10.1
Washington	12	10,425	1,296	8.0	869	108.0	11.7

Illinois, 1850–2

	1	2	3	4	5	6	7
Adams	22	26,508	881	30.0	1,205	40.0	7.2
Brown	12	7,198	308	23.3	606	25.6	5.7
Bureau	14	8,841	871	10.1	631	62.2	8.9
Calhoun	7	3,231	281	11.5	462	40.1	7.2
Fulton	22	22,508	883	25.4	1,023	40.1	7.2
Hancock	21	14,652	816	17.9	698	38.9	7.0
Henderson	7	4,612	399	8.5	656	57.0	8.5
Henry	12	3,807	828	4.5	317	69.0	9.4
Knox	13	13,279	729	18.2	1,021	56.0	8.5
MacDonough	13	7,616	582	13.0	586	44.8	7.5
Mercer	11	5,246	565	9.3	477	51.4	8.1
Peoria	19	17,547	632	27.7	923	33.2	6.5
Pike	22	18,819	615	22.2	855	27.9	5.9
Rock Island	10	6,937	453	15.3	694	45.3	7.6
Schuyler	12	10,573	438	24.1	881	36.5	6.8
Warren	12	8,176	542	15.0	681	45.1	7.6

Iowa, 1852

	1	2	3	4	5	6	7
Benton	2	672	718	0.8	336	359.0	21.4
Buchanan	2	517	572	0.9	259	286.0	19.1
Cedar	8	4,971	582	8.5	621	72.8	9.6
Clayton	n.a.	6,318	779	8.1			
Clinton	7	3,822	695	5.5	546	99.2	11.2
Delaware	3	2,654	578	4.6	885	192.6	15.7
Des Moines	12	12,418	414	30.0	1,034	34.5	6.6
Dubuque	10	12,508	607	20.6	1,251	60.7	8.8
Henry	14	9,633	436	22.1	668	31.1	6.3
Iowa	1	822	587	1.4	822	587.0	27.4
Jackson	12	8,231	638	12.9	686	53.2	8.2
Johnson	4	5,788	614	9.4	1,447	153.5	13.9
Jones	7	4,201	576	7.3	600	82.3	10.2
Keokuk	9	4,882	580	8.3	536	64.4	9.0
Lee	17	20,360	522	39.0	1,198	30.7	6.2
Linn	10	5,440	724	7.5	544	72.4	9.6
Louisa	13	5,476	402	13.6	421	30.9	6.3
Muscatine	9	6,812	442	15.4	757	49.1	7.9
Scott	10	8,612	459	18.8	862	45.9	7.6
Tama	0	8	721	0.1		0.0	
Van Buren	15	12,753	484	26.3	850	32.3	4.8
Washington	5	5,881	570	10.3	1,176	114.0	12.0

Note: 1 = number of towns in county; 2 = population; 3 = square miles per county; 4 = population density per square miles; 5 = population per town; 6 = square miles per town; 7 = average distance between towns (r = square root of [A/3.14].

ources: William Darby, *The emigrant's guide to the western and southwestern states and *rritories* (New York, 1818), 220; Edmund Dana, *Geographical sketches on the western)untry: designed for emigrants and settlers... Including a particular description of unsold ublic lands, collected from a variety of authentic sources. Also, a list of the principal roads* :incinnati, 1819), 72–3; William Creese Pelham, "Ohio," 1818, in *The Mapping of *hio,* ed. Thomas H. Smith (Kent, Ohio, 1977), 169–71; Donald R. Leet, *Population *ressure and Human Fertility Response, Ohio, 1810–1860* (New York, 1978), 15–16; *J.S. Census office, Census for 1820* (Washington, D.C., 1821); John M. Peck and John *Messinger, New Sectional Map of the State of Illinois Compiled from the United States Surveys* (New York, 1853); U.S. Census Office, *The seventh census of the United States:* *850* (Washington, D.C., 1853); *Colton's Township Map of Iowa Compiled from U.S. Surveys* (New York, 1852); U.S. Census Office, *Statistical view of the United States... being a ompendium of the seventh census...* (Washington, D.C., 1854), ed. J. D. B. DeBow.

Appendix B: *Town density and average population per town at population density thresholds, 1820–50*

County and year	1	2	3	4	5
Threshold less than 2 per square mile					
Benton, Iowa, 1852	0.9	2	359	336	21.4
Buchanan, Iowa, 1852	1.0	2	358	286	19.1
Iowa, Iowa, 1852	1.4	1	822	587	27.4
Average	1.1	2	411	505	22.6
Threshold 3–6 per square mile					
Pike, Ill., 1830	3.9	1	2,396	615	28.0
Henry, Ill., 1850	4.5	12	317	69	9.4
Delaware, Iowa, 1852	4.6	3	885	193	15.7
Scott, Iowa, 1840	4.7	2	1,070	229	17.0
Athens, Ohio, 1820	5.1	4	1,578	308	19.8
Clinton, Iowa, 1852	5.5	7	546	100	11.2
Clark, Mo., 1844	5.6	22	130	23	5.4
Average	4.8	7	989	219.5	15.2
Threshold 10–14 per square mile					
Mercer, Ill., 1850	9.3	11	447	51	8.1
Tuscarawas, Ohio, 1820	9.6	6	1,388	144	13.2
Knox, Ohio, 1820	9.6	5	1,665	173	14.8
Pike, Ohio, 1820	9.6	2	2,127	71	16.7
Pike, Ill., 1836	9.8	24	252	26	5.7
Hardin, Ohio, 1844	9.8	1	3,032	135	13.1
Bureau, Ill., 1850	10.1	14	631	62	8.9
Madison, Ohio, 1820	10.3	6	800	78	9.9

Washington, Iowa, 1852	10.3	5	1,176	114	12.0
Trumbull, Ohio, 1820	10.8	19	818	76	9.8
Clark, Mo., 1851	10.9	14	395	36	6.7
Henderson, Ill., 1852	11.5	7	659	57	8.5
Calhoun, Ill., 1850	11.5	7	462	40	7.2
Lee, Iowa, 1840	11.7	4	1,523	131	12.8
Van Buren, Iowa, 1840	12.7	9	683	54	8.3
Jackson, Iowa, 1852	12.9	12	686	53	8.2
Louisa, Iowa, 1852	13.6	13	421	31	6.3
Average	10.8	9	1,189	77.5	9.4

Threshold 18–24 per square mile

Knox, Ill., 1850	18.2	13	1,021	56	8,5
Scioto, Ohio, 1844	18.3	6	1,865	102	11.4
Scott, Iowa, 1852	18.7	10	862	46	7.6
Clinton, Ohio, 1820	19.7	3	2,695	137	13.2
Van Buren, Iowa 1845	20.4	10	987	49	7.8
Dubuque, Iowa, 1852	20.6	10	1,209	61	8.8
Madison, Ohio, 1854	21.4	6	1,669	78	9.9
Henry, Iowa, 1852	22.1	14	688	31	6.3
Pike, Ill., 1845	22.8	30	466	21	5.1
Hocking, Ohio, 1844	23.0	2	4,871	212	16.4
Brown, Ill., 1850	23.3	12	606	26	5.7
Average	20.6	10	1,519	73.7	9.2

Threshold 27–35 per square mile

Peoria, Ill., 1850	27.7	19	923	33	6.5
Muskingum, Ohio, 1850	27.7	11	1,620	28	8.7
Ross, Ohio, 1820	29.8	16	1,289	43	7.4
Adams, Ill., 1850	30.0	22	1,200	40	7.2
Scott, Ohio, 1854	30.1	16	1,152	39	6.9
Jackson, Ohio, 1854	30.2	4	3,179	105	11.6
Pike, Ill., 1850	30.6	32	588	19	4.9
Clermont, Ohio, 1820	30.7	8	1,977	119	12.2
Marion, Ohio, 1854	31.3	7	1,802	58	8.6
Harrison, Ohio, 1820	31.9	1	14,345	450	23.9
Washington, Ohio, 1844	32.5	8	2,603	80	12.7
Van Buren, Ohio, 1855	32.8	21	758	23	5.4
Lawrence, Ohio, 1854	33.4	18	847	25	5.7
Hocking, Ohio, 1854	33.4	6	2,353	71	9.5
Lee, Iowa, 1851	33.7	12	1,468	44	7.4
Ashtabula, Ohio, 1844	33.7	16	1,483	44	7.5
Darke, Ohio, 1854	33.8	9	2,253	67	9.2
Shelby, Ohio, 1854	34.1	15	931	27	5.9
Average	31.4	13	2,265	72.9	8.9

Threshold 45–51 per square mile

	1	2	3	4	5
Brown, Ohio, 1844	46.1	10	2,272	49	7.9
Franklin, Ohio, 1844	46.1	8	3,131	68	9.3
Butler, Ohio, 1820	46.2	9	2,416	52	8.2
Washington, Ohio, 1854	46.2	12	2,462	53	8.5
Ross, Ohio, 1854	46.3	12	2,673	58	8.6
Highland, Ohio, 1854	46.6	16	1,611	35	6.6
Scott, Iowa, 1855	46.9	13	1,656	35	6.7
Miami, Ohio, 1844	48.0	5	3,939	82	10.2
Warren, Ohio, 1820	48.2	5	3,567	81	10.1
Delaware, Ohio, 1854	49.2	11	1,983	40	7.2
Morgan, Ohio, 1844	49.6	9	2,317	47	7.7
Jefferson, Ohio, 1820	51.5	15	1,235	24	5.5
Average	47.7	10	2,439	52	8.1

Note: 1 = population density per square mile; 2 = number of towns; 3 = number of people per town; 4 = square miles per town; 5 = average distance in miles between towns.

Source: See Appendix A.

Appendix C: *Population of river towns, 1820–60*

Town and year	Population	Source
Galena, Ill.		
1826	150	*Northwestern Gazette and Galena Advertiser,* January 13, 1843
1828	800	Ibid.
1830	900	Ibid.
1832	1,000	Ibid.
1837	1,500	Ibid.
1837	1,200	S. Augustus Mitchell, *Illinois in 1837* (Philadelphia, 1837), 122
1839	1,800	*Northwestern Gazette and Galena Advertiser,* January 13, 1843
1841	2,200	Ibid.
1843	3,000	Ibid.
1845	4,008	*Galena Gazette and Advertiser,* December 2, 1845
1845	5,500	*Burlington Hawkeye,* November 20, 1845
1850	6,004	*Galena Gazette and Advertiser,* June 13, 1854; U.S. Census Office, *The seventh census of the United States: 1850* (Washington, D.C., 1853)
1857	14,000	*Illinois state gazetteer and business directory for 1858 and 1859,* ed. George Hawes (Chicago, 1858), 91

Dubuque, Iowa

1850	3,108	*The 1880 Census of Iowa* (Des Moines, Iowa, 1883), 474
1850	4,000	*Dubuque Miner's Express,* October 23, 1850; *The Dubuque city directory and annual advertiser* (Dubuque, Iowa, 1856), 36
1852	5,500	Ibid.
1854	8,500	Ibid.
1854	6,715	*Galena Gazette and Advertiser,* June 20, 1854
1854	6,634	Ibid., September 12, 1854; *The 1880 Census of Iowa,* 474
1855	12,000	*Dubuque City Directory* (1856), 36
1855	12,052	*Dubuque Express Herald,* January 1, 1858
1856	16,000	*Dubuque City Directory* (1856), 36
1856	12,334	*Dubuque Express Herald,* January 1, 1858
1857	15,957	Ibid.
1860	13,000	*The 1880 Census of Iowa,* 474

Davenport, Iowa

1837	160	Harry E. Downer, *History of Davenport and Scott County, Iowa* (Chicago, 1910), 156
1839	300	Ibid.
1840	600	Ibid., 157
1842	817	Ibid., 164
1844	1,750	Ibid., 174
1844	900	Ibid.
1847	1,300	*Appleton's Southern and Western Traveller's Guide* (New York, 1852), 44
1849	1,200	Downer, *History of Davenport and Scott County, Iowa,* 190
1850	1,848	*Seventh census of the United States: 1850*
1850	4,837	*Davenport city directory and advertiser* (Davenport, Iowa, 1855), xxvi
1850	2,000	Downer, *History of Davenport and Scott County, Iowa,* 194
1851	3,000	Ibid., 195
1851	1,700	*Davenport Gazette,* February 3, 1853
1852	6,016	*Davenport city directory* (1855), xxvi
1853	4,500	Downer, *History of Davenport and Scott County, Iowa,* 196
1853	5,000	*Davenport Gazette,* February 3, 1853
1853	4,560	*Directory for the city of Davenport for 1856, '57* (Davenport, Iowa, 1856), 133
1854	5,203	*The 1880 Census of Iowa,* 577
1854	12,570	*Davenport City Directory* (1855), xxvi
1854	6,000	*Directory for the city of Davenport for 1856, '57,* 133

1855	7,000	Downer, *History of Davenport and Scott County, Iowa*, 198
1856	11,000	*Directory for the city of Davenport for 1856, '57*, 133
1858	15,190	Downer, *History of Davenport and Scott County, Iowa*, 208
1860	11,267	*The 1880 Census of Iowa*, 577

Muscatine, Iowa

1850	2,540	*Seventh census of the United States: 1850; The 1880 Census of Iowa*, 552
1850	3,100	*Dubuque Miner's Express*, October 23, 1850
1854	3,694	*Galena Gazette and Advertiser*, September 12, 1854
1854	3,693	*The 1880 Census of Iowa*, 552
1856	9,000	Nathan Parker, *Iowa as it is: A handbook for immigrants* (Chicago, 1856), 72
1859	4,828	*The 1880 Census of Iowa*, 552
1860	5,324	Ibid.

Burlington, Iowa

1844	1,831	*Galena Gazette and Advertiser*, December 2, 1845
1850	4,082	*Seventh census of the United States: 1850; The 1880 Census of Iowa*, 473
1850	2,000	Parker, *Iowa as it is*, 85
1854	7,206	*Galena Gazette and Advertiser*, September 12, 1854
1854	8,000	Parker, *Iowa as it is*, 85
1854	7,310	*The 1880 Census of Iowa*, 473
1856	16,000	Parker, *Iowa as it is*, 85
1859	9,033	*The 1880 Census of Iowa*, 473
1860	6,706	Ibid.

Keokuk, Iowa

1845	500	William Rees, *Rees' Description of the city of Keokuk, Lee County, Iowa* (Keokuk, Iowa, 1854), 14
1847	620	Orion Clemens, *City of Keokuk in 1856* (Keokuk, Iowa, 1856), 3; *Keokuk city directory for 1856–57* (Keokuk Iowa, 1856), 23; *Keokuk directory and business mirror for the year 1857* (Keokuk, Iowa, 1857), 155
1850	2,478	*Seventh census of the United States: 1850; The 1880 Census of Iowa*, 524
1850	2,773	*Rees' description of the city of Keokuk, Lee County, Iowa*, 14
1852	4,663	Ibid.
1854	4,769	*Galena Gazette and Advertiser*, September 12, 1854
1854	5,000	*Keokuk directory and business mirror for the year 1857*, 155
1854	6,000	William Rees, *Rees' Description of Keokuk, the "Gate City," Lee County, Iowa* (Keokuk, Iowa, 1855), 17

1854	5,044	*The 1880 Census of Iowa,* 524; *A History of Keokuk from its founding in 1820 to date* (Keokuk, Iowa, 1906), 7
1855	8,000	Rees, *Description of Keokuk, the "Gate City,"* 17
1856	9,000	Ibid.
1856	13,500	Clemens, *Keokuk in 1856,* 27
1857	17,500	*Keokuk directory and business mirror for the year 1857,* 155
1858	17,000	*A History of Keokuk from its founding in 1820 to date,* 7
1860	8,136	*The 1880 census of Iowa,* 524

Quincy, Ill.

1835	700	Pat Redmond, *A History of Quincy and its men of mark* (Quincy, Ill., 1869), 14
1837	1,500	Augustus Mitchell, *Illinois in 1837* (Philadelphia, 1837), 127
1837	1,653	*Illinois state gazette and business directory for 1858 and 1859,* 178
1841	2,686	Ibid.
1842	2,686	John Tilson, *A History of Quincy* (Chicago, n.d.), 89
1843	3,148	Ibid., 91
1845	4,007	Ibid., 101
1845	4,300	*Quincy Whig,* June 25, 1845
1849	5,500	Redmond, *A History of Quincy,* 14; *Illinois state gazette and business directory for 1858 and 1859,* 178
1850	6,902	*Seventh census of the United States: 1850*
	6,000	*Appleton's Western and Southern Traveller's Guide,* 44
1857	14,500	*Illinois state gazette and business directory for 1858 and 1859,* 179
1857	18,000	*Quincy Whig,* January 24, 1857

Alton, Ill.

1837	2,500	Mitchell, *Illinois in 1837,* 113
1850	3,585	*Seventh census of United States: 1850*
1852	3,000	*Appleton's Western and Southern Traveller's Guide,* 44
1854	10,000	John Reynolds, *Sketches of the country, on the northern route from Belleville, Illinois, to the city of New York* (Belleville, Ill., 1854), 32
1857	12,000	*Illinois state gazetteer and business directory for 1858 and 1859,* 4

St. Louis Mo.

1820	4,123	*Annual Review, The commercial statistics and history of St. Louis* (St. Louis, 1854), 8

1830	6,694	Ibid.
1837	6,634	Reynolds, *Sketches of the country on the northern route*, 32
1840	16,649	*Annual Review*, 8
1850	81,000	*Appleton's Western and Southern Traveller's Guide*, 44
1850	77,860	*Seventh census of the United States: 1850*
1850	77,439	*Annual Review*, 8
1852	94,000	Ibid.
1853	100,000	Reynolds, *Sketches of the country on the northern route*, 32

ppendix D *Data for Figure 5.1: Isochronous map of travel times from St. Louis by fastest means, 1840–60*

he following data were used to compute average travel times between various aces across the upper Mississippi region.

Burlington Hawkeye, March 7, 1844: "Steamboat Arrangement for Season": rom St. Louis on Saturday afternoon, arrive in Galena Tuesday morning (66 urs up). Galena depart Tuesday morning, to Oquawka by Wednesday orning (24 hours to Oquawka) to Keokuk early Thursday morning (20 hours wn from Oquawka to Keokuk) and to St. Louis Thursday (Galena to St. ouis 58 hours).

Peoria Register and Northwestern Gazette, February 28, 1844: St. Louis to lton, 4:00–8:00 P.M. Thursday (4 hours up). Alton to St. Louis 1:00–2:30 M. (1.5 hours down).

Galena Daily Advertiser, May 20, 1852: Packets for St. Louis leave St. ouis Saturday at 4:00 P.M. and arrive in Galena Tuesday morning (65 hours). Leave Galena Tuesday night, arrive in St. Louis Friday 4:00 P.M. (40 urs down). Packet to St. Louis leaves Galena Monday 5:00 P.M. and arrives St. Louis Friday 4:00 P.M., stops at all intermediate points (82 hours down).

Keokuk Gate City, April 14, 1857: "1857 Arrangement": Leave St. ouis 4:00 P.M., Hannibal 5:00 A.M., Quincy 7:00 A.M., arrive at Keokuk 12 on (20 hours up). Leave Keokuk 8:00 A.M., Warsaw 9:00 A.M., La Grande :00 A.M., Quincy 2:00 P.M., Hannibal 4:00 P.M., arrive at St. Louis 10:00 M. (14 hours down).

Keokuk Gate City, July 21, 1856: Leave Keokuk 6:00 A.M., Quincy 9:00 M., arrive in St. Louis 5:00 A.M. (23 hours down).

he following are special cases:

Keokuk Gate City, June 2, 1855: "The *Jennie Dean* up from St. Louis in 18 urs with a strong back wind. Breaks record of *Lucy Betram*."

Keokuk Gate City, August 20, 1850: "*Lucy Betram* race from St. Louis ▮ hours, 45 mintues."

Galena Daily Advertiser, July 14, 1852: "A Pretty Quick Trip": *Golden E▮* left St. Louis at 6:00 P.M. Friday, arrived in Montrose Saturday evening ▮ 8:30 P.M. (up 26.5 hours), having made her usual landings, arrived towing barge at Galena at 7:00 A.M. Monday (34.5 hours up from Montrose, 61 hou▮ up from St. Louis).

Galena Daily Advertiser, May 14, 1852: "The splendid *Die Vernon* arrive▮ sometime Sunday evening in 49 hours from St. Louis – This is making ver▮ good time indeed!" (49 hours up from St. Louis).

Galena Daily Advertiser, May 14, 1852: "But the *Dubuque* did better on h▮ trip down on the 19th, having made the Galena to St. Louis run in 34. hours."

Diary of Benjamin F. Felt, 1849, Galena, Illinois, Galena Public Librar▮ September 5–7, 1849: Leave Galena 5:00 P.M. on September 5. On Septembe▮ 6 left LeClaire at daylight, at Oquawka by sunset. On September 7 arrived i▮ St. Louis at 9:00 A.M. (40 hours down).

Ibid.: September 12–17, 1849, return home. September 11 left St. Louis i▮ evening. September 12, at Clarksville 4:00 to 5:00 P.M. September 13, a▮ Quincy between 11:00 A.M. and 12:00 P.M. At Keokuk about 2:00 P.M. It too▮ until sunset to get the cargo out of the boat. September 14, crossed the rapids detained at Montrose until dark. September 15, at Oquawka about 8:00 A.M▮ Put out a good deal of cargo here. At Muscatine by sunset. September 16, sto▮ at Davenport to spend the Sabbath. September 17, left for home via stage t▮ Maquoteka. Arrive home at 5:00 P.M. (St. Louis to Quincy, 39 hours; St. Loui▮ to Galena up over 100 hours).

Ibid.: October 1–4, 1849: Galena to St. Louis (72 hours down).

Ibid.: October 8–12, 1849: Four days to return. On October 10 at rapids a▮ 5:00 A.M. At Burlington before sundown (Keokuk to Burlington, 12 hours).

Ibid.: October 22–27, 1849: St. Louis to Galena. Five days with stop i▮ Hannibal, Mo.

Ibid.: March 22–23, 1849: Galena to St. Louis (50 hours down).

Ibid.: March 28–31, 1849: St. Louis to Galena (68 hours up). March 22▮ 6:00 P.M., depart St. Louis to Quincy at 5:00 P.M. (St. Louis to Quincy, 2▮ hours); rapids at midnight on March 30 (Quincy to LeClaire, 34 hours); rapid▮ to Galena (11 hours up).

Fragment of an anonymous letter, October 16, 1858, Missouri Historica▮ Society, St. Louis, Mo.: St. Louis to Alton 9:30 A.M. to 12:00 P.M. (2.5 hour▮ up).

Letters of Horatio Newhall, Galena, Ill., 1827–45, Illinois State Historia▮ Society, Springfield, Ill.: April 23, 1828: Passed lower rapids at Keokuk befor▮ dark and arrived at St. Louis 3:00 P.M. (Keokuk to St. Louis, 22 hours down▮

4 hours down from Galena). 7:00 P.M. to 8:00 A.M., Galena to Rock Island
(1 hours down); Burlington, 3:00 P.M. to St. Louis 3:00 P.M. (24 hours down).
Diary of Martha Minor Hall, June 18, 1853, Missouri Historical Society, St.
Louis, Mo.: Remained in Galena until Saturday morning at 11:00 A.M.,
reached St. Louis Monday at 7:00 A.M. (44 hours down).

William V. Pooley, "The Settlement of Illinois from 1830 to 1850," *Bulletin
of the University of Wisconsin*, History Series 1 (May 1908): 364: "Steamboats
make 2–3 miles per hour against the current."

Abner D. Jones, *Illinois and the West* (Boston, 1838), 40: "reached Alton in
our hours (from St. Louis). The distance is twenty-five miles...the
downward trip in half the time it takes to ascend the same distance."

Appendix E.1 *Agricultural specialization in St. Louis's northern hinterland,*
1840

	Production per farmer			
County	Wheat (bu.)	z	Corn (bu.)	z
Southern lowlands				
Bond	14.1	−.54	115.3	−.66
Boone (Mo.)	11.2	−.66	127.4	−.55
Callaway	11.8	−.64	116.0	−.65
Clay (Ill.)	3.1	−1.02	110.5	−.70
Clinton (Ill.)	7.4	−.83	49.0	−1.25
Cole	12.0	−.63	116.3	.65
Cooper	16.5	−.43	224.0	.32
Gasconade	5.2	−.93	101.0	−.79
Franklin	15.7	−.47	125.0	−.57
Howard	10.3	−.71	175.9	−.11
Jefferson (Ill.)	7.7	−.82	181.2	−.06
Jefferson (Mo.)	14.7	−.51	201.0	.12
Madison	48.2	.98	410.9	1.01 [a]
Marion (Ill.)	7.4	−.83	204.3	.14
Miller	7.8	−.82	145.6	−.38
Moniteau				
Monroe (Ill.)	22.9	−.15	299.7	1.01 [a]
Montgomery	9.9	−.72	95.7	−.83
Osage				
Perry	9.0	−.76	104.2	−.76
Randolph (Ill.)	29.9	.17	159.0	−.26
St. Charles	36.4	.45	182.3	−.05
St. Clair	11.4	−.66	490.0	2.72 [a]
St. Louis	14.8	−.51	119.6	−.62

Warren (Mo.)	11.5	−.65	111.0	−.70
Washington	33.0	.30	253.6	.59
Middle Mississippi border				
Adair				
Adams	75.4	2.18 [a]	377.9	1.71
Audrain	5.6	−.91	148.4	−.36
Brown (Ill.)	13.4	−.57	198.8	.10
Calhoun	5.8	−.90	149.7	−.35
Cass	44.3	.80	331.3	1.27
Chariton	4.2	−.98	92.4	.86
Christian	17.6	−.38	316.9	1.16
Clark	10.8	−.68	200.0	.11
De Witt	28.9	.12	326.4	1.25
Effingham	3.3	−1.02	123.7	−.58
Fayette	13.2	−.58	197.5	−.08
Green	8.7	−.78	96.2	−.83
Jersey	30.6	.20	200.0	.11
Knox (Mo.)				
Lewis	27.8	.07	229.9	.38
Lincoln	15.0	−.50	191.6	.03
Logan	18.7	−.33	354.2	1.50
Macon (Ill.)				
Macon (Mo.)	5.3	−.93	321.1	1.20
Macoupin	32.1	.26	404.3	1.95
Marion (Mo.)	17.2	−.40	237.4	.44
Mason				
Menard	17.8	−.37	392.6	1.84
Monroe (Mo.)	7.7	−.82	198.9	.10
Montgomery (Ill.)	9.9	−.72	95.7	−.83
Morgan	49.4	1.03 [a]	648.2	4.15
Moultrie				
Piatt				
Pike (Ill.)	28.7	.11	104.2	−.76
Pike (Mo.)	13.4	−.57	159.0	−.26
Ralls	18.3	−.35	183.2	−.04
Randolph (Mo.)	62.3	−.89	168.1	−.18
Sangamon	24.2	−.09	451.6	2.37
Schuyler (Ill.)				
Schuyler (Mo.)				
Scotland				
Scott (Ill.)	46.7	.91	473.1	2.57
Shelby (Ill.)	10.9	−.68	225.5	.34
Shelby (Mo.)	6.2	−.89	160.7	−.25
Prairie Peninsula				
Appanoose				

enton				
lack Hawk				
oone (Ill.)	43.2	.75	66.9	−1.09
oone (Iowa)				
uchanan				
ureau	70.2	1.95[a]	151.6	−.33
edar	3.7	−1.00	127.1	−.55
linton (Iowa)	23.2	−.13	79.8	−.98
avis				
eKalb	105.2	3.50[a]	137.2	−.46
elaware (Iowa)	30.0	.17	419.4	2.08[a]
es Moines	13.5	−.56	162.0	−.24
ulton (Ill.)	27.1	.04	168.4	−.18
rundy (Ill.)				
rundy (Iowa)				
ancock	27.9	.08	145.0	−.39
enderson				
enry (Ill.)	39.9	.61	135.0	−.48
enry (Iowa)	10.4	−.70	260.0	.65
wa				
ckson				
efferson (Iowa)	8.9	−.77	190.8	.02
ohnson	1.7	−1.09	32.4	−1.40
ones	12.4	−.61	52.3	−1.22
eokuk				
nox (Ill.)	64.3	1.69[a]	382.2	1.75[a]
aSalle	10.2	−.71	137.4	−.46
ee (Ill.)	63.0	1.63[a]	104.6	−.75
ee (Iowa)	21.1	−.23	201.4	.12
inn	4.6	−.96	19.1	−1.53
ivingston	58.1	1.42[a]	249.4	.55
ouisa	21.6	−.20	164.6	−.21
ahaska				
arshall (Ill.)	79.3	2.36[a]	225.4	.34
arshall (Iowa)				
cDonough	20.0	−.28	174.0	−.13
cHenry	67.2	1.82[a]	69.5	−1.07
cLean	33.9	.34	267.8	.72
ercer	40.6	.64	167.0	−.19
onroe (Iowa)				
uscatine	17.3	−.39	135.0	−.48
eoria	34.1	.35	172.4	−.14
oweshiek				
utnam	71.6	2.01[a]	124.8	−.57
ock Island	37.9	.52	191.0	.03

Scott (Iowa)	39.9	.61	71.4	−1.05
Stark	55.2	1.29[a]	180.2	−.07
Tama				
Tazewell	80.0	2.39[a]	346.4	1.43[a]
Van Buren	5.8	−.90	100.8	−.79
Wapello				
Warren (Ill.)	45.7	.87	178.5	−.09
Washington (Iowa)	4.1	−.98	184.3	−.03
Whiteside	4.1	−.98	94.2	−.85
Woodford				
Lead Region				
Carroll	25.6	−.03	94.0	−.85
Clayton (Iowa)	6.3	−.88	93.0	−.86
Dubuque	27.8	.07	43.0	−1.30
Fayette				
Grant	17.9	−.37	165.7	−.20
Green (Wis.)	48.0	.97	102.9	−.77
Iowa (Wis.)	19.6	−.29	116.5	−.65
Jo Daviess	21.2	−.22	118.6	−.63
Lafayette				
Ogle	102.5	3.38[a]	158.3	−.27
Stephenson	53.1	1.19[a]	111.4	−.69
Winnebago (Ill.)	64.2	1.69[a]	119.7	−.62
Mean	26.19		188.15	
Standard deviation	22.55		110.99	
n = 103				

[a] A county with specialized production has a z-score greater than 1 ($z = (X - \overline{X})/sd$)
Source: For methodology, see Diane Lindstrom, *Economic Development of the Philadelphia Region* (New York, 1978), 141. U.S. Department of State, Census Office *Sixth census or enumeration of the inhabitants of the United States* (Washington, D.C. 1841), 298–301, 311–13, 348–9.

Appendix E.2 *Agricultural specialization in St. Louis's northern hinterland,*
1850

County	Wheat (bu.)	z	Corn (bu.)	z
		Production per improved acre		
Southern lowlands				
Bond (Mo.)	.16	−1.31	9.59	−.33
Boone	.67	−.87	9.61	−.33
Callaway	.54	−.99	8.76	−.51
Clay (Ill.)	.70	−.84	11.60	.09
Clinton (Ill.)	.49	−1.05	10.26	−.19
Cole	1.19	−.35	8.32	−.60
Cooper	1.25	−.40	13.50	.50
Gasconade	1.44	−.24	13.52	.50
Franklin	1.28	−.37	12.20	.22
Howard	1.03	−.58	8.46	−.57
Jefferson (Ill.)	.13	−1.34	10.21	−.20
Jefferson (Mo.)	.72	−.84	11.97	.17
Madison	.95	−.65	12.37	.26
Marion (Ill.)	.09	−1.37	6.65	−.96
Miller	1.09	−.53	10.79	.08
Moniteau	.72	−.84	10.15	−.22
Monroe (Ill.)	.58	−.96	10.60	.12
Montgomery	.74	−.83	12.14	.21
Osage	1.12	−.51	12.90	.37
Perry	.20	−1.28	11.23	.01
Randolph (Ill.)	1.20	−.44	8.75	−.51
St. Charles	2.18	.39	11.67	.11
St. Clair	1.98	.22	9.75	−.30
St. Louis	1.38	−.29	9.41	−.37
Warren (Mo.)	3.81	1.76[a]	31.70	4.36[a]
Washington	.25	−1.24	9.83	−.28
Middle Mississippi border				
Adair	.47	−1.05	11.50	.07
Adams	3.41	1.42[a]	14.20	.65
Audrain	.36	−1.15	8.99	−.46
Brown (Ill.)	2.19	.39	14.70	.75
Calhoun	.46	−1.06	20.00	1.87[a]
Cass	2.40	.57	26.00	3.15[a]
Chariton	.42	−1.09	10.89	−.06
Christian	.62	−.93	21.50	2.20[a]
Clark	1.60	−.10	10.54	−.13
De Witt	.61	−.94	19.07	1.68[a]

Effingham	.36	−1.15	15.70	.96
Fayette	.48	−1.05	10.40	−.16
Green	1.93	.18	15.40	.90
Jersey	2.72	.84	13.40	.48
Knox (Mo.)	1.11	−.52	11.46	.06
Lewis	1.84	.10	9.09	−.44
Lincoln	1.33	−.33	11.71	.12
Logan	.57	−.97	17.89	1.45[a]
Macon (Ill.)	.66	−.89	20.94	2.08[a]
Macon (Mo.)	.57	−.97	12.60	.31
Macoupin	.79	−.78	16.30	1.09[a]
Marion (Mo.)	1.70	−.01	16.75	1.19[a]
Mason	3.08	1.15[a]	11.95	.17
Menard	1.11	−.52	22.95	2.50[a]
Monroe (Mo.)	.58	−.96	10.60	−.12
Montgomery (Ill.)	.44	−1.08	9.20	−.42
Morgan	.64	−.91	18.92	1.65[a]
Moultrie	.27	−1.22	16.15	1.06[a]
Piatt	.25	−1.24	18.32	1.52[a]
Pike (Ill.)	2.20	.40	15.60	.94[a]
Pike (Mo.)	1.46	−.22	10.30	−.18
Ralls	1.51	−.18	12.55	.30
Randolph (Mo.)	.57	−.97	10.70	−.10
Sangamon	.59	−.95	18.83	1.63[a]
Schuyler (Ill.)	2.11	.33	10.54	−.13
Schuyler (Mo.)	.46	1.06[a]	13.75	.55
Scotland	.62	−.93	10.67	−.11
Scott (Ill.)	1.75	.02	15.87	1.00[a]
Shelby (Ill.)	.04	−1.42	14.71	.75
Shelby (Mo.)	.99	−.62	12.36	.25
Prairie Peninsula				
Appanoose	.26	−1.22	17.13	1.27[a]
Benton	2.70	.83	6.53	−.99
Black Hawk	.55	−.99	7.43	−.79
Boone (Ill.)	1.78	.05	1.14	−2.13
Boone (Iowa)				
Buchanan	2.43	.60	7.25	−.83
Bureau	2.74	.86	8.68	−.53
Cedar	3.37	1.39[a]	9.21	−.42
Clinton (Iowa)	3.26	1.30[a]	4.95	−1.32
Davis	1.11	−.51	13.81	.56
DeKalb	3.47	1.48[a]	3.38	−1.65
Delaware (Iowa)	2.82	.93	6.16	−1.06
Des Moines	.21	−1.27	10.30	−.18
Fulton (Ill.)	2.19	.39	11.46	.06

Grundy (Ill.)	2.95	1.04 [a]	9.03	−.45
Grundy (Iowa)				
Hancock	2.36	.54	8.60	−.55
Henderson	3.40	1.42 [a]	9.86	−.28
Henry (Ill.)	2.66	.79	8.87	−.49
Henry (Iowa)	1.63	−.08	12.80	.35
Iowa	1.58	−.12	8.90	−.48
Jackson	3.40	1.41 [a]	5.21	−1.27
Jefferson (Iowa)	1.09	−.53	12.94	.38
Johnson	2.13	.34	8.88	−.49
Jones	2.80	.91	7.21	−.84
Keokuk	1.19	−.45	13.87	.58
Knox (Ill.)	1.95	.20	15.21	.86
LaSalle	2.72	.84	6.85	−.92
Lee (Ill.)	2.52	.67	6.00	−1.10
Lee (Iowa)	1.71	.01	8.65	−.53
Linn	2.30	.49	8.23	−.62
Livingston	1.16	.47	9.73	−.31
Louisa	1.69	−.03	12.87	.36
Mahaska	1.60	−.10	13.62	.52
Marshall (Ill.)	2.88	.98	10.81	−.08
Marshall (Iowa)	.22	−1.26	13.02	.40
McDonough	1.94	.18	10.69	−.10
McHenry	4.50	2.34 [a]	2.41	−1.86
McLean	.69	−.86	13.25	.44
Mercer	2.96	1.04 [a]	12.34	.25
Monroe (Iowa)	1.33	−.33	14.96	.79
Muscatine	2.71	.83	13.55	.51
Peoria	2.21	.41	12.10	.20
Poweshiek	1.04	−.57	9.10	−.44
Putnam	3.16	1.21 [a]	9.94	−.26
Rock Island	3.35	1.37 [a]	8.68	−.53
Scott (Iowa)	6.00	3.60 [a]	7.70	−.74
Stark	2.21	.41	12.73	.33
Tama				
Tazewell	1.98	.22	15.79	.88
Van Buren	1.47	−.21	9.89	−.27
Wapello	1.22	−.42	13.55	.51
Warren (Ill.)	1.63	−.07	13.56	.51
Washington (Iowa)	1.24	−.41	11.15	−.01
Whiteside	4.16	2.05 [a]	5.86	−1.13
Woodford	2.09	.31	11.03	−.03
Lead Region				
Carroll	4.16	2.05 [a]	6.65	−.96
Clayton (Iowa)	3.37	1.39 [a]	3.90	−1.54

Dubuque	2.76	.87	4.36	−1.45
Fayette	.83	−.75	8.55	−.55
Grant	3.10	1.24[a]	5.03	−1.30
Green (Wis.)	3.15	1.20[a]	2.82	−1.77
Iowa (Wis.)	2.95	1.04[a]	4.72	−1.37
Jo Daviess	3.44	1.45[a]	3.11	−1.71
Lafayette	2.21	.41	3.19	−1.70
Ogle	3.75	1.71[a]	6.23	−1.05
Stephenson	2.99	1.07[a]	3.97	−1.53
Winnebago (Ill.)	4.88	2.66[a]	4.33	−1.45
Mean	1.72		11.16	
Standard deviation	1.19		4.71	
n = 131				

Note: The figure of bushels per improved acre is calculated for accounting purposes, given the lack of figures that differentiated acres planted in either wheat or corn.
[a] A z-score greater than 1 indicates specialization.
Source: U.S. Census Office, *The seventh census of the United States: 1850* (Washington, D.C., 1853) 675–802, 728–35, 956–9.

Appendix E.3   *Agricultural specialization in St. Louis's northern hinterland, 1860*

	Production per improved acre			
County	Wheat (bu.)	z	Corn (bu.)	z
Southern lowlands				
Bond	.63	−.82	7.00	−.77
Boone (Mo.)	.36	−1.08	9.23	−.17
Callaway	.39	−1.06	8.71	−.31
Clay (Ill.)	.31	−1.14	10.54	.19
Clinton (Ill.)	1.78	.33	9.23	−.17
Cole	1.07	−.38	9.38	−.13
Cooper	.96	−.49	15.19	1.45[a]
Gasconade	1.34	−.11	9.20	−.18
Franklin	1.26	−.19	10.45	.16
Howard	.61	−.84	9.52	−.10
Jefferson (Ill.)	.70	−.75	9.79	−.02
Jefferson (Mo.)	1.19	−.26	9.10	−.21
Madison	2.06	.61	8.97	−.24
Marion (Ill.)	.79	−.66	9.34	−.14
Miller	.79	−.66	11.73	.51
Moniteau	.41	−1.04	11.00	.31

Monroe (Ill.)	4.79	3.34[a]	7.32	− .69
Montgomery	.37	− 1.08	8.59	− .34
Osage	1.55	.10	10.67	.22
Perry	1.52	.07	6.56	− .89
Randolph (Ill.)	3.56	2.11[a]	7.67	− .59
St. Charles	2.84	1.39[a]	9.51	− .09
St. Clair	4.50	3.05[a]	8.50	− .37
St. Louis	1.03	− .42	9.45	− .11
Warren (Mo.)	1.07	− .38	10.25	− .11
Washington	1.37	.08	9.09	− .21

Middle Mississippi border

Adair	.17	− 1.28	12.23	.64
Adams	1.87	.42	12.90	.83
Audrain	.14	− 1.31	9.55	− .08
Brown (Ill.)	1.34	− .11	11.92	.56
Calhoun	2.12	.67	14.51	1.26[a]
Cass	1.64	.19	15.03	1.40[a]
Chariton	.16	− 1.28	11.57	.46
Christian	1.08	− .37	10.41	.15
Clark	.42	− 1.03	20.37	2.85[a]
De Witt	1.30	− .15	12.14	.62
Effingham	.57	− .88	8.98	− .24
Fayette	1.04	− .41	6.65	− .87
Green	1.67	− .22	7.81	− .56
Jersey	2.98	1.53[a]	7.89	− .53
Knox (Mo.)	.11	− 1.34	9.71	− .04
Lewis	.39	− 1.06	9.80	− .02
Lincoln	.91	− .54	6.24	− .98
Logan	1.11	− .34	9.73	− .03
Macon (Ill.)	2.35	.90	14.10	1.15[a]
Macon (Mo.)	.07	− 1.38	11.93	.56
Macoupin	1.47	.02	6.42	− .93
Marion (Mo.)	.69	− .76	11.33	− .40
Mason	1.99	.54	16.25	1.73[a]
Menard	.75	− .69	14.82	1.21[a]
Monroe (Mo.)	.11	− 1.34	8.06	− .49
Montgomery (Ill.)	1.24	− .21	6.39	− .94
Morgan	1.03	− .42	12.09	.61
Moultrie	.57	− .88	15.23	1.46[a]
Piatt	.77	− .68	16.34	1.76[a]
Pike (Ill.)	2.71	1.26[a]	12.69	.77
Pike (Mo.)	.99	− .46	7.47	− .65
Ralls	.79	− .66	9.20	− .18
Randolph (Mo.)	.07	− 1.38	9.35	− .14
Sangamon	.97	− .48	11.45	.43

Schuyler (Ill.)	1.29	−.16	12.38	.68
Schuyler (Mo.)	.10	−1.35	9.46	−.11
Scotland	.17	−1.28	10.38	.14
Scott (Ill.)	2.72	1.27[a]	10.50	.17
Shelby (Ill.)	.91	−.54	11.72	.51
Shelby (Mo.)	.12	−1.33	14.17	1.17
Prairie Peninsula				
Appanoose	.51	−.94	15.16	1.44
Benton	2.81	1.36[a]	8.79	−.29
Black Hawk	3.00	1.55[a]	9.88	.01
Boone (Ill.)	2.27	.82	1.18	−2.35
Boone (Iowa)	1.17	−.28	12.96	.84
Buchanan	3.12	1.67[a]	7.03	−.77
Bureau	3.14	1.69[a]	5.37	−1.27
Cedar	3.59	2.14[a]	9.33	−.14
Clinton (Iowa)	4.24	2.79[a]	5.70	−1.13
Davis	.32	−1.13	14.38	1.23[a]
DeKalb	3.12	1.67[a]	1.86	−2.17
Delaware (Iowa)	2.28	.83	4.50	−1.45
Des Moines	1.14	−.31	11.64	.48
Fulton (Ill.)	1.43	−.02	14.32	1.21[a]
Grundy (Ill.)	.41	−1.04	5.34	−1.22
Grundy (Iowa)	2.93	1.48[a]	9.24	−.17
Hancock	1.03	−.42	9.68	−.05
Henderson	1.95	.50	14.79	1.34[a]
Henry (Ill.)	2.89	1.44[a]	6.92	−.79
Henry (Iowa)	1.03	−.42	11.54	.46
Iowa	2.42	.97	15.13	1.43[a]
Jackson	3.15	1.70[a]	7.07	−.76
Jefferson (Iowa)	.73	−.72	11.80	.53
Johnson	2.29	.84	14.25	1.22[a]
Jones	2.72	1.27[a]	7.44	−.66
Keokuk	1.27	−.18	14.50	1.26[a]
Knox (Ill.)	1.48	.03	10.56	.19
LaSalle	1.21	−.24	5.42	−1.20
Lee (Ill.)	4.18	2.73[a]	3.21	−1.80
Lee (Iowa)	1.08	−.37	11.44	.43
Linn	2.17	.72	9.05	−.22
Livingston	1.32	−.13	9.05	−.22
Louisa	1.92	.47	13.97	1.12[a]
Mahaska	1.44	−.01	17.85	2.17[a]
Marshall (Ill.)	2.82	1.37[a]	9.02	−.23
Marshall (Iowa)	2.40	.95	14.00	1.12[a]
McDonough	1.30	−.15	11.32	.40
McHenry	3.09	1.64[a]	1.65	−2.22

McLean	1.39	−.06	9.68	−.05
Mercer	2.29	.84	13.66	1.03 [a]
Monroe (Iowa)	.75	−.70	14.30	1.20 [a]
Muscatine	3.07	1.62 [a]	10.14	.08
Peoria	1.87	.42	14.20	1.18 [a]
Poweshiek	1.95	.50	14.76	1.33 [a]
Putnam	2.30	.85	9.74	.03
Rock Island	2.67	1.22 [a]	10.64	.21
Scott (Iowa)	4.94	3.49 [a]	6.72	−.85
Stark	2.87	1.42 [a]	5.49	−1.18
Tama	2.77	1.32 [a]	11.99	.58
Tazewell	1.43	−.02	12.04	.59
Van Buren	.69	−.76	12.57	.74
Wapello	.69	−.76	15.15	1.43 [a]
Warren (Ill.)	1.50	.05	17.03	1.94 [a]
Washington (Iowa)	1.50	.05	12.84	.81
Whiteside	3.77	2.25 [a]	4.91	−1.34
Woodford	1.88	.43	10.08	.06
Lead Region				
Carroll	4.22	2.77 [a]	4.99	−1.32
Clayton (Iowa)	4.13	2.68 [a]	4.97	−1.32
Dubuque	2.97	1.52 [a]	6.50	−.91
Fayette	3.75	2.30 [a]	5.40	−1.21
Grant	4.10	2.65 [a]	5.33	−1.23
Green (Wis.)	2.80	1.35 [a]	2.84	−1.90
Iowa (Wis.)	4.94	3.49 [a]	3.82	−1.64
Jo Daviess	2.15	.70	6.56	−1.14
Lafayette	3.56	2.11 [a]	4.06	−1.57
Ogle	3.97	2.52 [a]	2.96	−1.87
Stephenson	3.92	2.47 [a]	4.26	−1.52
Winnebago (Ill.)	3.52	2.07 [a]	2.56	−1.98
Mean	1.79		9.86	
Standard deviation	1.24		3.69	
n = 134				

[a] A z-score greater than 1 indicates specialization.

Source: U.S. Census Office, *Agriculture of the United States in 1860: compiled from the original returns of the eighth census* (Washington, D.C., 1864), 30–7, 46–53, 88–95.

Appendix F *Sources of wheat and flour trade figures,*
1840–50 and 1850–8, in Tables 6.3, 6.4 and 6.5

Dubuque

1845–9: "90,000 barrels of flour produced each year." *History of Dubuque County, Iowa* (Chicago, 1880), 474.

Galena

1845: "exported 150,000 bushels of wheat." Delegates to the Chicago River and Harbor Convention, *The commerce and navigation of the valley of the Mississippi; and also that appertaining to the City of St. Louis; considered, with reference to the Improvement, the general government, of the Mississippi River and its principal tributaries* (St. Louis, 1847), 20.

1848: "exported 13,491 barrels of flour and 16,984 bushels of wheat." *Galena Gazette and Advertiser*, December 21, 1848.

1849: "exported 20,282 barrels of flour and 15,493 bushels of wheat." *Galena Gazette and Advertiser*, January 6, 1851.

1850: "exported 32,733 barrels of flour, 8000 bushels of wheat." *Galena Gazette and Advertiser*, January 6, 1851.

Davenport

1844: "1000 bushels of wheat received but no mill." Harry E. Downer, *History of Davenport and Scott County, Iowa* (Chicago, 1910), 174.

1849: "exported 30,200 barrels of flour, 16,700 bushels of wheat." Willard Barrows, *Annals of Iowa* (Iowa City, 1863; reprint, 1970) 114; *Davenport Gazette*, December 6, 1849; Downer, *History of Davenport and Scott County, Iowa*, 193.

Burlington

1846–7: "exported 32,821 barrels of flour." *Davenport Gazette*, June 10, 1847.

1847: "exported 207,948 bushels wheat and 32,821 barrels flour." Delegates to the Chicago River and Harbor Convention, *The commerce and navigation of the valley of the Mississippi*, 20; *History of Des Moines County* (Chicago, 1879), 482.

1849: "exported year ending September 1, 1849, 12,500 bushels wheat and 39,500 barrels flour." *Davenport Gazette*, November 8, 1849.

Oquawka, Ill.

1847–8: 130, 148 bushels of wheat, 7,084 bags of flour shipped. Robert P. Sutton, *Rivers, Railways, and Roads: A History of Henderson County* (Raritan, Ill., 1988) 32. Estimate for annual exports after 1845, 40,000 bushels of wheat and approximately 3,500 barrels of flour (2 bags barrel) in 1847–8.

Quincy

1837: "flour and wheat exports of $100,000." S. Augustus Mitchell, *Illinois 1837* (Philadelphia, 1837).

1841: "exported 295,000 bushels wheat, 40,000 barrels flour." *Quincy Whig*, January 24, 1857.

1841: "275,000 bushels exported." George Hawes, ed., *Illinois state gazetteer and business directory for 1858 and 1859* (Chicago, 1858), 178.

1844: "six mills produced 35,000 barrels flour." Downer, *History of Davenport and Scott County, Iowa*, 459.

1846: "exported 70,000 barrels flour." John Tilson, *A History of Quincy* (Chicago, n.d.), 107.

1847: "exported more than 10,000 barrels less." Ibid.

1847: "450,000 bushels of wheat shipped, 55,160 barrels of flour from eight mills." David Wilcox, ed., *A History of Quincy and Adams County and Its Representative Men*, 2 vols. (Chicago, 1919).

1849: "exported 550,000 bushels wheat." *Quincy Whig*, January 27, 1857.

Alton

1840: "Production of Madison County: 165,520 bushels wheat, and 47,900 barrels flour." St. Louis Chamber of Commerce, *Proceedings of the chamber of commerce, in relation to the improvement of the navigation of the Mississippi River, and Its principal tributaries and the St. Louis Harbor* (St. Louis, 1842), 9.

1841: "exported 200,000 bushels wheat." Ibid.

1846: "exported of flour, 18,000 barrels." *The History of Madison and Clinton Counties, Illinois* (Philadelphia, 181), 92.

St. Louis

1840:"seven-eighths of the flour milled in St. Louis was grown in Illinois." *Alton Telegragh*, February 25, 1840.

Dubuque

1850s: "Pratt and Manson Mills produced 90,000 barrels a year." *History of Dubuque County, Iowa*, 474.

1854: "exports 180 tons flour and 880 tons wheat (about 29,300 bushels), or $1200. and $48,000 respectively." Nathan Parker, *Iowa as it is: A handbook for immigrants* (Chicago, 1856), 128.

1855: "Exported 540 tons wheat." *Dubuque city directory and annual advertiser, 1856–7* (Dubuque, Iowa, 1856). At 33 bushels a ton, that would amount to about 17,820 bushels of wheat.

Galena

1854: "wheat exports 20,684 bushels, of which only 1300 bushels by railroad. Flour 25,894 by river, 10,427 barrels by railroad, total: 36,321 barrels." *Galena Gazette and Advertiser*, January 30, 1855.

1855: "wheat exports 60,352 bushels by railroad, 35,840 by river, total: 96,192 bushels. Flour exports, 3891 barrels by railroad, 7729 by river, total: 11,620 barrels." *Galena Gazette and Advertiser*, January 15, 1856.

1857: "exports; flour 40,025 barrels by river, 5,600 by railroad, total: 45,625 barrels valued at $250,937." *The Galena city directory containing also advertisements of the principal merchants,* (Galena, Ill., 1858), 284.

1857: "226,000 bushels of wheat, 20,000 barrels flour." *Illinois state gazette and business directory for 1858 and 1859,* ed. George W. Hawes (Chicago, 1858), 91. Extrapolation in Table 6.4: in 1855, 63% by rail, 37% by river; let us assume in 1857, 66% by rail, 33% by river, or 226,000 bushels, 149,160 by rail and 74,580 by river.

1860: "20,000 bushels of wheat milled into 4000 barrels of flour." Manuscript Manufacturing Schedule, Jo Daviess County, Ill.; Eighth Census of the United States, 1860.

Davenport

1854: "50,000 barrels flour manufactured, value $350,000, 30,150 barrels exported, mostly to Chicago." *Davenport city directory and advertiser* (Davenport, Iowa, 1855), xxxviii, xl.

1855: "exported 30,000 bushels of wheat, 30,150 barrels of flour." Barrows, *Annals of Iowa,* 122; Downer, *History of Davenport and Scott County,* Iowa, 198. Assume exports are half by river and half by rail.

1856: "wheat received 450,000 bushels." Ibid., 199.

1857: "wheat received 1,019,000 bushels, wheat to flour 879,000 bushels; exported 30,072 bushels by river, 51,936 bushels by rail" (total: 82,008 bushels). "Exported 19,819 barrels flour by river, 86,509 barrels by rail" (total: 106,328 barrels). Downer, *History of Davenport and Scott County, Iowa,* 276.

Muscatine

1854: "received 393,570 bushels of wheat to make 29,515 barrels of flour." Parker, *Iowa as it is,* 162.

Oquawka, Ill.

1851: "shipments of grain purchased here amounted to 169,366 bushels wheat, corn, and oats." *A History of Mercer County,* Illinois (Chicago, 1882), 133.

1856: "May 10 to October 11, 1856, 270,727 bushels grain taken on (in addition to heavy shipments in April)." Ibid.

1851 estimate is 50% of 1851 figure, or 84,683, averaged with 1848 figure, 107,416. The 1854 figure is an average of 1851 and 1856 figures, 177,705. These figures indicate no milling or marketing activity there.

Burlington

1855: "exported 297,000 bushels of wheat, 268,000 by rail; rest by river and 21,900 barrels of flour." *History of Des Moines County* (Chicago, 1879), 112.

1856: "Wheat received 437,000 bushels. Exported 17,000 by river, 187,500 by rail, total: 204,500 bushels. Flour produced 54,000 barrels, exported 18,700." *The first annual directory, of the City of Burlington for 1859, comp. Watson Bowron* (Burlington, Iowa, 1859), 8.

1858: "exported 187,500 bushels wheat by rail, 10,000 by river, total: 197,500 bushels." Ibid., 8–9.

Keokuk

1857: "60,000 bushels of wheat exported." *Keokuk Gate City*, October 30, 1857.

Quincy

1850: 270,000 bushels of wheat used to make 54,000 barrels flour. Manuscript Manufacturing Schedules, Adams County, Ill.; Seventh Census of the United States, 1850.

1852: "Quincy consumed 300,000 bushels of wheat." Tilson, *History of Quincy*, 141.

1853: Exported 20,993 barrels of flour and 40,866 bushels of wheat. *Quincy Whig*, February 28, 1854.

1854: "exported 22,294 bushels of wheat, 48,000 barrels flour." Ibid., 157.

1856: "370,000 bushels of wheat exported, all by river." *Quincy Whig*, January 27, 1857.

1856: "flour mills produced 105,400 barrels of flour." Ibid., January 17, 1857.

1857: "six mills used 660,000 bushels of wheat to make 132,000 barrels of flour." Joseph T. Holmes, *Quincy in 1857. Or facts and figures* (Quincy, Ill., 1857), 29.

1860: "560,500 bushels received, 112,000 barrels produced." Manuscript Manufacturing Schedules, Adams County, Ill.; Eighth Census of the United States, 1860.

Alton

1850: "450,000 bushels of wheat used to make 115,000 barrels of flour." Manuscript Manufacturing Schedules, Madison County, Ill.; Seventh Census of the United states, 1850.

1853: "exported 84,780 bushels of wheat and 27,003 barrels of flour: received 225,883 bushels of wheat." John Reynolds, *Sketches of the country, on the northern route from Belleville, Illinois, to the city of New York* (Belleville, Ill., 1854), 61–2.

1854: "exports 192,849 bushels wheat, 58,800 barrels flour." *Alton city directory and business mirror* (Alton, Ill., 1856).

1860: "50,000 bushels of wheat ground into 10,000 barrels flour." Manuscript Manufacturing Schedule, Madison County, Ill.; Eighth Census of the United States, 1860.

Appendix G: *Documentation for Table 7.1:The local balance of trade; imports versus exports in river towns, 1840–60*

Data are organized in the following manner:
  I. Documented figures with source citation.
  II. Extrapolated or estimated figures:
    A. Those extrapolated as a percentage of a figure given in any year.
    B. Those extrapolated by population changes from year in which solid figure exists.

Dubuque

I. All figures 1851–5 documented. *Dubuque city directory and annual advertiser, 1856–7* (Dubuque, Iowa, 1856), 34; Nathan Parker, *Iowa as it is: A handbook for immigrants* (Chicago, 1856), 128.

Galena

I. 1842 imports: $1,250,000. *Northwestern Gazette and Galena Advertiser,* January 13, 1843.

1847 exports: $2,421,000. Delegates to the Chicago River and Harbor Convention, *The commerce and navigation of the valley of the Mississippi; and also that appertaining to the City of St. Louis; considered, with reference to the improvement, by the general government, of the Mississippi River and its principal tributaries* (St. Louis, 1847), 20.

1848 exports: $1,602,050. *Galena Gazette and Advertiser,* December 20, 1848.

1850 exports: $2,002,252. *Galena Gazette and Advertiser,* January 6, 1851.

1853 imports: $4,958,048. *The Galena City Directory, containing also advertisements of the principal merchants* (Galena, Ill., 1854), 2.

II. A. In the 1847 figures, the amount of lead produced is quoted at $2.25 million compared with the quote of $1.72 million in Table 6.6. Given the nature of the convention report, it is probable that the figure is overstated and that the actual figure is closer to that in Table 6.6. The total return on lead, nevertheless, amounted to 71% of the full quoted total in the 1847 report, while the amount reported in the 1847 convention report equaled over 90% of total exports. I will estimate that lead exports were 80% of total exports for the town economy.

Year	Lead exports (see Table 6.6)	% of total	Total estimated exports
1842	$ 700,000	80	$ 875,000
1846	1,481,650	80	1,852,063
1850	1,671,650	80	2,089,563
1851	1,354,670	80	1,693,338
1853	1,639,390	80	2,049,238
1855	1,777,435	80	2,221,793
1857	1,800,000 (est.)	80	2,250,000
1860	660,000 (est.)	50	1,320,000

II. B. Import figures extrapolated from 1853 as percent of population:

Year	Population % of 1853	Estimate
1842	33	$
1846	72	3,569,795
1850	80	3,966,438
1851	80 (est.)	3,966,438
1853	100	
1855	140	6,941,267
1857	184	9,122,808
1860	136	6,742,945

Davenport

I. 1848 imports: $148,500. *Davenport Gazette*, December 6, 1849; *Harry E. Downer, History of Davenport and Scott County, Iowa* (Chicago, 1910), 193.

1855 imports: $3,542,670. *Twin cities directory* (Davenport, Iowa 1856), 60–1.

1857 imports: $4,738,340. Franc B. Wilkie, *Davenport, past and present: including the early history and personal and anecdotal reminiscences of Davenport* (Davenport, Iowa, 1858), 270–6.

II. A. From a detailed account of 1849 figures in Downer, *History of Davenport and Scott County, Iowa*, 193, it is estimated that wheat and flour export figures were about 33% of the total exports figure. For wheat and flour figures, see Appendix F. For price estimates, see Figure 6.3. Estimated figures are marked with an asterisk.

Year	Wheat and flour exports	Value 1845
1847	Flour < 1000 bbls. * @ $2.25 = $2,250	
	Wheat ~40,000 bu. * @ .45 = 18,000. = 20,250/.33 = 60,750	
1848	Flour 35,000 bbls @ 3.00 = 105,000	
	Wheat 16,000 bu. @ .60 = 9,600 = 114,600/.33 = 343,800	
1852	Flour 20,000 bbls. * @ 3.00 = 60,000	
	Wheat 20,000 bu. @ .60 = 12,000 = 72,000/.33 = 216,000	
1855	Flour 30,000 bbls @ 5.25 = 157,500	
	Wheat 30,000 bu. @ 1.05 = 31,500 = 189,000/.33 = 567,000	
1857	Flour 100,000 bbls. @ 4.50 = 450,000	
	Wheat 90,000 @ .90 = 81,000 = 531,000/.33 = 1,593,000	

II. B. In 1845 Davenport's population was 1.4 times that in 1848; hence estimated 1845 imports are set at 1.4 × 148,500 = 207,900.

By 1853 Davenport's population had increased six times over its 1848 size, hence the estimate for 1852 imports is set at 6 × 148,500 = 891,000.

Burlington

I. 1847 imports and exports: $245,440 and $926,250. Both derived from calculations in Delegates to the Chicago River and Harbor Convention, *The commerce and navigation of the valley of the Mississippi*, 20.

1856 imports: calculated at $1,702,935. Convention Report estimate of value of $65 a ton times given imports of 26,199 tons in *The first annual directory, of the city of Burlington for 1859*, comp. Watson Bowron (Burlington, Iowa, 1859). Given the fact that prices were much higher in 1856, this figure is probably much too low and will be replaced by an extrapolated figure from population estimates.

1858 imports: $3,426,923. Ibid.

II. A. Estimated from claim by the Delegates to the Chicago River and Harbor Convention, *The commerce and navigation of the Mississippi*, 20, that flour and wheat account for approximately 25% of Burlington's more diversified exports. Asterisk signifies estimated figure.

Year	Wheat and flour	Value	Total exports

1847   Flour 37,821 bbls. @ 3.00 = 112,563
       Wheat 207,948 bu. @ .60 = 124,769 = 237,332/.25 = 949,328
       Approximate to solid figure above +/− 5%
1856   Flour 18,700 bbls. @ 5.50 = 102,850
       Wheat 204,000 bu. @ 1.10 = 224,000 = 326,850/.25 = 1,307,400
1858   Flour 20,000 * bbls. @ 4.00 = 80,000
       Wheat 197,500 bu. @ .80 = 158,000 = 238,000/.25 = 952,000

II. B. Between 1847 and 1858 population increased 9 times and imports, according to offical figures, increased 14 times. Therefore, it is estimated that imports increased 1.5 times faster than population. In 1856 Burlington's population of 16,000 was 8 times greater than its population in 1848. It is estimated, therefore, that imports may have been as high as 12 times greater than the 1847 figures: $245,440 × 12 = 2,945,280. This figure seems more likely than the figure calculated from a tonnage report listed above.

Keokuk

     I. 1854 imports: $1,960,515. Orion Clemens, *City of Keokuk in 1856* (Keokuk, 1856), 19.
     1855 imports: $2,913,653. Ibid.
     1856 imports: $5,037,543. *Keokuk directory and business mirror for 1857* (Keokuk, Iowa, 1857), 182.

     II. A. Percentage of total for wheat and flour same as at Burlington, 25%. Unfortunately there are few sound figures for trade, requiring that one resort to extrapolating by population figures for exports as well as imports. Asterisks signify estimated figures.

Year	Wheat and flour	Value	Total exports

1854   Flour 30,000 * bbls. @ 5.00 = 150,000
       Wheat 70,000 bu. * @ 1.00 = 70,000 = 220,000/.25 = $880,000
1854   estimate, 850,000

Year	Population index: 1854 = 1.0	Estimated exports
1850	.45	$ 382,500
1855	1.5	1,275,000
1856	1.6	1,360,000
1857	1.2	1,020,000
1859	1.3	1,050,000

II. B.

Year	Population index: 1856 = 1.0 for 1857 and 1859 calculations	Estimated imports
1850	.45 of 1854	$ 882,231
1857	1.2 × 1856	6,045,052
1859	1.3 × 1856	6,548,805

Quincy

I. 1837 exports; $112,500. Joseph T. Holmes, *Quincy in 1857. Or facts and figures* (Quincy, Ill., 1857), 12.

1853 imports: $1,248,000. *Quincy Whig*, February 28, 1854.

1854 imports: $1,279,500. John Tilson, *A History of Quincy* (Chicago, n.d.), 217.

II. A. Wheat and flour are estimated to have accounted for 30% of total exports. Estimated figures are marked by an asterisk.

Year	Wheat and flour	Value	Estimated total
1841	Flour 40,000 bbls. @ 2.50 = 100,000		
	Wheat 295,000 bu. @ .50 = 147,500 = 247,500/.30 = 825,000		
1846	Flour 70,000 bbls. @ 3.00 = 210,000		
	Wheat 200,000 * bu. @ 60 = 120,000 = 330,000/.30 = 1,100,000		
1850	Flour 20,000 bbls. @ 3.25 = 65,000		
	Wheat 400,000 bu. @ .65 = 260,000 = 325,000/.30 = 1,083,333		
1852	Flour 40,000 bbls. @ 2.50 = 100,000		
	Wheat 100,000 bu. * @ .50 = 50,000 = 150,000/.30 = 500,000		
1854	Flour 50,000 @ 5.00 = 250,000		
	Wheat 23,000 @ 1.000 = 23,000 = 273,000/.30 = 910,000		
1859	Flour 20,000 bbls. @ 3.50 = 70,000		
	Wheat 300,000 bu. * @ .70 = 210,000 = 280,000/.30 = 933,333		

II. B.

Year	% of 1854 population	Estimated imports
1841	36	$ 460,620
1846	61	780,495
1850	79	1,010,805
1852	86	1,100,370
1854	100	
1859	230	2,942,850

Index

Adams County, Ill.: corn production (1850), 136; population of, 108, 109t; town sites in, 92
Alton, Ill.: banking and finances, 167, 168t; communications with, by mail, 148–9; economic development, 64, 94, 197, 422–6; financial crisis of 1857, 238; flood of 1844, 59, 60, 73–4, 76; flour trade, 189–90, 192t, 194t, 244–5; hinterland, 24, 43, 180, 244; hinterland corn production, 180; hog packing at, 165, 196–7, 245–6; land traffic, to and from, 141; lead trade, 124–5; merchandising, wholesale and retail, 214–15, 216–17, 244–6; population, 108; produce trade, 112, 180, 244; steamboating, to and from, 113, 245; wheat trade, 157, 158f, 160, 190, 193t, 244
American Bottom, the: corn production, 179; floods, 59, 74; roads across, 37, 148; settlement of, 32, 33, 42, 45, 46–7, 58–9, 60; site of urban development, 94, 95; timber, 31
Amphlett, William, 17, 33

Baltimore, Maryland: communications with West, 149; financial crisis of 1857, 237
Baltimore and Ohio Railroad, extensions to St. Louis, 221
banking and finances: bills of exchange in West, 167, 168t; credit cycle, 168–72, 227; financial crisis of 1857, 234–41; transmission of money from West, 167
Beardstown, Ill.: hog packing, 196; merchandising, wholesale and retail, 214; roads, to and from, 129, 130, 131, 132; wheat trade, 158f, 160
Belleville, Ill.: flour trade, 189; land traffic, 133; settlement, 46; soil quality, 44
Bellevue, Iowa: wheat trade, 158f
Belvedere, Ill.: railroad, 185

Birkbeck, Morris: floods, 58; health of river bottoms, 60, 61; market, 30; settlement, 17, 36, 40, 41; town settlement, 90
Bloomington, Iowa: see Muscatine, Iowa
Boonslick country (Missouri): assessment of, 23, 24; communications with, 149; roads, 37; settlement of, 32, 47
Booth, Caleb: steamboat investment, 126
Boston, Mass.: communications with West, 149; financial crisis of 1857, 237; merchandising in the West, 219
Brown County, Ill.: town sites in, 92; wheat trade, 160
Browning, Orville: travel, 148
Buffalo, Iowa: county seat competition, 106; economic development, 111; founding, 104, 105f; steamboating, to and from, 111
Bureau County, Ill.: hog production, 182; roads across, 129
Burlington, Iowa: balance of trade, 223t; *Burlington Hawkeye*, 157; economic development, 64, 273; financial crisis of 1857, 238; floods, 60; flour production, 191; flour trade, 192t, 194t; founding of, 104; hog packing, 197; merchandising, wholesale and retail, 218, 219, 247; railroads, to and from, 191, 218; roads, to and from, 131, 132; steamboat arrivals, 116t, 117n, 117, 120, 121f; steamboat ownership, 125; steamboating, to and from, 111, 118, 147; wheat trade, 156t, 157, 158f, 158, 162, 190, 193t
Burrows, James D.: association with Antoine LeClaire, 267–8; county seat fight with Rockingham, Iowa, 107; financial dealings, 239; merchandising, 215, 250; produce trade, 112; wheat trade, 155, 159

Cahokia, Ill.,: settlement, 42; flood, 60
Cairo, Ill.: closing of navigation, 81; floods,

311